CISSP EXAM PREP:

Disclaimer: This book is intended for educational and informational purposes only. The content within this book is provided "as is" and without warranties of any kind, either express or implied. The authors, publishers, and contributors to this book do not warrant or make any representations concerning the accuracy, likely results, or reliability of the use of the materials in this book or otherwise relating to such materials or on any sites linked to this book.

The information provided in this book does not constitute legal, professional, or career advice, and should not be treated as such. While every effort has been made to ensure that the information provided in this book is accurate and up-to-date, laws, regulations, and best practices in the field of information security are constantly evolving. The authors, publishers, and contributors cannot be held responsible for any errors or omissions, or for any actions taken based on the information contained in this book.

This book is not affiliated with, authorized, endorsed by, or in any way officially connected with the International Information System Security Certification Consortium, Inc., (ISC)², or any of its subsidiaries or affiliates. The Certified Information Systems Security Professional (CISSP) is a registered trademark of (ISC)², Inc. This book is designed to provide information about the subject matter covered, but it is sold with the understanding that the publisher is not engaged in rendering legal, accounting, or other professional services.

If legal advice or other expert assistance is required, the services of a competent professional person should be sought. The use of this book does not guarantee passing any certification or qualification exams, and users should direct specific questions regarding such exams to the respective certifying bodies.

The authors, publishers, and contributors shall not be liable for any loss of profit or any other commercial damages, including but not limited to special, incidental, consequential, or other damages. By using this book, you agree that the limitations of liability set out in this disclaimer are reasonable. If you do not think they are reasonable, you must not use this book.

The views and opinions expressed in this book are those of the authors and do not necessarily reflect the official policy or position of any agency of the U.S. government or any other government or corporate entity.

INTRO:

Welcome to your journey towards mastering the CISSP certification. This guide is more than just a collection of information; it's a roadmap designed to navigate the complexities of information security and to clear the path toward achieving your CISSP certification.

In the pages that follow, you'll find a comprehensive breakdown of the CISSP domains, from the nuances of Security and Risk Management to the intricacies of Software Development Security. Each chapter is structured to build your understanding from the ground up, ensuring no stone is left unturned.

But this guide offers more than just knowledge. It's a source of encouragement, acknowledging the challenges ahead while reinforcing your capability to overcome them. The CISSP journey is demanding, but with determination and the right resources, achieving certification is entirely within your reach.

Remember, this book isn't just about passing an exam; it's about shaping your future in the information security field. Each chapter is crafted to not only prepare you for the CISSP exam but to equip you with real-world insights that will serve you long beyond test day.

So, let's embark on this journey together. With each page turned, you'll be one step closer to not only earning a prestigious certification but also to advancing your career and realizing your full potential in the world of information security. Your dream is not only possible; it's waiting for you to make it a reality.

The Certified Information Systems Security Professional (CISSP) is a globally recognized credential in the information security field, awarded by the International Information Systems Security Certification Consortium, commonly known as (ISC)². This certification is a testament to an individual's expertise and skills in designing, implementing, and managing a best-in-class cybersecurity program.

Importance and Value of CISSP in the Information Security Field

The CISSP certification is esteemed for its rigorous standards and comprehensive coverage of information security topics. It validates a professional's ability to effectively manage and mitigate security risks in a variety of environments, making it a valuable asset for career advancement. CISSP holders are often seen as authorities in information security, leading to enhanced credibility, higher earning potential, and better job opportunities in roles such as Chief Information Security Officer, Security Analyst, and Security Manager.

Exam Format, Structure, and Scoring

The CISSP exam employs a Computerized Adaptive Testing (CAT) format for English language exams, adjusting the difficulty of questions based on the candidate's responses. The exam comprises 100 to 150 questions, covering eight domains of the CISSP Common Body of Knowledge (CBK), which must be completed within a 4-hour timeframe. The types of questions include multiple-choice and advanced innovative questions. To pass, candidates must achieve a scaled score of 700 out of 1000 points.

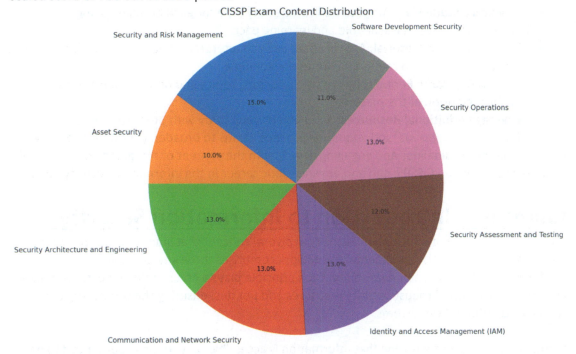

As shown above, this is the typical exam content distribution:

Security and Risk Management - 15%
Asset Security - 10%
Security Architecture and Engineering - 13%
Communication and Network Security - 13%
Identity and Access Management (IAM) - 13%
Security Assessment and Testing - 12%
Security Operations - 13%
Software Development Security - 11%

Eligibility Requirements and the Path to Certification
Candidates aiming for the CISSP certification must have a minimum of five years of cumulative, paid work experience in two or more of the eight domains of the CISSP CBK. A one-year experience waiver is available for candidates holding a four-year college degree, a master's degree in Information Security, or for possessing another approved credential. The path to certification involves preparing for and passing the CISSP exam, followed by an endorsement process where an active (ISC)² credential holder verifies the candidate's professional experience.
How to Use This Book Effectively
This guide is structured to provide a comprehensive review of all eight domains covered by the CISSP exam. To use this book effectively, it's recommended to:

- **Assess Your Knowledge**: Start by evaluating your current understanding of each domain to identify areas that require more focus.
- **Develop a Study Plan**: Allocate dedicated study time for each domain, taking into account your personal schedule and learning pace.
- **Engage with the Material**: Actively read each chapter, taking notes, and performing the practice questions to reinforce your understanding.
- **Review Regularly**: Periodically revisit challenging topics and practice questions to ensure retention of the material.
- **Leverage Additional Resources**: Supplement your study with other resources like forums, study groups, and additional practice exams to broaden your understanding.

By following these guidelines and engaging deeply with the content of this guide, you'll be well-equipped to tackle the CISSP exam and advance your career in the information security field.

Chapter 1: Introduction to Information Security:

Diving into the realm of Information Security, a pivotal concept that stands at the core of this field is the CIA Triad. This fundamental framework comprises three key principles: Confidentiality, Integrity, and Availability. Each principle plays a crucial role in the development and implementation of robust security measures and policies, ensuring the protection and resilience of information systems.

Confidentiality is about ensuring that information is accessible only to those authorized to have access. It's akin to keeping a secret; only those who are meant to know the information can see it. In practice, confidentiality is implemented through measures like encryption, access controls, and authentication mechanisms. For instance, when you send an encrypted email, the content is scrambled into an unreadable format for everyone except the intended recipient, who has the key to decrypt the message.

Integrity involves maintaining the accuracy and completeness of data. It ensures that information has not been tampered with or altered by unauthorized parties. This principle is crucial because even the slightest unauthorized modification can have significant consequences. Integrity controls include checksums, digital signatures, and audit trails. For example, a digital signature on a document verifies that it hasn't been altered since the signature was applied, providing assurance that the content is genuine and intact.

Availability ensures that information and resources are accessible to authorized users when needed. This aspect of the triad focuses on making sure that systems, networks, and data are up and running when required. Measures to ensure availability include redundant systems, backups, and disaster recovery plans. An example of availability in action is a website that uses load balancers to manage traffic; even if one server goes down, the website remains accessible via other servers.

In designing security measures and policies, the CIA Triad serves as a guiding framework, helping organizations to balance and prioritize their security efforts. For instance, a bank's online service must ensure the confidentiality of customer information through encryption, maintain the integrity of transaction records with digital signatures, and guarantee the availability of its services even in the face of cyber attacks or technical failures.

Understanding and applying the principles of the CIA Triad is essential for anyone involved in information security, as it shapes the way we protect and manage our digital assets.

In the landscape of information security, the terms threats, vulnerabilities, and risks are often used interchangeably, yet they hold distinct meanings. Grasping these differences is fundamental for implementing effective risk management strategies.

Threats are potential causes of unwanted incidents, which may result in harm to a system or organization. They can originate from various sources, such as natural disasters, technical failures, or human actions (both intentional and accidental). For example, a cybercriminal launching a phishing attack is a threat to an organization's information security.

Vulnerabilities refer to weaknesses or gaps in a system's design, implementation, operation, or internal controls that could be exploited by a threat to cause harm. Vulnerabilities can exist in software, hardware, processes, or people. An example of a vulnerability might be an outdated operating system on a computer that lacks the latest security patches, making it susceptible to malware infections.

Risks are defined as the potential for loss, damage, or any other undesirable outcome resulting from a combination of a threat exploiting a vulnerability. Risk quantifies the likelihood and the impact of a threat materializing. For instance, if an organization's servers are running outdated software (vulnerability), and there is a known hacking group targeting this type of software (threat), the organization faces a risk of a data breach.

Understanding the distinctions between threats, vulnerabilities, and risks is crucial for effective risk management. This understanding allows organizations to:

Identify and Prioritize: Recognize existing vulnerabilities within their systems and the potential threats that could exploit these weaknesses. This knowledge helps prioritize security efforts and resources towards the most significant risks.

Implement Protective Measures: Develop and apply appropriate security measures to mitigate vulnerabilities, deter threats, and reduce risks to an acceptable level. For example, patching software vulnerabilities reduces the risk of exploitation by threats.

Strategic Decision Making: Make informed decisions about where to allocate resources for the greatest impact on reducing security risks. This might involve choosing between enhancing security training for employees (reducing human vulnerabilities) or investing in advanced intrusion detection systems (countering threats).

Continual Assessment and Adaptation: Security is not a one-time effort but a continuous process. By understanding the dynamic nature of threats, vulnerabilities, and risks, organizations can adapt their security measures in response to evolving challenges.

Risk management in information security is a structured approach to identifying, assessing, and addressing risks to ensure the confidentiality, integrity, and availability (CIA) of information assets. This process is vital for maintaining the CIA Triad, as it helps organizations to proactively manage potential security threats and vulnerabilities.

Risk Assessment

The first step in risk management is risk assessment, which involves:

Identifying Risks: This involves recognizing potential threats to information assets and the vulnerabilities within the system that could be exploited by these threats. Identification can be achieved through various means, including security audits, vulnerability scanning, and threat intelligence.

Analyzing Risks: Once identified, each risk must be analyzed to determine its likelihood and impact. This analysis considers the nature of the threat, the vulnerability's extent, and the value of the affected assets to the organization. Techniques such as qualitative analysis (high, medium, low ratings) or quantitative analysis (numerical values) can be used.

Evaluating Risks: This step involves comparing the analyzed risk against predefined risk criteria set by the organization. It helps in understanding which risks are acceptable and which require mitigation. The goal is to prioritize risks based on their potential impact on the organization's objectives and the CIA Triad.

Risk Mitigation Strategies

Following risk assessment, organizations must develop and implement risk mitigation strategies to manage identified risks effectively. These strategies include:

Risk Avoidance: Eliminating the risk entirely by discontinuing the activities that generate the risk or by changing processes, practices, or technologies.

Risk Reduction: Implementing controls to lessen the likelihood or impact of a risk. This could involve updating security policies, strengthening access controls, or patching vulnerabilities.

Risk Sharing: Transferring part of the risk to another party, such as through insurance policies or outsourcing certain functions to third-party vendors with specialized security expertise.

Risk Acceptance: Deciding to accept the risk without taking any specific actions to mitigate it, usually because the cost of mitigation exceeds the potential loss or the risk is within the organization's risk appetite.

Integrating Risk Management with the CIA Triad
Risk management is inherently tied to the CIA Triad in the following ways:

Confidentiality: Risk management processes help identify and mitigate risks associated with unauthorized access to sensitive information, ensuring that data remains confidential and accessible only to those with legitimate rights.

Integrity: By identifying risks related to data tampering and implementing controls to prevent unauthorized modifications, risk management supports the integrity of information, ensuring its accuracy and reliability.

Availability: Risk management strategies address risks that could disrupt access to information and services, such as hardware failures, natural disasters, or cyber-attacks, thus supporting the continuous availability of critical systems and data.

So, risk management is a critical component of information security that supports the CIA Triad by identifying, assessing, and addressing risks to ensure that information assets are protected against potential threats and vulnerabilities. Through a systematic approach to risk management, organizations can maintain the confidentiality, integrity, and availability of their information assets, thereby safeguarding their operations and reputation.

Chapter 2: Legal, Regulations, Compliance, and Investigation:

Navigating the legal and regulatory environment of information security is crucial for organizations operating in today's digital landscape. Compliance with key laws and regulations not only ensures legal adherence but also significantly enhances an organization's security posture. Three pivotal regulations that have a profound impact on information security are the General Data Protection Regulation (GDPR), the Health Insurance Portability and Accountability Act (HIPAA), and the Sarbanes-Oxley Act (SOX).

General Data Protection Regulation (GDPR)
GDPR, implemented by the European Union in May 2018, has set a global benchmark for data protection and privacy. Its primary aim is to give individuals control over their personal data and to simplify the regulatory environment for international business by unifying the regulation

within the EU. GDPR impacts any organization, regardless of location, that processes the personal data of EU residents. Key requirements include obtaining clear consent from individuals before processing personal data, implementing measures to protect data privacy (such as data minimization and encryption), and reporting data breaches within 72 hours. Non-compliance can result in substantial fines, up to 4% of the annual global turnover or €20 million, whichever is greater.

Health Insurance Portability and Accountability Act (HIPAA)
In the United States, HIPAA sets the standard for protecting sensitive patient data. Entities covered by HIPAA, including healthcare providers, health plans, and healthcare clearinghouses, must ensure the confidentiality, integrity, and availability of protected health information (PHI). This involves physical, network, and process security measures, such as access controls, audit controls, and secure data transmission protocols. Violations of HIPAA can lead to significant financial penalties, criminal charges, and reputational damage.

Sarbanes-Oxley Act (SOX)
SOX, enacted in 2002, focuses on protecting investors from fraudulent financial reporting by corporations. It mandates strict reforms to improve financial disclosures and combat corporate and accounting fraud. For information security, SOX emphasizes the integrity of the data used in financial reporting. Organizations must implement internal controls and auditing practices to ensure the accuracy and reliability of their financial statements. Non-compliance with SOX can result in penalties, including fines and imprisonment for executives.

Importance of Compliance for Organizations
Compliance with these regulations is not just a legal requirement but also a critical component of an organization's risk management strategy. Adhering to GDPR, HIPAA, SOX, and other relevant regulations helps organizations:

Enhance Trust and Reputation: Demonstrating compliance with data protection and privacy standards can significantly boost an organization's reputation and foster trust among customers, partners, and stakeholders.

Avoid Legal and Financial Penalties: Compliance helps organizations avoid potentially crippling fines and legal costs associated with non-compliance.

Improve Security Posture: The security controls and practices mandated by these regulations contribute to strengthening an organization's overall security posture, protecting against breaches and other security incidents.

Foster Competitive Advantage: Organizations that are compliant can leverage their adherence as a competitive advantage, especially in industries where data security and privacy are paramount.

Navigating the legal and regulatory environment of information security is integral to an organization's operational, legal, and financial well-being. Compliance with regulations like GDPR, HIPAA, and SOX not only fulfills legal obligations but also plays a crucial role in safeguarding sensitive information, maintaining customer trust, and ensuring the long-term success of the organization.

Intellectual property (IP) law plays a pivotal role in information security, serving as a legal framework to protect the intangible creations of the mind, such as inventions, literary and artistic works, designs, symbols, names, and images used in commerce. In the realm of information security, understanding and adhering to intellectual property law is crucial, as breaches can lead to significant legal, financial, and reputational damages.

Copyrights

Copyrights protect original works of authorship, including literary, dramatic, musical, and artistic works, as well as software code. In the context of information security, copyright law safeguards software programs and databases from unauthorized copying, redistribution, or modification. Breaching copyright laws, intentionally or unintentionally, can result in legal actions, fines, and mandates to cease and desist from using the copyrighted material.

Patents

Patents grant inventors exclusive rights to their inventions, allowing them to exclude others from making, using, selling, or distributing the patented invention without permission. In information security, patents can cover a wide range of inventions, including algorithms, business methods, and computer-implemented inventions. Unauthorized use of patented technology can lead to patent infringement lawsuits, potentially resulting in injunctions, monetary damages, and the payment of royalties.

Trademarks

Trademarks protect symbols, names, and slogans used to identify goods or services. The role of trademarks in information security primarily relates to brand protection, ensuring that entities cannot use similar marks in a way that would confuse consumers or dilute the brand's value. Cybersecurity measures are essential to prevent practices like domain squatting, phishing, and brand impersonation, which can mislead consumers and tarnish the brand's reputation.

Trade Secrets

Trade secrets encompass formulas, practices, processes, designs, instruments, patterns, or compilations of information that provide a business advantage over competitors who do not know or use it. Information security measures are critical in protecting trade secrets from unauthorized access, theft, or espionage. Breaches of trade secrets can lead to loss of competitive advantage, legal battles, and significant financial losses.

Implications of Intellectual Property Breaches

Breaches of intellectual property rights in the digital realm can have far-reaching implications. Organizations may face legal challenges, including lawsuits and penalties, which can be costly and damage business relationships. Furthermore, breaches can lead to loss of trust among customers and partners, tarnishing the organization's reputation. In severe cases, breaches can disrupt business operations and lead to financial losses.

Protecting intellectual property requires robust information security practices, including access controls, encryption, regular audits, employee training, and legal measures such as non-disclosure agreements (NDAs). Organizations must remain vigilant in safeguarding their intellectual assets while respecting the intellectual property rights of others to navigate the complex interplay between IP law and information security effectively.

Preventing and responding to data breaches are critical components of an organization's information security strategy. Effective prevention measures reduce the risk of breaches, while a well-defined response plan ensures swift action to mitigate damage when a breach occurs. Legal requirements for disclosure and the use of encryption are integral to these strategies.

Prevention Strategies
Risk Assessment: Regularly conducting risk assessments helps identify potential vulnerabilities and threats, allowing organizations to prioritize and address security gaps.

Access Controls: Implementing strict access controls ensures that only authorized personnel have access to sensitive data, minimizing the risk of unauthorized access.

Employee Training: Educating employees about security best practices, phishing schemes, and other social engineering tactics reduces the risk of breaches caused by human error.

Regular Software Updates: Keeping all systems and software up-to-date with the latest security patches helps protect against known vulnerabilities.

Network Security: Utilizing firewalls, intrusion detection systems (IDS), and intrusion prevention systems (IPS) to monitor and protect the network perimeter.

Data Encryption: Encrypting data at rest and in transit protects the confidentiality and integrity of data, making it unreadable without the proper decryption keys.

Response Strategies
Incident Response Plan: Having a well-defined incident response plan ensures that the organization can act swiftly and effectively to contain and mitigate a data breach.

Breach Detection: Implementing advanced threat detection tools helps identify breaches early, reducing the potential impact.

Communication Plan: A clear communication plan is essential for informing affected parties, stakeholders, and regulatory bodies in compliance with legal requirements.

Forensic Analysis: Conducting a forensic investigation helps understand the breach's scope, the data affected, and how the breach occurred, informing future prevention strategies.

Legal Compliance and Disclosure: Adhering to legal requirements for breach disclosure is crucial. Laws such as GDPR and state-specific regulations in the US mandate timely notification to affected individuals and authorities, often within a specific timeframe.

Role of Encryption in Data Privacy
Encryption plays a pivotal role in protecting data privacy, both at rest and in transit. By transforming data into a format unreadable without the correct decryption key, encryption ensures that even if data is intercepted or accessed by unauthorized parties, the information remains confidential. This is particularly important for sensitive information such as personal identification details, financial records, and health information.

Implementing strong encryption algorithms and managing encryption keys securely are fundamental to maintaining data privacy. Additionally, encryption can aid in compliance with data protection regulations, which often specify the need for encryption as a measure to safeguard personal data.

A multi-faceted approach encompassing prevention strategies, a robust response plan, adherence to legal disclosure requirements, and the strategic use of encryption is essential for preventing data breaches and protecting data privacy. These measures collectively help organizations safeguard sensitive information, maintain trust with stakeholders, and comply with regulatory standards.

Ethical considerations in information security are foundational to professional conduct, guiding how practitioners manage data, engage with systems, and interact with stakeholders. Ethical frameworks and best practices ensure that information security professionals uphold integrity, confidentiality, and respect for privacy in their operations.

Professional Conduct
Adhering to a code of ethics, such as those provided by (ISC)² or ISACA, is essential for information security professionals. These codes emphasize:
- **Integrity**: Professionals should provide truthful, transparent, and complete information, avoiding deceptive practices.
- **Confidentiality**: Maintaining the confidentiality of information encountered in the course of professional activities is paramount, ensuring that data is disclosed only with proper authorization.

- **Objectivity**: Decisions and actions should be free from conflicts of interest, ensuring impartiality and fairness in all professional matters.

Handling of Data

Responsible data management is a cornerstone of ethical information security practice:

- **Data Minimization**: Collect and retain only the data necessary for the defined purpose, reducing the risk of harm from potential breaches.
- **Privacy by Design**: Incorporate privacy controls into systems and processes from the outset, ensuring that data protection is an integral part of the lifecycle.
- **Consent and Transparency**: Obtain clear consent for data collection and processing, providing individuals with information about how their data is used, stored, and protected.

Ethical Hacking Framework

Ethical hacking, or penetration testing, involves authorized attempts to bypass system defenses to identify vulnerabilities. An ethical hacking framework guides these activities, ensuring they are conducted responsibly:

- **Authorization**: Obtain explicit, written permission from the system owner before attempting any security assessment activities.
- **Scope**: Clearly define the scope of the assessment, ensuring that activities do not extend beyond agreed boundaries.
- **Disclosure**: Report all found vulnerabilities to the organization in a responsible manner, providing sufficient detail to facilitate remediation without exposing the system to further risk.

Best Practices for Ethical Standards

- **Continual Education**: Stay informed about emerging ethical dilemmas, legal standards, and best practices in information security.
- **Professional Collaboration**: Engage with the broader information security community to share knowledge, debate ethical issues, and develop consensus on best practices.
- **Responsibility to the Public**: Recognize the broader impact of information security on society, advocating for responsible use of information technology and the protection of public interests.

Adhering to ethical standards and best practices in information security not only fosters trust and respect among peers and stakeholders but also contributes to the integrity and reliability of information systems and the data they protect.

Chapter 3: Security and Risk Management:

Security governance encompasses the set of responsibilities and practices exercised by an organization's senior leadership to provide strategic direction, ensure objectives are achieved, manage risk effectively, and verify that the organization's resources are used responsibly. The foundational principles of security governance are crucial for establishing and maintaining a robust information security program that aligns with business objectives and meets regulatory requirements.

Foundational Principles of Security Governance
Responsibility and Accountability: Assigning clear responsibility and accountability for information security activities within the organization is fundamental. This ensures that decision-makers at all levels understand their roles in maintaining security and are accountable for their actions.

Risk Management: Identifying, assessing, and managing risks to the organization's information assets is central to security governance. This involves not only technological risks but also business, operational, and reputational risks, ensuring that risk management is integrated into business processes.

Resource Allocation: Effective security governance involves allocating resources strategically to address security needs. This includes budget, personnel, and technology resources, prioritizing based on risk assessment and business impact.

Performance Measurement: Establishing metrics and monitoring mechanisms to evaluate the effectiveness and efficiency of the information security program. This enables continuous improvement and ensures that the program remains aligned with business objectives.

Strategic Alignment: Aligning the information security strategy with the organization's overall business strategy is essential. This ensures that security measures support business objectives and that security considerations are integrated into business decisions.

Compliance and Ethical Conduct: Ensuring compliance with applicable laws, regulations, and ethical standards is a key principle of security governance. This not only involves adhering to legal requirements but also upholding ethical responsibilities to stakeholders.

Importance in Establishing and Maintaining an Organization's Information Security Program
These principles are vital for several reasons:

Strategic Direction: They provide a framework for setting the strategic direction of the information security program, ensuring that it supports the organization's overall goals and objectives.

Risk Management: By emphasizing risk management, these principles ensure that the organization can identify, prioritize, and address security risks effectively, protecting critical assets and information.

Resource Optimization: Clear governance principles help optimize the use of resources, ensuring that investments in security are made wisely and in areas that offer the greatest benefit to the organization.

Regulatory Compliance: Adhering to governance principles helps organizations meet regulatory requirements, avoiding legal penalties and reputational damage.

Stakeholder Confidence: Effective governance builds confidence among stakeholders, including customers, employees, and partners, that the organization takes information security seriously and manages it professionally.

Adaptability and Resilience: A well-governed security program is more adaptable to changes in the business environment and more resilient to threats, ensuring the organization's long-term success and stability.

The foundational principles of security governance are essential for aligning security strategies with business objectives and regulatory requirements, ensuring the effectiveness, efficiency, and adaptability of the organization's information security program.

The involvement of C-suite executives and board members is pivotal in shaping and endorsing security governance within an organization. Their strategic oversight, commitment, and understanding of security governance significantly influence the organization's security posture and its alignment with overall business objectives.

C-suite Executives
Chief Information Security Officer (CISO): The CISO plays a central role in developing and implementing the information security strategy. Responsibilities include identifying and assessing security risks, proposing appropriate mitigation strategies, and ensuring the deployment of effective security controls. The CISO also plays a crucial role in communicating security-related issues and strategies to other C-suite executives and the board, advocating for necessary resources, and ensuring compliance with regulatory requirements.

Chief Executive Officer (CEO): The CEO's engagement in security governance underscores its importance across the organization. The CEO ensures that information security is integrated into corporate governance, aligning security initiatives with business goals, and fostering a culture that values and practices robust security. The CEO also supports the CISO's initiatives at the board level and ensures that security considerations are part of strategic business decisions.

Chief Financial Officer (CFO): The CFO is responsible for overseeing the financial aspects of security governance, including budgeting for security initiatives, assessing the financial impact of security risks, and ensuring that investments in security align with the organization's risk appetite and financial goals.

Chief Operating Officer (COO): The COO ensures that operational practices across the organization incorporate security measures. This includes overseeing the integration of security practices in day-to-day operations and ensuring that security policies are effectively implemented and adhered to.

Board Members
Board members have the ultimate responsibility for the governance of an organization, which includes oversight of information security governance. Their roles involve:

Strategic Oversight: Board members ensure that the organization's information security strategy aligns with its overall business strategy and objectives. They provide guidance on the organization's risk appetite and ensure that security governance is integrated into broader corporate governance frameworks.

Resource Allocation: The board approves budgets and resources for security initiatives, based on the strategic importance of these initiatives and their expected contribution to risk management.

Policy Endorsement: Board members endorse information security policies, demonstrating their commitment to security governance and ensuring that these policies have the necessary authority and visibility across the organization.

Risk Management: They are involved in high-level risk management decisions, including understanding the organization's risk profile, major security risks, and the measures in place to mitigate these risks.

Performance Monitoring: Board members monitor the effectiveness of the organization's security governance through regular reports from C-suite executives, including the CISO, and ensure that the organization responds appropriately to evolving security threats.

The active engagement of C-suite executives and board members in security governance ensures that information security is not siloed as a technical issue but is recognized as a critical component of the organization's overall strategy and risk management framework. Their leadership in security governance helps build a security-aware culture, ensures adequate resources are allocated to protect critical assets, and fosters resilience against evolving cyber threats.

Ensuring compliance with applicable laws, regulations, and standards is a multi-step process that requires a strategic approach and ongoing vigilance. Key regulations such as the General Data Protection Regulation (GDPR), Health Insurance Portability and Accountability Act (HIPAA), and Payment Card Industry Data Security Standard (PCI-DSS) have specific requirements that organizations must adhere to in order to protect sensitive information and maintain data privacy and security.

Compliance Process

Understanding Applicable Regulations: The first step is to thoroughly understand the laws, regulations, and standards that apply to the organization. This includes identifying the types of data protected, the scope of the regulations, and the specific compliance requirements.

Gap Analysis: Conduct a gap analysis to assess the current state of the organization's practices against the requirements of the regulations. This involves reviewing current data handling practices, security measures, and policies and procedures.

Risk Assessment: Perform a risk assessment to identify potential vulnerabilities and threats that could lead to non-compliance. This helps prioritize areas that require immediate attention.

Implementation of Controls: Based on the gap analysis and risk assessment, implement necessary security controls, policies, and procedures to address compliance requirements. This may include technical controls like encryption and access controls, as well as administrative controls such as training and awareness programs.

Documentation and Record-Keeping: Maintain detailed documentation of compliance efforts, including policies, procedures, training records, and evidence of compliance with specific requirements. This documentation is crucial for demonstrating compliance during audits.

Continuous Monitoring and Auditing: Establish ongoing monitoring and regular auditing processes to ensure continuous compliance and to identify and address any compliance gaps promptly.

Incident Response and Reporting: Develop and maintain an incident response plan that includes procedures for reporting breaches or non-compliance issues to the relevant regulatory bodies, as required by the regulations.

Consequences of Non-Compliance

Legal Penalties: Non-compliance can result in legal actions, fines, and sanctions from regulatory bodies. For example, GDPR violations can lead to fines of up to 4% of annual global turnover or €20 million, whichever is greater.

Financial Impact: Beyond fines, non-compliance can lead to costly legal battles, compensation to affected parties, and the need for remediation measures, which can significantly impact an organization's financial health.

Reputational Damage: Breaches of regulations can lead to loss of trust among customers, partners, and the public. The negative publicity associated with non-compliance can harm an organization's brand and reputation, leading to loss of business and competitive disadvantage.

Operational Disruptions: Regulatory violations may result in operational restrictions imposed by regulatory bodies, affecting the organization's ability to conduct business.

Increased Scrutiny: Organizations that fail to comply with regulations may face increased scrutiny and more frequent audits from regulatory bodies, leading to higher compliance costs in the future.

Ensuring compliance with laws, regulations, and standards is not just about avoiding negative consequences; it's also about protecting sensitive data, maintaining customer trust, and ensuring the long-term success and sustainability of the organization. A proactive and comprehensive approach to compliance can help organizations navigate the complex regulatory landscape effectively.

Key legal concepts play a significant role in shaping information security policies and practices. Understanding these concepts is crucial for organizations to navigate the legal landscape, protect their assets, and avoid legal liabilities.

Privacy Laws
Privacy laws regulate the collection, storage, processing, and sharing of personal information. Examples include the General Data Protection Regulation (GDPR) in the European Union, which sets stringent requirements for handling personal data, and the California Consumer Privacy Act (CCPA) in the United States, which gives consumers rights over their personal information held by businesses.

Impact on Security Policies: Organizations must implement data protection measures such as data encryption, access controls, and data minimization to comply with privacy laws. Policies must also outline procedures for obtaining consent, handling data subject access requests, and reporting data breaches.

Intellectual Property Rights
Intellectual property rights protect creations of the mind, such as inventions (patents), literary and artistic works (copyrights), symbols, names, and images used in commerce (trademarks), and trade secrets.

Impact on Security Practices: To safeguard intellectual property, organizations implement measures like digital rights management (DRM), secure access controls, and network segmentation. Policies may include guidelines on the use of copyrighted material, protection of trade secrets, and enforcement actions against IP infringements.

Cybercrime Legislation

Cybercrime legislation addresses crimes committed using or against computers and networks. Examples include the Computer Fraud and Abuse Act (CFAA) in the United States, which penalizes unauthorized access to computers, and the Directive on security of network and information systems (NIS Directive) in the EU, which requires critical infrastructure operators to take measures to manage cybersecurity risks.

Impact on Security Policies: Organizations need to establish policies for incident response, cyber threat reporting, and cooperation with law enforcement in the case of cyber incidents. Security practices may involve regular security assessments, intrusion detection systems, and employee training on recognizing and preventing cyber threats.

Contractual Obligations

Contractual obligations related to information security arise from agreements with customers, partners, and vendors. These contracts may include clauses on data protection, confidentiality, and security standards that the parties must adhere to.

Impact on Security Practices: Compliance with contractual obligations requires organizations to align their security measures with the agreed-upon standards. This might involve conducting regular audits, achieving certifications (e.g., ISO/IEC 27001), and implementing specific controls required by the contract.

Examples:

Privacy Law Compliance: A retail company operating online must ensure its website complies with GDPR by implementing features for cookie consent, easy access to privacy policies, and secure mechanisms for customers to request data deletion or access.

Protecting Intellectual Property: A software company uses encryption and digital watermarking to protect its source code and multimedia content from unauthorized copying and distribution, in line with copyright laws.

Adhering to Cybercrime Legislation: A financial institution deploys advanced cybersecurity measures, including multi-factor authentication and real-time monitoring, to prevent unauthorized access and comply with regulations like the NIS Directive.

Fulfilling Contractual Obligations: A cloud service provider includes data security clauses in its contracts with clients, committing to maintaining specific security standards and undergoing regular third-party security audits to verify compliance.

Navigating these legal concepts requires a comprehensive approach to information security, ensuring that policies and practices not only protect the organization's assets and data but also comply with legal and contractual requirements.

Major information security organizations such as (ISC)² and ISACA have established codes of ethics to guide the professional and personal conduct of their members. These codes of ethics are foundational to maintaining professional integrity and public trust in the information security domain.

(ISC)² Code of Ethics
The (ISC)² Code of Ethics emphasizes four mandatory canons that its members and certified professionals must follow:

1. **Protect Society, the Common Good, and Infrastructure**: Information security professionals are committed to protecting society, the commonwealth, and the infrastructure by working to safeguard the confidentiality, integrity, and availability of information and systems.
2. **Act Honorably, Honestly, Justly, Responsibly, and Legally**: Professionals are expected to demonstrate honesty, integrity, fairness, and respect in all their professional activities, adhering to the highest standards of ethical and legal behavior.
3. **Provide Diligent and Competent Service to Principals**: Members must serve their clients and employers with dedication, competence, and diligence, ensuring that they provide only those services for which they are qualified.
4. **Advance and Protect the Profession**: Professionals are encouraged to advance the integrity and reputation of the profession, sharing their knowledge, and fostering professional growth among their peers.

ISACA Code of Ethics
ISACA's Code of Ethics promotes similar principles, focusing on four main tenets:

1. **Support the Implementation of, and Encourage Compliance with, Appropriate Standards, Procedures, and Controls**: ISACA members are expected to support the creation and implementation of standards, procedures, and controls that protect the information systems and information of their organizations and clients.
2. **Perform Duties with Objectivity, Due Diligence, and Professional Care**: This involves carrying out professional responsibilities with the highest sense of objectivity, avoiding conflicts of interest, and ensuring that their work is performed with due diligence and care.
3. **Maintain the Privacy and Confidentiality of Information**: Professionals must respect and protect the confidentiality and privacy of all information they encounter in their professional roles, disclosing it only when legally obligated or with proper authorization.

4. **Maintain Competence and Improve Professional Skills**: ISACA members are required to maintain their professional competence and strive for continual improvement in their skills and knowledge, contributing to the development of others in the field.

Importance of Ethical Behavior

Ethical behavior is crucial in the information security domain for several reasons:

- **Maintaining Professional Integrity**: Adherence to ethical standards ensures that professionals conduct themselves with honesty and integrity, making decisions that are not only legally compliant but also morally sound.
- **Building Public Trust**: In an era where data breaches and privacy concerns are prevalent, ethical behavior builds trust between information security professionals, their clients, organizations, and the public. It assures stakeholders that their information is in safe hands.
- **Protecting Information**: Ethical conduct ensures that sensitive information is handled with care and respect, safeguarding the confidentiality, integrity, and availability of data.
- **Fostering Collaboration and Knowledge Sharing**: Ethical principles encourage professionals to share knowledge and mentor others, fostering a collaborative environment that advances the field and promotes continuous learning.
- **Mitigating Risks**: Ethical decision-making helps in identifying and mitigating potential risks associated with information security practices, ensuring that actions taken do not harm individuals, organizations, or society.

The codes of ethics promoted by (ISC)², ISACA, and other information security organizations play a vital role in guiding the professional conduct of security practitioners. Adherence to these ethical standards is essential for maintaining professional integrity, building public trust, and ensuring the responsible management and protection of information in an increasingly digital world.

Ethical dilemmas in information security often involve complex situations where the right course of action may not be immediately clear. Presenting scenarios that test ethical boundaries can help in understanding these challenges and developing frameworks for ethical decision-making.

Scenario 1: Handling of Vulnerabilities

An information security professional discovers a significant vulnerability in a widely used software product. Reporting this vulnerability could lead to early remediation but might also risk public exposure and exploitation by malicious actors before a fix is implemented.

Ethical Considerations:

- Duty to protect the broader user community from potential harm.
- Responsibility to the software vendor to allow for remediation before public disclosure.

Ethical Framework:

- **Responsible Disclosure**: The professional could follow a responsible disclosure process, notifying the vendor of the vulnerability and allowing a reasonable timeframe for remediation before making the information public.

- **Balancing Harm**: Weigh the potential harm of immediate disclosure against the harm of delayed action. If the vulnerability is actively being exploited, quicker public disclosure might be justified.

Scenario 2: Privacy Dilemmas

A security team monitoring network traffic identifies activity that suggests an employee is leaking sensitive company data. Investigating further could confirm the breach but would require intrusive monitoring of the employee's communications, potentially violating their privacy.

Ethical Considerations:
- The need to protect company assets and sensitive information.
- The employee's right to privacy and the potential for wrongful accusation.

Ethical Framework:
- **Minimum Necessary Intrusion**: Limit monitoring to the least intrusive methods necessary to confirm or refute the suspicions.
- **Oversight and Authorization**: Ensure that any monitoring is authorized at the highest level and is subject to oversight to prevent abuse.
- **Transparency and Communication**: If the investigation is confirmed, communicate with the employee about the concerns and the actions taken, respecting their rights and dignity.

Scenario 3: Ethical Hacking

An ethical hacker, hired to test an organization's defenses, discovers an unrelated but critical security flaw in a third-party system used by the organization. Reporting the flaw to the third party could lead to its remediation but falls outside the agreed scope of work with the hiring organization.

Ethical Considerations:
- The ethical hacker's responsibility to the client and the boundaries of the contracted work.
- The potential risk to users of the third-party system if the flaw remains unaddressed.

Ethical Framework:
- **Client Consultation**: Discuss the discovery with the client first, explaining the potential risks and implications. Seek their guidance or permission to report the flaw to the third party.
- **Responsible Disclosure to the Third Party**: If the client agrees, or if the ethical hacker believes there is a significant risk to the public, proceed with a responsible disclosure to the third party, allowing them time to remediate before any public disclosure.

In all these scenarios, ethical decision-making frameworks should incorporate key principles such as transparency, accountability, minimization of harm, and respect for privacy and dignity. Adopting established ethical guidelines from professional organizations, seeking peer advice, and maintaining a clear focus on the broader implications of decisions can help navigate these complex dilemmas.

Developing, implementing, reviewing, and updating information security policies are critical steps in establishing a robust security framework within an organization. These policies serve as formal guidelines that dictate how an organization's information assets are protected, guiding organizational security practices and behavior.

Developing Information Security Policies
Identify Objectives: Begin by identifying the main objectives of the information security program, aligning with the organization's overall business goals and compliance requirements.

Assess Risks: Conduct a comprehensive risk assessment to identify potential threats to the organization's information assets and determine the level of risk associated with each threat.

Define Scope: Clearly define the scope of the policies, specifying the information assets, departments, and personnel they apply to.

Draft Policies: Based on the objectives, risk assessment, and scope, draft the security policies. Common policy areas include access control, data classification, incident response, and remote access.

Stakeholder Review: Engage stakeholders from various departments, including IT, legal, HR, and operations, to review the drafted policies, ensuring they are practical and aligned with business operations.

Approval: Obtain formal approval for the policies from senior management, ensuring they have the authority and support for implementation.

Implementing Information Security Policies
Communication: Clearly communicate the policies to all relevant personnel through training sessions, workshops, and written communications.

Integration: Integrate the policies into daily operations and business processes, ensuring they are practical and enforceable.

Training and Awareness: Provide ongoing training and awareness programs to ensure that employees understand the policies and their roles in maintaining information security.

Tools and Controls: Implement necessary security tools, technologies, and controls to enforce the policies, such as firewalls, encryption, and access controls.

Reviewing and Updating Policies
Regular Reviews: Schedule regular reviews of the information security policies to ensure they remain relevant and effective in addressing current security challenges.

Feedback Mechanism: Establish a feedback mechanism that allows employees to report issues, concerns, or suggestions regarding the policies.

Adapt to Changes: Update the policies to reflect changes in the organization's business processes, technological environment, legal and regulatory landscape, and emerging threats.

Audit and Compliance: Conduct regular audits to assess compliance with the policies and identify areas for improvement.

Role of Information Security Policies
Guidance: Security policies provide clear guidelines to employees on the expected behaviors and practices related to information security, helping to standardize responses to common security scenarios.

Risk Management: By establishing controls and procedures for managing risks, policies help minimize the potential impact of security threats on the organization.

Compliance: Policies ensure that the organization complies with legal, regulatory, and contractual obligations, reducing the risk of legal penalties and reputational damage.

Incident Response: Policies outline procedures for responding to security incidents, ensuring a coordinated and effective response that minimizes damage and recovery time.

Culture of Security: Well-defined policies contribute to creating a culture of security within the organization, where protecting information assets becomes a shared responsibility.

The process of developing, implementing, reviewing, and updating information security policies is a continuous cycle that requires active engagement from all levels of the organization. These policies are foundational to guiding organizational security practices and behaviors, ensuring that information assets are adequately protected against threats.

In the realm of information security, policies, standards, procedures, and guidelines form a structured framework that governs how an organization protects its information assets. Understanding the distinctions between these elements is crucial for effectively implementing and operationalizing security policies.

Standards
Standards are specific, mandatory requirements that establish a consistent framework for implementing policies. They define the minimum acceptable controls to safeguard information assets and provide a benchmark for measuring compliance.

Example: ISO/IEC 27001 is a widely recognized international standard for information security management. It outlines requirements for establishing, implementing, maintaining, and continually improving an Information Security Management System (ISMS). Organizations adopt ISO/IEC 27001 to demonstrate their commitment to information security best practices and to achieve certification, which can enhance credibility with clients and stakeholders.

Procedures

Procedures are detailed, step-by-step instructions that describe exactly how to comply with standards and policies. They are designed to be followed exactly as written, ensuring consistency and repeatability in the execution of tasks.

Example: A procedure for handling data breaches might include specific steps such as immediately isolating affected systems, notifying the security team, documenting the incident, and following legal and regulatory reporting requirements. This procedure ensures that every data breach is managed systematically, reducing the potential impact and aiding in recovery.

Guidelines

Guidelines are recommended practices that provide guidance on how policies and standards might be implemented. Unlike standards and procedures, guidelines are not mandatory and can be adapted to fit the specific needs or circumstances of different parts of an organization.

Example: A guideline for password management might suggest best practices such as using complex passwords, changing passwords regularly, and not reusing passwords across multiple accounts. While the organization's standard might require passwords to be at least 12 characters long, the guideline might suggest using a mix of letters, numbers, and special characters to increase password strength.

Supporting and Operationalizing Security Policies

Standards operationalize security policies by translating broad policy objectives into specific, measurable requirements. For instance, a policy stating that "access to sensitive data must be controlled" might be operationalized by a standard requiring two-factor authentication and strict access controls based on job roles.

Procedures ensure that standards are implemented consistently across the organization. They provide a clear roadmap for employees, reducing ambiguity and ensuring that security measures are applied effectively. For example, a procedure for installing software updates could help maintain the integrity and security of systems in line with a standard requiring regular patch management.

Guidelines offer flexibility in implementing security measures, allowing departments or teams to adapt best practices to their unique operational contexts. This flexibility ensures that security measures are both effective and practical, enhancing overall compliance with security policies and standards.

Standards, procedures, and guidelines each play a distinct role in supporting and operationalizing security policies within an organization. Standards provide the concrete requirements, procedures offer the "how-to" for meeting those requirements, and guidelines suggest best practices for effective implementation. Together, these elements form a comprehensive framework that ensures security measures are consistently applied, adapted to specific needs, and aligned with the organization's overall security objectives.

Organizational culture significantly influences the effectiveness of security policies and practices. A culture that values and prioritizes information security can enhance adherence to policies and encourage proactive security behaviors among employees. Conversely, a culture that views security as a secondary concern or a hindrance to productivity can lead to lax adherence to security policies and increased vulnerability to threats.

Impact of Organizational Culture on Security

- **Compliance and Adherence**: In organizations where security is integrated into the corporate culture, employees are more likely to understand, accept, and adhere to security policies. They perceive security measures not as restrictions but as essential practices that protect the organization and its stakeholders.
- **Employee Engagement**: A positive security culture fosters higher levels of employee engagement with security initiatives. Engaged employees are more likely to report security incidents, suggest improvements, and participate actively in security training and awareness programs.
- **Risk Management**: Cultures that emphasize proactive risk management encourage employees to consider the potential security implications of their actions and decisions, leading to more secure practices and reduced risk exposure.
- **Innovation and Improvement**: Security-aware cultures are typically more open to innovation and continuous improvement in security practices. Employees feel empowered to contribute ideas and feedback, which can lead to more effective and efficient security solutions.

Strategies for Fostering a Security-Aware Culture

1. **Leadership Commitment**: Security culture starts at the top. Leaders must demonstrate a commitment to security through their actions and communications, setting a clear example for the rest of the organization.
2. **Integration into Business Processes**: Security should be integrated into all business processes and decisions. When employees see that security is considered at all levels of the organization, they are more likely to recognize its importance and adhere to related policies.
3. **Comprehensive Training and Awareness Programs**: Regular, engaging training programs can increase security awareness and knowledge across the organization. Training should be tailored to different roles and departments, emphasizing the relevance of security to each employee's responsibilities.

4. **Open Communication Channels**: Encourage open communication about security concerns and incidents. Employees should feel comfortable reporting security issues without fear of reprisal, knowing that their concerns will be taken seriously.
5. **Positive Reinforcement**: Recognize and reward compliance with security policies and proactive security behaviors. Positive reinforcement can motivate employees to maintain and improve their security practices.
6. **Security as Part of Organizational Values**: Embed security within the core values of the organization. When employees understand that security is a fundamental aspect of the organizational ethos, they are more likely to internalize and reflect these values in their daily activities.
7. **Regular Feedback and Adaptation**: Solicit feedback from employees about security policies and practices, and be willing to adapt based on that feedback. A culture that values employee input is more likely to foster a sense of ownership and responsibility for security.
8. **Real-World Examples and Simulations**: Use real-world examples, simulations, and gamification to illustrate the importance of security and the potential consequences of security failures. Relatable, hands-on experiences can make security concepts more tangible and meaningful.

Organizational culture plays a crucial role in the effectiveness of security policies and practices. By fostering a security-aware culture, organizations can enhance policy adherence, encourage proactive security behaviors, and build a more resilient security posture. This requires commitment from leadership, integration of security into all aspects of the business, effective training and communication, and an environment that values and rewards secure practices.

Chapter 4: Asset Security:

Information classification is a fundamental aspect of asset security, serving as the cornerstone for safeguarding an organization's data. By categorizing information based on its sensitivity and value, organizations can apply appropriate protective measures, control access, and ensure that resources are allocated efficiently to protect the most critical assets.

Importance of Information Classification

- **Risk Management**: Classification helps in identifying the levels of risk associated with different types of information, enabling organizations to focus their security efforts where they are needed most.
- **Regulatory Compliance**: Many regulations require the protection of specific types of information. Classification ensures that such data is identified and adequately protected to meet legal and regulatory requirements.
- **Data Handling and Access Control**: Classification dictates how information should be handled, stored, transmitted, and destroyed, and it determines who should have access to it, thereby reducing the risk of unauthorized access and data breaches.
- **Resource Allocation**: By classifying information, organizations can allocate security resources more effectively, focusing on the protection of assets that are of the highest value or sensitivity.

Standard Classification Levels

While classification levels can vary by organization and industry, a commonly used hierarchy includes the following levels:

1. **Public**: Information intended for public disclosure, such as press releases, marketing materials, and published financial reports. Public information requires minimal protection and can be accessed by anyone without significant risk to the organization.
2. **Confidential**: Information that, if disclosed, could cause some level of harm or inconvenience to the organization or individuals. Confidential information might include employee personal details, internal policies, and certain contractual agreements. Access should be restricted to those with a legitimate need to know.
3. **Secret**: Information whose unauthorized disclosure could cause serious damage to the organization, its operations, or its stakeholders. This might include strategic plans, proprietary technologies, and sensitive financial data. Secret information requires stringent access controls and protection measures.
4. **Top Secret**: The highest level of classification, reserved for information whose disclosure could cause exceptionally grave damage to the organization, national security, or public safety. Examples might include details of critical infrastructure, advanced research and development projects, and high-level strategic decisions. Protection of top-secret information involves the most rigorous security controls and access is highly restricted.

Criteria for Assigning Classification Levels

The criteria for assigning classification levels to information include:

- **Value to the Organization**: The importance of the information to the organization's mission and objectives.
- **Potential Impact of Disclosure**: The degree of harm that could result from unauthorized access, including financial loss, reputational damage, legal liability, and impact on national security or public safety.
- **Legal and Regulatory Requirements**: The need to comply with laws and regulations governing the protection of certain types of information, such as personal data, health records, and financial information.
- **Lifespan of the Information**: The period during which the information retains its value or sensitivity, which can affect decisions on how long it needs to be protected.

Information classification is vital for effective asset security, guiding how different types of information are protected and managed throughout their lifecycle. By adhering to a structured classification system and carefully considering the criteria for assigning classification levels, organizations can ensure that their information assets receive an appropriate level of protection, commensurate with their value and sensitivity.

Developing and implementing an effective information classification program is a systematic process that involves multiple steps and the participation of various stakeholders within an organization. The program aims to ensure that information assets are appropriately classified and protected based on their sensitivity and value.

Steps in Developing an Information Classification Program
Define Classification Levels: Establish clear, organization-specific classification levels (e.g., Public, Confidential, Secret, Top Secret) that reflect the organization's needs and the types of information it handles.

Develop Classification Criteria: Create criteria for each classification level, detailing the type of information that falls into each category and the potential impact of unauthorized disclosure.

Assign Roles and Responsibilities: Identify key stakeholders responsible for classifying information, managing the classification program, and ensuring compliance. This typically involves senior management, IT security teams, legal departments, and data owners.

Create Classification Policies and Procedures: Develop formal policies and procedures that outline the classification process, handling requirements for each classification level, and responsibilities of employees. Policies should also cover declassification and reclassification processes.

Implement Classification Tools and Technologies: Deploy tools and technologies that support the classification process, such as data discovery and classification software, which can automate the identification and labeling of data based on predefined criteria.

Train and Educate Employees: Conduct training sessions to educate employees about the classification program, their roles and responsibilities, and the importance of adhering to classification policies.

Integrate with Data Handling and Security Measures: Ensure that classification levels are integrated into data handling processes and security measures, influencing access controls, encryption, data storage, and transmission protocols.

Monitor and Enforce Compliance: Establish mechanisms for monitoring compliance with the classification program and enforcing policies, including regular audits and reviews.

Review and Update: Periodically review and update the classification program to reflect changes in the organization's information assets, risk environment, and regulatory requirements.

Roles and Responsibilities of Key Stakeholders
Senior Management: Endorse and support the classification program, ensuring it aligns with organizational goals and provides necessary resources.
CISO/Security Team: Lead the development and implementation of the classification program, provide security expertise, and ensure integration with overall security policies.
Data Owners: Responsible for classifying information they own or manage according to the established criteria and ensuring proper handling and protection.

Employees: Comply with classification policies, handle information appropriately based on its classification, and report any classification issues or incidents.

Legal/Compliance Departments: Ensure the classification program complies with legal and regulatory requirements and addresses contractual obligations.

Impact on Data Handling and Security Measures

An effective information classification program significantly impacts how data is handled and protected within an organization:

Access Controls: Classification levels dictate who can access certain information, leading to more granular and effective access control policies.

Data Protection Measures: Higher classification levels may require stronger encryption, both at rest and in transit, and more secure storage solutions.

Incident Response: The classification level of involved data influences the response to security incidents, with higher classifications necessitating more urgent and comprehensive responses.

Compliance and Auditing: Classification simplifies compliance with regulations by clearly identifying which data sets require specific protections, facilitating more targeted and efficient audits.

Implementing an information classification program enhances an organization's ability to protect sensitive information, comply with regulatory requirements, and manage data more effectively. By involving key stakeholders and integrating classification into data handling and security measures, organizations can establish a strong foundation for information security.

The legal and regulatory frameworks governing privacy protection, notably the General Data Protection Regulation (GDPR) in the European Union and the California Consumer Privacy Act (CCPA) in the United States, have profound implications for information security practices, particularly concerning personal data protection. These frameworks establish comprehensive requirements for the handling of personal data, significantly influencing how organizations implement their information security and privacy measures.

GDPR

The GDPR, effective as of May 25, 2018, applies to any organization, regardless of location, that processes personal data of individuals in the EU. It introduces several key principles and requirements:

- **Lawfulness, Fairness, and Transparency**: Personal data must be processed lawfully, fairly, and transparently, with clear communication to data subjects about how their data is used.
- **Data Minimization**: Organizations should collect and process only the personal data necessary for the specified purpose.
- **Consent**: In many cases, explicit consent is required for the processing of personal data, and individuals have the right to withdraw consent at any time.
- **Data Subject Rights**: Individuals have enhanced rights, including the right to access their data, the right to rectification, the right to erasure ("right to be forgotten"), and the right to data portability.

- **Data Protection by Design and by Default**: Security measures must be integrated into the design of data processing operations and systems, ensuring that personal data is protected by default.
- **Breach Notification**: Data breaches likely to result in a risk to the rights and freedoms of individuals must be reported to the relevant supervisory authority within 72 hours, and, where the breach is likely to result in a high risk to individuals, those individuals must be notified without undue delay.

CCPA

The CCPA, effective as of January 1, 2020, applies to for-profit businesses that collect personal data of California residents and meet certain thresholds. It grants California residents several rights regarding their personal data:

- **Right to Know**: Individuals have the right to know what personal data is being collected about them, the sources from which it is collected, the purpose for collecting or selling the data, and the third parties with whom it is shared.
- **Right to Delete**: Individuals can request the deletion of their personal data held by businesses.
- **Right to Opt-Out**: Consumers can opt-out of the sale of their personal data by businesses.
- **Non-Discrimination**: The CCPA prohibits businesses from discriminating against consumers who exercise their rights under the Act.

Implications for Information Security Practices

Both GDPR and CCPA have significant implications for information security practices:

- **Data Inventory and Mapping**: Organizations must maintain a comprehensive inventory of personal data they hold, including its source, purpose, and basis for processing, to comply with transparency and data subject rights requirements.
- **Enhanced Security Measures**: To comply with the principles of data protection by design and by default, organizations must implement robust security measures, such as encryption, access controls, and secure data storage and transmission protocols.
- **Incident Response Plans**: The breach notification requirements necessitate having a well-defined incident response plan that enables quick detection, assessment, and reporting of data breaches.
- **Vendor Management**: Organizations must ensure that third-party vendors who process personal data on their behalf also comply with GDPR or CCPA requirements, necessitating stricter vendor assessments and contractual agreements regarding data protection.
- **Training and Awareness**: Employees must be trained on the importance of data privacy, the organization's obligations under GDPR, CCPA, and other relevant regulations, and their role in maintaining compliance.

The GDPR and CCPA represent a shift towards greater accountability and transparency in the processing of personal data, compelling organizations to integrate privacy into their information security frameworks. Compliance requires a holistic approach, combining legal, technological, and organizational measures to protect personal data effectively.

Privacy-Enhancing Technologies (PETs) play a crucial role in safeguarding individual privacy by embedding privacy protections into technology itself. PETs enable organizations to collect, process, and share data while minimizing personal data exposure and complying with privacy regulations. Key PETs and best practices include encryption, anonymization, and data minimization techniques.

Encryption

Encryption is a fundamental PET that protects the confidentiality and integrity of data by converting it into a coded format that can only be decoded with the correct key. It's essential for safeguarding data both at rest (stored data) and in transit (data being transmitted over networks).

- **Best Practices**:
  - Use strong encryption standards such as AES (Advanced Encryption Standard) for data at rest and TLS (Transport Layer Security) for data in transit.
  - Manage encryption keys securely, ensuring they are stored separately from encrypted data and accessed only by authorized personnel.

Anonymization and Pseudonymization

Anonymization removes or modifies personal data so that individuals cannot be identified, either directly or indirectly, by anyone without additional information. Pseudonymization is a related technique that replaces private identifiers with fake identifiers or pseudonyms, allowing data to be matched with its source without revealing the actual source.

- **Best Practices**:
  - Apply anonymization techniques such as data aggregation, noise addition, or hashing to reduce the risk of re-identification.
  - Ensure that pseudonymized data cannot be linked back to the individual without access to additional, securely stored information.
  - Regularly assess the effectiveness of anonymization and pseudonymization techniques, especially as data analysis methods evolve.

Data Minimization

Data minimization involves collecting only the data necessary for a specific purpose and retaining it only for as long as needed. This principle reduces the risk of privacy breaches and aligns with privacy regulations like GDPR.

- **Best Practices**:
  - Clearly define the purpose of data collection and limit the data gathered to what is strictly necessary for that purpose.
  - Establish data retention policies that specify how long data is kept and ensure that data is securely deleted when it is no longer needed.
  - Regularly review data collection practices and inventories to ensure ongoing compliance with data minimization principles.

Other PETs and Practices

- **Differential Privacy**: Introduces randomness into data queries, allowing organizations to share aggregate information about datasets without revealing individual entries.

- **Homomorphic Encryption**: Allows computations to be performed on encrypted data, producing an encrypted result that, when decrypted, matches the result of operations performed on the plaintext.
- **Secure Multi-party Computation**: Enables parties to jointly compute a function over their inputs while keeping those inputs private.

Implementing PETs
- **Integration into Systems and Processes**: PETs should be integrated into the design phase of systems and processes (privacy by design) to ensure that privacy protections are inherent and not just add-ons.
- **User Consent and Control**: Whenever possible, give users control over their data, including consent mechanisms that are clear and easy to use.
- **Training and Awareness**: Educate employees and stakeholders about the importance of privacy, the role of PETs, and the organization's privacy practices.

PETs and associated best practices are instrumental in enhancing privacy protections in an increasingly data-driven world. By implementing these technologies and adhering to privacy principles, organizations can protect individual privacy, build trust with users, and comply with regulatory requirements.

The secure handling, storage, and disposal of physical media and hardware assets are critical components of an organization's information security program. Effective strategies ensure that sensitive data remains confidential and is not inadvertently exposed or compromised during any phase of the asset lifecycle.

Secure Handling and Storage
Access Controls: Implement strict access controls to restrict physical access to storage areas containing sensitive media and hardware. This may include key card access systems, locks, and surveillance cameras.

Inventory Management: Maintain an up-to-date inventory of all physical media and hardware assets, including their location and the data they contain. This facilitates tracking and management of assets throughout their lifecycle.

Environmental Controls: Ensure that storage areas are equipped with appropriate environmental controls to protect media and hardware from damage. This includes temperature and humidity controls, fire suppression systems, and protection from water damage.

Encryption: Encrypt sensitive data stored on physical media such as hard drives and USBs to protect the confidentiality and integrity of the data, even if the media is lost or stolen.

Secure Transport: When physical media need to be transported, use secure containers and trusted couriers. Consider encrypting data before transport to mitigate the risk of interception.

Secure Disposal and Data Destruction

Data Wiping: Use software-based methods to overwrite all areas of a hard drive or storage device multiple times, ensuring that the original data cannot be recovered. Tools that adhere to standards such as NIST 800-88 can provide assurance of thorough data removal.

Degaussing: For magnetic media, degaussing can be used to disrupt the magnetic field and effectively erase the data. Note that degaussing renders the media unusable.

Physical Destruction: Physical destruction methods, such as shredding, crushing, or incineration, can be used for media and devices that are no longer needed. Ensure that the destruction method is appropriate for the media type and results in the data being irretrievable.

Certificate of Destruction: When using third-party services for data destruction, obtain a certificate of destruction that details the method of destruction, the date, and the assets destroyed, providing an audit trail.

Environmental Considerations: Dispose of electronic waste in an environmentally responsible manner, adhering to local regulations and best practices for e-waste recycling and disposal.

Best Practices

Policy and Procedures: Develop and document clear policies and procedures for the handling, storage, and disposal of physical media and hardware assets, ensuring that all employees understand their responsibilities.

Employee Training: Regularly train employees on the importance of secure handling and disposal practices, including recognizing sensitive data and understanding the procedures for securely disposing of media and hardware.

Regular Audits: Conduct regular audits of storage areas and disposal practices to ensure compliance with policies and identify any areas for improvement.

Vendor Management: When outsourcing disposal or data destruction, carefully vet vendors for compliance with industry standards and security best practices. Establish contracts that clearly define the scope of services, security requirements, and liability in case of a data breach.

Implementing these strategies for the secure handling, storage, and disposal of physical media and hardware assets protects sensitive information from unauthorized access, loss, or theft, and ensures that data is irretrievably destroyed when no longer needed. This comprehensive approach to physical security is a crucial aspect of an organization's overall information security strategy.

Personnel security measures are crucial in safeguarding an organization's information assets. The human element often represents the most unpredictable variable in security, making it vital to implement robust personnel security practices. Background checks, security awareness training, and insider threat management are key components of a comprehensive personnel security program.

Background Checks

Background checks are a preventative measure used to vet potential employees before granting them access to sensitive information or critical infrastructure. They help ensure that individuals with a history of malicious activities, poor judgment, or other risk factors are identified early.

- **Importance**: By verifying an individual's employment history, criminal record, educational background, and references, organizations can make informed decisions about the suitability of candidates for specific roles, particularly those involving access to sensitive data.
- **Implementation**: Background checks should be proportional to the level of access or sensitivity of the position. For high-security roles, more extensive checks, including financial history and security clearances, may be warranted.

Security Awareness Training

Security awareness training educates employees about various security threats, the organization's security policies, and their role in maintaining security. Regular, engaging training ensures that employees are aware of the latest threats, such as phishing, social engineering, and malware.

- **Importance**: Training empowers employees to act as a first line of defense against external threats and helps foster a security-conscious culture. It reduces the likelihood of accidental breaches caused by employee negligence or ignorance.
- **Implementation**: Training programs should be ongoing and tailored to different roles within the organization. They should include practical exercises, such as phishing simulations, to reinforce learning and assess employee vigilance.

Insider Threat Management

Insider threat management involves identifying and mitigating risks posed by individuals within the organization who might intentionally or unintentionally misuse their access to harm the organization. This includes employees, contractors, and business partners.

- **Importance**: Insiders already have legitimate access to the organization's systems and data, potentially allowing them to bypass security measures more easily than external attackers. Effective insider threat management is critical for early detection and response to such risks.
- **Implementation**: Implement a comprehensive insider threat program that includes behavioral monitoring, access controls, and user activity logging to detect unusual or unauthorized activities. Promote an organizational culture of trust and transparency while ensuring that privacy and legal requirements are met.

Best Practices

- **Role-based Access Control (RBAC)**: Limit access to information and systems based on the individual's role and the minimum access required to perform their job duties, reducing the potential impact of insider threats.
- **Regular Security Assessments**: Conduct regular assessments to identify potential security weaknesses related to personnel, including susceptibility to social engineering attacks.
- **Clear Policies and Procedures**: Develop clear policies and procedures regarding acceptable use, data handling, incident reporting, and disciplinary actions for security violations.
- **Employee Offboarding**: Ensure that access rights and credentials of departing employees are promptly revoked and conduct exit interviews to assess potential security risks.

Personnel security measures are integral to an organization's overall security strategy. By vetting individuals through background checks, fostering a security-aware culture through training, and managing insider threats with vigilance, organizations can significantly enhance the protection of their information assets. These measures not only mitigate risks but also contribute to a resilient security posture that adapts to evolving threats.

Integrating asset security practices into broader organizational security policies and procedures is essential for ensuring that the protection of information assets aligns with business objectives and compliance requirements. This integration involves establishing a cohesive framework that encompasses asset identification, risk assessment, access control, and continuous monitoring, all tailored to support the organization's strategic goals and adhere to regulatory standards.

Alignment with Business Objectives
Asset Identification and Classification: The process begins with identifying and classifying assets based on their value and sensitivity to the organization's operations and business objectives. This ensures that security measures are proportionate to the criticality of assets, focusing resources on protecting assets that are most vital to achieving business goals.

Risk Management: Asset security practices are aligned with business objectives through a risk management framework that evaluates threats and vulnerabilities in the context of their potential impact on business operations. This approach ensures that security efforts are directed towards mitigating risks that could significantly disrupt business processes or objectives.

Access Control: Access to assets is managed according to the principle of least privilege, ensuring that individuals have access only to the information and resources necessary for their job functions. This practice supports business efficiency by facilitating necessary access while minimizing the risk of unauthorized disclosure or alteration of sensitive information.

Integration into Organizational Policies and Procedures

Security Policies: Asset security practices are codified in organizational security policies, which set out the principles and standards for protecting assets. These policies cover aspects such as data classification, physical security, encryption, and secure disposal of assets, providing a clear framework for employees to follow.

Procedures and Guidelines: Detailed procedures and guidelines operationalize the security policies, offering step-by-step instructions for implementing security controls and handling assets securely. These documents ensure consistency in security practices across the organization and provide a reference point for employees.

Incident Response: Asset security is integrated into incident response plans, ensuring that there are predefined procedures for addressing security incidents that affect assets. This includes protocols for containment, eradication, and recovery, minimizing the impact of incidents on business continuity.

Compliance with Regulatory Requirements
Regulatory Mapping: Asset security practices are mapped to relevant legal and regulatory requirements, ensuring that the organization's approach to asset protection meets compliance standards. This involves understanding the specific protections required for different types of information, such as personal data under GDPR or health information under HIPAA.

Compliance Documentation: Security policies and procedures document how the organization complies with applicable regulations, serving as evidence of due diligence in protecting sensitive information. This documentation is crucial for demonstrating compliance during audits and regulatory assessments.

Continuous Monitoring and Improvement: Compliance is maintained through continuous monitoring of security controls and regular reviews of asset security practices. This proactive approach ensures that the organization adapts to changes in the regulatory landscape and evolving business objectives.

Integrating asset security practices into broader organizational security policies and procedures ensures a holistic approach to protecting information assets. By aligning these practices with business objectives and compliance requirements, organizations can safeguard their critical assets while supporting business operations and fulfilling regulatory obligations. This integrated approach fosters a secure and resilient organizational environment that is conducive to achieving strategic goals.

Case Study 1: Healthcare Data Breach
Scenario: A large healthcare provider experienced a data breach when unauthorized access was gained through a phishing attack. The attacker obtained login credentials from an employee and accessed patient health records, including personal and medical information.

Consequences:

- **Legal and Financial Penalties**: The healthcare provider faced significant fines under HIPAA for failing to protect patient data adequately.
- **Loss of Trust**: The breach eroded patient trust, with many individuals expressing concerns about their privacy and the security of their data.
- **Operational Disruption**: The organization had to temporarily suspend some services to address the breach, leading to operational disruptions and financial losses.

Lessons Learned:

- **Enhanced Employee Training**: The importance of regular and comprehensive security awareness training for employees to recognize and respond to phishing attempts.
- **Improved Access Controls**: Implementation of multi-factor authentication (MFA) and regular audits of access privileges to minimize the risk of unauthorized access.
- **Incident Response Plan**: The necessity of having a robust incident response plan that can be quickly activated in the event of a breach.

Case Study 2: Financial Institution Insider Threat

Scenario: A disgruntled employee at a financial institution intentionally leaked sensitive customer information online as an act of retaliation against the company. The employee had authorized access to the data but misused it for malicious purposes.

Consequences:

- **Reputational Damage**: The institution's reputation suffered as customers questioned the security of their investments and personal information.
- **Regulatory Scrutiny**: The institution faced intense scrutiny from financial regulators, resulting in stricter oversight and mandatory improvements to security practices.
- **Customer Litigation**: Affected customers filed lawsuits for damages caused by the exposure of their personal and financial data, leading to costly legal battles.

Lessons Learned:

- **Insider Threat Programs**: The critical need for insider threat detection programs that can identify and mitigate risks from within the organization.
- **Behavioral Monitoring**: Implementing behavioral monitoring tools to detect unusual activity patterns that could indicate malicious intent or unauthorized access by insiders.
- **Role-based Access Control**: Ensuring that access to sensitive information is strictly controlled and based on the principle of least privilege, limiting potential damage from insider threats.

Case Study 3: Retailer Point-of-Sale System Hack

Scenario: A major retailer experienced a breach of its point-of-sale (POS) systems, resulting in the theft of millions of customers' credit card details. The attackers exploited a vulnerability in the POS software that had not been patched.

Consequences:

- **Financial Losses**: The retailer faced direct financial losses from the breach, including the cost of credit monitoring services for affected customers, fines from payment processors, and a decrease in sales due to eroded customer confidence.

- **Brand Impact**: The breach had a long-lasting impact on the retailer's brand, with customers expressing concerns about the safety of their data and hesitating to make purchases.
- **Regulatory Fines**: The retailer was fined for failing to comply with PCI-DSS standards, which mandate the secure processing and storage of payment card information.

Lessons Learned:
- **Regular Software Updates**: The importance of keeping all systems, especially those handling sensitive data like POS systems, up-to-date with the latest security patches.
- **Network Segmentation**: Segmenting networks to ensure that a breach in one area, such as the POS system, cannot easily spread to other parts of the organization's network.
- **Continuous Monitoring**: The need for continuous monitoring of network and system activity to quickly detect and respond to suspicious behavior or unauthorized access attempts.

These case studies highlight the multifaceted nature of asset security breaches and underscore the importance of a comprehensive security strategy that includes employee training, access control, insider threat management, timely software updates, and effective incident response plans to mitigate risks and protect sensitive information.

Chapter 5: Security Architecture and Engineering:

Fundamental security models like Bell-LaPadula, Biba, and Clark-Wilson provide theoretical frameworks for understanding and implementing information security principles, specifically addressing confidentiality, integrity, and in some aspects, availability. Each model has unique features tailored to specific security requirements.

Bell-LaPadula Model

Principles: The Bell-LaPadula model is primarily focused on maintaining the confidentiality of data. It is known for two main access control rules:
- **The Simple Security Rule (no read up, "ss-property")**: A subject (e.g., a user or process) at a certain security level cannot read data at a higher security level (prevents unauthorized access to confidential information).
- **The *-property (star property, no write down)**: A subject at a certain security level cannot write to any object at a lower security level (prevents the flow of information from higher to lower security levels, avoiding information leakage).

Applications: This model is widely applied in government and military organizations where confidentiality and the classification of information are of paramount importance.

Addressing CIA:
- **Confidentiality**: Directly addresses confidentiality by preventing unauthorized access and disclosure of information.
- **Integrity and Availability**: Not explicitly designed to address integrity or availability. The model's restrictions could, in theory, prevent certain types of unauthorized modifications but at the cost of potentially limiting necessary data access and manipulation.

Biba Model

Principles: The Biba model is designed to ensure data integrity and is often viewed as the counterpart to the Bell-LaPadula model. It includes two primary rules:

- **The Simple Integrity Axiom (no write up)**: A subject cannot modify objects at a higher integrity level, preventing the corruption of more trusted data by less trusted sources.
- **The *-integrity Axiom (no read down)**: A subject at a high integrity level should not read data from a lower integrity level to prevent contamination by less reliable information.

Applications: Useful in environments where data integrity is critical, such as financial systems, safety-critical systems, and certain scientific research databases.

Addressing CIA:

- **Confidentiality**: Not the focus of the Biba model; it does not provide mechanisms for protecting data confidentiality.
- **Integrity**: Directly addresses data integrity by controlling how data is modified and accessed based on integrity levels.
- **Availability**: Not explicitly addressed, but like Bell-LaPadula, the restrictions could impact data accessibility.

Clark-Wilson Model

Principles: The Clark-Wilson model emphasizes data integrity through well-formed transactions and separation of duties. Key concepts include:

- **Constrained Data Items (CDIs)**: Data that must be maintained in a consistent state.
- **Integrity Verification Procedures (IVPs)**: Procedures that check the correctness and consistency of CDIs.
- **Transformation Procedures (TPs)**: The only means by which CDIs can be altered, ensuring all changes maintain system integrity.

Applications: This model is widely applicable in commercial environments where transaction integrity and non-repudiation are crucial, such as banking systems, e-commerce platforms, and enterprise resource planning systems.

Addressing CIA:

- **Confidentiality**: While not its primary focus, the model's principles of separation of duties and least privilege can indirectly contribute to confidentiality by limiting access to sensitive functions and data.
- **Integrity**: Directly addresses integrity by ensuring that only authorized transactions can alter data, maintaining consistency and accuracy.
- **Availability**: Indirectly supports availability by promoting the reliability and trustworthiness of data and systems, although it doesn't specifically address availability protection mechanisms.

Each of these fundamental security models offers a unique approach to addressing specific aspects of the CIA triad, with Bell-LaPadula focusing on confidentiality, Biba on integrity, and Clark-Wilson offering a comprehensive framework for integrity through controlled processes. Understanding these models helps in designing and implementing security architectures tailored to an organization's specific needs and regulatory requirements.

Architectural frameworks and design patterns in security architecture play crucial roles in ensuring that security measures are systematically integrated with business objectives and risk management strategies. Key frameworks like SABSA (Sherwood Applied Business Security Architecture) and TOGAF (The Open Group Architecture Framework), along with various security design patterns, provide structured approaches to designing, implementing, and managing an enterprise's security posture.

SABSA
Overview: SABSA is a security architecture framework that adopts a business-driven approach, ensuring that security measures align with business goals and requirements. It is based on a six-layer model that covers everything from business requirements to infrastructure.

Key Principles:

Business Focus: SABSA starts with defining the business requirements and objectives, ensuring that security architecture is driven by business needs and adds value to the organization.
Risk-Based Approach: It emphasizes a risk management strategy, where security controls are implemented based on a thorough risk assessment, ensuring that resources are allocated efficiently to mitigate significant risks.
Applications:

SABSA is used to develop customized security architectures that support business objectives, manage risks effectively, and ensure compliance with regulatory requirements.
It's applicable across various sectors, providing a holistic view of security that encompasses people, processes, and technology.
TOGAF
Overview: TOGAF is a comprehensive framework used to design, plan, implement, and manage enterprise information architecture. While not exclusively a security framework, TOGAF includes considerations for integrating security into enterprise architecture.

Key Principles:

Enterprise-wide Scope: TOGAF addresses the full spectrum of enterprise architecture, including business, data, application, and technology architectures, with security considerations integrated into each domain.
Adaptive and Iterative Process: The TOGAF ADM (Architecture Development Method) provides a structured approach for architecture development, which is iterative and can adapt to changing business and security requirements.
Applications:

TOGAF can be used to ensure that security is an integral part of the overall enterprise architecture, aligning with business goals and facilitating effective risk management.

It's suitable for organizations looking to harmonize their IT and security architectures with broader business strategies.

Security Design Patterns

Security design patterns are reusable solutions to common security problems within a given context. They provide best practices that can be applied to various scenarios, ensuring consistent and effective implementation of security controls.

Examples:

Layered Security (Defense in Depth): Involves creating multiple layers of security controls throughout an IT system, ensuring that if one layer is breached, others still provide protection. Principle of Least Privilege: Ensures that users and systems have only the minimum levels of access – or permissions – needed to perform their tasks, reducing the risk of unauthorized access or actions.

Secure Defaults: Systems and applications are configured with the most secure settings by default, minimizing the risk of misconfiguration and vulnerabilities.

Applications:

Design patterns can be applied across various aspects of security architecture, from network design to application development, ensuring that security considerations are consistently addressed.

They help in creating secure systems that are resilient to attacks and aligned with the organization's risk posture and business objectives.

Integrating architectural frameworks like SABSA and TOGAF, along with security design patterns, into the security architecture planning process ensures that security measures are not only technically effective but also aligned with business goals and risk management strategies. This alignment is essential for creating a security posture that supports the organization's objectives while protecting its assets and information.

Symmetric key cryptography is a method of encryption where the same key is used for both encrypting and decrypting information. This approach relies on shared secret keys, making key distribution and management critical aspects of its implementation. Symmetric cryptography is widely used for its efficiency, especially in scenarios requiring high-speed encryption and decryption of large volumes of data.

Key Principles
- **Shared Secret Key**: Both the sender and receiver use the same secret key, which must be known to both parties and kept confidential.
- **Encryption and Decryption Process**: The same algorithm and key are used for both processes. The sender uses the key to encrypt plaintext into ciphertext, which the receiver then decrypts back into plaintext using the same key.

- **Speed and Efficiency**: Symmetric algorithms are generally faster and less computationally intensive than asymmetric algorithms, making them suitable for encrypting large amounts of data.

Key Distribution Challenges
- **Secure Key Exchange**: The biggest challenge in symmetric cryptography is the secure exchange of the secret key. If the key is intercepted during transmission, an attacker could decrypt confidential communications.
- **Key Management**: Managing the keys, especially in systems with numerous users, can be complex. Each unique pair of users typically requires a separate shared key, increasing the complexity of key management.
- **Scalability**: As the number of participants in a system increases, the number of required keys grows exponentially, making symmetric systems less scalable than their asymmetric counterparts.

Common Algorithms

Advanced Encryption Standard (AES)
- **Overview**: AES is a widely used encryption standard adopted by the U.S. government and numerous other entities worldwide. It has replaced the older DES (Data Encryption Standard) due to its stronger security features.
- **Key Features**: AES operates on block ciphers of 128 bits, with key sizes of 128, 192, or 256 bits, providing a high level of security.
- **Use Cases**: AES is used in various applications requiring high security, including VPNs, file encryption, and securing wireless networks (WPA2 and WPA3).
- **Strengths**: AES offers a strong encryption level, is efficient in both software and hardware, and has been extensively tested and analyzed by the cryptographic community.
- **Vulnerabilities**: While AES itself is considered secure, vulnerabilities can arise from weak key management practices or poor implementation.

Data Encryption Standard (DES)
- **Overview**: DES was one of the first widely adopted symmetric encryption algorithms but is now considered obsolete for many applications due to its relatively short key length.
- **Key Features**: DES uses a 56-bit key to encrypt data in 64-bit blocks, which was sufficient in the early days of its use but is now vulnerable to brute-force attacks.
- **Use Cases**: Once used broadly in banking, communications, and government, DES has been largely replaced by AES but is still used in some legacy systems.
- **Strengths**: DES was widely supported and standardized, making it one of the first encryption algorithms to be adopted universally.
- **Vulnerabilities**: The primary vulnerability of DES is its short key length, making it susceptible to brute-force attacks. Triple DES (3DES) was introduced to improve security by encrypting data three times, but it is also being phased out in favor of more secure algorithms.

Symmetric key cryptography remains a cornerstone of modern encryption practices due to its efficiency and speed. However, the challenges of secure key distribution and management necessitate robust protocols and systems to ensure the confidentiality and integrity of the keys. As cryptographic practices evolve, the use of strong, well-implemented algorithms like AES in conjunction with secure key management practices is essential for maintaining the security of encrypted communications and data.

Advanced cryptographic techniques and tools in symmetric cryptography enhance data security by providing various modes of operation for block ciphers, utilizing cryptographic hash functions, and employing additional mechanisms to ensure confidentiality, integrity, and authentication of data.

Block Cipher Modes of Operation
Block cipher modes of operation define how block ciphers process plaintext blocks to produce ciphertext. Each mode offers different properties and is suitable for various applications:

Electronic Codebook (ECB): The simplest form, where each plaintext block is encrypted independently. While fast and parallelizable, ECB is not recommended for sensitive data as identical plaintext blocks produce identical ciphertext blocks, revealing patterns.

Cipher Block Chaining (CBC): Each plaintext block is XORed with the previous ciphertext block before encryption, introducing dependency between blocks. An initialization vector (IV) is used for the first block. CBC mode provides better security than ECB but requires sequential processing, which can be a limitation in parallelized environments.

Counter (CTR): Converts a block cipher into a stream cipher by encrypting successive values of a "counter." CTR mode allows for parallel encryption and decryption, making it suitable for high-speed applications. It's important to never reuse the same counter value with the same key.

Galois/Counter Mode (GCM): An extension of CTR mode, GCM provides both confidentiality and integrity by incorporating an authentication tag. It's widely used in protocols like TLS due to its efficiency and security.

Cryptographic Hash Functions
Cryptographic hash functions are algorithms that take an input (or 'message') and return a fixed-size string of bytes, typically a digest that is unique to each unique input. They are used in various security applications to ensure data integrity and authenticity.

Properties: A good cryptographic hash function has certain essential properties, including pre-image resistance (difficult to find input from its hash), second pre-image resistance (difficult to find another input with the same hash), and collision resistance (difficult to find two different inputs with the same hash).

Applications:

Data Integrity: Hash functions are used to verify the integrity of data by generating a hash of the data and comparing it with a previously computed hash.

Password Storage: Storing hashed values of passwords instead of plaintext passwords enhances security. Salting (adding a random value to the password before hashing) further increases protection against rainbow table attacks.

Digital Signatures: Hash functions are used in digital signatures, where a hash of the message is encrypted with a private key. The recipient decrypts it with the corresponding public key and compares the hash to ensure the message's integrity and authenticity.

Advanced Techniques

Authenticated Encryption: This approach combines encryption and authentication in a single step, providing confidentiality, integrity, and authenticity. Examples include GCM and CCM (Counter with CBC-MAC).

Key Derivation Functions (KDFs): KDFs derive one or more secret keys from a secret value such as a master key, password, or passphrase. They are used in various applications, including generating keys for encryption algorithms from passwords.

Cryptographic Salt: In the context of password hashing, a salt is a random value added to the password before hashing. This ensures that the same password will generate different hashes, thwarting pre-computed rainbow table attacks.

Advanced cryptographic techniques and tools play a pivotal role in enhancing the security of symmetric cryptography, addressing its inherent limitations, and ensuring the robust protection of data in a wide array of applications. Proper implementation and understanding of these techniques are crucial for maintaining data confidentiality, integrity, and authenticity.

Public Key Infrastructure (PKI) is a framework that provides security services and enables secure, encrypted communication over networks like the Internet. PKI relies on a set of roles, policies, hardware, software, and procedures needed to create, manage, distribute, use, store, and revoke digital certificates. At the heart of PKI are several key components and operations:

Components of PKI

1. **Digital Certificates**: A digital certificate, often compared to a digital passport, is an electronic document that uses a digital signature to bind a public key with an individual's identity. The certificate includes the public key, information about the identity of the holder, the validity period, the issuing authority, and other metadata.
2. **Certificate Authority (CA)**: A CA is a trusted entity that issues digital certificates. The CA verifies the certificate applicant's credentials before issuing a certificate, ensuring that the public key contained in the certificate belongs to the person, organization, system, or device it claims to represent.
3. **Registration Authority (RA)**: An RA is responsible for accepting requests for digital certificates and authenticating the individual or organization making the request. The

RA is often seen as an intermediary between the user and the CA, although its duties can sometimes be performed directly by a CA.

4. **Certificate Repository**: A secure location (often accessible online) where digital certificates are stored and can be accessed by parties needing to validate a certificate's status.

5. **Certificate Revocation Lists (CRLs)**: CRLs are lists of certificates that have been revoked by the CA before their expiration dates for various reasons, such as compromise of the private key or change in the holder's information.

Operations of PKI

1. **Certificate Issuance**: The process begins with an entity requesting a certificate from the CA, often through an RA. The CA verifies the entity's identity and, once satisfied, issues a digital certificate containing the entity's public key.

2. **Certificate Validation**: When a party receives a digital certificate, it contacts the issuing CA (or checks a certificate repository) to confirm that the certificate is valid, has not been revoked, and belongs to the sender.

3. **Encryption and Decryption**: PKI enables secure communication by allowing the sender to encrypt data using the recipient's public key (ensuring only the recipient can decrypt the message with their private key) and vice versa for secure message transmission.

4. **Digital Signatures**: A digital signature, created using the sender's private key, is attached to a document or message to ensure the integrity and authenticity of the message. The recipient uses the sender's public key to verify the signature.

Role in Establishing Trust

- **Authentication**: Digital certificates authenticate the identity of the entities involved in the communication, ensuring that the parties are who they claim to be.

- **Confidentiality**: By encrypting data with the recipient's public key, PKI ensures that only the intended recipient can decrypt and read the message, maintaining confidentiality.

- **Integrity**: Digital signatures verify that the message or document has not been altered in transit, maintaining its integrity.

- **Non-Repudiation**: Digital signatures also provide non-repudiation, meaning the sender cannot deny the authenticity of the message they signed.

PKI is foundational in establishing a trusted environment for digital communications, providing the mechanisms for secure data transmission, authentication, and non-repudiation in various applications, from secure email to online banking and confidential document exchange. Its effectiveness hinges on the trustworthiness of the CAs and the robustness of the underlying technologies and policies.

Asymmetric cryptography, also known as public-key cryptography, uses a pair of keys for encryption and decryption—a public key that can be shared openly and a private key that is kept secret by the owner. This cryptographic method underpins many security protocols and applications, playing a pivotal role in modern security architectures.

SSL/TLS for Secure Communications

Secure Socket Layer (SSL) and its successor, Transport Layer Security (TLS), are cryptographic protocols that provide secure communication over a computer network. They are widely used on the Internet for securing web traffic, indicated by "https://" in web addresses.

- **Process**: During the SSL/TLS handshake process, the server presents its digital certificate (containing the public key) to the client. The client verifies the certificate with the issuing Certificate Authority (CA) to ensure its legitimacy. The client then uses the server's public key to encrypt a session key, which is sent back to the server. The server decrypts this with its private key, and both parties use the session key for symmetric encryption during the session, combining the efficiency of symmetric encryption with the security of asymmetric encryption.
- **Importance**: SSL/TLS encryption protects the confidentiality and integrity of data in transit, preventing eavesdropping and tampering by malicious actors. It's essential for securing online transactions, personal information, and any data exchange over the Internet.

Digital Signatures for Non-Repudiation

Digital signatures use asymmetric cryptography to verify the authenticity and integrity of digital messages or documents, providing non-repudiation—assurance that a specific person sent the message and that it hasn't been altered.

- **Process**: The sender generates a hash of the message and encrypts the hash with their private key to create a digital signature. The signature is attached to the message and sent to the recipient. The recipient decrypts the signature using the sender's public key, obtains the hash, and compares it with the hash they generate from the received message. If the hashes match, the message is authentic and unchanged.
- **Importance**: Digital signatures are crucial for secure electronic transactions, legal documents, and any digital communication where authenticity and integrity are paramount. They ensure that parties in a transaction cannot deny their participation (non-repudiation) and that the content has not been altered.

Key Exchange Protocols

Key exchange protocols, such as Diffie-Hellman, enable two parties to securely establish a shared secret key over an insecure channel, which can then be used for symmetric encryption.

- **Process**: In the Diffie-Hellman key exchange, both parties agree on a large prime number and a base (public values). Each party then generates a private value, calculates a public value (using the agreed prime, base, and their private value), and exchanges the public value with the other party. Both parties can then compute the same shared secret, which is used as the key for symmetric encryption.
- **Importance**: Key exchange protocols are fundamental in setting up secure communication channels, especially in environments where prior secure exchange of symmetric keys is not feasible. They enable the secure initiation of encrypted sessions, ensuring confidentiality even before secure communication is established.

Asymmetric cryptography forms the backbone of many security protocols and mechanisms in today's digital world. Its applications in SSL/TLS, digital signatures, and key exchange protocols are integral to achieving confidentiality, integrity, authentication, and non-repudiation in digital communications, making it indispensable in modern security architectures.

Secure design principles are foundational guidelines that help in the development of systems and applications with robust security from the outset. These principles aim to minimize vulnerabilities, deter potential attacks, and ensure that systems remain secure even when unforeseen threats arise. Key principles include least privilege, defense in depth, fail-safe defaults, and security by design.

Least Privilege

Principle: The principle of least privilege dictates that individuals, systems, and applications should have only the minimum levels of access—or permissions—needed to perform their tasks. This limits the potential damage from accidents, errors, and unauthorized use.

Application: In practice, this involves creating user accounts with the least amount of privilege necessary, using role-based access control, and regularly reviewing and revoking unnecessary permissions. For instance, a database administrator might have access to sensitive data, but an application developer would have access restricted to only the development environment.

Defense in Depth

Principle: Defense in depth is a layered approach to security that establishes multiple barriers across different points in a system. The idea is that if one security measure fails, others will continue to provide protection.

Application: This principle is applied through the implementation of various security controls such as firewalls, intrusion detection systems, encryption, and security policies, creating a multi-layered defense. For example, sensitive data might be encrypted at rest (one layer), transmitted over secure protocols (another layer), and accessible only through authenticated and authorized sessions (yet another layer).

Fail-Safe Defaults

Principle: The principle of fail-safe defaults ensures that, in the event of a failure or security breach, the system defaults to a secure state that minimizes damage and exposure. Access decisions should deny by default, granting permission only when explicit access rights are provided.

Application: This can involve setting systems to lock down access in the case of an anomaly or failure, such as closing network ports, terminating sessions, or locking user accounts after multiple failed authentication attempts. For example, a web application might default to not displaying any content unless it has been explicitly marked as safe to display.

Security by Design

Principle: Security by design means integrating security considerations into every phase of the system development lifecycle, rather than adding them as an afterthought. This approach ensures that security is a core component of system functionality and architecture.

Application: This involves conducting threat modeling and risk assessments during the design phase, using secure coding practices during development, performing security testing throughout the development lifecycle, and maintaining security during deployment and maintenance. For instance, developers might use parameterized queries to prevent SQL injection attacks when designing database interactions.

Application in Secure Systems and Applications Development
Applying these principles in the development of secure systems and applications involves a holistic approach that encompasses planning, implementation, and maintenance stages:

Planning and Design: Security requirements are defined early, based on a thorough understanding of the threats and risks. Security by design and defense in depth are key considerations, ensuring that security controls are layered and integrated from the start.
Implementation: Developers adhere to secure coding practices, minimizing vulnerabilities and ensuring that applications operate with least privilege. Security features are tested rigorously.
Deployment and Maintenance: Systems are deployed with fail-safe defaults, ensuring that they revert to a secure state in case of failure. Regular updates and patches are applied to address new vulnerabilities, maintaining the security posture over time.
By adhering to these secure design principles, organizations can build systems and applications that are resilient to threats, protect sensitive data, and ensure the continuity and integrity of their operations.

Evaluating and enhancing the security of systems and applications is a multifaceted process that involves a combination of proactive measures, such as secure coding practices and adherence to security frameworks, as well as reactive measures like security testing. These methods work in tandem to identify vulnerabilities, mitigate risks, and ensure that systems and applications adhere to best security practices.

Security Testing
Security testing involves various techniques designed to uncover vulnerabilities and weaknesses in systems and applications, providing insights into potential security gaps.

Penetration Testing: Penetration testing, or pen testing, simulates cyber attacks on a system to identify exploitable vulnerabilities. Ethical hackers use the same tools and techniques as attackers but do so with permission, with the aim of strengthening the system's defenses.
Code Review: Security code reviews involve a systematic examination of application source code to identify security flaws. This can be done manually by experienced developers or using automated tools that scan code for known vulnerabilities.

Vulnerability Scanning: Automated tools are used to scan systems and applications for known vulnerabilities, providing a list of weaknesses that need to be addressed.

Dynamic Application Security Testing (DAST): DAST tools test applications from the outside, simulating attacks on a running application to identify vulnerabilities that could be exploited during operation.

Secure Coding Practices

Secure coding practices are preventive measures that developers can take to minimize vulnerabilities in the codebase and protect against common attack vectors.

Input Validation: Ensuring that all input received from users or external systems is validated to prevent common attacks such as SQL injection or cross-site scripting (XSS).

Error Handling: Implementing secure error handling that does not expose sensitive information or system details to users, which could be leveraged by an attacker.

Authentication and Authorization: Enforcing strong authentication mechanisms and ensuring that users are authorized to access only the resources that are necessary for their role (principle of least privilege).

Use of Cryptography: Properly implementing cryptographic functions to protect sensitive data in transit and at rest, including the secure storage of encryption keys.

Security Frameworks and Standards

Adhering to established security frameworks and standards can guide organizations in implementing best practices and achieving a baseline level of security.

OWASP: The Open Web Application Security Project (OWASP) is a nonprofit foundation that works to improve the security of software. OWASP's Top 10 is a widely recognized list of the most critical web application security risks, providing a starting point for developers and security professionals to address common vulnerabilities.

CIS Benchmarks: The Center for Internet Security (CIS) provides well-defined, unbiased security configuration benchmarks and best practices to help organizations secure their systems.

ISO/IEC 27001: This international standard specifies the requirements for establishing, implementing, maintaining, and continually improving an information security management system (ISMS), providing a systematic approach to managing sensitive company information.

Implementation

Implementing these methods involves a continuous cycle of assessment, remediation, and improvement:

Integration into the Development Lifecycle: Security practices should be integrated into every stage of the development lifecycle, from initial design through deployment and maintenance.

Regular Training and Awareness: Ensuring that development teams are trained in secure coding practices and are aware of the latest security threats and mitigation techniques.

Continuous Monitoring and Response: Establishing mechanisms for continuous monitoring of systems and applications for security incidents, coupled with a well-defined incident response plan.

By combining thorough security testing, adherence to secure coding practices, and the integration of established security frameworks and standards, organizations can significantly enhance the security of their systems and applications. This comprehensive approach ensures that security considerations are embedded in the fabric of system and application development, leading to more resilient and trustworthy software.

Emerging technologies like cloud computing, the Internet of Things (IoT), and blockchain introduce transformative opportunities for businesses and individuals alike. However, they also present unique security challenges that require careful consideration and strategic mitigation within the frameworks of security architecture and engineering.

Cloud Computing

Challenges:

- **Data Security and Privacy**: Sensitive data stored in the cloud can be vulnerable to breaches if not properly secured, raising concerns about data confidentiality and privacy.
- **Access Control and Identity Management**: Managing access to cloud resources can be complex, especially with the proliferation of users and devices.
- **Multi-Tenancy and Shared Resources**: The shared nature of cloud services could lead to potential data leaks and breaches if isolation controls fail.

Mitigation Strategies:

- **Encryption**: Implement encryption for data at rest and in transit to protect sensitive information.
- **Robust Access Management**: Employ strong authentication mechanisms and identity management solutions to control access to cloud resources.
- **Compliance and Standards**: Adhere to industry standards and regulatory requirements specific to cloud security, such as ISO/IEC 27017, and leverage cloud providers' compliance certifications.

Internet of Things (IoT)

Challenges:

- **Device Security**: Many IoT devices have limited processing capabilities, making it challenging to implement traditional security measures.
- **Network Security**: The interconnectivity of IoT devices increases the attack surface, exposing networks to potential breaches.
- **Data Privacy**: IoT devices often collect vast amounts of personal data, necessitating stringent data privacy measures.

Mitigation Strategies:

- **Secure Device Lifecycle Management**: Ensure security is integrated throughout the device lifecycle, from secure design and development to deployment and decommissioning.
- **Segmentation and Network Controls**: Use network segmentation to isolate IoT devices and implement strict network access controls to reduce the risk of lateral movement by attackers.

- **Regular Updates and Patch Management**: Maintain a process for regularly updating and patching IoT devices to address known vulnerabilities.

Blockchain

Challenges:

- **Smart Contract Vulnerabilities**: Flaws in smart contract code can be exploited, leading to significant losses or unauthorized actions within blockchain applications.
- **Privacy Concerns**: Public blockchains store transaction data transparently, which can raise privacy issues for certain applications.
- **Scalability and Performance**: The decentralized nature of blockchain can lead to scalability issues and reduced transaction processing speed, impacting its usability.

Mitigation Strategies:

- **Smart Contract Audits**: Conduct thorough audits and security assessments of smart contract code before deployment to identify and remediate vulnerabilities.
- **Privacy-Enhancing Technologies**: Utilize privacy-focused blockchain technologies or features, such as zero-knowledge proofs, to enhance transaction privacy without sacrificing transparency.
- **Layered Solutions and Off-Chain Transactions**: Explore layered blockchain architectures and off-chain transaction mechanisms to address scalability and performance challenges while maintaining security.

General Considerations for Security Architecture and Engineering

- **Security by Design**: Integrate security considerations into the design phase of emerging technology solutions, ensuring that security is built in from the ground up.
- **Continuous Risk Assessment**: Conduct ongoing risk assessments to identify and address new threats and vulnerabilities as they emerge.
- **Cross-Domain Expertise**: Foster collaboration between security professionals, developers, and domain experts to ensure a comprehensive understanding of the unique challenges and opportunities presented by emerging technologies.

Emerging technologies undoubtedly bring new security challenges, but with proactive risk management, adherence to security best practices, and a focus on resilience and adaptability, organizations can navigate these challenges effectively. Security architecture and engineering must evolve continuously to address the dynamic threat landscape and leverage the opportunities presented by innovation in cloud computing, IoT, blockchain, and beyond.

Chapter 6: Communication and Network Security:

Foundational principles of secure network design, such as segmentation, isolation, and the use of demilitarized zones (DMZs), are critical for enhancing the security and resilience of networks. By applying these principles, organizations can mitigate risks, limit the scope of potential breaches, and ensure the continuity of their operations even in the face of security threats.

Segmentation

Principle: Network segmentation involves dividing a network into smaller, distinct segments or subnets. Each segment can have its own security policies and controls tailored to the specific needs and risk profiles of the assets or applications it contains.

Contribution to Security:

- **Containment of Breaches**: By compartmentalizing the network, segmentation limits the lateral movement of attackers, containing breaches within isolated segments and preventing widespread network compromise.
- **Targeted Security Controls**: Segmentation allows for the application of more granular security controls, enabling tighter security for sensitive segments while maintaining usability for less critical areas.
- **Reduced Attack Surface**: By limiting the interaction between segments, the attack surface of the network is reduced, making it more difficult for attackers to exploit the entire network.

Isolation

Principle: Isolation involves separating critical systems and networks from the rest of an organization's network infrastructure to protect sensitive data and critical operations. This can be achieved through physical isolation (using separate hardware) or logical isolation (using virtualization technologies).

Contribution to Security:

- **Enhanced Protection for Critical Assets**: Isolating critical systems ensures that they are protected by dedicated security measures, reducing the risk of exposure to threats targeting the broader network.
- **Improved Performance and Stability**: Isolation can also protect critical systems from performance degradation and stability issues arising from the broader network, ensuring the reliability of essential services.
- **Regulatory Compliance**: For certain industries, isolation helps in complying with regulatory requirements that mandate strict controls and separation for sensitive data and systems.

Demilitarized Zones (DMZs)

Principle: A DMZ is a network segment that acts as a buffer zone between an organization's internal network and untrusted external networks, such as the internet. It typically hosts public-facing services (e.g., web servers, email servers) that need to be accessible from the outside but also need to be secured against unauthorized access.

Contribution to Security:

- **Controlled Access**: The DMZ allows for strict control over inbound and outbound traffic, ensuring that only authorized communications pass through to the internal network.

- **Layered Defense**: By placing public-facing services in a DMZ, organizations can implement a layered defense strategy, where multiple security controls work together to protect both the DMZ and the internal network.
- **Incident Containment**: If a public-facing service in the DMZ is compromised, the damage can be contained within the DMZ, protecting the internal network from direct exposure to the attack.

Integration into Secure Network Design

Integrating these principles into a secure network design involves careful planning and implementation:

- **Network Architecture Planning**: Design the network architecture with segmentation, isolation, and DMZs in mind, considering the specific security requirements of different business units, applications, and data types.
- **Access Control Policies**: Implement robust access control policies that define who can access various network segments, under what conditions, and what resources they can use.
- **Continuous Monitoring and Review**: Regularly monitor network traffic and segment configurations to ensure compliance with security policies and identify any deviations that might indicate a security threat.

By adhering to these foundational principles, organizations can create a network architecture that is not only secure but also resilient, ensuring that even if certain parts of the network are compromised, the integrity and continuity of critical operations are maintained.

Architectural frameworks provide structured approaches for designing and managing network infrastructures, while network topologies describe the physical or logical arrangement of network devices. Understanding these frameworks and topologies is crucial for developing secure and efficient networks. Here, we'll explore some common network topologies—star, mesh, and hybrid—and discuss their security considerations and best practices.

Star Topology
In a star topology, all network devices are connected to a central hub or switch. The hub acts as a conduit to transmit messages.

Security Considerations:

Central Point of Failure: The central hub represents a single point of failure. If the hub is compromised or fails, the entire network can become inoperative.
Traffic Analysis: An attacker compromising the central hub could potentially monitor all traffic passing through the network.
Best Practices:

Redundancy: Implement redundant central devices or failover mechanisms to mitigate the risk of a single point of failure.

Secure Hub: Ensure the central hub is securely configured and monitored, applying regular security updates and patches.

Network Segmentation: Use VLANs or similar technologies to segment the network at the hub level, limiting the spread of potential attacks.

Mesh Topology

In a mesh topology, each network device is connected to one or more other devices, with no central point of control, allowing for multiple paths between any two nodes.

Security Considerations:

Complex Configuration: The complexity of fully connected mesh networks can make security configurations and updates challenging.

Scalability: As the number of devices increases, the complexity of managing secure connections between every pair of devices can become unmanageable.

Best Practices:

Automated Security Policies: Leverage automated tools to manage security policies and ensure consistent security configurations across the network.

Regular Audits: Conduct frequent security audits to identify potential vulnerabilities or misconfigurations in the network's interconnected structure.

Encryption: Use strong encryption for data transmitted between devices to protect against eavesdropping and man-in-the-middle attacks.

Hybrid Topology

Hybrid topologies combine elements of different topologies (e.g., star, mesh, bus) to meet specific network requirements and optimize performance and security.

Security Considerations:

Complexity: The combination of different topologies can introduce complexity, making it harder to identify security vulnerabilities and manage security configurations.

Inconsistent Security Policies: Different parts of the network might have varying security requirements and policies, leading to potential gaps in protection.

Best Practices:

Unified Security Framework: Adopt a unified security framework that can be applied consistently across different parts of the network.

Segmentation and Isolation: Use segmentation and isolation to separate different network segments, applying appropriate security controls to each segment based on its specific requirements and risks.

Centralized Monitoring: Implement centralized security monitoring and management tools to maintain visibility and control over the diverse components of the network.

Architectural Frameworks

Architectural frameworks such as TOGAF (The Open Group Architecture Framework) or SABSA (Sherwood Applied Business Security Architecture) provide methodologies for designing, planning, implementing, and governing enterprise network architectures. These frameworks help ensure that network designs align with business goals, are adaptable to changing requirements, and incorporate security as a foundational element.

Security Integration:

Alignment with Business Objectives: Ensure network designs support business objectives while providing the necessary security controls to protect business assets.
Risk Management: Integrate risk management processes into the network design, identifying potential threats and vulnerabilities and implementing appropriate mitigation strategies.
Compliance: Design networks to comply with relevant industry standards, regulations, and best practices, ensuring that security measures meet required compliance levels.
Incorporating security considerations and best practices into network topologies and adhering to structured architectural frameworks are essential for developing secure, resilient, and efficient networks. These strategies enable organizations to protect their assets while maintaining flexibility and scalability to support evolving business needs.

Key network security devices like firewalls, Intrusion Detection Systems (IDS), Intrusion Prevention Systems (IPS), and Virtual Private Networks (VPNs) play crucial roles in protecting networked systems. Each device serves specific functions in the broader context of network security, and their effective configuration is essential for optimal security.
Firewalls
Role and Functions: Firewalls act as a barrier between secure internal networks and untrusted external networks, such as the internet. They filter incoming and outgoing traffic based on an organization's security policies, blocking or permitting data packets based on predefined rules.
Optimal Configuration:
- **Default Deny**: Configure the firewall with a default deny rule, ensuring that only traffic explicitly allowed by the security policy is permitted to pass.
- **Least Privilege**: Establish rules that grant the minimum necessary access for network services and users, reducing the potential attack surface.
- **Egress Filtering**: Implement outbound traffic filtering to prevent sensitive data exfiltration and block connections to known malicious IP addresses.

Intrusion Detection Systems (IDS)
Role and Functions: IDS monitor network and system activities for malicious activities or policy violations. When an intrusion is detected, the IDS generates alerts, allowing security personnel to take appropriate action.
Optimal Configuration:
- **Placement**: Position IDS sensors at strategic points within the network, such as at the network perimeter and key internal network segments, to maximize visibility of potential attacks.

- **Signature Updates**: Regularly update the IDS with the latest signature definitions to ensure it can detect new and evolving threats.
- **Anomaly-Based Detection**: Configure anomaly-based detection rules to identify deviations from normal network behavior, which could indicate a potential security threat.

Intrusion Prevention Systems (IPS)

Role and Functions: IPS are similar to IDS but with the ability to automatically block or prevent detected threats in real-time, without the need for manual intervention.

Optimal Configuration:

- **Inline Deployment**: Deploy IPS devices inline, allowing them to actively analyze and take action on traffic passing through the network.
- **Tuning**: Tune IPS rules and thresholds to the specific network environment to minimize false positives and false negatives, ensuring that legitimate traffic is not inadvertently blocked.
- **Integration**: Integrate IPS with other security systems, such as firewalls and SIEM (Security Information and Event Management) systems, for a coordinated response to threats.

Virtual Private Networks (VPNs)

Role and Functions: VPNs create a secure, encrypted tunnel between a device and a network over the internet, ensuring that data transmitted remains confidential and secure from interception.

Optimal Configuration:

- **Strong Encryption**: Use strong encryption protocols, such as IKEv2/IPSec or OpenVPN, to protect the confidentiality and integrity of data in transit.
- **Two-Factor Authentication**: Implement two-factor authentication for VPN access, adding an extra layer of security beyond just usernames and passwords.
- **Split Tunneling**: Avoid split tunneling, where only part of the traffic is sent through the VPN, as it can expose the network to security risks. Ensure all traffic from the device is routed through the VPN tunnel.

Examples

- A company might configure its **firewall** to block all incoming traffic to certain sensitive ports (e.g., RDP, SSH) from the internet, except from known, trusted IP addresses, while also setting up rules to block access to malicious websites.
- An **IDS** could be configured to alert administrators when there is an unusually high volume of traffic to a particular server, indicating a potential DDoS attack, or when there are repeated login failures, suggesting a brute force attack attempt.
- An **IPS** might be set up to automatically block IP addresses that are identified as sources of malicious traffic, such as known malware distribution points or command and control servers for botnets.
- A **VPN** configuration for remote employees could enforce the use of strong encryption, require two-factor authentication, and ensure that all remote desktop and file sharing activities are conducted through the VPN to maintain data security.

The effective configuration and integration of network security devices like firewalls, IDS, IPS, and VPNs are foundational to creating a secure network environment. By tailoring configurations to the specific needs and risks of the organization, security teams can ensure robust protection against a wide range of threats.

Securing wireless networks presents unique challenges due to their inherent nature, including the broadcast of data over the air, which can be intercepted by unauthorized individuals if not properly protected. Implementing robust security measures and protocols is essential for safeguarding wireless communication channels.

Challenges in Securing Wireless Networks
Eavesdropping: Wireless signals can extend beyond the physical boundaries of a location, making it possible for attackers to intercept and eavesdrop on wireless communications from a distance.
Unauthorized Access: Unsecured wireless networks can be easily accessed by unauthorized users, leading to potential data breaches and unauthorized use of network resources.
Spoofing and Rogue Access Points: Attackers can set up rogue access points or spoof legitimate ones to deceive users into connecting to malicious networks, facilitating man-in-the-middle attacks and data interception.
Encryption Weaknesses: Older wireless security protocols like WEP (Wired Equivalent Privacy) have significant vulnerabilities, making it crucial to use strong and up-to-date encryption standards.
Security Protocols and Strategies
WPA3 (Wi-Fi Protected Access 3)
Overview: WPA3 is the latest security certification for Wi-Fi networks, providing significant improvements over its predecessor, WPA2, including enhanced cryptographic strength.
Features:
Individualized Data Encryption: WPA3 uses Simultaneous Authentication of Equals (SAE) to provide individualized data encryption, even on open networks, protecting against eavesdropping.
Protection Against Brute-Force Attacks: WPA3 implements measures to protect against brute-force attacks, limiting the data available to attackers attempting to guess passwords.
Implementation: Ensure that all wireless devices and access points are configured to use WPA3. For devices that do not support WPA3, consider a separate network segment that uses WPA2 with a strong and complex passphrase.
EAP (Extensible Authentication Protocol)
Overview: EAP provides a framework for various authentication mechanisms over wireless (and wired) networks, allowing for the use of credentials beyond simple passwords, such as tokens, smart cards, and certificates.
Features:
Flexibility: EAP supports multiple authentication methods, catering to different security requirements and scenarios.

Integration with Enterprise Systems: EAP is commonly used in conjunction with 802.1X for network access control, allowing integration with enterprise-level authentication services like RADIUS and Active Directory.

Implementation: Use EAP methods that provide mutual authentication, such as EAP-TLS, to ensure both the client and the server authenticate each other, reducing the risk of rogue access points.

Additional Strategies

SSID Hiding and MAC Filtering: While not foolproof, hiding the SSID (Service Set Identifier) of a wireless network and implementing MAC address filtering can provide an additional layer of obscurity and control.

Network Segmentation: Separate wireless networks based on user roles and device types (e.g., guest network, employee network, IoT devices) to minimize the potential impact of a compromised device or network segment.

Regular Updates and Monitoring: Keep firmware on wireless access points and devices up to date to address known vulnerabilities. Implement continuous monitoring to detect and respond to suspicious activities on the wireless network.

Physical Security Measures: Consider the physical placement of wireless access points to minimize signal spillage outside the intended coverage area, reducing the risk of eavesdropping from outside the premises.

Securing wireless networks requires a multifaceted approach that combines the use of advanced security protocols like WPA3 and EAP with strategic measures such as network segmentation and regular security updates. By addressing the unique vulnerabilities of wireless communications and implementing robust security practices, organizations can significantly enhance the security and resilience of their wireless networks.

Encryption protocols like SSL/TLS, SSH, and IPsec play crucial roles in securing data in transit across networks by providing confidentiality, integrity, and authentication. These protocols are foundational to many security architectures, ensuring that data remains protected as it moves between devices and across networks.

SSL/TLS (Secure Sockets Layer/Transport Layer Security)
Mechanisms:

SSL/TLS operates between the transport and application layers, encrypting data before it's transmitted over the network.

The protocol uses asymmetric cryptography for key exchange (usually RSA or Diffie-Hellman) during the SSL/TLS handshake, where the client and server agree on encryption algorithms and exchange session keys.

Once the session is established, symmetric encryption (like AES) is used for data transfer, ensuring efficiency and confidentiality.
Applications:

SSL/TLS is widely used to secure web communications, indicated by "https://" in URLs. It's essential for online transactions, email, and any application requiring secure data exchange over the internet.
Beyond web browsers and servers, SSL/TLS is used in other applications like email (SMTPS, POPS, IMAPS) and VoIP.
Security Contributions:

Provides end-to-end encryption, ensuring that data cannot be read by third parties in transit.
Authenticates the server (and optionally the client) using digital certificates, preventing man-in-the-middle attacks.
Ensures data integrity, verifying that data has not been tampered with during transmission.
SSH (Secure Shell)
Mechanisms:

SSH is a protocol for secure network services over an unsecured network, providing a secure channel over which commands and data can be transmitted.
It uses public-key cryptography to authenticate users and devices, typically through RSA or DSA keys.
Once authentication is successful, all communication is encrypted using symmetric encryption algorithms, with keys negotiated at the start of the session.
Applications:

SSH is commonly used for secure remote login to computer systems, enabling secure command execution on remote machines.
It's also used for securely transferring files (using SCP or SFTP) and for securely tunneling other protocols (e.g., HTTP, SMTP).
Security Contributions:

Encrypts all communications, protecting data from eavesdropping and interception.
Authenticates both the client and server, ensuring that users are connecting to the correct server and vice versa.
Can be configured to use key-based authentication, which is more secure than traditional password-based authentication methods.
IPsec (Internet Protocol Security)
Mechanisms:

IPsec operates at the network layer, securing IP communications by authenticating and encrypting each IP packet of a communication session.

It can operate in two modes: Transport mode (encrypts only the payload of each packet) and Tunnel mode (encrypts the entire IP packet).

IPsec uses the IKE (Internet Key Exchange) protocol to negotiate and establish secure sessions, exchanging keys and agreeing on encryption and authentication methods.

Applications:

IPsec is used to secure VPN connections, enabling secure site-to-site or remote access connections over the internet.

It's also used to secure private data communications over IP networks, including the protection of data flows between a pair of hosts (host-to-host), between a pair of security gateways (network-to-network), or between a security gateway and a host (network-to-host).

Security Contributions:

Provides confidentiality through encryption, ensuring that data cannot be read by unauthorized parties.

Ensures data integrity, verifying that packets have not been tampered with in transit.

Supports data origin authentication, confirming the identity of the sender of the data.

These encryption protocols are fundamental to securing modern digital communications, offering robust mechanisms to protect data in transit against a variety of threats. Their widespread adoption is a testament to their effectiveness in providing secure, reliable, and confidential communications over potentially insecure networks.

Network Access Control (NAC) is a comprehensive approach to securing networks by enforcing policies that regulate access to network resources based on the user's identity and the compliance status of their devices. Endpoint security management complements NAC by ensuring that devices meet security standards before they connect to the network, thereby protecting network resources against unauthorized access and threats.

Implementation of NAC Measures

Endpoint Assessment: Before granting access, NAC systems evaluate devices attempting to connect to the network to ensure they comply with the organization's security policy. This includes checking for up-to-date antivirus software, required security patches, and appropriate system configurations.

Access Control Policies: NAC solutions enforce access control policies that define who can access the network, what resources they are allowed to access, and under what conditions. Policies can be based on user roles, device types, connection methods, and other attributes.

Authentication and Authorization: NAC systems integrate with authentication services like RADIUS, LDAP, or Active Directory to authenticate users. Following successful authentication, they determine the level of network access based on predefined policies.

Network Segmentation: NAC can dynamically assign devices to specific network segments based on policy compliance and user credentials. This limits access to sensitive areas of the network and contains potential security breaches within isolated segments.

Continuous Monitoring and Response: NAC systems continuously monitor connected devices for changes in compliance status. If a device becomes non-compliant (e.g., due to a disabled firewall or detected malware), the system can automatically restrict its access or quarantine the device for remediation.

Importance of Endpoint Security Management
Threat Prevention: Endpoint security management involves deploying security solutions on devices to prevent malware infections, data breaches, and other security threats. This includes antivirus and antimalware software, personal firewalls, and intrusion prevention systems.

Compliance and Patch Management: Ensuring that endpoints are regularly updated with the latest security patches and configurations is vital to protect against vulnerabilities. Endpoint management tools can automate the deployment of patches and monitor compliance across all devices.

Data Protection: Endpoint security management tools often include data loss prevention (DLP) capabilities to protect sensitive information. This can involve encrypting data on endpoints and monitoring data transfer to prevent unauthorized exfiltration.

Incident Detection and Response: Advanced endpoint security solutions offer capabilities for detecting and responding to security incidents in real-time. This includes isolating infected devices, removing malware, and restoring affected systems to a secure state.

Integration of NAC and Endpoint Security
Integrating NAC with endpoint security management creates a synergistic security posture where network access is controlled based on the real-time security status of devices, and endpoints are kept secure and compliant with organizational policies. For example, a device that fails a security check due to outdated antivirus definitions can be automatically directed to a remediation VLAN where it must update its antivirus software before gaining access to the main network.

This holistic approach ensures that only secure, policy-compliant devices can access network resources, significantly reducing the risk of security breaches and enhancing the overall security posture of the organization. By combining the dynamic control of network access with robust endpoint security measures, organizations can effectively protect their networks and data from a wide range of threats.

Effective network security management is critical in safeguarding an organization's digital assets against evolving threats. Best practices in this area encompass a range of strategies and tools designed to identify vulnerabilities, apply necessary updates, and detect threats in real-time. Here are some key practices:

Regular Vulnerability Assessments

- **Scheduled Scans**: Conduct regular vulnerability scans to identify weaknesses in the network infrastructure, including outdated software, misconfigurations, and open ports.
- **Penetration Testing**: Supplement vulnerability scans with periodic penetration testing, which involves simulating cyber-attacks to evaluate the effectiveness of security measures.
- **Risk Analysis**: After identifying vulnerabilities, perform a risk analysis to prioritize remediation efforts based on the potential impact and likelihood of exploitation.

Patch Management

- **Automated Patching Tools**: Utilize automated patch management tools to streamline the process of applying software updates, ensuring that all systems are consistently protected against known vulnerabilities.
- **Patch Testing**: Before widespread deployment, test patches in a controlled environment to ensure they do not disrupt system functionality or introduce new vulnerabilities.
- **Patch Prioritization**: Given the volume of updates, prioritize patching based on the severity of the vulnerabilities, focusing first on those that pose the greatest risk to the network.

Advanced Threat Detection Tools

- **Intrusion Detection and Prevention Systems (IDPS)**: Deploy IDPS solutions to monitor network traffic for suspicious activities, providing real-time alerts and the capability to block malicious traffic.
- **Security Information and Event Management (SIEM)**: Implement SIEM systems to aggregate and analyze log data from various sources within the network, offering a comprehensive view of the security posture and facilitating the early detection of potential threats.
- **Endpoint Detection and Response (EDR)**: Use EDR tools to continuously monitor endpoints for signs of malicious activities, providing detailed forensic data and the ability to respond to threats quickly.

Additional Best Practices

- **Zero Trust Model**: Adopt a zero-trust security model that assumes all users and devices, both inside and outside the network, could be compromised and therefore must be verified before granting access to resources.
- **Network Segmentation**: Divide the network into segments, limiting access to sensitive information and containing potential breaches within isolated sections of the network.
- **Security Awareness Training**: Educate employees about security best practices, phishing, and other social engineering tactics, as human error remains a significant vulnerability in network security.

- **Encryption**: Use encryption for data in transit and at rest to protect sensitive information from interception and unauthorized access.
- **Regular Backups**: Maintain regular backups of critical data and systems, ensuring that they can be quickly restored in the event of a data loss incident.
- **Disaster Recovery and Business Continuity**: Develop and test disaster recovery and business continuity plans to ensure that the organization can maintain operations in the face of a significant network security event.

Implementing these best practices in network security management helps organizations build a resilient security posture capable of withstanding and rapidly recovering from cyber threats. By proactively identifying vulnerabilities, keeping systems up to date, and employing sophisticated tools to monitor and respond to threats, organizations can protect their networks and ensure the confidentiality, integrity, and availability of their digital assets.

Case Study 1: DDoS Attack on a Financial Institution

Scenario: A major financial institution faced a Distributed Denial of Service (DDoS) attack, where multiple compromised systems were used to flood the bank's online services with excessive traffic, overwhelming the servers and causing downtime for online banking services.

Lessons Learned:
- **Inadequate Preparedness**: The institution's infrastructure was not equipped to handle sudden, massive spikes in traffic, highlighting a lack of preparedness for DDoS attacks.
- **Impact on Reputation and Trust**: The downtime significantly impacted customer trust and the institution's reputation, emphasizing the importance of maintaining service availability.

Measures Implemented:
- **Increased Infrastructure Scalability**: Enhanced server capacity and network bandwidth to handle sudden surges in traffic.
- **DDoS Mitigation Services**: Engaged third-party DDoS mitigation services specializing in identifying and filtering malicious traffic before it reached the institution's network.
- **Incident Response Plan**: Developed a comprehensive incident response plan specifically addressing DDoS attacks, including communication strategies to manage customer expectations and trust.

Case Study 2: Man-in-the-Middle Attack on an E-commerce Platform

Scenario: An e-commerce platform experienced a man-in-the-middle (MitM) attack where an attacker intercepted communications between customers and the website. The attacker was able to capture sensitive information, including login credentials and payment details.

Lessons Learned:
- **Encryption Gaps**: The attack exploited unencrypted data transmission points, revealing the need for end-to-end encryption across the platform.
- **Lack of Monitoring**: The absence of effective monitoring tools delayed the detection of unusual patterns in network traffic that could have indicated an ongoing MitM attack.

Measures Implemented:

- **SSL/TLS Enforcement**: Implemented SSL/TLS encryption across the entire website, ensuring that all data transmitted between the server and clients is encrypted.
- **Network Monitoring and Anomaly Detection**: Deployed advanced network monitoring solutions with anomaly detection capabilities to identify and alert on suspicious activities indicative of MitM attempts.
- **Customer Authentication Enhancements**: Introduced multi-factor authentication (MFA) for customer accounts to add an extra layer of security beyond just username and password.

Hypothetical Scenario: Insider Threat in a Corporate Network

Scenario: A disgruntled employee in the IT department abused their access privileges to exfiltrate sensitive corporate data, including intellectual property and customer information, intending to sell it to competitors.

Lessons Learned:

- **Access Control Lapses**: Excessive access privileges granted to employees can lead to significant security risks if those privileges are abused.
- **Insufficient Insider Threat Detection**: The lack of a robust system to monitor and analyze user behavior allowed the malicious activities to go unnoticed for an extended period.

Measures Implemented:

- **Principle of Least Privilege**: Reviewed and revised access control policies to ensure employees only have access to resources necessary for their job functions.
- **User and Entity Behavior Analytics (UEBA)**: Implemented UEBA solutions to detect unusual behavior patterns that might indicate insider threats, such as abnormal data access or exfiltration attempts.
- **Regular Audits and Access Reviews**: Instituted regular audits of system access and user activities, along with periodic access reviews, to ensure that access rights remain appropriate and are promptly revoked when no longer needed.

These case studies and hypothetical scenarios underscore the diverse nature of network security breaches and the importance of adopting a multi-layered security approach. Lessons learned from such incidents inform the development of more robust security measures, helping organizations enhance their resilience against future threats.

Chapter 7: Identity and Access Management (IAM):

Physical and logical access control systems are fundamental components of an organization's security posture, each serving to protect different aspects of the organization's assets. While physical access control systems secure the tangible assets and environments, logical access control systems safeguard digital assets like data and information systems.

Physical Access Control Systems

Description: Physical access control systems manage and monitor access to physical spaces, such as buildings, rooms, or secure facilities. These systems ensure that only authorized individuals can enter specific physical areas.

Examples:

- **Locks and Keys**: Traditional lock-and-key mechanisms are the simplest form of physical access control.
- **Electronic Door Locks**: Card readers, keypads, or biometric systems control access to secured doors, elevators, and other entry points.
- **Surveillance Cameras**: While not controlling access directly, they monitor and record activities, acting as a deterrent and providing evidence of unauthorized access attempts.
- **Turnstiles and Barriers**: Used in high-traffic areas to control entry and exit points, often integrated with badge or ticketing systems.

Contexts:

- Used in virtually all organizations to protect assets such as office buildings, data centers, warehouses, and restricted areas where sensitive activities occur or critical infrastructure is located.

Logical Access Control Systems

Description: Logical access control systems manage access to digital resources, including networks, databases, files, and other data. They ensure that only authorized users can access specific digital assets and perform predefined actions.

Examples:

- **Password Authentication**: The most basic form of logical access control, requiring users to enter a username and password.
- **Multi-Factor Authentication (MFA)**: Enhances security by requiring additional verification factors, such as a fingerprint or a one-time code sent to a mobile device.
- **Role-Based Access Control (RBAC)**: Grants access rights based on the user's role within the organization, ensuring they have access only to the resources necessary for their job functions.
- **Encryption**: Protects data by encoding it, allowing only those with the decryption key to access the information.

Contexts:

- Implemented in environments where data needs to be protected from unauthorized access or modification, such as in corporate networks, cloud services, banking systems, and any scenario involving sensitive or regulated data.

Similarities

- **Authorization**: Both systems require a process of verifying that an individual or entity has the right to access certain assets or resources.
- **Audit Trails**: They provide logs and records of access attempts and activities, which are crucial for security audits, investigations, and compliance.
- **Layered Security**: Often used in conjunction with other security measures to provide a multi-layered defense (defense in depth).

Differences
- **Scope of Protection**: Physical access control systems focus on securing tangible assets and locations, whereas logical access control systems protect digital assets and information.
- **Types of Threats**: Physical systems are designed to prevent threats like trespassing or theft, while logical systems guard against cyber threats like hacking, data breaches, and unauthorized data access or modification.

Contribution to Overall Security Posture

Together, physical and logical access control systems form a comprehensive security strategy that protects an organization's broad spectrum of assets. By ensuring that only authorized individuals can access sensitive areas and information, these systems significantly reduce the risk of theft, espionage, vandalism, data breaches, and other security incidents. They also contribute to regulatory compliance by enforcing policies and procedures that safeguard personal and sensitive data against unauthorized access. In essence, the integration of both physical and logical access controls is crucial for maintaining the integrity, confidentiality, and availability of an organization's assets, thereby strengthening its overall security posture.

Access control methodologies and models are fundamental to information security, determining how access to resources is granted and restricted. The choice of an access control model impacts the security, flexibility, and manageability of systems. Here, we explore Discretionary Access Control (DAC), Mandatory Access Control (MAC), and Role-Based Access Control (RBAC), along with their implementation considerations and security implications.

Discretionary Access Control (DAC)

Description: DAC allows resource owners to decide who can access their resources and the level of access. In DAC systems, users have control over the permissions of their files, allowing them to grant or revoke access to others at their discretion.

Implementation Considerations:
- **Flexibility**: DAC offers flexibility, allowing users to easily share resources. However, this flexibility can lead to potential security risks if users are not cautious about how they assign permissions.
- **Ease of Administration**: DAC systems are relatively easy to administer in environments with fewer users and resources but can become complex and unwieldy in larger organizations.

Security Implications:

- **Potential for Misconfiguration**: The discretionary nature of DAC can lead to misconfigurations, where sensitive data might be inadvertently exposed by users with the authority to set access controls.
- **Insider Threats**: DAC is more susceptible to insider threats, as compromised user accounts can be used to grant unauthorized access to sensitive resources.

Mandatory Access Control (MAC)

Description: MAC is a more rigid model where access decisions are enforced by a central authority based on predefined security policies and classifications for both users and data. Users cannot change access controls at their discretion.

Implementation Considerations:
- **Strict Policy Enforcement**: MAC requires the definition and enforcement of a comprehensive security policy that classifies all users and resources.
- **Complexity in Administration**: The administration of MAC systems can be complex, requiring careful planning and ongoing management to ensure policies remain relevant and effective.

Security Implications:
- **Enhanced Security**: MAC provides a higher level of security by minimizing the chances of data leakage or unauthorized access, as users cannot alter access controls.
- **Limited Flexibility**: The rigidity of MAC can limit users' ability to share resources dynamically, potentially hindering collaboration and productivity in environments that require frequent data sharing.

Role-Based Access Control (RBAC)

Description: RBAC assigns permissions to roles rather than individual users. Users are then assigned roles, inheriting the permissions associated with those roles. This model simplifies administration by grouping permissions into roles based on job functions.

Implementation Considerations:
- **Role Definition**: Defining roles that accurately reflect the organization's job functions and access needs is critical. Overly broad or narrow role definitions can lead to excessive or insufficient access.
- **Scalability**: RBAC scales well in larger organizations where many users perform similar roles, making it easier to manage permissions as users change roles or leave the organization.

Security Implications:
- **Principle of Least Privilege**: RBAC supports the principle of least privilege by granting users only the access necessary to perform their roles, reducing the risk of unauthorized access to sensitive information.
- **Role Creep**: Without regular audits and role management, there's a risk of "role creep," where roles accumulate excessive permissions over time, potentially violating the principle of least privilege.

Each access control model offers a different approach to managing how resources are secured and accessed within an organization. DAC provides flexibility but requires users to be security-aware; MAC offers high security but can be inflexible and complex to administer; RBAC strikes a balance by offering scalability and easier management but requires careful role definition and management to avoid privilege creep. The choice of model depends on the organization's specific security requirements, regulatory environment, and operational needs. Implementing a combination of these models, tailored to different parts of an organization's IT environment, can often provide a more nuanced and effective security posture.

Identification and authentication are foundational processes in securing systems and data. Identification is the process by which a system recognizes a user, often through a username or ID number. Authentication, on the other hand, verifies the identity through various mechanisms, ensuring the user is who they claim to be. These mechanisms can be categorized into three main factors: something you know, something you have, and something you are.

Something You Know (Passwords)

Mechanism: This category includes passwords, PINs, and security questions. Users must provide the correct information, which they have previously set or been given, to gain access.

Strengths:

- **Ubiquity**: Passwords and PINs are widely used and understood, requiring no special hardware or software for implementation.
- **Simplicity**: They are easy to implement and use, with users familiar with the concept from various services.

Weaknesses:

- **Vulnerability to Attack**: Passwords can be vulnerable to various attacks, including brute force, dictionary attacks, and social engineering.
- **Human Factor**: Users often choose weak passwords or reuse them across multiple services, increasing vulnerability. They may also forget complex passwords, leading to access issues.

Something You Have (Tokens)

Mechanism: This category involves physical or digital objects the user possesses, such as security tokens, smart cards, or mobile devices used in two-factor authentication (2FA) setups.

Strengths:

- **Harder to Duplicate**: Physical tokens and devices add a layer of security that's harder to replicate remotely, compared to knowledge-based methods.
- **Dynamic Codes**: Many tokens generate dynamic, time-based codes, offering protection against replay attacks.

Weaknesses:

- **Loss or Theft**: Physical devices can be lost or stolen, potentially allowing unauthorized access if additional authentication factors are not used.
- **Cost and Logistics**: Deploying and managing physical tokens can incur significant costs and logistical challenges, especially in large organizations.

Something You Are (Biometrics)

Mechanism: Biometric authentication uses unique physical characteristics, such as fingerprints, facial recognition, iris scans, or voice recognition, to verify identity.

Strengths:

- **Uniqueness**: Biometric traits are unique to individuals, making them difficult to replicate or steal.
- **Convenience**: Biometrics can offer a seamless user experience, with authentication processes that are fast and require minimal user action.

Weaknesses:
- **False Positives/Negatives**: Biometric systems can sometimes reject legitimate users (false negatives) or accept impostors (false positives), although advancements continue to reduce these rates.
- **Privacy Concerns**: The collection and storage of biometric data raise significant privacy issues, requiring stringent data protection measures.
- **Immutability**: Unlike passwords or tokens, biometric traits cannot be changed. If biometric data is compromised, it represents a permanent loss of security for that authentication factor.

Evaluation

Each authentication mechanism offers a balance of strengths and weaknesses. Passwords are familiar and easy to use but are vulnerable to poor security practices. Tokens provide a physical barrier to unauthorized access but introduce challenges related to cost, logistics, and the potential for loss or theft. Biometrics offer a high level of security and convenience but raise significant privacy concerns and challenges related to false rejections and acceptances.

In practice, the most secure systems often rely on multi-factor authentication (MFA), combining two or more of these mechanisms to compensate for the weaknesses of any single method. For example, a system might require a user to provide a password (something they know) and a fingerprint (something they are) to authenticate, significantly enhancing security by layering different types of defenses.

Authorization within an Identity and Access Management (IAM) framework is a critical process that determines what resources or actions an authenticated user is permitted to access or perform. Unlike authentication, which verifies identity, authorization ensures that users have appropriate permissions aligned with their roles and responsibilities. Effective authorization mechanisms are essential for enforcing security policies and minimizing the risk of unauthorized access to sensitive resources.

Techniques for Implementing Authorization

Role-Based Access Control (RBAC): This is one of the most common methods of implementing authorization. In RBAC, permissions are not assigned directly to individual users but rather to roles that users assume within an organization. For example, a "Human Resources Manager" role might have permissions to access employee records, while an "IT Technician" role might have permissions to access server logs.

Attribute-Based Access Control (ABAC): ABAC uses a set of policies that evaluate attributes (or characteristics) of users, resources, and the environment to make authorization decisions. For instance, a system might allow access to a financial report only to users with the role of "Finance Analyst" and only during business hours.

Discretionary Access Control (DAC): In DAC systems, the owner of the resource (e.g., a file or database) determines who can access it and what actions they can perform. For example, a document owner might grant read-only access to certain users and read-write access to others.

Mandatory Access Control (MAC): MAC is a more rigid approach where access permissions are based on information classification and user clearances. This model is often used in government and military contexts. For example, a classified document might be accessible only to users with a "Top Secret" clearance.

Examples of Authorization Management
Enterprise Systems: In enterprise environments, an IAM system might use RBAC to manage employee access to different applications and services. When an employee's role changes, their access permissions are automatically updated based on the new role, ensuring that they have appropriate access to perform their job functions.

Cloud Platforms: Cloud service providers often offer ABAC mechanisms, allowing organizations to define complex policies that control access to cloud resources. For instance, an IAM policy in AWS (Amazon Web Services) can specify that only certain IP addresses can access a specific S3 bucket, and only if the request is signed with Multi-Factor Authentication (MFA).

Operating Systems: Modern operating systems implement a combination of DAC and RBAC for file and system resource management. For example, in Windows, file owners can set permissions defining which users or groups can read, write, or execute a file, while system roles like "Administrator" have broader system-wide permissions.

Web Applications: Many web applications use session-based authorization mechanisms. After a user logs in, the application assigns them a session with specific permissions based on their role or account settings, which determine the actions they can perform and the data they can access within the application.

Managing Permissions
Effective authorization requires not just the initial setup of permissions but also ongoing management to adapt to changes within the organization:

Regular Audits and Reviews: Periodic audits of role definitions and user assignments ensure that permissions remain aligned with current job functions and organizational policies.
Principle of Least Privilege: Users should be granted only the permissions necessary to perform their duties, minimizing the potential impact of compromised accounts.

Separation of Duties: Critical tasks should be divided among multiple roles to prevent fraud or errors and to ensure no single user has excessive control over sensitive operations. Authorization within an IAM framework is a nuanced process that involves defining, implementing, and managing access controls to ensure users have appropriate permissions. By leveraging techniques like RBAC, ABAC, DAC, and MAC, organizations can enforce security policies, protect sensitive resources, and adapt to evolving security requirements.

Accountability in Identity and Access Management (IAM) involves tracing actions back to individual users to ensure that all activities within the system can be attributed to authenticated and authorized entities. Maintaining accountability is crucial for security, compliance, and operational integrity. This is achieved through rigorous auditing, logging, and monitoring activities, which collectively provide a comprehensive view of user actions and system events.

Auditing

Description: Auditing in IAM involves systematically reviewing and examining access controls, user activities, and system changes to ensure compliance with security policies and standards. Audits can be conducted internally or by external entities, especially for compliance with regulatory standards.

Importance:
- **Compliance Verification**: Regular audits help organizations verify compliance with internal policies, industry standards, and legal requirements.
- **Policy and Procedure Effectiveness**: Audits assess the effectiveness of current access controls and policies, identifying gaps and areas for improvement.

Logging

Description: Logging involves the automatic recording of events and user activities within the system. Logs typically include information about access requests, system changes, authentication attempts, and any actions performed on resources.

Importance:
- **Forensic Analysis**: In the event of a security incident, logs provide crucial forensic evidence that can help in tracing the sequence of events, understanding the impact, and identifying the perpetrator.
- **Trend Analysis**: Analyzing log data over time can reveal patterns of normal behavior and deviations that may indicate security threats or operational issues.

Monitoring

Description: Monitoring entails the continuous observation of system activities and performance metrics to identify unusual or unauthorized activities in real-time. Monitoring can be manual but is often automated using specialized tools that alert administrators to potential security incidents.

Importance:
- **Real-time Detection**: Monitoring allows for the immediate detection of potential security incidents, enabling rapid response to mitigate threats.

- **Proactive Security Posture**: Continuous monitoring helps organizations move from a reactive to a proactive security stance, identifying and addressing vulnerabilities before they can be exploited.

Implementing Accountability Mechanisms
- **Comprehensive Log Management**: Implement log management solutions that aggregate, normalize, and analyze log data from various sources, ensuring that logs are secure, tamper-proof, and readily available for analysis.
- **Automated Alerting and Reporting**: Use monitoring tools that provide automated alerting for suspicious activities, along with detailed reporting capabilities for audit and compliance purposes.
- **Regular Review and Analysis**: Establish processes for the regular review of logs and monitoring data, along with routine security audits, to ensure ongoing accountability and compliance.
- **Integration with Incident Response**: Ensure that auditing, logging, and monitoring systems are integrated with the organization's incident response plan, providing actionable intelligence for responding to and recovering from security incidents.

Importance in Security Incident Detection and Response
- **Early Detection**: Effective monitoring and logging enable the early detection of security breaches, often before significant damage can occur.
- **Incident Analysis**: Detailed logs are invaluable for analyzing the tactics, techniques, and procedures (TTPs) used by attackers, improving the organization's defensive strategies.
- **Post-Incident Review**: After a security incident, auditing and logging data play a critical role in post-incident reviews and root cause analysis, helping to prevent future incidents.

Maintaining accountability through auditing, logging, and monitoring is fundamental to effective IAM. These activities not only ensure that user actions are traceable and compliant with policies but also enhance the organization's ability to detect, respond to, and recover from security incidents, thereby strengthening the overall security posture.

Identity as a Service (IDaaS) is a cloud-based service that provides identity and access management (IAM) functionalities to businesses over the internet. It offers a range of services and features aimed at managing user identities, credentials, and access rights efficiently and securely. IDaaS solutions are designed to simplify the implementation of IAM capabilities, providing scalability, flexibility, and cost-effectiveness.

Common Features and Services Offered by IDaaS Providers
Single Sign-On (SSO): Allows users to access multiple applications and services with a single set of credentials, enhancing user convenience and reducing password fatigue.

Multi-Factor Authentication (MFA): Adds an extra layer of security by requiring users to provide two or more verification factors to gain access, significantly reducing the risk of unauthorized access.

User Provisioning and De-provisioning: Automates the process of creating, managing, and removing user accounts and access rights, ensuring timely access to resources and revocation upon role change or departure.

Directory Services: Maintains a centralized directory of user information, roles, and permissions, facilitating efficient user management and authentication.

Access Management: Controls user access to applications and data based on predefined policies, roles, and permissions, ensuring that users have appropriate access levels.

Federated Identity Management: Enables secure sharing of identity information across different security domains, allowing users to use the same identity to access resources across multiple systems.

Audit and Compliance Reporting: Provides detailed logs and reports on user activities, access changes, and authentication events, supporting compliance with regulatory requirements and internal audits.

Benefits of Adopting IDaaS Solutions
Scalability: IDaaS solutions can easily scale to accommodate growing numbers of users and applications, making them suitable for businesses of all sizes.

Cost-Effectiveness: By leveraging cloud services, organizations can reduce the costs associated with on-premise IAM infrastructure, including hardware, software, and maintenance expenses.

Simplified Management: IDaaS offers a centralized platform for managing identities and access across multiple applications and systems, reducing administrative overhead.

Enhanced Security: With features like MFA and federated identity management, IDaaS solutions strengthen security by ensuring that only authorized users can access sensitive resources.

Regulatory Compliance: IDaaS providers often offer built-in compliance controls and reporting tools, helping organizations meet regulatory requirements related to data protection and privacy.

Risks Associated with IDaaS Solutions
Data Privacy Concerns: Storing sensitive identity and access data in the cloud raises concerns about data privacy and potential exposure to breaches.

Dependence on Third-Party Providers: Relying on external IDaaS providers can introduce risks related to service availability, provider security practices, and the potential for vendor lock-in.

Integration Challenges: Integrating IDaaS solutions with existing on-premise systems and applications can be complex and may require significant effort to ensure seamless operation.

Limited Customization: While IDaaS solutions offer flexibility, there may be limitations in terms of customization to meet specific organizational requirements or workflows.

Compliance and Legal Implications: Organizations must ensure that their use of IDaaS complies with relevant data protection regulations and that contractual agreements with providers address compliance and liability issues.

IDaaS presents a compelling solution for managing identities and access in the cloud era, offering scalability, cost savings, and enhanced security features. However, organizations must carefully weigh the benefits against the potential risks, considering factors such as data privacy, compliance, and integration requirements, to ensure that the chosen IDaaS solution aligns with their security posture and business objectives.

Integrating and managing third-party identity services in an organization's Identity and Access Management (IAM) framework poses various challenges. These challenges stem from ensuring interoperability, maintaining data security, and adhering to compliance requirements. Addressing these challenges effectively requires adherence to best practices that prioritize security, efficiency, and regulatory compliance.

Challenges
Interoperability: Integrating third-party identity services with existing systems can be complex, especially if there are compatibility issues or if the systems use different standards for identity management and authentication.

Data Security: Third-party identity services require sharing sensitive user data across organizational boundaries, raising concerns about data protection, potential data breaches, and unauthorized access.

Compliance: Organizations must ensure that their use of third-party identity services complies with relevant data protection and privacy regulations (e.g., GDPR, HIPAA), which may impose specific requirements on data handling, storage, and processing.

Vendor Dependence: Relying on third-party services for critical identity management functions can create dependency on vendors, making organizations vulnerable to service disruptions and changes in vendor policies or pricing.

Complexity in Management: Managing multiple third-party identity services increases the complexity of the IAM ecosystem, potentially leading to configuration errors, inconsistent access controls, and challenges in auditing and reporting.

Best Practices
Standardization and Protocols: Prioritize third-party services that adhere to widely accepted standards and protocols for identity management (e.g., SAML, OpenID Connect, OAuth) to ensure compatibility and ease of integration.

Thorough Vendor Assessment: Conduct comprehensive security and compliance assessments of potential third-party identity service providers. Evaluate their security practices, compliance certifications, and track record to ensure they meet your organization's standards.

Data Encryption: Ensure that all data transmitted to and from third-party identity services is encrypted in transit and at rest. Use strong, industry-standard encryption algorithms to protect sensitive information.

Access Control and Monitoring: Implement strict access controls for data shared with third-party services, adhering to the principle of least privilege. Continuously monitor the services for unusual activities or security incidents.

Contractual Agreements and SLAs: Establish clear contractual agreements and Service Level Agreements (SLAs) with third-party providers, specifying security requirements, data handling procedures, and responsibilities in the event of a data breach.

Compliance and Data Sovereignty: Ensure that third-party services comply with relevant regulatory requirements, especially those related to data protection and privacy. Consider data sovereignty issues, ensuring data is stored and processed in jurisdictions that comply with your regulatory obligations.

Regular Reviews and Audits: Conduct regular reviews and audits of third-party identity services to ensure ongoing compliance with security policies and standards. Be prepared to adjust or revoke access based on audit findings or changes in service provision.

Disaster Recovery and Redundancy: Plan for contingencies, including service disruptions and vendor changes. Ensure you have backup and recovery procedures in place, and consider redundant services to mitigate the risk of downtime.

User Education and Training: Educate users about the proper use of third-party identity services, emphasizing the importance of security practices such as safeguarding credentials and recognizing phishing attempts.

By addressing these challenges with comprehensive best practices, organizations can effectively integrate and manage third-party identity services, enhancing their IAM capabilities while maintaining a strong security posture and compliance with regulatory standards.

Federated identity management and Single Sign-On (SSO) are pivotal concepts in modern identity and access management (IAM) that streamline the authentication process across multiple systems, domains, or organizations. By leveraging underlying technologies like SAML (Security Assertion Markup Language) and OAuth, these concepts enhance both user experience and security, albeit with some considerations.

Federated Identity Management

Concept: Federated identity management involves linking and managing identities across multiple systems or organizations, allowing users to use the same identification data to obtain access to all networks within the federation. It eliminates the need for multiple usernames and passwords, simplifying access to a wide array of resources across different domains.

Underlying Technologies:

- **SAML**: An XML-based standard used to exchange authentication and authorization data between parties, particularly between an identity provider (IdP) and a service provider (SP). SAML assertions, which are packages of information confirming a user's identity, are used to make access decisions.
- **OAuth**: An open standard for access delegation commonly used as a way for users to grant websites or applications access to their information on other websites but without giving them the passwords. OAuth is often used in federated identity scenarios to authorize devices, APIs, servers, and applications with access tokens rather than credentials.

Single Sign-On (SSO)

Concept: SSO is a user authentication service that permits a user to use one set of login credentials (e.g., name and password) to access multiple applications. The primary goal of SSO is to improve user experience by reducing the number of times a user has to log in to different applications within the same organization or federated group.

Impact on User Experience:

- **Enhanced Convenience**: SSO simplifies the user's experience by reducing the need to remember and enter different sets of credentials for various services.
- **Increased Productivity**: With SSO, users spend less time logging in and managing multiple accounts, leading to increased efficiency and productivity.

Impact on Security:

- **Centralized Control**: SSO provides centralized management of user access, allowing for consistent application of security policies across all accessed services.
- **Reduced Phishing Risks**: By minimizing the number of login prompts, SSO can reduce the likelihood of phishing attacks, as users become more accustomed to a single, secure method of authentication.
- **Potential Single Point of Failure**: While SSO improves convenience, it also means that if the primary authentication mechanism is compromised, an attacker could potentially

gain access to all linked services. Therefore, robust security measures, including strong authentication methods and regular monitoring, are vital.

Considerations and Best Practices

- **Implementation of Strong Authentication**: Implementing strong authentication methods, such as Multi-Factor Authentication (MFA), within SSO and federated systems can significantly enhance security.
- **Regular Monitoring and Auditing**: Continuous monitoring of authentication processes and regular auditing of access controls and user activities are essential to detect and respond to potential security incidents promptly.
- **Privacy and Compliance**: Ensure that federated identity and SSO implementations comply with relevant data protection and privacy regulations, carefully managing and protecting user identity data.
- **User Education**: Educate users about the security aspects of SSO and federated identity management, emphasizing the importance of securing their primary authentication credentials.

Federated identity management and SSO, supported by technologies like SAML and OAuth, offer significant benefits in terms of user experience and operational efficiency. However, their implementation must be carefully managed to balance convenience with security, ensuring that robust authentication methods are in place and that potential risks are mitigated through continuous monitoring and user education.

Chapter 8: Security Assessment and Testing:

Security assessments are essential for identifying vulnerabilities, evaluating risks, and ensuring the effectiveness of security controls within an organization. Various frameworks and methodologies guide these assessments, each with specific objectives, scope, and methodologies. Three key types of security assessments include risk assessments, vulnerability assessments, and penetration testing.

Risk Assessments

Objectives: The primary goal of a risk assessment is to identify potential threats to an organization's assets and evaluate the likelihood and impact of these threats materializing. It aims to prioritize risks based on their severity and guide the allocation of resources to mitigate them effectively.

Scope:

- **Asset Identification**: Identifying and categorizing assets within the organization, including data, hardware, software, and personnel.
- **Threat and Vulnerability Analysis**: Identifying potential threats to each asset and the vulnerabilities that could be exploited by these threats.
- **Impact and Likelihood Evaluation**: Assessing the potential impact of each threat and the likelihood of its occurrence.

Methodologies:

- **Qualitative Risk Assessment**: Uses subjective judgment to assess the impact and likelihood of risks, often categorizing them as low, medium, or high.

- **Quantitative Risk Assessment**: Employs numerical values and statistical methods to estimate the probability of risks and their potential impact in financial terms.
- **Frameworks**: NIST SP 800-30, ISO 31000, and OCTAVE are among the frameworks that provide guidelines for conducting risk assessments.

Vulnerability Assessments

Objectives: Vulnerability assessments aim to identify, classify, and prioritize vulnerabilities in systems and applications. The focus is on uncovering existing vulnerabilities that could be exploited by attackers and recommending measures to mitigate them.

Scope:

- **System and Network Scanning**: Scanning systems, networks, and applications to identify known vulnerabilities, such as outdated software, missing patches, and misconfigurations.
- **Vulnerability Classification**: Categorizing identified vulnerabilities based on their nature and potential impact.
- **Prioritization**: Prioritizing vulnerabilities based on their severity, exploitability, and impact on the organization.

Methodologies:

- **Automated Scanning Tools**: Utilizing automated tools and scanners (e.g., Nessus, OpenVAS) to identify known vulnerabilities across systems and networks.
- **Manual Review**: Complementing automated tools with manual reviews and inspections to identify vulnerabilities that automated tools might miss.

Penetration Testing

Objectives: Penetration testing (pen testing) simulates cyber-attacks on an organization's systems to evaluate the effectiveness of existing security controls and identify exploitable vulnerabilities. The objective is to understand how an attacker could breach the system and the potential consequences of such a breach.

Scope:

- **Target Identification**: Selecting the systems, applications, and network segments to be tested.
- **Threat Modeling**: Developing scenarios based on potential attackers, their goals, and methods.
- **Exploitation**: Attempting to exploit identified vulnerabilities to gain unauthorized access or perform malicious activities.

Methodologies:

- **Black Box Testing**: The tester has no prior knowledge of the target system, simulating an external attacker's perspective.
- **White Box Testing**: The tester has comprehensive knowledge of the target system, including network maps, source codes, and credentials, simulating an insider threat or a highly skilled attacker.
- **Grey Box Testing**: A combination of black and white box testing, where the tester has limited knowledge of the target system.

Frameworks like the Penetration Testing Execution Standard (PTES) and methodologies like the Open Source Security Testing Methodology Manual (OSSTMM) provide guidelines for conducting penetration tests.

Each type of security assessment plays a vital role in an organization's overall security strategy. Risk assessments provide a broad overview of potential threats and their impacts, vulnerability assessments focus on identifying specific weaknesses in systems and applications, and penetration testing actively exploits those weaknesses to understand the real-world implications of a breach. Together, these assessments enable organizations to identify security gaps, prioritize remediation efforts, and strengthen their defenses against cyber threats.

Planning and executing a security assessment involves a systematic approach to identify vulnerabilities, assess risks, and evaluate the effectiveness of security controls within an organization. The process requires careful planning, selection of appropriate tools and techniques, and management to ensure minimal impact on operations. Here are the key steps involved:

1. Define Objectives

- **Scope Definition**: Clearly define the scope of the assessment, including the systems, networks, and applications to be evaluated. Specify what is in scope and what is out of scope to focus the assessment efforts effectively.
- **Assessment Goals**: Identify the specific goals of the assessment, such as compliance with regulatory standards, identification of vulnerabilities, or validation of security controls. Goals should align with the organization's overall security strategy.

2. Obtain Necessary Approvals

- **Stakeholder Engagement**: Engage with key stakeholders to discuss the assessment plan, objectives, and potential impact. Stakeholders might include IT management, security teams, legal departments, and operational leaders.
- **Authorization**: Obtain formal authorization to conduct the assessment, ensuring that all legal and compliance requirements are met. This is particularly important for activities like penetration testing, which simulate real attack scenarios.

3. Select Assessment Tools and Techniques

- **Tool Selection**: Choose appropriate tools for the assessment based on the objectives and scope. This might include vulnerability scanners, penetration testing tools, code analysis tools, and more.
- **Methodology**: Decide on the assessment methodology, whether it be risk assessment, vulnerability assessment, or penetration testing. Consider industry best practices and frameworks that guide these methodologies.

4. Plan Assessment Execution

- **Timing**: Schedule the assessment at a time that minimizes impact on operations, avoiding peak business hours or critical operational periods.
- **Resource Allocation**: Allocate sufficient resources, including personnel and technical resources, to conduct the assessment effectively. Ensure that team members have the necessary skills and access rights.

- **Communication Plan**: Develop a communication plan to keep stakeholders informed throughout the assessment process, particularly if any critical issues are identified.

5. Conduct the Assessment

- **Data Collection**: Gather information relevant to the assessment, such as network diagrams, system configurations, and existing security policies.
- **Execution**: Carry out the assessment using the selected tools and techniques. This might involve scanning for vulnerabilities, attempting to exploit vulnerabilities during penetration testing, or evaluating compliance with security policies.

6. Analyze Findings and Generate Reports

- **Data Analysis**: Analyze the data collected during the assessment to identify vulnerabilities, assess risks, and evaluate the effectiveness of current security controls.
- **Report Generation**: Generate a comprehensive report detailing the findings, including identified vulnerabilities, their potential impact, and recommendations for remediation. The report should be tailored to the audience, providing technical details for IT and security teams and executive summaries for leadership.

7. Review and Remediation Planning

- **Findings Review**: Review the assessment findings with relevant stakeholders, discussing the implications and prioritizing issues based on risk.
- **Remediation Plan**: Develop a plan to address identified vulnerabilities and weaknesses. The plan should include timelines, responsible parties, and required resources.

8. Implement Remediation Measures

- **Remediation Execution**: Implement the necessary remediation measures to address the identified vulnerabilities and weaknesses. This might involve patching systems, reconfiguring network devices, updating policies, or enhancing security controls.

9. Post-Assessment Activities

- **Validation**: Conduct follow-up assessments to validate that remediation measures have been effectively implemented and that vulnerabilities have been addressed.
- **Lessons Learned**: Review the assessment process to identify lessons learned and opportunities for improvement in future assessments.

Planning and executing a security assessment requires a structured approach, careful coordination, and clear communication to ensure that objectives are met, stakeholders are engaged, and operations are minimally impacted. By following these steps, organizations can effectively assess their security posture, identify areas for improvement, and enhance their overall security defenses.

Testing the effectiveness of security controls is crucial for identifying vulnerabilities and security gaps within an organization's IT infrastructure. Various techniques and tools, including static and dynamic analysis, code review, and simulation exercises, are employed to evaluate security measures' efficiency and robustness. Here's an overview of these approaches:

Static Analysis

Description: Static analysis involves examining the code of an application without executing it. The process uses automated tools to scan the source code, bytecode, or binary code for patterns that may indicate security vulnerabilities.

Tools: Tools like Fortify, Checkmarx, and SonarQube are commonly used for static code analysis. These tools can identify vulnerabilities such as SQL injection, cross-site scripting (XSS), and buffer overflows by analyzing the codebase against a database of known vulnerability patterns.

Application: Static analysis is particularly useful in the development phase, allowing developers to identify and fix security issues before the application is deployed. It's an essential part of secure coding practices and can be integrated into the CI/CD pipeline for continuous security assessment.

Dynamic Analysis

Description: Dynamic analysis, or dynamic application security testing (DAST), involves testing an application by executing it and analyzing its behavior. This approach simulates real-world attacks to identify vulnerabilities that may not be apparent through static analysis alone.

Tools: Tools like OWASP ZAP, Burp Suite, and IBM AppScan simulate attacks on running applications and analyze responses to identify security issues such as input validation errors, session management vulnerabilities, and misconfigurations.

Application: Dynamic analysis is used to test applications in their running state, often as part of the QA and security testing phase. It provides insights into how an application behaves under attack and can identify vulnerabilities that are dependent on the application's runtime environment.

Code Review

Description: Code review is a manual examination of application source code by security experts or developers to identify security flaws. Unlike automated static analysis, manual code review involves a more in-depth and contextual examination of the code by individuals.

Application: Code review is often conducted as part of the development process, especially for critical applications or when significant changes are made. It complements automated analysis by identifying logic errors, insecure coding practices, and other issues that automated tools might miss.

Simulation Exercises

Description: Simulation exercises, including penetration testing and red team exercises, simulate real-world attack scenarios to test the effectiveness of security controls and incident response procedures.

- **Penetration Testing**: Pen testers, or ethical hackers, attempt to exploit vulnerabilities in systems, networks, and applications to assess the effectiveness of security controls.
- **Red Team Exercises**: Red team exercises involve a comprehensive attack simulation against an organization's security posture, including social engineering, physical security breaches, and cyber attacks, to test the organization's detection and response capabilities.

Application: These exercises provide a realistic assessment of an organization's security defenses and its ability to detect and respond to attacks. They are typically conducted periodically and after significant changes to the IT environment or security controls.

Identifying Vulnerabilities and Security Gaps

- **Comprehensive Assessment**: Combining static and dynamic analysis with manual code review and simulation exercises provides a comprehensive assessment of an organization's security posture, identifying vulnerabilities across different layers of the IT infrastructure.
- **Contextual Understanding**: Manual reviews and simulation exercises offer contextual insights into how vulnerabilities could be exploited in real-world scenarios, helping prioritize remediation efforts based on actual risk.
- **Continuous Improvement**: Regular testing and assessment facilitate continuous improvement of security controls, enabling organizations to adapt to evolving threats and technologies.

By employing these techniques and tools, organizations can proactively identify and address vulnerabilities and security gaps, enhancing their overall security posture and resilience against cyber threats.

Assessing compliance with internal policies and external regulations such as the General Data Protection Regulation (GDPR) and the Health Insurance Portability and Accountability Act (HIPAA) is crucial for organizations to ensure they meet required legal, security, and operational standards. Effective compliance assessment strategies involve clear planning regarding the scope, frequency, and documentation of the assessments.

Scope of Compliance Assessments

- **Identify Applicable Regulations**: Determine which laws and regulations are relevant to the organization's operations. For instance, GDPR applies to organizations processing the personal data of EU citizens, while HIPAA concerns U.S. entities handling protected health information (PHI).
- **Understand Requirements**: Thoroughly understand the requirements of each regulation, including data protection, privacy, security measures, and reporting obligations.
- **Internal Policy Alignment**: Ensure internal policies align with external regulatory requirements. This involves reviewing data handling practices, security policies, incident response plans, and employee training programs.
- **Critical Areas and Processes**: Focus on areas most impacted by the regulations, such as data collection, storage, processing, and sharing practices, as well as IT systems and security measures safeguarding sensitive information.

Frequency of Compliance Assessments

- **Regular Scheduled Assessments**: Conduct compliance assessments at regular intervals, typically annually, to ensure ongoing adherence to regulations and policies.
- **Triggered Assessments**: In addition to scheduled assessments, trigger additional reviews following significant changes to regulations, internal policies, IT infrastructure, or business processes.
- **Continuous Monitoring**: Implement continuous monitoring mechanisms for critical compliance aspects, enabling real-time detection of potential compliance deviations.

Documentation of Compliance Assessments

- **Detailed Assessment Plans**: Document the objectives, scope, methodology, and criteria for each compliance assessment. This plan serves as a blueprint for the assessment process and ensures consistency.
- **Evidence Collection**: Maintain comprehensive records of evidence gathered during assessments, such as system configurations, data protection measures, training records, and incident management logs.
- **Assessment Reports**: Produce detailed reports summarizing the findings of the compliance assessments, including identified gaps, areas of non-compliance, and recommendations for remedial actions.
- **Remediation Tracking**: Document the actions taken to address compliance gaps, including responsible parties, timelines, and outcomes. This tracking ensures accountability and closure of identified issues.
- **Audit Trails**: Keep audit trails of all compliance-related activities, providing a historical record that can be invaluable during external audits or investigations.

Considerations for Effective Compliance Assessments

- **Stakeholder Engagement**: Involve relevant stakeholders from across the organization, including legal, IT, security, HR, and operations, to ensure a comprehensive understanding of compliance requirements and practices.
- **External Expertise**: Consider engaging external consultants or legal experts specializing in specific regulations to complement internal assessments, especially for complex or highly specialized regulatory environments.
- **Training and Awareness**: Ensure that employees at all levels are aware of compliance requirements and their roles in maintaining compliance through regular training and communication.
- **Technology Use**: Leverage technology solutions, such as compliance management software, to automate aspects of the compliance assessment and monitoring process, enhancing efficiency and accuracy.

By outlining clear strategies for assessing compliance with internal policies and external regulations, organizations can ensure they not only meet legal and regulatory requirements but also maintain high standards of security and privacy, thereby protecting their interests and those of their customers and stakeholders.

Internal audits play a pivotal role in maintaining security and compliance within an organization by providing an independent assessment of its processes, controls, and policies. Unlike routine security assessments, which are typically more technical and focused on identifying vulnerabilities and threats, internal audits offer a broader evaluation of governance, risk management, and compliance (GRC) practices, ensuring that organizational activities align with internal standards and external regulatory requirements.

Role of Internal Audits

- **Compliance Verification**: Internal audits verify adherence to applicable laws, regulations, and industry standards, such as GDPR, HIPAA, or PCI-DSS, as well as internal policies and procedures.
- **Risk Management**: Audits assess the effectiveness of an organization's risk management strategies, identifying areas where risk mitigation measures might be inadequate or misaligned with the organization's risk appetite.
- **Operational Efficiency**: By examining processes and controls, internal audits can identify inefficiencies or redundancies in operations, providing recommendations for improvement.
- **Governance and Accountability**: Audits reinforce governance structures by evaluating the roles, responsibilities, and performance of management and ensuring accountability in security and compliance efforts.

Process of Internal Audits

1. **Planning**: Define the audit's scope, objectives, and timeline, focusing on areas of high risk or significance to security and compliance. This phase involves understanding the business context, regulatory landscape, and previous audit findings.
2. **Evidence Collection**: Gather documentation, logs, records, and other forms of evidence that demonstrate the organization's adherence to policies and controls. This includes reviewing configurations, access controls, encryption standards, incident response plans, and employee training records.
3. **Testing and Evaluation**: Conduct detailed testing of controls to verify their effectiveness. This might involve walkthroughs of processes, interviews with staff, and technical tests to validate security measures.
4. **Reporting**: Compile audit findings, highlighting areas of non-compliance, control weaknesses, and potential risks. The audit report should offer clear recommendations for remediation and improvement.
5. **Follow-up**: Monitor the implementation of audit recommendations, verifying that corrective actions have been effectively enacted to address identified issues.

Internal Audits vs. Security Assessments

- **Scope and Focus**: Internal audits have a broader scope, assessing the entirety of governance, risk, and compliance practices, whereas security assessments typically focus more narrowly on technical vulnerabilities and threats.
- **Objective and Purpose**: The primary objective of internal audits is to ensure organizational activities comply with internal and external standards, while security assessments aim to identify and mitigate specific security risks.
- **Frequency and Regularity**: Internal audits are often conducted on a regular schedule, dictated by audit plans and regulatory requirements, whereas security assessments might be more frequent and driven by changes in the threat landscape or IT environment.

Importance of Audit Trails and Evidence Collection

- **Accountability**: Audit trails provide a chronological record of user activities and system events, offering transparency and accountability for actions taken within the organization.
- **Incident Investigation**: In the event of a security incident, audit trails can be invaluable for forensic analysis, helping to trace the origin, impact, and progression of the incident.
- **Compliance Verification**: Detailed evidence collection and audit trails are crucial for demonstrating compliance with regulatory requirements, supporting claims of due diligence and adherence to prescribed standards.

Internal audits, with their comprehensive review of an organization's GRC practices, are indispensable for ensuring security and compliance. By maintaining robust audit trails and diligently collecting evidence, organizations can not only validate their compliance efforts but also enhance their overall security posture and operational efficiency.

Managing third-party audits involves coordinating with external entities to assess various aspects of an organization's operations, such as compliance with regulations, security posture, financial health, or quality management. This process presents unique challenges but also opportunities for improvement and validation of practices. Here's a breakdown of the challenges and best practices involved in managing third-party audits:

Challenges
Auditor Selection: Choosing the right auditor or audit firm that has the requisite expertise, industry knowledge, and impartiality is crucial. The wrong choice can lead to inadequate or irrelevant audit findings.

Defining Audit Scope: Clearly defining the scope of the audit can be challenging but is essential to ensure the audit addresses the right areas and provides meaningful insights.

Operational Disruptions: Audits can be disruptive to day-to-day operations, particularly if they require extensive documentation or direct involvement from key personnel.

Interpretation of Findings: Audit findings, especially those related to complex regulations or technical standards, can be difficult to interpret and may require specialized knowledge to understand fully.

Implementing Changes: Addressing audit findings can involve significant changes to processes, policies, or systems, which can be resource-intensive and challenging to implement.

Best Practices
Thorough Auditor Vetting: Conduct a comprehensive vetting process for auditors, including reviewing their credentials, industry experience, and references. Ensure they understand the specific context and requirements of your organization.

Clear Scope Definition: Work collaboratively with the auditor to establish a clear and detailed audit scope that aligns with your organization's objectives and regulatory requirements. Ensure the scope is documented and agreed upon before the audit begins.

Minimizing Disruption: Plan the audit schedule in consultation with relevant stakeholders to minimize disruption. Prepare documentation and responses in advance to expedite the audit process.

Stakeholder Engagement: Engage stakeholders from relevant departments early in the process to ensure they understand the purpose of the audit, the expectations, and their roles in supporting the audit.

Training and Preparation: Provide training or briefing sessions for staff involved in the audit to ensure they understand the process, the information required, and how to interact effectively with the auditors.

Open Communication: Maintain open lines of communication with the audit team throughout the process to clarify requirements, discuss preliminary findings, and address any issues that arise.

Actionable Findings: Work with the auditor to ensure findings are presented in an actionable format, with clear explanations of any deficiencies, the associated risks, and recommended corrective actions.

Findings Review and Validation: Conduct a thorough review of the audit findings with relevant internal teams to validate the results and interpretations. This may involve discussing complex or unexpected findings with the auditors for clarification.

Remediation Planning: Develop a structured remediation plan to address audit findings, assigning responsibilities, setting timelines, and allocating resources. Prioritize actions based on risk and impact.

Follow-up and Continuous Improvement: Implement a process for regular follow-up on remediation actions to ensure they are completed effectively. Use the insights gained from the audit to drive continuous improvement in processes and controls.

Managing third-party audits effectively requires careful planning, coordination, and communication, both with the external auditors and within the organization. By addressing the challenges and adhering to best practices, organizations can ensure that third-party audits provide valuable insights, validate compliance and security efforts, and contribute to overall operational improvement.

Addressing findings from security assessments and audits is a critical process that ensures vulnerabilities and non-compliance issues are effectively remediated. This process involves prioritizing remediation efforts, implementing corrective actions, and establishing feedback loops for continuous improvement. Here's a detailed look at each step:

1. Prioritization of Remediation Efforts

- **Risk Assessment**: Evaluate the risk associated with each finding, considering the potential impact on the organization and the likelihood of exploitation. High-risk vulnerabilities that could lead to significant data breaches or compliance violations should be prioritized.
- **Business Impact Analysis**: Consider the business impact of each finding, including potential financial losses, reputational damage, and operational disruptions. Prioritize issues that could significantly affect critical business processes or objectives.
- **Regulatory Requirements**: Take into account any legal or regulatory implications of the findings. Non-compliance with laws and regulations like GDPR, HIPAA, or PCI-DSS should be addressed promptly to avoid penalties and legal issues.

2. Implementation of Corrective Actions

- **Action Plan Development**: For each prioritized finding, develop a detailed action plan outlining the steps required to remediate the issue. The plan should include technical fixes, policy updates, training programs, or other corrective measures as needed.
- **Resource Allocation**: Assign responsibility for implementing each action plan to specific individuals or teams, ensuring they have the necessary resources and authority to carry out the remediation efforts.
- **Timeline Establishment**: Set realistic timelines for the completion of corrective actions, taking into account the urgency of the issue and the complexity of the required remediation.

3. Documentation and Communication

- **Documentation**: Maintain comprehensive documentation of all findings, risk assessments, action plans, and remediation efforts. This documentation serves as a record of the organization's response to security issues and can be valuable for future audits and assessments.
- **Stakeholder Communication**: Communicate the findings and planned corrective actions to relevant stakeholders, including management, affected departments, and external parties if necessary. Transparency helps build trust and ensures organizational alignment.

4. Implementation and Monitoring

- **Execution of Action Plans**: Implement the corrective actions as outlined in the action plans, monitoring progress to ensure compliance with the established timelines.
- **Effectiveness Assessment**: After implementing corrective actions, assess their effectiveness in addressing the original findings. This may involve re-testing the affected systems or processes to ensure vulnerabilities have been mitigated and compliance has been achieved.

5. Feedback Loops and Continuous Improvement

- **Lessons Learned**: Conduct a review of the remediation process to identify lessons learned, including any challenges encountered, effective strategies, and areas for improvement.
- **Feedback Integration**: Incorporate feedback and lessons learned into future security practices, policies, and training programs. This continuous improvement cycle helps strengthen the organization's overall security posture.
- **Ongoing Monitoring and Assessment**: Establish mechanisms for ongoing monitoring of the remediated areas to ensure continued compliance and security. Regularly scheduled audits and assessments can help identify new vulnerabilities and compliance issues, maintaining the security and integrity of the organization's systems and data.

Addressing findings from security assessments and audits is an iterative process that requires careful planning, effective execution, and ongoing evaluation. By prioritizing remediation efforts based on risk and impact, implementing corrective actions diligently, and leveraging feedback for continuous improvement, organizations can enhance their security posture and ensure compliance with relevant standards and regulations.

Effectively reporting and communicating the outcomes of security assessments and audits is crucial for ensuring that stakeholders understand the implications of the findings and are aligned on the necessary steps for remediation and improvement. Best practices in this area focus on creating actionable reports, effectively presenting findings, and providing clear recommendations for improvement.

Creating Actionable Reports
- **Executive Summary**: Begin with a concise executive summary that highlights key findings, overall risk levels, and urgent action items. This allows senior management to quickly grasp the critical issues without delving into technical details.
- **Clear and Concise Language**: Use clear, non-technical language whenever possible, especially when the report is intended for a broader audience that may not have specialized security knowledge.
- **Structured Format**: Organize the report into sections that cover methodology, findings, impact analysis, and recommendations. A structured format helps readers navigate the report and understand its contents.
- **Detail Findings**: For each finding, provide a detailed description, including the context, the identified vulnerability or non-compliance issue, the potential impact, and the risk level. Use visuals, charts, and tables to enhance comprehension.
- **Prioritized Recommendations**: Offer clear, prioritized recommendations for each finding, specifying actionable steps for remediation. Include a rationale for each recommendation to help stakeholders understand its importance.
- **Reference Frameworks and Standards**: Reference relevant security frameworks, standards, and best practices to provide a benchmark for the findings and recommendations. This adds credibility and can help justify the need for certain actions.

Presentation of Findings

- **Tailored Presentations**: Customize presentations based on the audience. Senior management may require a high-level overview focusing on business impacts and strategic recommendations, while technical teams may need a detailed discussion of specific vulnerabilities and remediation strategies.
- **Use of Visual Aids**: Incorporate charts, graphs, and other visual aids to illustrate risk levels, trends, and the distribution of vulnerabilities. Visual representations can make complex data more accessible.
- **Interactive Sessions**: Encourage questions and discussions during presentations to engage the audience and clarify any uncertainties. This interactive approach can foster a better understanding of the issues and the commitment to the recommended actions.

Recommendations for Improvement

- **Actionable Steps**: Provide specific, actionable steps for remediation, avoiding vague or generic advice. Clearly define who is responsible for each action, along with proposed timelines.
- **Best Practices and Resources**: Where applicable, include references to industry best practices, guidelines, and resources that can assist in implementing the recommendations.
- **Cost-Benefit Analysis**: For significant recommendations that require substantial investment or resources, include a cost-benefit analysis to help stakeholders understand the value and impact of the proposed actions.
- **Follow-Up Mechanisms**: Suggest mechanisms for follow-up and review of the implementation progress. This could include scheduled status meetings, progress reports, or subsequent audits.

Continuous Communication

- **Regular Updates**: Provide regular updates to stakeholders on the progress of implementing the recommendations, highlighting any challenges, successes, and adjustments to the plan.
- **Feedback Loops**: Establish feedback loops to gather input from stakeholders on the report and the remediation process. This feedback can be invaluable for improving future assessments and reports.

Effective reporting and communication are integral to the success of security assessments and audits. By delivering actionable reports, engaging presentations, and well-founded recommendations, security professionals can ensure that stakeholders are informed, aligned, and committed to strengthening the organization's security posture.

Chapter 9: Security Operations:

Security operations play a crucial role in an organization's overall security posture, involving various specialized roles and responsibilities that work together to monitor, assess, and defend against cybersecurity threats. Central to these operations is the Security Operations Center (SOC), which acts as the hub for all security activities.

Security Operations Center (SOC)

Function: The SOC is a centralized unit that deals with security issues on an organizational level. It's equipped with a suite of security technologies and a team of security professionals who monitor, analyze, and respond to cybersecurity incidents round the clock.

- **Monitoring and Detection**: Continuous monitoring of the organization's networks, systems, and applications for unusual activities or signs of security threats.
- **Incident Response**: Coordinating and managing responses to cybersecurity incidents, including containment, eradication of threats, and recovery of affected systems.
- **Threat Intelligence**: Gathering and analyzing information about emerging threats and vulnerabilities to stay ahead of potential security risks.

Security Analysts

Security analysts are key players within the SOC, responsible for various tasks aimed at protecting the organization from cyber threats.

- **Monitoring and Analysis**: Continuously monitoring security access logs and alerts to identify and analyze potential security threats.
- **Incident Investigation**: Conducting in-depth investigations of suspected security incidents, using various forensic tools and techniques to understand the scope and impact of the threat.
- **Vulnerability Management**: Regularly assessing systems and applications for vulnerabilities, recommending security measures, and applying necessary patches or updates.

Coordination Between Operational and Executive Teams

Effective security operations require close coordination between the operational teams, such as the SOC and security analysts, and the executive leadership. This collaboration ensures that security operations align with the broader organizational goals and risk management strategies.

- **Strategic Alignment**: Operational teams should understand the organization's strategic goals and risk appetite to tailor their security efforts accordingly. Regular communication between SOC leaders and executive management ensures that security operations support business objectives.
- **Reporting and Escalation**: Establish clear protocols for reporting security incidents and escalating significant threats to executive management. This ensures that leadership is informed of critical security issues and can make timely decisions on risk management and resource allocation.
- **Policy Development and Compliance**: Operational teams contribute to the development and enforcement of security policies, ensuring they reflect current threat landscapes and compliance requirements. Executives must ensure that these policies align with legal and regulatory obligations and organizational values.

- **Budgeting and Resource Allocation**: Executives are responsible for allocating resources to security operations, including funding for technologies, staffing, and training. Regular reviews of security operations' needs and performance help ensure that the SOC has the necessary resources to effectively protect the organization.

The effectiveness of security operations hinges on the well-defined roles and responsibilities of the SOC, security analysts, and the seamless coordination between operational and executive teams. This collaborative approach ensures that the organization can rapidly detect, respond to, and recover from cybersecurity threats, minimizing their impact on business operations and reputation.

A Security Operations Center (SOC) is a centralized unit within an organization that continuously monitors, analyzes, and responds to cybersecurity incidents. The SOC is the nerve center of an organization's cybersecurity efforts, equipped with advanced tools and staffed by a team of security professionals dedicated to protecting the organization from cyber threats.

Structure of a SOC
Personnel: The SOC team typically consists of security analysts, engineers, and managers with various levels of expertise and specialization. Roles within the SOC can include Tier 1 analysts (frontline defenders who monitor alerts), Tier 2 analysts (more experienced professionals who conduct in-depth investigations), and Tier 3 analysts (experts who handle advanced threat detection and response).
Processes: Effective SOCs operate according to well-defined processes and procedures for incident detection, analysis, response, and reporting. These processes are often based on industry standards and best practices, such as the NIST Cybersecurity Framework or the Incident Handling steps outlined by SANS.
Technology: SOCs utilize a range of cybersecurity tools and technologies to facilitate the monitoring, detection, and response to threats. This technology stack includes Security Information and Event Management (SIEM) systems, intrusion detection systems (IDS), firewalls, endpoint detection and response (EDR) tools, and threat intelligence platforms.
Function of a SOC
Proactive Monitoring: SOCs continuously monitor network traffic, system logs, and other data sources for signs of suspicious activity. This proactive approach allows the SOC to detect potential security incidents before they escalate into serious breaches.
Threat Detection: Utilizing a combination of technology and human expertise, the SOC identifies and validates security threats. This involves analyzing alerts generated by SOC tools, correlating data from multiple sources, and leveraging threat intelligence to understand emerging threats.
Incident Response: Once a threat is confirmed, the SOC coordinates the response to contain and mitigate the incident. This can involve isolating affected systems, removing malware, and applying patches or other security measures.
Recovery and Remediation: Post-incident, the SOC is responsible for ensuring that affected systems are cleaned, restored, and returned to normal operation. They also analyze the incident to identify root causes and implement measures to prevent future occurrences.

Communication and Reporting: The SOC keeps stakeholders informed about security incidents and their status. They also produce reports detailing incident analysis, response activities, and lessons learned for continuous improvement.

Tools and Technologies Used in a SOC

SIEM Systems: SIEM systems collect and aggregate log data from various sources, providing real-time analysis and alerting of potential security incidents. They are central to SOC operations, enabling the correlation of events across the network.

Intrusion Detection Systems (IDS) and Intrusion Prevention Systems (IPS): These tools monitor network traffic and system activities for malicious patterns or policy violations, generating alerts for further investigation.

Endpoint Detection and Response (EDR): EDR tools provide continuous monitoring and response capabilities for endpoints (e.g., laptops, servers), offering insights into threats and enabling remote response actions.

Threat Intelligence Platforms: These platforms collect and analyze data on emerging threats, providing the SOC with actionable intelligence to inform detection and response efforts.

Forensic Tools: In the aftermath of an incident, forensic tools are used to conduct in-depth analyses of how an attack occurred, the extent of the breach, and the data or systems affected. The SOC is a critical component of an organization's cybersecurity infrastructure, offering a dedicated and focused approach to detecting, responding to, and recovering from cyber threats. By combining skilled personnel, effective processes, and advanced technologies, SOCs play a vital role in maintaining the security and resilience of organizational assets.

The Incident Response Lifecycle is a structured approach to managing and resolving security incidents effectively. It consists of several key stages: Preparation, Detection and Analysis, Containment, Eradication, Recovery, and Post-Incident Analysis. An Incident Response Plan (IRP) plays a critical role in this lifecycle, providing a predefined set of guidelines and procedures for responding to incidents.

1. Preparation

- **Developing an IRP**: The preparation stage involves developing a comprehensive Incident Response Plan that outlines roles, responsibilities, communication protocols, and procedures for responding to incidents.
- **Training and Awareness**: Regular training and awareness programs for the incident response team and employees are essential to ensure everyone understands their role in the response process.
- **Tools and Resources**: Ensuring that the necessary tools, technologies, and resources are available and properly configured for incident detection, analysis, and mitigation.

2. Detection and Analysis

- **Detection**: The initial detection of potential security incidents through monitoring tools, alerts, user reports, or other sources.
- **Initial Analysis**: Assessing the validity and severity of the incident to determine the appropriate response. This may involve triaging alerts, analyzing logs, and gathering evidence.

- **Documentation**: Documenting all findings, actions, and observations from the outset, maintaining a detailed incident log for future reference.

3. Containment
- **Short-term Containment**: Implementing immediate measures to limit the spread of the incident and prevent further damage. This could involve isolating affected systems, blocking malicious traffic, or changing access credentials.
- **Long-term Containment**: Developing a strategy for long-term containment to ensure that the threat cannot re-emerge, potentially involving system changes, network reconfigurations, or other broader measures.

4. Eradication
- **Removing Threats**: Identifying and eliminating the root cause of the incident, such as malware, unauthorized access points, or vulnerabilities that were exploited.
- **System Cleanup**: Ensuring that affected systems are thoroughly cleaned and that any malicious artifacts are removed.

5. Recovery
- **System Restoration**: Restoring systems and services to normal operation, ensuring that they are no longer compromised and are fully functional.
- **Monitoring**: Closely monitoring affected systems for any signs of abnormal activity or re-emergence of the threat.
- **Validation**: Verifying the integrity and security of systems before bringing them back online.

6. Post-Incident Analysis (Lessons Learned)
- **Review and Debrief**: Conducting a thorough review of the incident, response efforts, and outcomes to identify what was successful and what could be improved.
- **Actionable Improvements**: Developing actionable steps to improve response capabilities, update policies and procedures, and mitigate the risk of future incidents.
- **Knowledge Sharing**: Sharing lessons learned with relevant stakeholders, potentially including employees, management, and external partners, to enhance organizational resilience.

Importance of an Incident Response Plan (IRP)
- **Guidance and Clarity**: An IRP provides clear guidelines and procedures for responding to incidents, ensuring a coordinated and efficient response.
- **Roles and Responsibilities**: Clearly defines the roles and responsibilities of the incident response team, management, and other stakeholders, ensuring that everyone knows what is expected of them during an incident.
- **Legal and Regulatory Compliance**: Helps ensure compliance with legal and regulatory requirements related to incident response, potentially reducing legal risks and penalties.
- **Minimizing Impact**: A well-executed IRP can significantly reduce the impact of security incidents on the organization, protecting assets, reputation, and the bottom line.

The Incident Response Lifecycle, guided by a comprehensive IRP, is essential for preparing for, managing, and recovering from security incidents effectively. By following this structured approach, organizations can minimize the impact of incidents and strengthen their overall security posture.

Effectively handling security incidents requires a structured approach, clear communication, adherence to legal requirements, and thorough forensic analysis. Here are some best practices for each aspect of incident handling:

Initial Response

- **Activate the Incident Response Plan (IRP)**: Immediately activate the IRP to guide the response efforts. The plan should outline the steps to be taken, roles and responsibilities, and escalation procedures.
- **Incident Triage**: Quickly assess the severity and scope of the incident to prioritize response efforts. Determine which systems, data, or services are affected and the potential impact on the organization.
- **Containment**: Implement immediate containment measures to limit the spread of the incident and minimize damage. This may involve isolating affected systems, blocking malicious network traffic, or temporarily disabling compromised accounts.

Communication Strategies

- **Internal Communication**: Establish clear lines of communication within the response team and with key stakeholders, including IT staff, management, legal counsel, and public relations. Ensure everyone is informed about the situation and their expected roles.
- **External Communication**: Prepare for external communications with customers, partners, regulators, and possibly the public. Communications should be carefully crafted to provide necessary information without compromising security or ongoing investigations. Legal and PR teams should review all external messages.
- **Notification Requirements**: Be aware of and comply with any legal or contractual notification obligations. Many regulations and industry standards require organizations to notify affected individuals, partners, or regulatory bodies within a specific timeframe.

Legal Considerations

- **Legal and Regulatory Compliance**: Understand the legal and regulatory landscape related to incident response, including data protection laws (e.g., GDPR) and industry-specific regulations. Ensure all response activities comply with these requirements.
- **Preservation of Evidence**: Maintain the integrity of evidence related to the incident for potential legal proceedings or regulatory investigations. This includes securely logging all actions taken, maintaining chain of custody for digital evidence, and documenting decisions and findings.
- **Engagement with Law Enforcement**: Determine when and how to engage with law enforcement or regulatory agencies. In some cases, involving these entities early can provide additional resources and support for addressing the incident.

Forensic Analysis

- **Data Collection**: Collect and preserve data from affected systems for analysis, including logs, memory dumps, and disk images. This data can provide valuable insights into how the breach occurred and how to prevent similar incidents in the future.
- **Root Cause Analysis**: Conduct a thorough analysis to identify the root cause of the incident. Understanding how attackers gained access and what vulnerabilities were exploited is crucial for preventing recurrence.
- **Timeline Reconstruction**: Create a timeline of events leading up to, during, and following the incident. This helps in understanding the sequence of actions, the extent of the compromise, and the effectiveness of the response.

Post-Incident Activities
- **Lessons Learned**: Conduct a post-incident review with all involved parties to discuss what happened, how it was handled, and what could be improved. This review should result in actionable recommendations to strengthen security measures and response processes.
- **Remediation and Recovery**: Implement the necessary remediation measures to address the root causes of the incident and restore affected services and systems to normal operation. Ensure that all vulnerabilities are patched, and security gaps are closed.
- **Continuous Improvement**: Incorporate the lessons learned into the IRP and ongoing security practices. Update training programs, policies, and technologies based on the insights gained from the incident.

Effectively handling security incidents involves a combination of prompt action, clear communication, adherence to legal and regulatory requirements, and comprehensive forensic analysis. By following these best practices, organizations can minimize the impact of incidents, maintain stakeholder trust, and enhance their resilience against future threats.

Disaster recovery planning is a critical aspect of organizational resilience, ensuring that businesses can recover from significant disruptions such as natural disasters, cyber-attacks, or system failures. The planning process involves identifying essential components of operations, setting recovery objectives, and developing strategies to restore functions after a disaster. Key principles and components include Recovery Time Objectives (RTOs), Recovery Point Objectives (RPOs), and the development of comprehensive recovery strategies.

Recovery Time Objective (RTO)
Definition: The RTO is the maximum acceptable amount of time that a service, application, or function can be unavailable after a disaster occurs. It essentially defines the target time within which business processes must be restored to avoid unacceptable consequences.
Application: RTOs guide the prioritization of recovery efforts and resources allocation. Critical services with shorter RTOs require more immediate attention and robust backup solutions to ensure quick restoration.
Recovery Point Objective (RPO)

Definition: The RPO represents the maximum acceptable amount of data loss measured in time. It specifies the maximum age of files or data that must be recovered from backup storage for normal operations to resume without significant losses.

Application: RPOs influence the frequency of backups and the choice of data protection strategies. Services with stringent RPOs necessitate more frequent backups and potentially, real-time replication to minimize data loss.

Development of Disaster Recovery Strategies

Risk Assessment and Business Impact Analysis (BIA): Begin by identifying potential threats and vulnerabilities that could lead to a disaster. Conduct a BIA to understand the impact of these threats on business operations, which helps in setting appropriate RTOs and RPOs.

Identification of Critical Systems and Functions: Determine which systems, applications, and functions are critical to the organization's operations. This includes assessing dependencies between different areas of the business to ensure comprehensive recovery planning.

Data Protection Measures: Implement data protection strategies that align with established RPOs. This may involve solutions like on-site and off-site backups, cloud storage, and data replication technologies.

Infrastructure and Application Recovery Solutions: Develop solutions for the rapid recovery of IT infrastructure and critical applications. This could involve standby systems, cloud-based solutions, or agreements with third-party providers for temporary infrastructure.

Communication Plan: Establish a communication plan that outlines how employees, customers, partners, and other stakeholders will be informed before, during, and after a disaster. This plan should include predefined channels of communication and templates for messages.

Emergency Response Team: Form an emergency response team with clearly defined roles and responsibilities. Team members should be trained and familiar with the disaster recovery procedures.

Testing and Drills: Regularly test the disaster recovery plan through simulations and drills to ensure its effectiveness and the team's preparedness. Testing helps identify gaps in the plan and areas for improvement.

Documentation and Training: Document all aspects of the disaster recovery plan, including procedures for declaring a disaster, activation of the recovery plan, and step-by-step recovery processes. Provide training for all relevant personnel to ensure they understand their roles in the plan.

Review and Update: Continuously review and update the disaster recovery plan to reflect changes in the business environment, technology, and potential threats. Incorporate lessons learned from tests and actual disaster events to improve the plan's effectiveness.

Disaster recovery planning is an ongoing process that prepares organizations to respond effectively to disruptions, minimizing downtime and data loss. By establishing clear recovery objectives, developing robust recovery strategies, and ensuring regular testing and updates, businesses can enhance their resilience and continuity in the face of disasters.

Business Continuity Planning (BCP) is a strategic process designed to ensure that an organization can continue to operate and recover quickly in the event of a disruption. The goal is to minimize the impact on business operations, protect assets, and maintain services to customers. The process from conducting a Business Impact Analysis (BIA) to developing and testing Business Continuity Plans (BCPs) involves several critical steps:

1. Business Impact Analysis (BIA)
- **Objective**: The BIA aims to identify and prioritize critical business functions and processes, assessing the potential impact of disruptions on these areas.
- **Data Collection**: Gather detailed information about all business processes, including dependencies, resources required, and the potential financial and non-financial impacts of disruptions.
- **Criticality Assessment**: Determine the criticality of each business function based on factors like impact on revenue, legal or regulatory compliance, and customer service. This helps in prioritizing recovery efforts.

2. Risk Assessment
- **Threat Identification**: Identify a wide range of potential threats and disruptions that could impact the organization, such as natural disasters, cyber-attacks, supplier failures, or utility outages.
- **Vulnerability Analysis**: Assess the organization's vulnerabilities to these threats, considering current controls and mitigation strategies.
- **Risk Prioritization**: Prioritize risks based on the likelihood of occurrence and the potential impact on critical business functions identified in the BIA.

3. Strategy Development
- **Recovery Strategies**: Develop strategies for recovering critical business functions and processes within the recovery time objectives (RTOs) established during the BIA. Strategies may involve alternate work locations, outsourcing, or leveraging technology solutions like cloud services.
- **Resource Requirements**: Identify the resources required to support recovery strategies, including personnel, information technology, facilities, equipment, and communication tools.

4. Plan Development

- **BCP Documentation**: Document the business continuity plan, detailing the recovery strategies, resource requirements, and step-by-step procedures for responding to a disruption.
- **Roles and Responsibilities**: Clearly define the roles and responsibilities of the business continuity team and other key personnel within the BCP, ensuring everyone understands their tasks during a disruption.
- **Communication Plan**: Develop a communication plan that outlines how employees, customers, suppliers, and other stakeholders will be informed about disruptions and recovery efforts.

5. Training and Awareness
- **Training Programs**: Conduct training programs for the business continuity team and all employees to ensure they understand the BCP and their roles in it.
- **Awareness Campaigns**: Implement awareness campaigns to keep business continuity planning top of mind for all employees, emphasizing the importance of preparedness and resilience.

6. Testing and Exercises
- **Testing Objectives**: Define clear objectives for each test or exercise, focusing on specific components of the BCP or simulating particular types of disruptions.
- **Testing Methods**: Employ various testing methods, including tabletop exercises, simulations, and full-scale drills, to evaluate the effectiveness of the BCP and the preparedness of the organization.
- **Improvement Plan**: Document the lessons learned from testing and exercises, identifying gaps and areas for improvement in the BCP.

7. Maintenance and Continuous Improvement
- **Regular Reviews**: Schedule regular reviews of the BCP to ensure it remains current and effective, considering changes in the business environment, new threats, and lessons learned from tests and actual incidents.
- **Change Management**: Establish a process for updating the BCP in response to significant changes in the organization, such as mergers, acquisitions, new products or services, or changes in key suppliers or partners.

Business Continuity Planning is an iterative process that enhances an organization's resilience to disruptions. By conducting thorough BIAs, developing effective recovery strategies, and regularly testing and updating BCPs, organizations can ensure they are prepared to maintain critical operations and recover swiftly in the face of adversity.

Operational controls and techniques are essential for protecting organizational assets, encompassing a broad range of measures designed to ensure the security, integrity, and availability of these assets. These controls include physical security measures, environmental controls, and the management of critical infrastructure, each playing a vital role in the overall security posture of an organization.

Physical Security Measures

Physical security measures are designed to prevent unauthorized access to facilities, protect personnel, and safeguard physical assets such as hardware, documents, and other tangible assets.

- **Access Control Systems**: Implement electronic access control systems to manage entry to secure areas. These systems can include card readers, biometric scanners, and PIN codes to authenticate individuals.
- **Surveillance Systems**: Deploy surveillance cameras around the perimeter and within critical areas to monitor and record activities, deterring unauthorized access and enabling incident investigation.
- **Physical Barriers**: Utilize fences, gates, bollards, and other barriers to enhance perimeter security and control access points to the facility.
- **Security Personnel**: Employ trained security personnel to conduct physical patrols, respond to incidents, and enforce access control policies.
- **Secure Storage**: Provide secure storage for sensitive documents, equipment, and other assets. This can include safes, locked cabinets, and secure rooms with additional access controls.

Environmental Controls

Environmental controls are implemented to protect assets from damage due to environmental factors and ensure the continuity of operations.

- **Fire Detection and Suppression**: Install fire detection systems and suppression mechanisms, such as smoke detectors and sprinkler systems, to mitigate the risk of fire damage.
- **Climate Control**: Use heating, ventilation, and air conditioning (HVAC) systems to maintain optimal environmental conditions for technology infrastructure and personnel comfort.
- **Power Management**: Implement uninterruptible power supply (UPS) systems and backup generators to ensure continuous power supply during outages, protecting against data loss and system failures.
- **Water Damage Prevention**: Employ leak detection systems and design facilities to prevent water damage from leaks, floods, or other water-related issues.

Management of Critical Infrastructure

The management of critical infrastructure involves ensuring the resilience and security of essential systems and networks that support core organizational functions.

- **Redundancy and Failover**: Design critical systems with redundancy and failover capabilities to ensure availability in the event of a component failure or other disruption.
- **Patch Management**: Establish a robust patch management process to regularly update software and firmware on critical systems, addressing vulnerabilities and ensuring system integrity.
- **Network Segmentation**: Utilize network segmentation to isolate critical infrastructure from less secure networks, reducing the risk of lateral movement by attackers within the organization's network.

- **Monitoring and Incident Response**: Implement continuous monitoring of critical infrastructure for signs of security incidents or operational issues. Develop and maintain an incident response plan specifically for critical systems to ensure rapid recovery.
- **Vendor Risk Management**: Conduct thorough assessments of vendors and third-party service providers involved in the management of critical infrastructure to ensure they meet security standards and contractual obligations.

Operational controls and techniques are integral to protecting organizational assets from a wide range of threats. By implementing comprehensive physical security measures, environmental controls, and effective management of critical infrastructure, organizations can enhance their resilience, protect against potential damages, and ensure the continuity of essential operations.

Maintaining secure operations is crucial for protecting organizational assets, data, and infrastructure from evolving threats. Implementing best practices in areas such as patch management, change management, and the secure disposal or repurposing of equipment can significantly enhance an organization's security posture.

Patch Management

Patch management is the process of managing updates for software and systems, including the deployment of patches to address vulnerabilities, bugs, and enhance functionality.

- **Vulnerability Assessment**: Regularly scan systems and software to identify vulnerabilities that need to be patched. Use reputable vulnerability scanning tools to automate this process.
- **Patch Testing**: Before widespread deployment, test patches in a controlled environment to ensure they do not introduce new issues or conflicts with existing systems.
- **Prioritization**: Prioritize patches based on the severity of the vulnerability, the criticality of the affected system, and the potential impact of exploitation. Critical security patches should be deployed as soon as possible.
- **Automated Patch Deployment**: Utilize automated patch management tools to streamline the deployment process, ensuring timely and consistent patch application across all systems.
- **Audit and Compliance**: Maintain records of patching activities, including details of deployed patches and systems affected, to ensure compliance with internal and external audit requirements.

Change Management

Change management involves the systematic approach to managing all changes made to the IT infrastructure, ensuring that changes do not compromise system integrity or security.

- **Formal Process**: Establish a formal change management process that includes submission, review, approval, implementation, and post-implementation review of all changes.
- **Risk Assessment**: Assess the potential security and operational impacts of proposed changes, considering both the direct effects and potential unintended consequences.

- **Stakeholder Communication**: Communicate planned changes to all relevant stakeholders, ensuring they are aware of potential impacts and any required actions on their part.
- **Documentation**: Document all changes, including the rationale, implementation steps, testing results, and any issues encountered. This documentation is essential for audit trails and future reference.
- **Rollback Plans**: Develop contingency plans for rolling back changes in case they lead to unforeseen issues or security vulnerabilities.

Secure Disposal or Repurposing of Equipment

Properly disposing of or repurposing IT equipment is essential to prevent unauthorized access to sensitive data and ensure environmental responsibility.

- **Data Sanitization**: Before disposal or repurposing, ensure that all data is securely erased from storage devices using methods that meet industry standards for data destruction, such as degaussing, physical destruction, or cryptographic erasure.
- **Inventory Management**: Maintain an accurate inventory of all IT assets, and ensure that the disposal or repurposing of any equipment is documented and tracked.
- **Certification of Destruction**: When using third-party services for equipment disposal, obtain certification of destruction that confirms the secure disposal of devices in compliance with legal and environmental standards.
- **Environmental Considerations**: Adhere to environmentally responsible practices for disposing of electronic waste, following local regulations and industry best practices.

By implementing these best practices, organizations can maintain secure operations, mitigate risks associated with vulnerabilities, unauthorized changes, and improperly disposed equipment, and ensure the ongoing confidentiality, integrity, and availability of their systems and data.

Emerging trends like cloud computing, the proliferation of IoT (Internet of Things) devices, and the increasing reliance on automation are significantly impacting traditional security operations frameworks. These trends introduce new challenges but also offer opportunities for enhancing security posture through innovative approaches.

Impact of Cloud Computing

Trends:

- Organizations are increasingly adopting cloud services for their flexibility, scalability, and cost-effectiveness. This shift from on-premises infrastructure to cloud-based solutions necessitates a reevaluation of traditional security operations.

Challenges:

- **Shared Responsibility Model**: In cloud environments, security responsibilities are shared between the cloud service provider (CSP) and the customer. Organizations often struggle to fully understand the extent of their responsibilities, leading to potential security gaps.
- **Visibility and Control**: Migrating to the cloud can result in reduced visibility and control over data and infrastructure, complicating security monitoring and management.

- **Complex Multi-Cloud Environments**: As organizations adopt services from multiple CSPs, managing security consistently across different platforms becomes challenging.

Opportunities:
- **Advanced Security Features**: CSPs often offer advanced security features and services that can enhance an organization's security posture, such as identity and access management (IAM), encryption, and threat intelligence.
- **Scalability**: Cloud environments can easily scale security controls alongside organizational growth, allowing for more efficient resource allocation and management.

Proliferation of IoT Devices

Trends:
- The rapid expansion of IoT devices across various sectors introduces numerous endpoints into organizational networks, expanding the attack surface.

Challenges:
- **Device Security**: Many IoT devices have inherent security weaknesses, such as default passwords, unpatchable firmware, or lack of encryption, making them vulnerable to attacks.
- **Network Complexity**: The integration of countless IoT devices into corporate networks increases complexity and potential entry points for attackers.
- **Data Privacy Concerns**: IoT devices often collect sensitive data, raising significant data privacy and protection concerns that need to be addressed.

Opportunities:
- **Enhanced Monitoring and Automation**: IoT devices can contribute valuable data for security monitoring and enable automated responses to certain security events.
- **Innovative Security Applications**: IoT technology can be leveraged for security purposes, such as surveillance systems, access control, and environmental monitoring.

Automation in Security Operations

Trends:
- Automation and orchestration are becoming integral to security operations, enabling more efficient threat detection, analysis, and response.

Challenges:
- **Integration with Existing Systems**: Integrating automation tools with existing security infrastructure and workflows can be complex.
- **Over-reliance on Automation**: Excessive reliance on automation may lead to complacency, with potentially unusual or sophisticated threats being overlooked if they fall outside predefined automation parameters.
- **Skill Gaps**: Implementing and managing automation tools requires specific skills and knowledge, which may be lacking within current security teams.

Opportunities:
- **Efficiency and Speed**: Automation significantly enhances the efficiency and speed of security operations, enabling rapid responses to threats and reducing manual workloads.

- **Consistency**: Automated processes ensure consistent application of security policies and procedures, reducing the likelihood of human error.

The evolving landscape of security operations, influenced by cloud computing, IoT, and automation, requires organizations to adapt and innovate. Embracing these trends while being mindful of the associated challenges enables the development of more resilient, responsive, and effective security operations frameworks.

Chapter 10: Software Development Security:

Software security is a critical aspect of overall cybersecurity, focusing on ensuring that software systems are designed, developed, and maintained to protect against vulnerabilities and threats. Core principles such as secure coding practices, the principle of least privilege, and defense-in-depth are fundamental to achieving robust software security. These principles should be integrated and enforced throughout the software development lifecycle (SDLC) to mitigate risks and enhance the security posture of software products.

Secure Coding Practices

Description: Secure coding practices involve writing code with security in mind, aiming to prevent the introduction of vulnerabilities that could be exploited by attackers.

Application:
- **Input Validation**: Ensure that all input received from users, systems, or external sources is validated to prevent common attacks such as SQL injection and cross-site scripting (XSS).
- **Output Encoding**: Properly encode output to avoid injection vulnerabilities, especially when displaying data received from untrusted sources.
- **Error Handling**: Implement secure error handling that does not expose sensitive information or system details to users, which could be leveraged by attackers.
- **Authentication and Authorization**: Enforce strong authentication mechanisms and ensure that users are authorized to perform only actions allowed by their roles, adhering to the principle of least privilege.

Enforcement:
- **Code Reviews**: Conduct regular code reviews to identify security issues and enforce secure coding standards.
- **Automated Scanning**: Utilize static application security testing (SAST) tools to automatically identify potential vulnerabilities in the codebase.
- **Developer Training**: Provide ongoing security training for developers to keep them informed about secure coding practices and emerging threats.

Principle of Least Privilege

Description: The principle of least privilege dictates that software and users should have only the minimum levels of access—or permissions—needed to perform required tasks, reducing the potential impact of a compromise.

Application:

- **Access Controls**: Implement fine-grained access controls within the software, ensuring that users and components have access only to the resources necessary for their functionality.
- **Privilege Escalation Prevention**: Design the software to prevent unauthorized privilege escalation, which could allow attackers to gain higher levels of access.

Enforcement:
- **Role-Based Access Control (RBAC)**: Utilize RBAC to define roles and associated permissions based on job functions, applying the principle of least privilege at the role level.
- **Regular Audits**: Conduct regular audits of user privileges and software components to ensure compliance with the principle of least privilege.

Defense-in-Depth
Description: Defense-in-depth is a layered approach to security, implementing multiple defensive mechanisms to protect software in case one layer is bypassed or fails.
Application:
- **Multiple Security Layers**: Incorporate various security controls at different layers, such as network security, application security, and data encryption, to provide comprehensive protection.
- **Redundancy**: Ensure that critical security controls are redundant, so that the failure of one control does not leave the software unprotected.

Enforcement:
- **Security Testing**: Conduct a range of security testing methodologies, including dynamic application security testing (DAST), penetration testing, and vulnerability assessments, to evaluate the effectiveness of the layered defenses.
- **Continuous Monitoring**: Implement continuous monitoring to detect and respond to threats in real-time, ensuring that all layers of defense are functioning as intended.

Integrating and enforcing these core principles of software security throughout the SDLC—from planning and design to development, testing, deployment, and maintenance—helps in building resilient software systems that are capable of withstanding threats and reducing the likelihood of successful attacks. Collaboration across development, security, and operations teams, alongside ongoing education and adherence to best practices, are essential for maintaining robust software security.

Defining security requirements and conducting threat modeling at the early stages of software development are crucial steps for ensuring the security of the software system. These proactive measures help identify potential security issues and guide the development of security controls to mitigate identified risks.

Defining Security Requirements
Process:
1. **Gather Requirements**: Start by understanding the software's intended functionality, users, data flow, and interaction with other systems. Engage with stakeholders,

including developers, security teams, and business units, to gather security requirements.
   2. **Analyze the Software Context**: Consider the software's operating environment, including the technology stack, deployment scenarios, and integration points, which could influence security requirements.
   3. **Identify Regulatory and Compliance Obligations**: Determine if there are specific regulatory or compliance standards (e.g., GDPR, HIPAA, PCI-DSS) that the software must adhere to and derive security requirements from these obligations.
   4. **Develop Security Requirements**: Translate the gathered information into specific security requirements, addressing aspects such as authentication, authorization, data protection, and audit logging. Requirements should be clear, measurable, and aligned with the overall security policy.

Conducting Threat Modeling

Process:
   1. **Model the Software Architecture**: Create a detailed representation of the software architecture, including data flows, entry points, and trust boundaries. Diagrams such as Data Flow Diagrams (DFDs) can be particularly useful for visualizing these aspects.
   2. **Identify Threats**: Using methodologies like STRIDE (Spoofing, Tampering, Repudiation, Information Disclosure, Denial of Service, Elevation of Privilege), systematically identify potential threats against each component and interaction within the system.
   3. **Assess Threats**: Evaluate the identified threats to understand their potential impact and likelihood. Tools like DREAD (Damage, Reproducibility, Exploitability, Affected Users, Discoverability) can help quantify and prioritize threats.
   4. **Mitigate Threats**: For each identified threat, develop mitigation strategies that could involve architectural changes, implementing specific security controls, or accepting the risk if it's within the organization's risk tolerance.

Methodologies

   - **STRIDE**: A threat modeling methodology developed by Microsoft, used to identify threats based on six categories (Spoofing, Tampering, Repudiation, Information Disclosure, Denial of Service, Elevation of Privilege). STRIDE helps in understanding the types of attacks that could be made against a system.
   - **DREAD**: A risk assessment model used to quantify and compare the severity of threats identified during the threat modeling process. DREAD stands for Damage Potential, Reproducibility, Exploitability, Affected Users, and Discoverability, with each aspect rated to provide an overall risk score for each threat.

Best Practices

   - **Early and Continuous Involvement**: Integrate security requirements definition and threat modeling into the early stages of the SDLC and revisit them continuously as the project evolves.
   - **Cross-Functional Collaboration**: Ensure collaboration between security professionals, developers, architects, and business analysts to gain comprehensive insights and foster a shared understanding of security goals.

- **Documentation and Communication**: Document all security requirements and threat modeling outcomes clearly and communicate them effectively to all relevant stakeholders to ensure they are understood and implemented.
- **Iterative Approach**: Treat security requirements and threat modeling as iterative processes, revisiting and refining them as new information becomes available or as the project scope changes.

By defining security requirements and conducting threat modeling early in the software development process, organizations can proactively identify and mitigate potential security risks, leading to more secure and resilient software systems.

Integrating security into the Software Development Lifecycle (SDLC) is essential for building secure software systems. Different SDLC models, including Waterfall, Agile, and DevSecOps, offer various frameworks for integrating security, each with its benefits and challenges.

Waterfall Model

Integration:
- In the Waterfall model, security is integrated at specific stages of the linear, sequential process. Security requirements are defined upfront during the requirements gathering phase. Security design reviews and threat modeling occur during the design stage. Security testing, such as static and dynamic analysis, is conducted after the development phase, followed by security-focused acceptance testing.

Benefits:
- **Structured Approach**: The clear, sequential phases of the Waterfall model allow for thorough security planning and comprehensive testing at designated stages.
- **Comprehensive Documentation**: The emphasis on documentation in the Waterfall model ensures that security requirements and designs are well-documented.

Challenges:
- **Inflexibility**: The linear nature of the Waterfall model makes it challenging to address new security issues or changes in requirements once the project progresses past the initial stages.
- **Late Testing**: Security testing occurs late in the lifecycle, which can lead to the discovery of critical vulnerabilities at a stage where they are costly and time-consuming to fix.

Agile Model

Integration:
- Security in Agile is integrated continuously throughout the iterative development process. Security requirements are revisited and refined in each sprint. Security practices such as pair programming and code reviews are embedded into the development process. Automated security testing tools are integrated into the continuous integration pipeline to identify vulnerabilities early.

Benefits:
- **Flexibility**: Agile's iterative nature allows for the continuous refinement of security requirements and the ability to address new threats as they emerge.

- **Early Detection**: Continuous integration and testing enable early detection and remediation of security issues, reducing the cost and impact of fixes.

Challenges:
- **Rapid Pace**: The fast pace of Agile sprints can sometimes lead to security being overlooked or deprioritized in favor of new features and functionality.
- **Fragmentation**: Security efforts can become fragmented across sprints and teams without a coherent, overarching security strategy.

DevSecOps Model
Integration:
- DevSecOps integrates security as a fundamental component of the DevOps pipeline, embedding security practices and tools from the initial planning phase through development, deployment, and operations. Security is automated and made a part of the continuous delivery pipeline, with practices such as infrastructure as code (IaC) security scanning, container vulnerability scanning, and automated compliance checks.

Benefits:
- **Security as Culture**: DevSecOps fosters a culture where security is everyone's responsibility, leading to more secure development practices and outcomes.
- **Automation and Efficiency**: Automated security tools and processes enable efficient identification and remediation of vulnerabilities, reducing manual effort and accelerating the development cycle.

Challenges:
- **Integration Complexity**: Integrating and automating a comprehensive suite of security tools into the CI/CD pipeline can be complex and requires expertise.
- **Collaboration Barriers**: Achieving true collaboration between development, operations, and security teams can be challenging due to differing priorities and cultures.

Integrating security into the SDLC, regardless of the model, enhances the security posture of the software produced. Each approach requires a tailored strategy to effectively embed security practices while aligning with the model's inherent workflow and culture. The choice of model and integration approach should consider the organization's specific needs, capabilities, and the nature of the projects undertaken.

Secure coding practices are essential for developers to prevent common security vulnerabilities and protect applications from attacks. Adherence to security standards and guidelines, such as the OWASP Top 10 and CERT Secure Coding Standards, further strengthens the security posture of software systems. Here's a detailed overview of secure coding practices aligned with these standards:

Input Validation
- **Practice**: Ensure that all input received from users, files, databases, or any external source is validated for type, length, format, and range before processing.
- **OWASP Context**: Addresses issues like Injection (OWASP A1) by preventing malicious data from being executed as part of commands or queries.
- **CERT Standard**: FIO30-C. Exclude user input from format strings.

Output Encoding
- **Practice**: Encode data before displaying it to users to prevent attacks such as Cross-Site Scripting (XSS).
- **OWASP Context**: Mitigates XSS vulnerabilities (OWASP A7) by ensuring that user-controlled data is safely rendered in browsers.
- **CERT Standard**: IDS01-J. Normalize strings before validating them.

Authentication and Session Management
- **Practice**: Implement strong authentication mechanisms and secure session management practices, including the use of multi-factor authentication (MFA) and secure tokens.
- **OWASP Context**: Protects against Broken Authentication (OWASP A2) by ensuring that only authorized users can access the application.
- **CERT Standard**: SEC05-J. Do not store passwords directly.

Authorization and Access Controls
- **Practice**: Enforce the principle of least privilege and ensure that users can only access resources and perform actions that are necessary for their role.
- **OWASP Context**: Prevents Broken Access Control (OWASP A5) by restricting user access to unauthorized features or data.
- **CERT Standard**: OBJ06-J. Defensively copy private mutable class members before returning them to clients.

Secure Data Storage and Transmission
- **Practice**: Protect sensitive data at rest and in transit using encryption and secure protocols like HTTPS.
- **OWASP Context**: Addresses Sensitive Data Exposure (OWASP A3) by encrypting sensitive information such as passwords, credit card numbers, and personal data.
- **CERT Standard**: DRD04-J. Do not store sensitive information in non-volatile memory.

Error Handling and Logging
- **Practice**: Implement secure error handling that does not reveal sensitive information about the application or its environment. Ensure that logs do not contain sensitive data.
- **OWASP Context**: Helps mitigate Security Misconfiguration (OWASP A6) by avoiding verbose error messages that could assist attackers.
- **CERT Standard**: ERR01-J. Do not allow exceptions to expose sensitive information.

Use of Security Features and Libraries
- **Practice**: Utilize existing security features of frameworks and libraries, and keep them up-to-date to protect against known vulnerabilities.
- **OWASP Context**: Protects against Using Components with Known Vulnerabilities (OWASP A9) by ensuring the use of secure and updated components.
- **CERT Standard**: MSC56-J. Do not rely on unsupported or obsoleted APIs.

Secure Software Architecture
- **Practice**: Design software with security in mind, incorporating security controls and threat modeling from the earliest stages of development.

- **OWASP Context**: Encourages a proactive approach to security, addressing architectural weaknesses that could lead to vulnerabilities.
- **CERT Standard**: TPS00-J. Design for security.

Developers should continuously educate themselves on secure coding practices and stay updated with the latest security standards and guidelines. Regular code reviews, security training, and the use of automated security testing tools can further reinforce the application of these practices throughout the software development lifecycle.

Securing the development environment is crucial in safeguarding the software development lifecycle (SDLC) against unauthorized access, code tampering, and other security risks that could compromise the integrity and confidentiality of the software being developed. Key practices such as the use of version control systems, code signing, and the segregation of development, testing, and production environments play pivotal roles in ensuring a secure development process.

Version Control Systems
Importance:
- **Integrity and Traceability**: Version control systems maintain a history of code changes, including who made changes and when. This traceability helps in auditing changes and identifying potentially malicious modifications.
- **Collaboration and Access Control**: They facilitate collaboration while allowing for granular access controls to different parts of the codebase, ensuring that developers have access only to the segments necessary for their work.
- **Backup and Recovery**: Serve as a backup mechanism, enabling the recovery of previous versions of the code in case of accidental loss or corruption.

Code Signing
Importance:
- **Authenticity and Integrity**: Code signing uses digital signatures to verify the authenticity of the code source and ensure that the code has not been altered or tampered with since it was signed. This is critical for maintaining trust, especially in distributed environments where code is shared or downloaded.
- **Non-repudiation**: It provides a mechanism for non-repudiation, ensuring that the entity that signed the code can be reliably identified and cannot deny having signed it.
- **User and System Trust**: Signed code can be configured to generate warnings or prevent execution when the code's integrity is in question, thereby protecting end-users and systems from potentially malicious software.

Segregation of Development, Testing, and Production Environments
Importance:
- **Security and Stability**: Segregating environments ensures that experimental or untested code does not affect the stability or security of production systems. Each environment can have its own set of security controls appropriate to its level of exposure and risk.

- **Controlled Testing**: A separate testing environment allows for rigorous testing of software under conditions that mimic production without risking actual production data or services.
- **Access Control and Risk Mitigation**: By segregating environments, access can be tightly controlled based on roles, minimizing the risk of unauthorized access to sensitive production data and systems. It also prevents accidental changes to production systems by developers or testers.

Additional Considerations
- **Secure Configuration**: Ensure that all development tools, IDEs, and supporting infrastructure are securely configured and updated to protect against known vulnerabilities.
- **Sensitive Information Management**: Avoid storing sensitive information like credentials and API keys in the source code or version control repositories. Use secure secrets management tools to handle such data.
- **Monitoring and Auditing**: Implement monitoring and auditing mechanisms to detect unauthorized access or abnormal activities within the development environment, aiding in the early detection of potential security incidents.

Securing the development environment is a foundational aspect of software security, helping to protect code integrity, prevent unauthorized access, and ensure that the software development process contributes to the overall security posture of the final product. Organizations should adopt a comprehensive approach, incorporating best practices and tools that align with their specific development workflows and security requirements.

Using third-party components and libraries is a common practice in software development, offering significant benefits in terms of efficiency and functionality. However, this practice also introduces security risks, as vulnerabilities in these components can compromise the security of the entire application. Effective management of these risks involves several key strategies, including the use of software composition analysis (SCA) tools.

Inventory Management
- **Maintain an Inventory**: Keep an up-to-date inventory of all third-party components and libraries used in your applications, including versions and dependencies. This inventory is crucial for tracking the use of components and identifying potential vulnerabilities.

Due Diligence and Selection Process
- **Vet Third-Party Components**: Before integrating a third-party component, conduct due diligence to assess its security posture. This can include reviewing the component's security documentation, update history, known vulnerabilities, and the responsiveness of its maintainers to security issues.
- **Prefer Well-Supported Components**: Opt for components that are actively maintained and supported, with a strong community or commercial backing. Regular updates and patches are indicative of a commitment to security.

Use of Software Composition Analysis (SCA) Tools

- **Automated Vulnerability Identification**: SCA tools automatically identify third-party components within your codebase and check them against databases of known vulnerabilities, such as the National Vulnerability Database (NVD).
- **Continuous Monitoring**: Integrate SCA tools into your development and deployment pipelines to continuously monitor for new vulnerabilities as they are disclosed. This ensures that emerging threats are promptly identified.
- **Risk Assessment and Prioritization**: SCA tools often provide risk assessment and prioritization features, helping teams to focus on the most critical vulnerabilities based on severity, exploitability, and the potential impact on the application.

Patch Management and Dependency Updates
- **Regular Updates**: Regularly update third-party components to the latest stable versions to address known vulnerabilities. This should be part of a broader patch management process.
- **Automate Dependency Updates**: Utilize tools that can automate the process of updating dependencies, making it easier to keep third-party components up-to-date without manual intervention.

Secure Configuration
- **Default Configurations**: Be wary of default configurations of third-party components, which may not be secure. Customize configurations to adhere to security best practices and minimize the attack surface.
- **Minimize Component Use**: Only include the necessary functionalities of a third-party component to reduce the potential attack surface. Remove or disable unused features and services.

Legal and Compliance Considerations
- **License Compliance**: Ensure compliance with the licenses of third-party components to avoid legal issues. Some licenses may impose specific obligations or restrictions that could affect how you can use or distribute the component.
- **Data Protection**: Consider the data protection implications of using third-party components, especially those that may process or store sensitive information. Ensure that their use is compatible with data protection laws and regulations applicable to your application.

Education and Awareness
- **Developer Training**: Educate developers about the risks associated with third-party components and the importance of using SCA tools, secure configurations, and regular updates.
- **Security Guidelines**: Develop and disseminate guidelines on securely integrating and managing third-party components within your development teams.

Effectively managing the security of third-party components and libraries is an ongoing process that requires vigilance, automation, and a proactive approach. By integrating SCA tools into the software development lifecycle, continuously monitoring for vulnerabilities, and adhering to best practices for component selection and management, organizations can significantly reduce the risks associated with third-party dependencies.

Security testing is a critical component of the software development process, aimed at identifying and mitigating vulnerabilities to enhance the security posture of applications. Various security testing techniques, each with its unique approach and focus, are employed throughout the software development lifecycle (SDLC) to ensure comprehensive coverage of potential security issues. Among these techniques are Static Application Security Testing (SAST), Dynamic Application Security Testing (DAST), and Penetration Testing.

Static Application Security Testing (SAST)
Overview: SAST involves analyzing source code, byte code, or binary code of an application without executing it, to identify security vulnerabilities that could lead to potential breaches.

How It Works:

SAST tools scan an application's codebase to detect issues such as input validation errors, insecure dependencies, and improper error handling.
The analysis is conducted from the "inside out," allowing for a detailed examination of the application's inner workings.
Advantages:

Early Detection: SAST can be integrated early in the SDLC, enabling developers to identify and fix security issues during the coding phase.
Comprehensive Coverage: It provides comprehensive coverage of the codebase, identifying vulnerabilities that might be missed during manual reviews.
Challenges:

False Positives: SAST tools may generate false positives, requiring manual review to validate findings.
Limited Runtime Context: Since SAST does not execute the application, it may not identify vulnerabilities that only appear during runtime.
Dynamic Application Security Testing (DAST)
Overview: DAST involves testing an application from the "outside in" by simulating attacks against a running application to identify vulnerabilities that could be exploited by attackers.

How It Works:

DAST tools interact with a live application, sending various inputs and observing the outputs to detect issues like XSS, SQL injection, and authentication flaws.
The testing is typically black-box, with the tools having no knowledge of the application's internal workings.
Advantages:

Real-world Attack Simulation: DAST simulates real-world attacks, providing insights into how an attacker might exploit vulnerabilities in a live application.

Runtime Analysis: It identifies vulnerabilities that manifest during the application's execution, which SAST might miss.

Challenges:

Late Detection: DAST is usually conducted later in the SDLC, potentially making the remediation of identified vulnerabilities more time-consuming and costly.

Limited Code Insight: As a black-box testing method, DAST may not provide detailed insights into the source of vulnerabilities within the code.

Penetration Testing

Overview: Penetration testing, or pen testing, is a proactive and simulated cyberattack against an application or system to check for exploitable vulnerabilities.

How It Works:

Pen testers, or ethical hackers, use a variety of techniques and tools to simulate attacks, aiming to breach the application or system's defenses.

The testing can be white-box (with full knowledge of the application's environment), black-box (with no prior knowledge), or grey-box (with partial knowledge).

Advantages:

Comprehensive Evaluation: Penetration testing evaluates the application's security posture from an attacker's perspective, considering both technical vulnerabilities and potential business impacts.

Human Expertise: The involvement of skilled pen testers allows for the discovery of complex vulnerability chains and business logic flaws that automated tools might not detect.

Challenges:

Resource Intensive: Penetration testing can be time-consuming and requires skilled professionals to conduct effectively.

Snapshot in Time: Pen testing provides a snapshot of the application's security at a specific point in time and might not identify vulnerabilities introduced after the test.

Integrating a combination of these security testing techniques—SAST, DAST, and Penetration Testing—into the SDLC allows organizations to achieve a more holistic understanding of their applications' security posture. Each method contributes unique insights, enabling the early detection of vulnerabilities, the simulation of real-world attacks, and the in-depth evaluation of security from an attacker's perspective. Together, they form a comprehensive security testing strategy that significantly enhances the resilience of software systems against cyber threats.

Continuous monitoring and incident response are critical components of a robust security strategy for software applications, ensuring that potential security threats are identified, analyzed, and addressed promptly. This process involves the use of various tools and practices, such as intrusion detection systems, logging, and real-time monitoring, to maintain the security posture of applications.

Continuous Monitoring

Process:

1. **Establish Monitoring Goals**: Define what needs to be monitored, which could include network traffic, system performance, user behaviors, and security events. Goals should align with the organization's overall security objectives.

2. **Implement Monitoring Tools**: Deploy tools and technologies for continuous monitoring. This can include:

   - **Intrusion Detection Systems (IDS)**: Deploy network-based (NIDS) or host-based (HIDS) intrusion detection systems to monitor for suspicious activities or known attack patterns.

   - **Security Information and Event Management (SIEM)**: Implement SIEM systems to aggregate, correlate, and analyze logs and events from various sources within the application and underlying infrastructure.

   - **File Integrity Monitoring**: Use file integrity monitoring tools to detect unauthorized changes to critical system files, configuration files, or content files.

3. **Configure Alerts**: Set up alerts based on predefined thresholds or suspicious patterns that indicate a potential security incident. Alerts should be prioritized based on the severity and potential impact of the detected issue.

4. **Regular Updates and Maintenance**: Keep all monitoring tools up-to-date and maintain their configurations to adapt to evolving security threats and changes in the application environment.

Incident Response

Process:

1. **Preparation**: Develop an Incident Response Plan (IRP) detailing the response process, roles and responsibilities, communication protocols, and documentation requirements. Train the incident response team and relevant personnel on the IRP.

2. **Detection and Analysis**: Utilize continuous monitoring tools to detect potential incidents. Analyze alerts to confirm incidents, determine their scope, and assess their impact. Initial analysis should include reviewing logs, system states, and network traffic.

3. **Containment**: Implement short-term containment measures to limit the spread of the incident, such as isolating affected systems or blocking malicious traffic. Then, plan for long-term containment to prevent recurrence.

4. **Eradication**: Identify and eliminate the root cause of the incident. This may involve removing malware, closing vulnerabilities, and implementing additional security measures to prevent similar incidents.

5. **Recovery**: Restore affected systems and services to their normal operation, ensuring they are no longer compromised. Gradually reintegrate systems into the production environment, monitoring for any signs of issues.

6. **Post-Incident Review**: Conduct a post-incident review to analyze the incident's handling, document lessons learned, and update the IRP and security controls as necessary. Share findings with relevant stakeholders to improve overall security posture.

Importance of Logging and Monitoring

- **Evidence Collection**: Logs provide valuable forensic data that can help in reconstructing the sequence of events leading up to, during, and after an incident, aiding in the analysis and understanding of attackers' tactics.
- **Trend Analysis and Baseline Establishment**: Regular monitoring and logging enable the establishment of baseline behaviors for systems and networks, making it easier to identify anomalies or suspicious activities.
- **Compliance and Auditing**: Many regulatory standards require comprehensive logging and monitoring of security events. Well-maintained logs are essential for demonstrating compliance during audits.
- **Proactive Threat Detection**: Effective logging and monitoring can help in the early detection of potential threats, allowing for proactive measures to prevent incidents before they cause significant damage.

Continuous monitoring and incident response for software applications are ongoing processes that require a well-planned strategy, the right mix of tools, and a trained team ready to respond to security incidents. By maintaining vigilance through continuous monitoring and being prepared to respond effectively to incidents, organizations can protect their applications and data from emerging security threats.

After software deployment, ongoing security management is crucial to protect against evolving threats and vulnerabilities. Key considerations include patch management, vulnerability management, and end-of-life (EOL) planning. Implementing best practices in these areas ensures the continued security and reliability of software applications.

Patch Management
Considerations:

Timely Updates: Keep the software up-to-date with the latest patches, especially those addressing security vulnerabilities, to protect against exploitation by attackers.
Dependency Management: For applications dependent on third-party libraries or components, monitor these dependencies for updates or security patches and apply them as necessary.
Best Practices:

Automated Patching Tools: Utilize tools that automate the patch management process, ensuring patches are applied consistently and promptly across all instances of the software.
Patch Testing: Before deploying patches in a production environment, test them in a controlled setting to ensure they don't introduce new issues or incompatibilities.
Vulnerability Management

Considerations:

Continuous Monitoring: Stay vigilant for new vulnerabilities that may affect the software, including those in underlying platforms, libraries, or components.
Risk Assessment: Assess the risk posed by identified vulnerabilities, considering the potential impact and likelihood of exploitation.
Best Practices:

Vulnerability Scanning: Regularly perform vulnerability scans using reputable tools to detect potential security weaknesses in the software and its environment.
Remediation Prioritization: Prioritize the remediation of vulnerabilities based on their risk assessment, focusing first on those with the highest severity and impact.
Disclosure Policy: Have a clear vulnerability disclosure policy, encouraging responsible reporting of security issues and outlining the process for addressing reported vulnerabilities.
End-of-Life (EOL) Planning
Considerations:

EOL Policy: Establish a policy for handling software that reaches its end-of-life, including guidelines for decommissioning, data migration, and transitioning to supported alternatives.
Communication: Communicate EOL timelines and plans to all stakeholders, including users, developers, and support teams, well in advance.
Best Practices:

Migration Strategies: Develop strategies for migrating users and data to newer, supported versions of the software or alternative solutions, ensuring minimal disruption.
Security During Transition: Maintain security measures and monitoring for EOL software during the transition period, addressing critical vulnerabilities that may arise.
Data Handling and Preservation: Ensure that data from the EOL software is securely backed up, archived, or migrated to new systems, in compliance with data retention policies and regulations.
General Best Practices:

Security Training: Continuously train development, operations, and support teams on security best practices and emerging threats to foster a culture of security awareness.
Incident Response Plan: Maintain an up-to-date incident response plan, ensuring the team is prepared to quickly and effectively address security incidents post-deployment.
User Education: Educate users on secure usage practices, especially for software that interacts with sensitive or personal data, to minimize risks from the user side.
By adhering to these best practices for patch management, vulnerability management, and EOL planning, organizations can significantly enhance the security posture of their software applications post-deployment, protecting against threats and ensuring compliance with relevant security standards and regulations.

Chapter 11: Integrating Security Practices:

Case Study: Financial Services Firm Enhances Cybersecurity Posture

Background

A mid-sized financial services firm, "FinSecure," faced increasing cybersecurity threats, including phishing attacks, data breaches, and insider threats. Given the sensitivity of financial data and the regulatory requirements of the financial industry, FinSecure recognized the need to enhance its security posture.

Risk Assessment Process

1. **Identification of Assets**: FinSecure began by cataloging critical assets, including customer data, financial records, proprietary trading algorithms, and IT infrastructure.
2. **Threat Analysis**: The firm identified potential threats, such as cyber-attacks from external hackers, internal data leaks, and system failures due to outdated hardware.
3. **Vulnerability Assessment**: Using a combination of automated scanning tools and expert reviews, FinSecure assessed vulnerabilities in its systems, applications, and processes.
4. **Impact Analysis**: The firm evaluated the potential impact of various threat scenarios on its operations, reputation, and compliance obligations.
5. **Risk Prioritization**: Risks were prioritized based on their likelihood and impact, focusing on scenarios that could lead to significant financial loss or regulatory non-compliance.

Selection of Security Controls

Based on the risk assessment, FinSecure implemented a multi-layered security strategy:

1. **Employee Training and Awareness**: Recognizing that employees can be the weakest link in security, the firm instituted regular training sessions on cybersecurity best practices and phishing awareness.
2. **Enhanced Access Controls**: FinSecure implemented multi-factor authentication (MFA) and role-based access controls (RBAC) to ensure that only authorized personnel could access sensitive systems and data.
3. **Data Encryption**: All sensitive data, both at rest and in transit, was encrypted to protect against unauthorized access.
4. **Intrusion Detection and Prevention Systems (IDPS)**: The firm deployed advanced IDPS solutions to monitor network and system activities for malicious actions or policy violations.
5. **Regular Security Audits and Penetration Testing**: FinSecure conducted annual security audits and semi-annual penetration tests to identify and address vulnerabilities proactively.
6. **Incident Response Plan**: A comprehensive incident response plan was developed and tested, outlining procedures for detecting, containing, and recovering from security incidents.

Outcomes

- **Reduced Incidence of Phishing Attacks**: Employee training led to a significant reduction in successful phishing attacks, as employees became adept at recognizing and reporting suspicious emails.

- **Strengthened Data Security**: Encryption and access controls significantly reduced the risk of data breaches, ensuring the confidentiality and integrity of sensitive information.
- **Regulatory Compliance**: The enhanced security measures allowed FinSecure to meet stringent regulatory requirements, avoiding potential fines and legal issues.
- **Improved Incident Response**: The incident response plan enabled FinSecure to quickly contain and mitigate a ransomware attack, minimizing downtime and financial impact.
- **Enhanced Reputation**: By demonstrating a commitment to cybersecurity, FinSecure bolstered its reputation among clients and partners, contributing to business growth.

FinSecure's proactive approach to security and risk management exemplifies how a comprehensive risk assessment process, coupled with the strategic implementation of security controls, can protect an organization's assets and enhance its overall security posture. This case study underscores the importance of continuous risk management and the adoption of security best practices in safeguarding against evolving cyber threats.

Case Study: Healthcare Provider Responds to Data Breach
Background
A regional healthcare provider, "HealthCarePro," experienced a significant data breach that exposed the personal health information (PHI) of thousands of patients. The breach was due to a sophisticated phishing attack that led to unauthorized access to the email accounts of several employees.

Initial Detection
Alert from Security Systems: The intrusion detection system flagged unusual outbound data traffic from a server containing PHI.
Investigation: The IT security team immediately launched an investigation, which traced the source to compromised employee email accounts.
Response Actions
Containment: HealthCarePro's IT team quickly isolated the affected email accounts and servers to prevent further unauthorized access and data exfiltration.

Eradication: The team identified and removed the malicious payloads from the compromised systems and reset passwords for all affected accounts.

Recovery: Critical systems were restored from recent backups, ensuring that patient services remained uninterrupted. Enhanced monitoring was implemented to detect any residual threats.

Notification: In compliance with regulatory requirements and ethical obligations, HealthCarePro notified affected patients, regulatory bodies, and law enforcement about the breach. The organization offered credit monitoring services to impacted patients.

Post-Incident Analysis: An in-depth analysis was conducted to understand the breach's root cause, the extent of the data exposure, and the effectiveness of the response actions.

Lessons Learned

Employee Training: The incident highlighted the need for ongoing employee training on cybersecurity awareness and phishing detection.

Access Controls: It became evident that more stringent access controls and multi-factor authentication (MFA) were needed to secure sensitive systems and data.

Incident Response: While the incident response plan was generally effective, the event underscored the need for regular drills and updates to the plan to address emerging cyber threats.

Vendor Relationships: The breach prompted a review of third-party vendors with access to HealthCarePro's systems, leading to tighter security requirements and regular audits.

Impact on Future Security Policies and Practices

Enhanced Training Programs: HealthCarePro implemented a comprehensive cybersecurity training program for all employees, focusing on phishing, social engineering, and secure data handling practices.

Implementation of MFA: MFA was rolled out across the organization, particularly for accessing email and other critical systems.

Regular Security Assessments: The organization committed to more frequent security assessments, including penetration testing and vulnerability scanning, to identify and mitigate potential weaknesses proactively.

Improved Vendor Management: HealthCarePro established a formal process for assessing and managing the security postures of third-party vendors, incorporating regular security audits and compliance checks.

Culture of Security: The breach served as a catalyst for fostering a culture of security within the organization, with an emphasis on shared responsibility and proactive risk management.

The data breach at HealthCarePro was a wake-up call, leading to significant enhancements in the organization's cybersecurity posture. By learning from the incident and implementing comprehensive security improvements, HealthCarePro not only addressed the immediate issues but also strengthened its resilience against future threats. This case study underscores the importance of continuous vigilance, employee education, and the adoption of robust security controls in protecting sensitive information and maintaining trust in the digital age.

Scenario: Regional Bank Overcomes Natural Disaster

Background

A regional bank, "RegioBank," with multiple branches in a hurricane-prone area, had developed comprehensive Business Continuity and Disaster Recovery Plans (BCP and DRP) in anticipation of potential natural disasters. The plans were put to the test when a Category 4 hurricane hit the area, causing widespread damage, power outages, and flooding.

Planning Process

- **Risk Assessment**: RegioBank conducted a thorough risk assessment to identify potential threats to its operations, with natural disasters, particularly hurricanes, being identified as a high-risk factor due to the bank's geographical location.
- **Business Impact Analysis (BIA)**: The BIA highlighted critical functions such as customer transactions processing, data center operations, and customer support as areas requiring prioritization in continuity planning.
- **Strategy Development**: The bank developed strategies for maintaining critical functions, including redundant data centers, alternative work locations for key staff, and arrangements with third-party service providers for emergency services.

Challenges During the Disaster

- **Infrastructure Damage**: The hurricane caused significant damage to one of the bank's primary data centers and several branch offices, disrupting normal operations.
- **Communication Issues**: Widespread power outages and damage to communication infrastructure made it difficult to coordinate recovery efforts and communicate with employees and customers.
- **Staff Availability**: The disaster impacted the homes and families of many employees, making it challenging for them to participate in recovery efforts.

Recovery Actions

1. **Activation of the DRP**: RegioBank's disaster recovery team was activated, and the DRP was put into motion immediately following the disaster's onset.
2. **Relocation of Operations**: Critical operations were shifted to a secondary data center located outside the hurricane impact zone, ensuring the continuity of essential services like transaction processing.
3. **Alternative Work Arrangements**: Employees from affected branches and the primary data center were relocated to pre-designated recovery sites or enabled to work remotely where possible.
4. **Customer Communication**: RegioBank used social media, its website, and other available communication channels to update customers on the situation, available services, and recovery efforts.
5. **Resource Allocation**: Emergency resources, including backup generators, satellite phones, and mobile ATMs, were deployed to maintain operations and serve customers in affected areas.

Post-Disaster Recovery

- **Assessment and Repairs**: Once the hurricane passed, RegioBank assessed the damage to its facilities and initiated repairs to bring affected branches and the primary data center back online.

- **Review and Debrief**: The bank conducted a thorough review of its response to the hurricane, identifying successes and areas for improvement. Lessons learned were integrated into future iterations of the BCP and DRP.
- **Customer Support**: Special programs were implemented to support affected customers, including loan deferrals and emergency credit lines.

Lessons Learned

- **Importance of Redundancy**: The hurricane underscored the importance of having redundant systems and backup sites for critical operations.
- **Effective Communication**: Maintaining open lines of communication with employees and customers was crucial for managing expectations and ensuring trust during the recovery process.
- **Flexibility in Response**: The disaster highlighted the need for flexibility in response plans, as unforeseen challenges required quick adaptation and alternative solutions.

RegioBank's effective response to the hurricane demonstrated the value of having a well-thought-out and tested Business Continuity and Disaster Recovery Plan. By prioritizing the continuity of critical operations and maintaining clear communication throughout the disaster, RegioBank was able to minimize the impact on its operations and customers, ultimately emerging stronger and more resilient.

Zero Trust Architecture (ZTA) is a security concept centered on the belief that organizations should not automatically trust anything inside or outside their perimeters. Instead, they must verify anything and everything trying to connect to their systems before granting access. This approach is designed to protect modern digital environments by leveraging network segmentation, preventing lateral movement, providing Layer 7 threat prevention, and simplifying granular user-access control.

Application in Real-World Organizational Context

In a real-world scenario, an organization might implement ZTA to safeguard its distributed IT environment, which could include cloud services, remote workforces, and mobile devices. For instance, a financial institution facing threats from sophisticated cyber-attacks might adopt ZTA to ensure that only authenticated and authorized users and devices can access its banking applications and data, regardless of their location or network.

Challenges

Complex Implementation: Transitioning to a Zero Trust model can be complex, requiring significant changes in IT infrastructure and processes.

Legacy Systems Compatibility: Integrating ZTA with legacy systems that weren't designed with this model in mind can be challenging.

User Experience: Balancing security and user convenience is crucial, as stringent authentication processes might impede user productivity or satisfaction.

Benefits

Enhanced Security: By verifying all users and devices, ZTA minimizes the risk of unauthorized access and data breaches.

Reduced Attack Surface: Limiting access to resources on a need-to-know basis reduces the potential attack vectors within the organization.

Improved Compliance: ZTA can help organizations meet regulatory requirements by providing detailed access controls and audit trails.

Key Components of Zero Trust Model

Identity Verification: In ZTA, identity and access management (IAM) solutions are crucial. They ensure that only authenticated and authorized users can access specific resources. This involves strong authentication methods, such as multi-factor authentication (MFA), to verify user identities reliably.

Microsegmentation: This involves dividing the network into secure, distinct zones to control access and traffic flow among them. Microsegmentation limits the potential impact of breaches by restricting lateral movement within the network.

Least Privilege Access: Users are granted the minimum access necessary to perform their duties, reducing the risk of insider threats and limiting the potential damage from compromised accounts.

Continuous Monitoring and Validation: Continuous monitoring of network traffic and user behaviors allows for the detection of suspicious activities in real-time. The system continually validates the security posture of both the user and the device for the duration of the session.

Security Policies and Automation: Defining and enforcing security policies based on user roles, data types, and locations, combined with automated responses to detected threats, are integral to the Zero Trust approach.

Real-World Implementation Example

Consider a multinational corporation with employees accessing corporate resources from various locations and devices. By implementing ZTA, the corporation would require all users, whether they are on the corporate network or working remotely, to authenticate through a secure IAM system. Access to applications and data would be based on the user's role and the context of the access request, with all transactions logged for audit purposes. Network microsegmentation would ensure that even if attackers compromise a part of the network, they would be contained within that segment, preventing access to critical assets.

Zero Trust Architecture represents a paradigm shift in organizational security, moving away from traditional perimeter-based defenses to a model where trust is never assumed and must be continually earned. While the transition to ZTA presents challenges, its benefits in enhancing security and compliance make it a compelling approach for modern, distributed organizations.

Implementing ZTA requires careful planning, the right technological solutions, and a cultural shift towards security awareness and responsibility across the organization.

Advanced Persistent Threats (APTs) are sophisticated, covert, and continuous cyber-attacks orchestrated to infiltrate and remain inside a target's network for an extended period, often aiming to steal data or monitor internal activities. APTs are typically launched by well-resourced and skilled adversaries, such as nation-states or criminal organizations, making them particularly challenging to defend against.

Nature of APTs

- **Sophistication**: APTs use advanced hacking techniques, custom malware, and exploit zero-day vulnerabilities to evade detection.
- **Persistence**: Unlike other cyber threats that aim for quick gains, APTs focus on maintaining long-term access to the target's network.
- **Stealth**: APTs are designed to operate covertly, using methods to minimize detection and blend in with normal network traffic.
- **Targeted**: APTs usually have a specific target, such as government agencies, critical infrastructure, or high-value corporations, chosen for strategic, political, or financial reasons.

Countermeasures and Defense Strategies

Organizations employ a multi-layered defense strategy to combat APTs, focusing on detection, response, and mitigation.

Detection

- **Network Monitoring**: Continuous monitoring of network traffic to identify unusual patterns or behaviors that could indicate malicious activity. Advanced solutions like SIEM (Security Information and Event Management) systems are used to aggregate and analyze logs from various sources.
- **Endpoint Detection and Response (EDR)**: Implementing EDR solutions to monitor endpoint and server activities, detecting and investigating suspicious actions that could indicate the presence of an APT.
- **Threat Hunting**: Proactively searching for indicators of compromise (IoCs) within the network to identify threats that evade traditional detection methods.

Response

- **Incident Response Plan**: Having a well-defined incident response plan that includes specific procedures for dealing with APTs. This plan should outline roles, communication protocols, and steps for containment, eradication, and recovery.
- **Containment and Isolation**: Quickly isolating affected systems to prevent the spread of the threat. This can involve segmenting network areas, restricting access, or temporarily taking systems offline.
- **Forensic Analysis**: Conducting a thorough forensic investigation to understand the attack vectors, the extent of the compromise, and the tactics, techniques, and procedures (TTPs) used by the attackers.

Mitigation

- **Patching and Vulnerability Management**: Regularly updating software and systems to patch vulnerabilities that could be exploited by APTs. This includes not only operating systems and applications but also firmware on network and IoT devices.
- **Privileged Access Management (PAM)**: Implementing strict controls and monitoring around privileged accounts to reduce the risk of credential theft and misuse, a common tactic in APT attacks.
- **User Education and Awareness**: Training employees to recognize phishing attempts and other social engineering tactics that APT groups might use as initial entry points.
- **Microsegmentation**: Dividing the network into smaller, secure segments to limit lateral movement and restrict access to sensitive areas of the network.

Real-World Examples of Defense Strategies

- **Zero Trust Architecture**: An international financial institution adopted a Zero Trust model, requiring continuous verification of all users and devices, regardless of their location, before granting access to resources. This approach significantly reduced the attack surface and made it more difficult for APTs to move laterally within the network.
- **AI and Machine Learning**: A technology company leveraged AI and machine learning-based security tools to analyze behavior patterns and detect anomalies that could indicate APT activity, allowing for early detection and response.
- **Threat Intelligence Sharing**: A consortium of energy sector companies established a platform for sharing threat intelligence, including IoCs and TTPs associated with APT groups targeting the sector. This collective defense approach enhanced the individual and collective resilience of the participating organizations.

Combating APTs requires a comprehensive and adaptive security strategy that encompasses advanced detection techniques, rapid response capabilities, and robust mitigation measures. Given the evolving nature of APTs, organizations must continuously update their defense strategies to address emerging threats and tactics.

Emerging technologies like the Internet of Things (IoT), Artificial Intelligence (AI), and blockchain are revolutionizing industries but also bring complex security challenges. Understanding the potential risks and evolving threat landscape is crucial for developing effective security strategies.

Internet of Things (IoT)
Security Implications:

Device Vulnerability: Many IoT devices lack robust security features, making them susceptible to hacking and malware infections.
Data Privacy: IoT devices often collect sensitive data, raising concerns about data privacy and protection.
Network Security: The proliferation of IoT devices increases the attack surface, potentially introducing vulnerabilities into networks.
Strategies for Securing IoT:

Device Security: Implement strong authentication and encryption for device communication. Regular firmware updates are crucial for addressing vulnerabilities.

Network Segmentation: Segregate IoT devices onto separate network segments to limit their access to critical systems and reduce the risk of lateral movement by attackers.

Monitoring and Management: Employ comprehensive monitoring to detect anomalous behavior and manage device security centrally.

Artificial Intelligence (AI)

Security Implications:

Adversarial Attacks: AI systems can be susceptible to adversarial attacks, where manipulated inputs lead to incorrect outputs or decisions.

Data Poisoning: AI models can be compromised through data poisoning, where malicious data is introduced to skew the model's learning process.

Model Theft: AI models, particularly those with proprietary or sensitive logic, are at risk of theft or unauthorized access.

Strategies for Securing AI:

Robust Data Validation: Ensure the integrity of training data and implement mechanisms to detect and prevent data poisoning.

Secure Model Storage: Protect AI models with encryption and secure access controls to prevent unauthorized access and theft.

Adversarial Training: Incorporate adversarial examples into the training process to make AI models more resilient to adversarial attacks.

Blockchain

Security Implications:

51% Attacks: In blockchain networks, gaining control of more than 50% of the network's computing power can allow an attacker to alter transactions or double-spend cryptocurrencies.

Smart Contract Vulnerabilities: Flaws in smart contract code can be exploited to manipulate transactions or drain funds from blockchain-based applications.

Privacy Concerns: Public blockchains can expose transaction details, leading to potential privacy issues.

Strategies for Securing Blockchain:

Code Auditing and Testing: Conduct thorough audits and testing of smart contract code to identify and rectify vulnerabilities.

Decentralization: Ensure the blockchain network is sufficiently decentralized to mitigate the risk of 51% attacks.

Privacy Enhancements: Implement privacy-enhancing technologies such as zero-knowledge proofs or private transactions to protect user data.

Evolving Threat Landscape

The rapid advancement of these technologies presents a continuously evolving threat landscape. Attackers are increasingly leveraging sophisticated techniques to exploit vulnerabilities in these emerging technologies. The interconnectedness of IoT devices, the reliance on data for AI, and the immutable nature of blockchain transactions all present unique challenges.

Securing emerging technologies requires a proactive and multifaceted approach. It involves understanding the unique vulnerabilities of each technology, staying informed about the latest threats, and implementing layered security measures. Collaboration within the industry, ongoing research, and adopting best practices are crucial for mitigating risks and ensuring the secure adoption of these transformative

Chapter 12: Exam Preparation and Strategy:

Transitioning from the technical intricacies of cybersecurity, let's get into the equally critical realm of effective study techniques and time management, pivotal for conquering the CISSP exam. Mastering these strategies not only enhances comprehension of complex security concepts but also optimizes the vast preparation required for this certification.

Developing a Study Plan

Crafting a personalized study plan is paramount. Begin by assessing the CISSP exam's eight domains, pinpointing areas of strength and those necessitating further attention. Allocate study time proportionately, dedicating more hours to unfamiliar topics. It's advisable to set clear, achievable goals for each study session, fostering a sense of accomplishment and maintaining motivation.

Active Learning Approaches

Engaging actively with the material is essential. Employ diverse study methods to cater to various learning styles:

- **Interactive Learning**: Participate in study groups or forums to discuss complex topics, offering and receiving explanations from peers, which reinforces understanding.
- **Practical Application**: Where possible, apply theoretical knowledge to real-world scenarios or simulations. This practical application solidifies abstract concepts, making them more relatable and easier to recall.
- **Teaching Concepts**: Explaining topics to others, perhaps a study partner or even to oneself aloud, can significantly enhance comprehension and retention.

Time Management Techniques

Efficient time management is crucial for balancing extensive study sessions with other professional and personal commitments:

- **Pomodoro Technique**: This involves focused study sessions of 25 minutes, followed by a 5-minute break. Such short bursts can enhance concentration and prevent burnout.
- **Prioritization**: Utilize tools like the Eisenhower Matrix to prioritize study tasks, focusing on urgent and important topics while scheduling or delegating less critical tasks.

- **Scheduled Reviews**: Regularly spaced review sessions help in reinforcing memory. The spacing effect, a cognitive phenomenon, suggests that information is more easily recalled if learning sessions are spaced out over time.

Utilizing CISSP Resources Wisely

The CISSP exam covers a broad spectrum of topics, making it essential to select study materials judiciously:

- **Official ISC² Resources**: The official ISC² CISSP Study Guide and Practice Tests are tailored to the exam's latest version, ensuring relevancy.
- **Online Courses and Webinars**: Many reputable platforms offer CISSP preparation courses that include video tutorials, interactive quizzes, and live webinars, catering to different learning preferences.
- **Flashcards**: These are excellent for memorizing key concepts, terms, and definitions. Digital flashcard apps allow for studying on the go and often employ spaced repetition algorithms to optimize learning.

Health and Wellness

Maintaining physical and mental well-being is often overlooked but is vital for effective studying:

- **Regular Exercise**: Physical activity, even short walks, can boost cognitive function and reduce stress.
- **Adequate Rest**: Ensure sufficient sleep and take regular breaks during study sessions to prevent fatigue and retain information more effectively.
- **Mindfulness and Stress Management**: Techniques such as meditation or deep-breathing exercises can alleviate exam-related anxiety, enhancing focus and mental clarity.

In preparing for the CISSP exam, blending disciplined study habits with efficient time management and self-care practices lays the foundation for success. This holistic approach not only aids in mastering the expansive CISSP curriculum but also in developing the resilience and adaptability characteristic of accomplished information security professionals.

Building upon the foundational knowledge of effective study techniques and time management, we now turn our focus to the critical exam-taking strategies and tips specifically tailored for the CISSP exam. Mastering the art of exam-taking is as crucial as understanding the content itself, particularly for a comprehensive and challenging exam like the CISSP.

Understanding the Exam Format

Familiarize yourself with the CISSP exam format, which is adaptive in nature and consists of a range of 100 to 150 questions, covering multiple-choice and advanced innovative questions. The adaptive testing format means that the difficulty of the exam can adjust based on the test taker's responses, requiring a strategic approach to answering questions.

Time Management During the Exam

- **Pace Yourself**: Given the maximum time limit of 3 hours, it's essential to pace yourself. Allocate time slots for each question and keep track of the time without rushing, ensuring that you have enough time to review your answers.

- **Prioritize Questions**: Tackle questions you are confident about first, marking more challenging questions for review. This ensures that you secure all the points you can before dealing with more complex questions.

Reading Questions Carefully
- **Understand the Question**: Read each question carefully, paying attention to the details and the context. CISSP questions often contain critical information in the scenario that can guide you to the correct answer.
- **Identify Keywords**: Look for keywords or phrases in the question that indicate what it's truly asking, such as "BEST," "MOST," "LEAST," which can significantly alter the meaning of the question and the correct response.

Answering Strategies
- **Eliminate Wrong Answers**: Use the process of elimination to narrow down your choices. Even if you're unsure of the correct answer, dismissing clearly incorrect options increases your chances of selecting the right one.
- **Think Like a Manager**: The CISSP exam often requires a managerial perspective, focusing on risk management, cost-benefit analysis, and best practices rather than technical details alone. Approach questions from a strategic viewpoint.
- **Watch for Absolutes**: Be cautious of answer choices with absolute terms like "always" or "never," as these are seldom correct in the nuanced scenarios CISSP questions typically present.

Handling Difficult Questions
- **Don't Panic**: If you encounter particularly challenging questions, don't let them unsettle you. Mark them for review and move on, returning to them with a fresh perspective after answering other questions.
- **Use Logical Reasoning**: Apply logical reasoning to deduce the most plausible answer, drawing on your understanding of the CISSP domains and real-world applications of security principles.

Reviewing Answers
- **Review Marked Questions**: Make use of any remaining time to review questions you've marked. Re-reading with a clearer mind might help you catch details you missed initially.
- **Trust Your Instincts**: While reviewing, be cautious about changing your answers. Often, your first choice is correct unless you find clear evidence or recall information that justifies changing your response.

Mental and Physical Preparedness
- **Rest Well**: Ensure you get a good night's sleep before the exam day to be mentally alert and focused.
- **Stay Hydrated and Nourished**: Drink water and eat a light meal before the exam to maintain energy levels without discomfort.

Approaching the CISSP exam with these strategies in mind enhances your ability to navigate its complexities confidently. Remember, the exam not only tests your knowledge but also your decision-making and problem-solving skills under pressure. Combining a deep understanding of the content with these exam-taking strategies will position you for success in achieving your CISSP certification.

PRACTICE TEST SECTION:

Welcome you to the practice test section of this CISSP study guide. This segment is meticulously designed to simulate the real exam environment, challenging your understanding and application of the CISSP domains through a series of thought-provoking questions.

Each question in this section is crafted to test specific aspects of the CISSP curriculum, reflecting the complexity and depth of scenarios you may encounter in the actual exam. Following each question, you will find not only the correct answer but also a detailed explanation that delves into the rationale behind the answer. This immediate feedback mechanism is intended to reinforce your learning by providing clarity on why a particular answer is correct and elucidating the thought process that leads to it.

This approach eliminates the need to flip through pages to consult an answer key, streamlining your study experience and allowing for more efficient learning. By understanding the reasoning behind each answer, you can better grasp the underlying principles and concepts, enhancing your ability to apply this knowledge in varied contexts, both in the exam and in real-world situations.

Embark on this series of practice questions with a keen and analytical mind, embracing each challenge as an opportunity to fortify your knowledge and refine your test-taking strategies. Remember, each question is a step forward in your journey toward CISSP certification and a testament to your commitment to excellence in the field of information security.

1. An enterprise is planning to migrate their data center to a cloud service provider (CSP). As part of due diligence, the Chief Information Security Officer (CISO) needs to assess the risks associated with the CSP's data retention and destruction policies. Which of the following best ensures that the CSP adheres to the enterprise's data security standards?
a. Conducting an on-site audit of the CSP's facilities.
b. Reviewing the CSP's Service Level Agreements (SLAs).
c. Implementing strong encryption for data at rest and in transit.
d. Requiring the CSP to provide regular data recovery capability proofs.

Answer: b. Reviewing the CSP's Service Level Agreements (SLAs). Explanation: The Service Level Agreements (SLAs) will contain detailed information about the CSP's policies on data retention and destruction, as well as compliance with security standards. While on-site audits and encryption are important, they do not provide direct insight into the CSP's policies. Regular data recovery proofs ensure availability but do not address the security standards for data retention and destruction.

2. A multinational corporation with operations in multiple countries is developing a global data protection program. The program must comply with a variety of data protection laws, including GDPR. Which approach should be prioritized to address the variability in legal requirements?
a. Adopting the strictest data protection standards across all operations.
b. Customizing data protection policies for each country's specific laws.
c. Implementing a data protection policy based on the least stringent legal requirements.
d. Outsourcing data protection responsibilities to a third-party vendor in each region.

Answer: a. Adopting the strictest data protection standards across all operations. Explanation: When dealing with multiple jurisdictions with varying data protection laws, adopting the strictest data protection standards ensures compliance across all regions. This approach is often referred to as the 'highest common denominator' approach and helps avoid the complexity of tailoring policies to each specific set of laws, which can be resource-intensive and may still result in non-compliance due to overlapping legal frameworks.

3. During a routine audit, it was discovered that several employees have access to financial records beyond what their job roles require. What is the first step the organization should take to remediate this issue?
a. Revise the organization's access control policies.
b. Conduct a user access review for the financial system.
c. Implement role-based access control for the financial records.
d. Provide additional training to employees on proper data handling.

Answer: b. Conduct a user access review for the financial system. Explanation: The immediate step to remediate inappropriate access is to review who has access to the financial records. Conducting a user access review will identify all individuals with access and allow the organization to adjust permissions according to the principle of least privilege. While revising access control policies, implementing role-based access control, and training are important, they are subsequent steps after identifying the extent of the issue.

4. A security manager is evaluating vendors for a security information and event management (SIEM) solution. Which of the following criteria is the most critical for the selection process?
a. The user-friendliness of the SIEM dashboard.
b. The ability of the SIEM to integrate with existing security tools.
c. The cost of the SIEM solution compared to others in the market.
d. The vendor's market share and brand reputation.

Answer: b. The ability of the SIEM to integrate with existing security tools. Explanation: While all the factors are important, the primary purpose of a SIEM is to aggregate and correlate data from various security tools. Its ability to integrate with the organization's existing security infrastructure is critical to provide comprehensive monitoring and effective incident analysis.

5. A company's proprietary project data has been leaked, and an insider is suspected. Which of the following would be the most effective next step to identify the culprit?
a. Review network access logs for unusual activity.
b. Perform a full audit of physical access logs.
c. Implement a strict password change policy.
d. Increase the frequency of data backups.

Answer: a. Review network access logs for unusual activity. Explanation: Network access logs can provide evidence of unusual activity, such as data access at odd hours, large data transfers, and access from unusual locations, which can help identify the insider responsible for the data leak. While physical access logs are useful, data leaks more commonly occur over the network. Password policies and data backups are security measures but do not aid in identifying the source of a data leak.

6. During a recent security assessment, it was found that an organization's critical systems are running outdated software that cannot be immediately updated due to compatibility issues. What is the most effective compensating control to implement?
a. Install a firewall specifically for these systems.
b. Increase network intrusion detection capabilities.
c. Isolate the systems in a dedicated network segment.
d. Mandate frequent password changes for system access.

Answer: c. Isolate the systems in a dedicated network segment. Explanation: Isolating the outdated systems in a dedicated network segment, or microsegmentation, is a compensating control that can help limit the risk exposure and prevent potential compromise from affecting the broader network. While firewalls and intrusion detection systems are important, they do not provide the same level of isolation and containment as network segmentation does.

7. A Chief Information Security Officer (CISO) is evaluating a new security framework for their organization, which requires handling sensitive data across multiple international borders. To ensure compliance with varying data protection laws, the CISO should prioritize understanding which of the following?
a. The data localization requirements of each operational country
b. The export restrictions related to cryptographic products
c. The principles of the Payment Card Industry Data Security Standard (PCI DSS)
d. The guidelines outlined in ISO/IEC 27002

Answer: a. The data localization requirements of each operational country. Explanation: Data localization laws mandate that data about a country's citizens or residents be collected, processed, and/or stored inside the country, often before being transferred internationally. Understanding these laws is crucial for international operations to ensure compliance with different countries' data protection regulations. While export restrictions, PCI DSS, and ISO/IEC 27002 are important, they do not directly address the varying international data protection requirements as data localization laws do.

8. A financial institution is undergoing a merger, and the board of directors requires a risk assessment regarding the consolidation of digital assets. What is the FIRST step they should take in this process?
a. Identify all digital assets that will be consolidated in the merger
b. Conduct a cost-benefit analysis of the merger
c. Implement new access controls across both organizations
d. Purchase an insurance policy to cover potential cyber risks

Answer: a. Identify all digital assets that will be consolidated in the merger. Explanation: The first step in a risk assessment process is to identify the assets that are at risk, in this case, the digital assets that will be consolidated. Without knowing what assets are involved, it is impossible to accurately assess the risks, potential impacts, or to implement the appropriate security controls. Cost-benefit analysis, access controls, and cyber insurance are subsequent considerations after asset identification.

9. In an organization's data center, a server containing personally identifiable information (PII) has been compromised. Which of the following is the MOST critical immediate action to protect affected individuals' privacy?
a. Notify the public relations department to prepare a press release
b. Isolate the server and begin an investigation
c. Encrypt the PII on the remaining servers
d. Contact all individuals whose PII was on the server

Answer: b. Isolate the server and begin an investigation. Explanation: Isolating the compromised server is the most immediate and critical action to contain the breach and prevent further unauthorized access or data loss. While notifying affected individuals and public relations are important steps, they come after securing and containing the compromised system. Encryption of PII on other servers is a preventative measure for future security.

10. During a routine audit, it was discovered that several employees have access to financial records that are not required for their job functions. This situation violates which security principle?
a. Dual control
b. Job rotation
c. Least privilege
d. Mandatory vacations

Answer: c. Least privilege. Explanation: The principle of least privilege dictates that individuals should only have access to the information and resources necessary for their job functions. Granting employees unnecessary access to financial records increases the risk of data breaches or misuse. The other options, while important in a comprehensive security program, do not directly relate to limiting access based on job necessities.

11. A company's security team has noticed an increase in phishing attempts and has decided to implement an email filtering solution. Which of the following would be the BEST metric to assess the effectiveness of this solution?
a. The number of phishing emails reported by users
b. The time taken to resolve reported phishing incidents
c. The decrease in the volume of outbound emails
d. The increase in emails blocked by the new filter

Answer: a. The number of phishing emails reported by users. Explanation: The best metric to assess the effectiveness of an email filtering solution is the reduction in the number of phishing emails that users report. This indicates that fewer phishing attempts are reaching end-users, thereby demonstrating the solution's effectiveness. The other options may provide useful information but do not directly measure the performance of the email filtering solution regarding phishing attempts.

12. A global organization with offices in multiple countries is trying to implement a uniform security policy. However, they face legal and cultural differences that affect the acceptable use of IT resources. To reconcile these differences, the organization should FIRST:
a. Create a baseline security policy that adheres to the strictest legal requirements
b. Customize security policies for each location based on local laws and customs
c. Enforce the home country's security policies across all international offices
d. Seek a consensus from all regional managers before drafting a policy

Answer: b. Customize security policies for each location based on local laws and customs. Explanation: The most effective approach when dealing with diverse legal and cultural environments is to tailor security policies to reflect the specific legal requirements and cultural norms of each location. This ensures compliance and respects local practices while maintaining the organization's overall security posture. Starting with the strictest legal requirements or the home country's policies might not address all local nuances, and seeking consensus is time-consuming and may not result in clear guidance.

13. The IT department of a large corporation is implementing a new security information and event management (SIEM) system. What should be the PRIMARY focus during the initial phase of implementation?
a. Configuring alerts for all security events
b. Integrating the SIEM with existing security tools
c. Training the security team on using the SIEM dashboard
d. Establishing a process for responding to SIEM alerts

Answer: b. Integrating the SIEM with existing security tools. Explanation: The primary focus during the initial phase of implementing a SIEM system should be integrating it with existing security tools to ensure that it has access to all relevant data sources. This integration is crucial for the SIEM to provide comprehensive monitoring, correlation, and analysis of security events across the organization. While configuring alerts, training staff, and establishing response processes are important, these steps follow integration.

14. A cybersecurity analyst at a tech company is using an intrusion detection system (IDS) to monitor network traffic. After a system upgrade, the IDS starts generating an overwhelming number of false positives. What is the MOST effective strategy to address this issue?
a. Increase the IDS's traffic threshold settings
b. Conduct a review and fine-tuning of IDS signatures and rules
c. Switch the IDS to a less restrictive detection mode
d. Disable the IDS until the system upgrade can be rolled back

Answer: b. Conduct a review and fine-tuning of IDS signatures and rules. Explanation: The most effective way to reduce false positives in an IDS is to review and fine-tune its signatures and rules based on the network's normal traffic patterns. This helps to ensure that the IDS is accurately distinguishing between benign and malicious activity. Simply increasing thresholds or switching modes may reduce false positives but could also result in missing genuine threats, while disabling the IDS exposes the network to potential undetected intrusions.

15. A security manager is evaluating different risk treatment options for identified threats to the organization's information systems. Which of the following is an appropriate strategy for a risk with a low impact and low likelihood of occurrence?
a. Accept the risk and monitor for changes in the threat landscape.
b. Transfer the risk by purchasing cyber insurance.
c. Avoid the risk by discontinuing the affected business process.
d. Mitigate the risk by implementing costly controls.

Answer: a. Accept the risk and monitor for changes in the threat landscape. Explanation: In risk management, acceptance is a viable strategy for low-impact, low-likelihood risks. It is cost-effective to monitor such risks rather than invest in mitigation strategies that might not be proportional to the risk itself. The other options represent risk treatment strategies that are more suitable for higher levels of risk.

16. The Chief Information Security Officer (CISO) is developing an information security strategy aligned with business objectives. Which of the following best ensures that the security initiatives will have the support of the business leaders?
a. Designing technical controls that operate independently of business processes.
b. Creating security policies without consulting department heads to maintain impartiality.
c. Ensuring security investments are proportional to the potential impact on the business.
d. Focusing solely on regulatory compliance to guide security investments.

Answer: c. Ensuring security investments are proportional to the potential impact on the business. Explanation: By aligning security investments with the potential impact on the business, the CISO demonstrates that security initiatives are designed to protect the organization's most critical assets. This approach is more likely to garner support from business leaders, as it directly ties security to business value. The other options do not foster alignment with business objectives or stakeholder support.

17. During a routine security audit, it was discovered that an employee had unauthorized access to sensitive customer data. Which principle of access control was violated?
a. Authentication
b. Authorization
c. Accounting
d. Availability

Answer: b. Authorization. Explanation: Authorization is the process of granting or denying specific access rights to different resources, which was compromised in this scenario. Authentication refers to verifying identity, accounting refers to tracking user actions, and availability is about ensuring that authorized users have access to resources when needed.

18. An organization is considering adopting a new technology that would streamline customer service processes but also introduces new data privacy concerns. What should be the first step in deciding whether to proceed with the implementation?
a. Perform a cost-benefit analysis, including the potential privacy impact.
b. Purchase an insurance policy that covers privacy breach incidents.
c. Implement the technology on a trial basis to gather performance data.
d. Consult with the legal team about the implications of data privacy laws.

Answer: a. Perform a cost-benefit analysis, including the potential privacy impact. Explanation: A cost-benefit analysis that includes privacy impact considerations will provide a holistic view of the value and risks of the new technology, guiding informed decision-making. This should precede insurance considerations, trial implementations, or legal consultations, as it will inform whether the benefits outweigh the risks.

19. A company has implemented strict security controls to protect its network. Despite this, a recent incident revealed that a hacker was able to maintain persistent access to the network over several months. What is the most likely type of attack that was not adequately prevented?
a. Denial of Service (DoS) attack
b. Man-in-the-middle (MitM) attack
c. Advanced Persistent Threat (APT)
d. Phishing attack

Answer: c. Advanced Persistent Threat (APT). Explanation: APTs are characterized by the ability to gain long-term access to networks, often going undetected. They are sophisticated and can circumvent traditional security controls, unlike the other options, which generally do not result in long-term network access.

20. A global corporation is revising its risk management program. In accordance with ISO 31000, which action is essential for integrating risk management into organizational processes?
a. Assigning risk management tasks to a dedicated team
b. Ensuring the risk management process is a standalone procedure
c. Making risk management part of the responsibilities of every employee
d. Outsourcing risk management to specialized third-party vendors

Answer: c. Making risk management part of the responsibilities of every employee. Explanation: ISO 31000 emphasizes the integration of risk management into all organizational processes and decisions. Making it a part of every employee's responsibilities ensures that risk is considered at all levels and in all activities, fostering a risk-aware culture.

21. Following a merger, a company is consolidating its data centers. Which of the following actions aligns with ensuring data availability during the transition?
a. Decommissioning all legacy servers immediately to avoid confusion
b. Maintaining parallel operations of both data centers during a phased migration
c. Migrating all data to the cloud without maintaining any on-premises backup
d. Utilizing data deduplication across data centers to minimize storage needs

Answer: b. Maintaining parallel operations of both data centers during a phased migration. Explanation: Keeping both data centers operational during a phased migration ensures that data remains available to users and there is a fallback option in case of issues. Immediate decommissioning or lack of on-premises backup could risk data availability.

22. A software development company is implementing a DevSecOps approach. Which of the following best exemplifies this methodology?
a. Security assessments are performed once a year by an external auditor.
b. Developers are solely responsible for security in the software development lifecycle.
c. Security testing is integrated into the continuous integration/continuous deployment (CI/CD) pipeline.
d. Operations teams manage security controls post-deployment without developer involvement.

Answer: c. Security testing is integrated into the continuous integration/continuous deployment (CI/CD) pipeline. Explanation: DevSecOps involves integrating security practices within DevOps workflows, making security an integral part of the development and deployment process. By embedding security testing in the CI/CD pipeline, security becomes a continuous, shared responsibility between developers and operations.

23. In preparing for the implementation of the General Data Protection Regulation (GDPR), the data protection officer (DPO) of a multinational company is assessing the need for a data protection impact assessment (DPIA). Which type of project would most likely require a DPIA?
a. Updating the company's public website with a new design
b. Deploying a network upgrade to improve connectivity speeds
c. Introducing a new system for processing large volumes of personal data
d. Replacing office productivity software with a new version from the same vendor

Answer: c. Introducing a new system for processing large volumes of personal data. Explanation: Under GDPR, a DPIA is required for processing operations that are likely to result in a high risk to the rights and freedoms of individuals, particularly when involving large-scale processing of personal data. A new system that processes large volumes of personal data likely meets this criterion, necessitating a DPIA.

24. The IT department of a financial institution is deploying a new transaction processing system. Which security principle should be emphasized to ensure the integrity of transaction data?
a. Redundancy of data storage
b. Encryption of data in transit
c. Frequent backups of transaction logs
d. Input validation of transaction entries

Answer: d. Input validation of transaction entries. Explanation: Input validation is crucial for ensuring that only correct and intended data is entered into the system, thereby maintaining the integrity of transaction data. While encryption protects data confidentiality and backups ensure availability, input validation directly affects the accuracy and reliability of the data being processed.

25. A security analyst is reviewing an incident where confidential client information was leaked through an email breach. Which security control would be most effective in preventing such a breach in the future?
a. Implementing a RAID array to prevent data loss
b. Deploying an intrusion prevention system to monitor network traffic
c. Applying digital rights management to sensitive documents
d. Enforcing multi-factor authentication on email accounts

Answer: c. Applying digital rights management to sensitive documents. Explanation: Digital rights management (DRM) is a set of access control technologies that protect and control the use of digital content and devices. By applying DRM to sensitive documents, an organization can prevent unauthorized access and sharing, directly protecting the confidentiality of client information. RAID arrays are used for data availability, intrusion prevention systems for integrity and availability, and while multi-factor authentication secures account access, it does not protect the content once accessed or shared.

26. The IT department has implemented a new backup solution that encrypts data before transferring it to an off-site storage facility. This change primarily enhances which aspect of the CIA triad?
a. Confidentiality of the backup data
b. Integrity of the backup data
c. Availability of the backup data
d. Authenticity of the backup data

Answer: a. Confidentiality of the backup data. Explanation: Encryption protects data from being read by unauthorized parties, thus ensuring confidentiality. While encryption can also support integrity and authenticity, in this context, its primary function is to secure the confidentiality of the data during transfer and storage. Availability is ensured by the existence of backups themselves, not by the encryption process.

27. A company is designing a critical system that must maintain uptime even in the face of hardware failures. Which of the following best ensures high availability of the system?
a. Employing a WAF to protect against web-based attacks
b. Implementing load balancers and redundant servers
c. Encrypting data at rest and in transit
d. Conducting regular vulnerability scanning

Answer: b. Implementing load balancers and redundant servers. Explanation: Load balancers distribute workloads across multiple computing resources, such as servers, to optimize resource use and maximize throughput, minimizing response time. Redundant servers ensure that if one server fails, another can take over, maintaining system availability. While the other options are important for security, they do not directly contribute to the system's uptime and availability.

28. During a system upgrade, a database administrator mistakenly inputs a wrong command, leading to corruption of data. Which of the following would best mitigate this type of risk?
a. Implementing strong access control mechanisms
b. Regularly testing data restoration from backup
c. Applying strict change management procedures
d. Increasing the bandwidth of the network connection

Answer: c. Applying strict change management procedures. Explanation: Change management procedures are designed to manage changes systematically and efficiently while minimizing the impact on system stability and avoiding unintended service disruptions. By applying strict change management procedures, such as requiring peer review of changes or pre-approval for critical commands, the risk of human error leading to data corruption is significantly reduced.

29. A multinational organization is considering implementing an information classification program. What is the primary goal of classifying information?
a. To streamline the information retrieval process
b. To define the scope of information to be encrypted
c. To ensure appropriate protection levels based on sensitivity
d. To increase the transparency of information handling

Answer: c. To ensure appropriate protection levels based on sensitivity. Explanation: The primary goal of classifying information is to ensure that data receives an appropriate level of protection based on its sensitivity and value to the organization. This determines how information is handled, shared, and secured. The other options are secondary effects or specific actions that might result from the classification but are not the primary goal.

30. A security consultant recommends that a financial institution utilize hashing to protect the integrity of data at rest. Which of the following properties of hashing makes it suitable for this purpose?
a. Hash functions are reversible, allowing easy retrieval of original data
b. Hash algorithms generate a unique fixed-size hash value for the same input data
c. Hashing increases the size of the data, making it harder to tamper with
d. Hash functions can be easily decrypted with the institution's private key

Answer: b. Hash algorithms generate a unique fixed-size hash value for the same input data. Explanation: Hashing is used to ensure data integrity because it produces a unique hash value for the original data, which can be compared to the hash value of the data at any later point to verify that it has not been altered. If the data changes in any way, even slightly, the resulting hash will be significantly different, indicating a potential compromise of the data's integrity.

31. A cloud service provider is implementing security controls to protect data for a new client. The client's main concern is ensuring that their data cannot be accessed by unauthorized entities. Which of the following measures should be prioritized?
a. Enabling georedundancy of data centers
b. Implementing network segmentation
c. Utilizing strong symmetric encryption
d. Regular penetration testing of the cloud infrastructure

Answer: c. Utilizing strong symmetric encryption. Explanation: Strong symmetric encryption ensures that data cannot be accessed by unauthorized entities because it requires a secret key to decrypt the data. Georedundancy, network segmentation, and penetration testing are important for availability, controlling access within the network, and identifying vulnerabilities, respectively, but they do not directly protect data from unauthorized access like encryption does.

32. An organization's security team has noticed an increase in the number of phishing attempts. Which of the following measures could most effectively reduce the success rate of these attacks?
a. Deploying an IDS to monitor network traffic
b. Conducting security awareness training focused on phishing identification
c. Increasing the complexity of password requirements
d. Implementing CAPTCHAs on all external login pages

Answer: b. Conducting security awareness training focused on phishing identification. Explanation: Security awareness training that focuses on identifying phishing attempts equips employees with the knowledge to recognize and properly respond to phishing emails, which are often the first line of defense against such attacks. While IDS, complex passwords, and CAPTCHAs are valuable security measures, they do not address the human element of identifying and reporting phishing attempts.

33. In an effort to maintain data integrity during transmission, a security engineer is evaluating different cryptographic methods. Which of the following would provide assurance that the data has not been altered during transit?
a. Digital signatures
b. Data encryption
c. Tokenization
d. Steganography

Answer: a. Digital signatures. Explanation: Digital signatures provide integrity and non-repudiation by allowing the recipient to verify that the data has not been altered since it was signed by the sender. While encryption secures the confidentiality of the data, it does not by itself provide a mechanism for integrity verification. Tokenization substitutes sensitive elements with non-sensitive equivalents and is primarily used for protecting data at rest, and steganography hides data within other data, but neither ensures data integrity during transmission like digital signatures.

34. A financial analyst at a large bank is responsible for developing a new predictive model for credit risk. To maintain the integrity of the model outputs, which of the following measures should be prioritized?
a. Implementing robust data encryption at rest and in transit.
b. Applying rigorous data validation checks before model ingestion.
c. Ensuring high availability of the modeling system.
d. Conducting regular data privacy impact assessments.

Answer: b. Applying rigorous data validation checks before model ingestion. Explanation: Data integrity in predictive modeling is crucial to ensure accurate and reliable output. While encryption maintains confidentiality and high availability ensures the system is consistently operational, rigorous data validation checks directly impact the integrity of the model by ensuring that the input data is correct and unaltered.

35. The IT department is deploying a new mission-critical application that requires high availability. Which of the following architectural decisions best supports this requirement?
a. Implementing strong encryption for data at rest.
b. Deploying load balancers and redundant servers.
c. Enforcing multifactor authentication for system access.
d. Applying the principle of least privilege to system users.

Answer: b. Deploying load balancers and redundant servers. Explanation: Load balancers and redundant servers are key to achieving high availability by distributing the workload evenly and maintaining service in case of a server failure. Encryption and access control measures like multifactor authentication and least privilege are essential for security but do not directly contribute to system availability.

36. A law firm handling sensitive client information is evaluating their data storage solutions. To ensure client confidentiality is maintained, which of the following approaches should be emphasized?
a. Frequent data backup schedules.
b. Encryption of data both at rest and in transit.
c. Rapid failover capabilities in case of a system crash.
d. Implementation of write-once-read-many (WORM) storage.

Answer: b. Encryption of data both at rest and in transit. Explanation: Encryption is critical for maintaining the confidentiality of sensitive data. It ensures that even if data is intercepted or accessed by unauthorized parties, it remains unreadable and secure. While backups, failover capabilities, and WORM storage contribute to data integrity and availability, they do not primarily address confidentiality.

37. In a hospital's digital record system, ensuring the availability of patient records while maintaining their confidentiality and integrity is critical. Which of the following scenarios demonstrates a potential compromise of availability?
a. An unauthorized employee accessed patient records.
b. Patient records were altered by a malware infection.
c. A power outage rendered the record system temporarily inaccessible.
d. A clinician was unable to modify a patient's record due to access controls.

Answer: c. A power outage rendered the record system temporarily inaccessible. Explanation: Availability in the context of the CIA triad refers to ensuring that authorized users have reliable access to data and resources when needed. A power outage directly impacts availability by making the system inaccessible. The other scenarios impact confidentiality and integrity but not availability.

38. The security team of a multinational corporation is implementing a new data policy to enhance security. Which of the following measures is primarily aimed at ensuring data integrity?
a. Increasing bandwidth to improve system response times.
b. Installing anti-virus software on all corporate endpoints.
c. Introducing checksums and hashing for files before transmission.
d. Expanding the use of virtual private networks (VPNs) for remote work.

Answer: c. Introducing checksums and hashing for files before transmission. Explanation: Checksums and hashing are methods used to verify that data has not been altered or corrupted. They are directly related to maintaining data integrity by ensuring that files remain unchanged from their original state. While anti-virus software helps protect against malware, and VPNs secure data in transit, checksums and hashing specifically address integrity.

39. A cloud service provider is reviewing security controls to prevent data breaches. Which of the following is a preventive control for protecting the integrity of customer data?
a. Intrusion detection systems monitoring network traffic.
b. Regular backups of customer data.
c. Digital signatures for data transactions.
d. Incident response teams prepared to react to data leaks.

Answer: c. Digital signatures for data transactions. Explanation: Digital signatures provide authentication and integrity for data transactions. They ensure that the data received is the same as the data sent and has not been tampered with, directly protecting the integrity of customer data. While intrusion detection systems and incident response teams are important for identifying and reacting to breaches, and backups ensure data recovery, digital signatures prevent data integrity breaches at the transaction level.

40. An organization is implementing security controls to ensure the confidentiality of its strategic plans. Which of the following is most effective in preventing unauthorized disclosure of this information?
a. Data classification and labeling.
b. Load balancing across network servers.
c. Redundant array of independent disks (RAID) storage configuration.
d. Periodic vulnerability scanning of the network.

Answer: a. Data classification and labeling. Explanation: Data classification and labeling are essential processes for maintaining confidentiality. They ensure that sensitive information, such as strategic plans, is clearly marked and handled according to its classification level, reducing the risk of unauthorized disclosure. While load balancing and RAID storage are more about availability and vulnerability scanning is a component of integrity and overall security, classification, and labeling specifically target the protection of confidentiality.

41. The board of a tech startup is determining the strategic direction of their information security program. What should be the FIRST step according to best practices in security governance?
a. Developing an information security policy that aligns with the business strategy.
b. Purchasing cyber insurance to transfer risk.
c. Hiring a third-party consultant to implement security controls.
d. Conducting a penetration test to identify current vulnerabilities.

Answer: a. Developing an information security policy that aligns with the business strategy. Explanation: The first step in establishing a sound security governance framework is to create a security policy that aligns with and supports the business objectives and strategy. This will ensure that security processes and measures are integrated into the business effectively and that security considerations are included in strategic planning.

42. During a review of the company's security governance practices, it is noted that there is no formal approval process for information security policies. What is the MOST likely consequence of this oversight?
a. Reduced efficiency in policy distribution.
b. Increased risk of non-compliance with legal requirements.
c. Diminished alignment between security policies and business objectives.
d. Lower engagement in security awareness training.

Answer: c. Diminished alignment between security policies and business objectives. Explanation: Without a formal approval process, there is a risk that information security policies may not align with business objectives or may not be endorsed by senior management. Formal approval ensures that policies are both relevant to the organization's strategic goals and have the backing required for effective implementation and compliance.

43. A multinational corporation is assessing its adherence to security governance best practices. Which of the following activities is LEAST likely to be part of a governance framework?
a. Regularly updating the disaster recovery plan.
b. Ensuring all employees complete annual security awareness training.
c. Delegating the responsibility for security to the IT department.
d. Aligning security initiatives with organizational goals and objectives.

Answer: c. Delegating the responsibility for security to the IT department. Explanation: While the IT department plays a critical role in implementing security measures, responsibility for security should be shared across the organization. A governance framework would typically involve the establishment of an information security governance committee or similar body that spans beyond IT to ensure organization-wide accountability and integration of security practices.

44. The CEO of a financial institution is looking to establish a security governance committee. Who should be INCLUDED to ensure effective oversight and decision-making?
a. IT support staff and software developers.
b. Marketing representatives and sales associates.
c. Representatives from legal, human resources, and finance departments.
d. All employees in the organization for comprehensive representation.

Answer: c. Representatives from legal, human resources, and finance departments. Explanation: For effective oversight, a security governance committee should include members from key departments such as legal, human resources, and finance, as they can provide insights on compliance, employee-related matters, and financial implications of security decisions. IT support staff and developers are responsible for implementing security, but governance typically requires higher-level strategic decision-makers.

45. In the wake of a data breach, a large retailer is revising its security governance structure. What should be the PRIMARY focus to improve security governance?
a. Increasing the frequency of security audits.
b. Ensuring clear communication channels between the security team and executive management.
c. Replacing all outdated security technologies.
d. Mandating additional technical training for the security staff.

Answer: b. Ensuring clear communication channels between the security team and executive management.
Explanation: Clear communication channels between the security team and executive management are essential for effective security governance. This ensures that security risks are understood at the highest levels of the organization and that strategic decisions are made with a clear understanding of security implications.

46. A Chief Information Security Officer (CISO) is advocating for the adoption of a security framework. Which framework focuses primarily on improving risk management processes within an organization?
a. ISO/IEC 27001
b. NIST Cybersecurity Framework
c. COBIT
d. ITIL

Answer: b. NIST Cybersecurity Framework. Explanation: The NIST Cybersecurity Framework is designed to help organizations manage and mitigate cybersecurity risk more effectively. While ISO/IEC 27001 sets out the requirements for an information security management system (ISMS), COBIT provides a comprehensive framework for IT management and governance, and ITIL offers guidelines for IT service management, the NIST Framework is specifically tailored toward improving an organization's risk management processes.

47. An enterprise is deploying a new Security Information and Event Management (SIEM) system. In terms of security governance, what is the MOST important factor to consider?
a. The ability of the SIEM to generate compliance reports.
b. The speed at which the SIEM can process events.
c. Integration of the SIEM with existing organizational workflows.
d. The cost of the SIEM solution.

Answer: c. Integration of the SIEM with existing organizational workflows. Explanation: While all the options are relevant considerations, the most critical aspect from a governance perspective is how well the SIEM integrates with existing organizational workflows and processes. This ensures that the SIEM tool enhances, rather than disrupts, the organization's ability to detect and respond to security incidents effectively.

48. A healthcare provider is establishing governance for its newly implemented electronic health record (EHR) system. Which of the following would BEST ensure the security of patient data?
a. Implementing role-based access controls (RBAC) on the EHR system.
b. Training medical staff on the new features of the EHR system.
c. Posting privacy notices in patient care areas.
d. Conducting periodic performance evaluations of the EHR system.

Answer: a. Implementing role-based access controls (RBAC) on the EHR system. Explanation: Role-based access controls are essential for ensuring that only authorized individuals can access patient data, based on their roles within the healthcare provider. This is a direct and effective measure to safeguard the confidentiality and integrity of patient information, reflecting a governance approach to security.

49. The internal audit department of an organization is conducting a review to ensure alignment with security governance principles. Which of the following findings indicates a need for improvement?
a. The incident response plan has not been tested in the last year.
b. Security policies are reviewed and updated annually.
c. The data classification policy includes definitions for various levels of sensitivity.
d. Security training is mandatory for new employees.

Answer: a. The incident response plan has not been tested in the last year. Explanation: Regular testing of the incident response plan is a critical component of security governance, ensuring that the organization is prepared to respond effectively to incidents. An untested plan may contain outdated procedures or fail to address current threats, indicating a gap in governance that could have serious implications during a security incident.

50. In preparing for a security certification audit, a CISO must ensure that the security governance practices align with which of the following standards to demonstrate compliance with best practices for protecting cardholder data?
a. HIPAA
b. Sarbanes-Oxley Act
c. Payment Card Industry Data Security Standard (PCI DSS)
d. General Data Protection Regulation (GDPR)

Answer: c. Payment Card Industry Data Security Standard (PCI DSS). Explanation: PCI DSS is the relevant standard for protecting cardholder data and applies to all entities that store, process, or transmit cardholder information. Ensuring alignment with PCI DSS requirements is essential for passing a security certification audit in the context of payment card data protection.

51. An international software development company is seeking to expand its services into European markets. Which regulation must they ensure compliance with to protect the personal data of EU citizens?
a. Health Insurance Portability and Accountability Act (HIPAA)
b. Family Educational Rights and Privacy Act (FERPA)
c. Sarbanes-Oxley Act (SOX)
d. General Data Protection Regulation (GDPR)

Answer: d. General Data Protection Regulation (GDPR). Explanation: GDPR is the crucial regulation for any company processing the personal data of individuals within the EU, focusing on data protection and privacy. Compliance with GDPR is mandatory for operating in European markets, regardless of the company's location, and includes requirements such as data subject consent, data breach notifications, and data protection impact assessments.

52. A Chief Information Security Officer (CISO) of a healthcare organization is overseeing the transition to a new electronic health records (EHR) system. Which act governs the protection of patient health information in this context?
a. The Computer Fraud and Abuse Act (CFAA)
b. The Federal Information Security Management Act (FISMA)
c. The Health Insurance Portability and Accountability Act (HIPAA)
d. The Gramm-Leach-Bliley Act (GLBA)

Answer: c. The Health Insurance Portability and Accountability Act (HIPAA). Explanation: HIPAA sets the standard for protecting sensitive patient data. Any company that deals with protected health information (PHI) must ensure that all the required physical, network, and process security measures are in place and followed, including in EHR systems.

53. During a routine audit, a discrepancy is found between the organization's data retention policy and the requirements of the Sarbanes-Oxley Act (SOX). Which department should be FIRST to review the policy for necessary revisions?
a. Human Resources
b. Legal
c. Research and Development
d. Sales and Marketing

Answer: b. Legal. Explanation: The legal department should first review the data retention policy to ensure compliance with SOX, which includes mandates on how long business records and communications need to be stored. Legal professionals are best suited to interpret the requirements and guide the policy adjustments.

54. A data breach has exposed customer credit card information. Under the Payment Card Industry Data Security Standard (PCI DSS), which step should the company take FIRST?
a. Notify all affected customers immediately.
b. Launch an internal investigation to determine the breach cause.
c. Report the incident to the acquiring bank and card brands.
d. Encrypt all stored credit card data to prevent further incidents.

Answer: c. Report the incident to the acquiring bank and card brands. Explanation: PCI DSS requires that the company report the incident to the acquiring bank and card brands immediately after a breach is detected. This is to ensure that proper steps are taken to prevent fraud and to comply with contractual obligations related to the handling of cardholder data.

55. The legal team of a global corporation is revising its contracts to include clauses on information security. Which clause is MOST essential to include to mitigate the risk of third-party data processors?
a. Jurisdiction clause
b. Indemnity clause
c. Confidentiality clause
d. Force majeure clause

Answer: c. Confidentiality clause. Explanation: A confidentiality clause is critical when dealing with third-party data processors to ensure that sensitive information is handled securely and is not disclosed improperly. This clause should define the confidential information, outline the duty of care required, and specify the consequences of a breach of confidentiality.

56. After an update to the company's security policy, an employee is found using a personal device to access the corporate network, which is now against company policy. According to best practices, what is the FIRST action the company should take?
a. Terminate the employee's access to the network.
b. Conduct security awareness training for all employees.
c. Review the policy with the employee and issue a warning.
d. Update the network access control (NAC) system to block personal devices.

Answer: c. Review the policy with the employee and issue a warning. Explanation: Initially, the company should ensure that the employee is aware of the updated policy and understand the implications of their actions. A warning allows for corrective behavior and reinforces the importance of policy compliance. Subsequent violations would call for stronger measures.

57. A U.S.-based company with international operations is assessing its cybersecurity policies to ensure they protect against unauthorized access to controlled unclassified information (CUI). Which framework would be the MOST appropriate to follow?
a. NIST Special Publication 800-171
b. ISO/IEC 27002
c. COBIT 5
d. CIS Controls

Answer: a. NIST Special Publication 800-171. Explanation: NIST SP 800-171 provides guidelines for protecting CUI in non-federal information systems and organizations, making it the most appropriate framework for a U.S.-based company handling such information. The framework helps organizations ensure they are meeting the necessary security requirements to protect CUI.

58. The Information Security team is reviewing the company's incident response plan for regulatory compliance. Which regulation requires organizations to disclose data breaches involving personal data to the affected individuals?
a. California Consumer Privacy Act (CCPA)
b. Health Insurance Portability and Accountability Act (HIPAA)
c. Gramm-Leach-Bliley Act (GLBA)
d. Federal Information Security Modernization Act (FISMA)

Answer: a. California Consumer Privacy Act (CCPA). Explanation: The CCPA requires that organizations disclose data breaches involving personal data to the affected California residents. This regulation gives consumers rights over their personal information, including the right to be informed of breaches in their data privacy.

59. A multinational company is undergoing a third-party audit to assess compliance with various privacy laws. What is the PRIMARY purpose of this audit?
a. To ensure alignment with the company's internal security policies
b. To evaluate the effectiveness of the company's firewall configurations
c. To validate the company's adherence to applicable legal and regulatory requirements
d. To check the company's alignment with the latest technology trends

Answer: c. To validate the company's adherence to applicable legal and regulatory requirements. Explanation: The primary purpose of a third-party audit in this context is to provide an objective assessment of the company's compliance with relevant legal and regulatory requirements, ensuring that the company meets its legal obligations and avoids potential fines and penalties.

60. A cloud service provider is revising its standard service agreements in response to newly enacted data protection laws. What is the MOST important consideration when updating these agreements?
a. Detailed descriptions of the cloud services offered
b. Specification of the data protection standards to be upheld
c. Provisions for regular service availability reporting
d. Clauses related to the scalability and flexibility of cloud resources

Answer: b. Specification of the data protection standards to be upheld. Explanation: With the enactment of new data protection laws, the cloud service provider must ensure that its service agreements specify the data protection standards that will be upheld. This includes how data will be secured, processed, and maintained in compliance with legal requirements, which is critical for both the provider and the clients in terms of legal compliance and protection of personal data.

61. An information security consultant discovers a vulnerability in a client's network during a routine assessment. The client has no immediate plans to fix the vulnerability. What is the consultant's BEST course of action?
a. Document the vulnerability in the assessment report and advise the client on potential risks.
b. Keep the information confidential until the client decides to take action.
c. Notify the software vendor about the client's vulnerability.
d. Disclose the vulnerability publicly to pressure the client into taking action.

Answer: a. Document the vulnerability in the assessment report and advise the client on potential risks. Explanation: Professional ethics require the consultant to maintain client confidentiality while also ensuring that the client is fully informed of the risks associated with the vulnerability. The consultant should document their findings and provide a detailed risk assessment to the client, allowing them to make an informed decision on remediation.

62. A security professional is offered confidential information about a competitor by an unknown source. How should the professional respond according to ethical standards?
a. Accept the information to assess the potential threat to their own organization.
b. Decline the offer and report the incident to their organization's compliance department.
c. Use the information for personal gain.
d. Share the information with their team to improve company security posture.

Answer: b. Decline the offer and report the incident to their organization's compliance department. Explanation: Ethical standards require security professionals to refuse participation in any actions that involve the unauthorized sharing of confidential information. The incident should also be reported to the appropriate department within the organization to handle in accordance with company policy and legal requirements.

63. During a penetration test, a security professional accidentally accesses sensitive customer data. What is the FIRST action that should be taken?
a. Immediately delete the data to ensure there is no trace left.
b. Continue the test and review the data to help improve security.
c. Report the incident to the employer or client as per incident response procedures.
d. Secure the data and use it as leverage in negotiating the contract terms.

Answer: c. Report the incident to the employer or client as per incident response procedures. Explanation: Ethical conduct requires the professional to report any accidental access to sensitive information immediately, regardless of the circumstances. This maintains transparency and allows the client to take necessary steps to manage the data exposure.

64. A cybersecurity professional is approached by a friend to conduct an unofficial security audit of the company they work for. The friend suspects a coworker of malicious activities. How should the professional respond?
a. Agree to help the friend out of loyalty.
b. Decline and suggest that the friend report their suspicions through official channels.
c. Ask for payment in return for the security audit.
d. Agree to the audit if the friend provides insider information.

Answer: b. Decline and suggest that the friend report their suspicions through official channels. Explanation: Professional ethics dictate that security work should only be conducted through official and authorized means. The professional should advise the friend to follow their organization's official reporting procedures for such suspicions.

65. An IS auditor finds evidence of illegal activity while conducting an audit. There is no immediate threat to the organization. What should the auditor do?
a. Ignore the finding as it is outside the scope of the audit.
b. Report the activity to law enforcement without notifying the organization.
c. Discuss the finding with the organization to determine the appropriate action.
d. Use the finding to negotiate a higher fee for the audit.

Answer: c. Discuss the finding with the organization to determine the appropriate action. Explanation: While the auditor has an obligation to maintain confidentiality, they also have a duty to report illegal activities. Discussing the findings with the organization allows them to take appropriate legal and ethical action.

66. A security analyst receives a lucrative job offer from a company that is a direct competitor to their current employer. The analyst has access to sensitive strategic plans. What should the analyst do upon accepting the job offer?
a. Inform the new employer of the strategies to prove their value.
b. Refrain from sharing any information about their current employer's strategies.
c. Use the information as leverage to get a better offer from their current employer.
d. Delete all the information about the strategic plans before leaving.

Answer: b. Refrain from sharing any information about their current employer's strategies. Explanation: The analyst is ethically bound to protect the confidentiality of their current employer's sensitive information, even after employment ends. Sharing this information would be a breach of professional ethics and could lead to legal consequences.

67. A security manager discovers that their company's new security system was developed using stolen intellectual property. What is the most ETHICAL next step?
a. Keep the information secret to avoid legal repercussions for the company.
b. Report the finding to senior management and advise on ceasing the use of the system.
c. Reach out to the party whose intellectual property was stolen and negotiate a deal.
d. Use the information to gain a promotion or raise for keeping the company's reputation intact.

Answer: b. Report the finding to senior management and advise on ceasing the use of the system. Explanation: Ethical responsibility requires the security manager to report any illegal activities, such as the use of stolen intellectual property, to senior management. They should also recommend that the company cease using the system and seek to rectify the situation through legal means.

68. An IT professional is aware that their company routinely ignores security best practices, which could lead to a data breach. However, the company has not suffered any incidents yet. What is the professional's ethical obligation?
a. Remain silent as no real harm has occurred.
b. Attempt to fix the issues without bringing attention to them.
c. Report the practices to the appropriate authorities as a whistleblower.
d. Raise the concerns with management and document the communication.

Answer: d. Raise the concerns with management and document the communication. Explanation: The professional has an ethical obligation to raise concerns about practices that could lead to security incidents. Documentation is important to ensure there is a record of the communication and to protect the professional's position.

69. A member of an organization's security team is offered a kickback by a vendor if they influence the procurement process in the vendor's favor. What should be the team member's response?
a. Accept the offer as it benefits both parties.
b. Decline the offer and report the vendor's actions to the organization.
c. Request a higher kickback amount to reflect the risk involved.
d. Accept the offer but disclose it to the organization as a conflict of interest.

Answer: b. Decline the offer and report the vendor's actions to the organization. Explanation: Accepting a kickback is unethical and potentially illegal. The team member should decline any offers that compromise the integrity of the procurement process and report the vendor's attempt to engage in corrupt practices to the organization.

70. An information security consultant discovers a significant vulnerability in a client's system, which could potentially lead to a data breach. The client decides not to address the vulnerability due to cost concerns. What is the consultant's BEST course of action?
a. Accept the client's decision and take no further action.
b. Inform the client's customers about the vulnerability.
c. Document the findings and the client's decision to accept the risk.
d. Exploit the vulnerability to demonstrate the potential consequences.

Answer: c. Document the findings and the client's decision to accept the risk. Explanation: As per professional ethics, the consultant should respect the client's autonomy while ensuring due diligence is performed. Documenting the vulnerability and the client's decision not only provides a record that the consultant fulfilled their professional responsibility but also maintains confidentiality and respects the client's right to make their own risk management decisions.

71. A security professional is offered a bribe to overlook a minor security issue during an audit. Which (ISC)² Code of Ethics Canon does this situation directly violate?
a. Protect society, the common good, and necessary public trust and confidence.
b. Act honorably, honestly, justly, responsibly, and legally.
c. Provide diligent and competent service to principals.
d. Advance and protect the profession.

Answer: b. Act honorably, honestly, justly, responsibly, and legally. Explanation: Accepting a bribe is a direct violation of acting honorably and honestly, which are fundamental tenets of the (ISC)² Code of Ethics. It compromises the integrity of the professional and the audit process and is also illegal, thus falling under this canon.

72. During a penetration test, a security professional finds evidence of an unrelated and previously undetected breach. What is the FIRST action they should take?
a. Notify law enforcement authorities immediately.
b. Discuss the findings with their penetration testing team.
c. Report the breach to the client as soon as possible.
d. Continue with the penetration test and report the findings later.

Answer: c. Report the breach to the client as soon as possible. Explanation: The security professional has an ethical duty to report critical findings such as an active breach promptly to the client so they can take immediate action to contain and address the incident. While notifying law enforcement may be a subsequent step, the client should be informed first as per the contractual agreement of the engagement.

73. A cybersecurity expert is requested to conduct an assessment of a competitor's security posture on behalf of their employer, without the competitor's knowledge or consent. What should the expert do?
a. Refuse the assignment, as it could constitute an unauthorized action.
b. Accept the assignment, trusting that the employer has a good reason.
c. Suggest an alternative approach that involves the competitor's consent.
d. Carry out the assessment but only report on publicly available information.

Answer: a. Refuse the assignment, as it could constitute an unauthorized action. Explanation: Conducting a security assessment without the knowledge or consent of the target organization can be unethical and illegal. The expert should refuse to perform any actions that could be construed as hacking or corporate espionage, in line with professional ethics and legal obligations.

74. An information security manager is aware of non-compliance with data protection laws in their organization. The non-compliance is not being addressed due to budget constraints. What is the MOST ethical action?
a. Ignore the issue, assuming responsibility lies with senior management.
b. Anonymously report the organization to the relevant regulatory authority.
c. Document the issue, including the potential risks, and escalate it within the organization.
d. Leak the information to the media to force the organization to comply.

Answer: c. Document the issue, including the potential risks, and escalate it within the organization. Explanation: The ethical approach is to document the compliance issues and escalate them to senior management or the appropriate internal body, such as the compliance department or the board of directors, giving them the opportunity to address the legal risks.

75. A senior security analyst receives a significant monetary gift from a vendor after the completion of a successful project. What is the analyst's BEST course of action?
a. Keep the gift, as it was given after the project was completed.
b. Report the gift to their organization according to company policy.
c. Return the gift, stating it is against personal and professional principles.
d. Accept the gift but donate it to charity to avoid personal benefit.

Answer: b. Report the gift to their organization according to company policy. Explanation: Receiving gifts from vendors can lead to a conflict of interest and may violate company policies. The analyst should report the gift to ensure transparency and adhere to the organization's rules regarding gifts, which may result in returning it or other actions based on policy.

76. While reviewing the security measures of a new software, an employee realizes that implementing a particular encryption algorithm would violate export controls due to the strength of the encryption. What should the employee do?
a. Proceed with implementation, considering security as the highest priority.
b. Report the concern to management and seek guidance on compliance.
c. Choose a weaker encryption algorithm that complies with export controls.
d. Advise the development team to ignore the export controls for the benefit of security.

Answer: b. Report the concern to management and seek guidance on compliance. Explanation: The employee should report the compliance issue to management to address the legal implications of export controls. Ignoring such regulations can result in severe penalties for the organization, and the decision to proceed with implementation should involve a compliance review.

77. A security auditor discovers that a close friend in the organization has unintentionally violated a security policy, potentially causing a data leak. What is the MOST ethical action for the auditor to take?
a. Discuss the situation with the friend and provide advice on how to cover it up.
b. Report the incident through official channels, maintaining professional integrity.
c. Ignore the violation, considering it was an honest mistake.
d. Warn the friend and allow them to report the violation themselves.

Answer: b. Report the incident through official channels, maintaining professional integrity. Explanation: The auditor must maintain professional integrity and report the violation through official channels, regardless of personal relationships. Allowing personal relationships to influence professional conduct would be a breach of ethics and could compromise the security of the organization.

78. During a security clearance process, it is found that an employee has failed to disclose a previous employment where they were dismissed for misconduct. What action should the organization's security department take?
a. Dismiss the employee immediately for dishonesty.
b. Confront the employee for an explanation before taking any action.
c. Review the circumstances of the dismissal to determine if it impacts current responsibilities.
d. Ignore the issue if the employee's performance has been satisfactory.

Answer: c. Review the circumstances of the dismissal to determine if it impacts current responsibilities. Explanation: The security department should investigate the context and relevance of the previous dismissal to the employee's current role before taking appropriate action. Immediate dismissal or ignoring the issue could be premature or negligent, respectively. A fair and thorough review ensures that any action taken is justified and proportionate to the risk presented.

79. In the development of a Business Continuity Plan (BCP), what is the PRIMARY objective of conducting a Business Impact Analysis (BIA)?
a. To identify the financial impact of a disruptive event on the organization.
b. To ensure all business processes are compliant with industry regulations.
c. To determine the criticality of business functions and their resource dependencies.
d. To assess the organization's IT infrastructure resilience to cyber-attacks.

Answer: c. To determine the criticality of business functions and their resource dependencies. Explanation: The primary objective of a BIA is to identify and prioritize critical business functions and their dependencies on resources, systems, and processes. This analysis helps in understanding which functions must be recovered first following a disruption, guiding the development of effective recovery strategies in the BCP.

80. A company is evaluating recovery strategies for its data center. Which of the following would BEST ensure minimal downtime in the event of a major disaster?
a. Regular off-site backup of critical data.
b. Implementation of RAID technology in all servers.
c. Establishment of a mirrored data center at a geographically distant location.
d. Subscription to a cloud-based storage solution for critical data.

Answer: c. Establishment of a mirrored data center at a geographically distant location. Explanation: A mirrored data center, especially in a geographically distant location, offers real-time replication of data and systems, enabling quick switchover and minimal downtime in case the primary site is rendered inoperable. While other options contribute to data recovery, they may not ensure minimal downtime due to potential delays in data restoration or system recovery.

81. During a BCP test, it was observed that the recovery time objective (RTO) for a critical application was not met. What is the MOST likely action to take next?
a. Review and adjust the application's RTO to a more realistic timeframe.
b. Increase the frequency of BCP testing for the critical application.
c. Conduct a root cause analysis to identify and address the issues encountered.
d. Reassign the critical application to a less critical category in the BCP.

Answer: c. Conduct a root cause analysis to identify and address the issues encountered. Explanation: When an RTO is not met during a test, the immediate step is to perform a root cause analysis to understand why the recovery process failed or was delayed. Identifying and addressing these issues is crucial to ensure that the RTO can be met in future incidents, rather than adjusting the RTO or testing frequency, or changing the application's criticality level.

82. In updating its BCP, a multinational corporation decides to adopt a more flexible approach to disaster recovery due to the diverse nature of risks in its various operating regions. Which of the following strategies aligns BEST with this approach?
a. Centralizing all backup processes in the corporate headquarters.
b. Developing region-specific recovery protocols based on local risk assessments.
c. Contracting a single global vendor for all disaster recovery services.
d. Standardizing all IT systems across regions to simplify recovery processes.

Answer: b. Developing region-specific recovery protocols based on local risk assessments. Explanation: Given the diversity of risks across different regions, adopting region-specific recovery protocols ensures that each area's unique threats and challenges are addressed effectively. This approach allows for a more tailored and hence potentially more effective recovery strategy in the face of region-specific disasters.

83. A critical aspect of maintaining business continuity is ensuring effective communication during a crisis. Which of the following is MOST critical to include in a BCP's communication plan?
a. A single, centralized communication platform for all stakeholders.
b. Pre-defined templates for public announcements and stakeholder notifications.
c. An automated social media posting tool for real-time updates.
d. Detailed contact lists for all employees, vendors, and emergency services.

Answer: d. Detailed contact lists for all employees, vendors, and emergency services. Explanation: Having detailed and up-to-date contact lists is essential for effective communication during a crisis, ensuring that all relevant parties, including employees, vendors, and emergency services, can be reached promptly to coordinate recovery efforts. While other tools and templates can aid in communication, the foundation is having accurate contact information.

84. When considering insurance as part of a business continuity strategy, what is the PRIMARY role of such a policy?
a. To replace the need for a BCP by transferring all risks to the insurer.
b. To provide financial support to aid recovery following a disruptive event.
c. To ensure all employees are trained on business continuity procedures.
d. To guarantee the replacement or repair of all IT equipment in case of damage.

Answer: b. To provide financial support to aid recovery following a disruptive event. Explanation: Insurance policies in the context of business continuity are designed to provide financial support to help an organization recover from a disruptive event. While insurance is a critical component of a comprehensive BCP, it does not replace the need for a plan or ensure specific recovery actions like employee training or equipment replacement.

85. For a global e-commerce company, which of the following would be the MOST critical factor to consider in its BCP to ensure continuity of operations?
a. Ensuring all physical stores have backup power supplies.
b. Maintaining high availability of the online storefront and transaction processing systems.
c. Keeping a large inventory of products to prevent stockouts.
d. Diversifying the supplier base to include vendors from multiple countries.

Answer: b. Maintaining high availability of the online storefront and transaction processing systems. Explanation: For an e-commerce company, the continuity of online operations, including the storefront and transaction processing systems, is critical. Ensuring these systems are highly available, even in the face of disruptions, is key to maintaining business operations and customer service.

86. A financial services firm is reviewing its BCP in light of recent regulatory changes. Which of the following stakeholders should be MOST involved in this review to ensure compliance?
a. IT department heads
b. Legal and compliance teams
c. Marketing and sales executives
d. External BCP consultants

Answer: b. Legal and compliance teams. Explanation: Legal and compliance teams are critical in ensuring that the BCP adheres to regulatory requirements, especially in industries like financial services where regulations can be stringent. Their involvement ensures that the plan not only meets business needs but also complies with legal obligations.

87. In the aftermath of a natural disaster, a company realizes that its BCP did not adequately address the needs of remote workers. What is the BEST approach to rectify this oversight?
a. Implement a permanent work-from-home policy for all employees.
b. Develop a specific section in the BCP focusing on remote work scenarios.
c. Require all remote workers to relocate closer to the company's main office.
d. Increase the IT helpdesk's capacity to handle remote workers' queries.

Answer: b. Develop a specific section in the BCP focusing on remote work scenarios. Explanation: Incorporating a section dedicated to remote work in the BCP ensures that the needs and challenges of remote workers are specifically addressed, including access to systems, communication protocols, and support structures, which is essential for maintaining business operations during a disruption.

88. During a business continuity exercise, it was noted that the RTO for the customer service department was significantly longer than planned, leading to potential reputational damage. What should be the IMMEDIATE next step?
a. Revise the RTO to align with the exercise findings.
b. Analyze the exercise to identify bottlenecks and inefficiencies.
c. Increase the customer service department's staff to meet the RTO.
d. Conduct a customer survey to assess the impact of the delay.

Answer: b. Analyze the exercise to identify bottlenecks and inefficiencies. Explanation: The immediate step following the exercise should be to analyze the results to identify why the RTO was not met, focusing on bottlenecks or inefficiencies in the recovery process. Understanding these issues allows for targeted improvements to meet the established RTO and prevent reputational damage in a real incident.

89. In the process of risk assessment, a company identifies a threat that could potentially exploit a vulnerability in its software, leading to unauthorized data access. The estimated annual loss from this risk is $200,000, and a proposed control can reduce the probability of this risk by 50%. The cost of implementing the control is $70,000 annually. Should the company implement the control based on a cost-benefit analysis?
a. Yes, because the control costs less than the estimated annual loss.
b. No, because the control does not eliminate the risk entirely.
c. Yes, because the reduction in risk outweighs the cost of the control.
d. No, because the residual risk is still too high.

Answer: a. Yes, because the control costs less than the estimated annual loss. Explanation: A cost-benefit analysis involves comparing the cost of implementing a control against the potential savings from reducing the risk. In this case, implementing the control would cost $70,000 annually, but it would reduce the risk by $100,000 (50% of $200,000), resulting in a net savings of $30,000 annually. Therefore, it's financially justified to implement the control.

90. A security analyst is conducting a qualitative risk assessment for a new online transaction system. Which of the following factors should the analyst consider FIRST to prioritize the identified risks?
a. The potential impact of each risk on the company's reputation.
b. The total cost of implementing controls for all identified risks.
c. The likelihood of each risk occurring within the next fiscal year.
d. The number of affected users for each identified risk.

Answer: a. The potential impact of each risk on the company's reputation. Explanation: In a qualitative risk assessment, the impact of a risk, especially on the company's reputation, is a critical factor to consider when prioritizing risks. Reputation can affect customer trust and business continuity. While likelihood, cost, and the number of affected users are important, the impact on reputation can have more far-reaching consequences.

91. During a risk analysis meeting, it's determined that the likelihood of a cyber-attack on the company's main server is once every five years, with an estimated financial loss of $500,000 per incident. What is the Annual Loss Expectancy (ALE) for this risk?

a. $100,000
b. $500,000
c. $1,000,000
d. $2,500,000

Answer: a. $100,000 Explanation: The Annual Loss Expectancy (ALE) is calculated by multiplying the Single Loss Expectancy (SLE), which is the financial loss per incident, by the Annual Rate of Occurrence (ARO), the expected frequency of the incident per year. In this case, the ARO is 0.2 (1 occurrence every 5 years), and the SLE is $500,000. Therefore, ALE = SLE * ARO = $500,000 * 0.2 = $100,000.

92. A multinational corporation is evaluating risks associated with geopolitical instability in a region where it has significant operations. Which of the following risk strategies would be MOST appropriate for dealing with this type of risk?
a. Mitigation, by diversifying investment to more stable regions.
b. Acceptance, considering it an inherent part of international business.
c. Avoidance, by immediately withdrawing all operations from the region.
d. Transfer, by purchasing insurance against geopolitical risks.

Answer: a. Mitigation, by diversifying investment to more stable regions. Explanation: Mitigation involves taking steps to reduce the impact of a risk. In the context of geopolitical instability, diversifying investments to more stable regions can reduce the potential impact on the corporation's overall operations. While acceptance acknowledges the risk, avoidance may not be feasible or strategic, and transferring such a broad risk through insurance might not cover all potential losses or be cost-effective.

93. The IT department has identified a vulnerability in the company's email system that could lead to data breaches. However, the vendor has not yet released a patch. What is the BEST immediate risk management action?
a. Accept the risk until a patch is available.
b. Implement a workaround to reduce the risk.
c. Transfer the risk by notifying the insurance company.
d. Avoid the risk by shutting down the email system until a patch is released.

Answer: b. Implement a workaround to reduce the risk. Explanation: When a patch is not available, the best immediate action is to implement a workaround or compensating control to mitigate the risk. This might involve additional security measures or changes in user behavior to reduce the likelihood or impact of a potential breach. Shutting down the system is impractical, and while risk transfer and acceptance are valid strategies, they do not proactively address the vulnerability.

94. A risk manager is evaluating the threats to an organization's physical assets. Which of the following would MOST likely be categorized as a natural threat?
a. Vandalism
b. Earthquake
c. Phishing attack
d. Insider sabotage

Answer: b. Earthquake Explanation: Natural threats include events like earthquakes, floods, hurricanes, and other environmental phenomena that can cause damage to physical assets. Vandalism, phishing attacks, and insider sabotage are categorized as human threats, either intentional or unintentional.

95. During the risk assessment process, it was determined that a critical system has no feasible technical solution to a known vulnerability. What should be the NEXT step according to risk management best practices?
a. Document the vulnerability as an accepted risk.
b. Continue searching for a technical solution indefinitely.
c. Explore non-technical controls to mitigate the risk.
d. Transfer the risk to a third-party vendor associated with the system.

Answer: c. Explore non-technical controls to mitigate the risk. Explanation: When a technical solution is not feasible, exploring non-technical controls or compensating controls is the next best step. This could include policy changes, training, or increased monitoring to mitigate the risk associated with the vulnerability. Acceptance is a final resort, and transferring the risk may not be feasible if the third party cannot address the vulnerability.

96. A company is considering the implementation of a new cloud-based CRM system. Which of the following risk assessment methods would be MOST effective in understanding the potential impact on data privacy?
a. Quantitative risk assessment
b. Qualitative risk assessment
c. Delphi technique
d. Monte Carlo simulation

Answer: b. Qualitative risk assessment Explanation: A qualitative risk assessment, which assesses the impact and likelihood of risks in non-numerical terms, is effective for understanding nuanced risks such as data privacy. It allows for expert opinions and industry knowledge to be incorporated, providing a comprehensive view of potential privacy concerns associated with a cloud-based CRM system.

97. In reviewing the risk management process, it's noted that the organization has not conducted regular reviews of its risk register. What is the PRIMARY risk of this oversight?
a. Increased insurance premiums due to outdated risk assessments.
b. Inability to effectively respond to newly emerging threats.
c. Reduced effectiveness of the organization's internal audit function.
d. Decreased stakeholder confidence in the organization's risk management practices.

Answer: b. Inability to effectively respond to newly emerging threats. Explanation: Regular reviews of the risk register are essential to ensure that it remains relevant and covers newly emerging threats. Failure to update the risk register could leave the organization unprepared for new risks, impacting its ability to respond effectively.

98. A new regulation requires companies in the financial sector to maintain a higher standard of data protection. In assessing this regulatory risk, what is the FIRST action the company should take?
a. Review current data protection measures against the new regulatory requirements.
b. Train employees on the importance of data protection.
c. Increase the cybersecurity budget to accommodate potential new technologies.
d. Hire a consultant to advise on compliance with financial regulations.

Answer: a. Review current data protection measures against the new regulatory requirements. Explanation: The first step in addressing regulatory risk is to review and assess the company's current data protection measures against the new standards set by the regulation. This assessment will identify gaps in compliance and inform the subsequent actions needed to meet the higher standard of data protection required.

99. In the process of updating its risk management framework, a company decides to incorporate more rigorous tracking of risk indicators. Which of the following would be considered a Key Risk Indicator (KRI) for cyber security risks?
a. The number of sales transactions processed daily.
b. The percentage of employees who have completed cybersecurity training.
c. The company's stock price.
d. The average time taken to resolve customer complaints.

Answer: b. The percentage of employees who have completed cybersecurity training. Explanation: KRIs are metrics used to provide an early signal of increasing risk exposure in various areas of an organization. The percentage of employees who have completed cybersecurity training is a KRI for cyber security risks as it can indicate the organization's preparedness and potential vulnerability to cyber threats.

100. When applying the STRIDE threat modeling methodology, what does the "S" stand for, and how is it typically mitigated?
a. Spoofing; mitigated through strong authentication mechanisms.
b. Sniffing; mitigated through network encryption.
c. Sabotage; mitigated by implementing physical security controls.
d. Scanning; mitigated through intrusion detection systems.

Answer: a. Spoofing; mitigated through strong authentication mechanisms. Explanation: In the STRIDE model, "S" stands for Spoofing, which refers to impersonating another user or device to gain unauthorized access. This threat is typically mitigated through the implementation of strong authentication mechanisms like two-factor authentication, biometrics, or digital certificates to verify the identity of users and devices.

101. During the development of a new web application, a security team employs the DREAD model to assess the risks associated with potential threats. What aspect does the "D" in DREAD specifically evaluate?
a. Damage potential if the threat is realized.
b. Difficulty of removing the vulnerability.
c. Detection capabilities to identify the threat.
d. Duration of time the threat could be active.

Answer: a. Damage potential if the threat is realized. Explanation: In the DREAD threat modeling framework, the first "D" stands for Damage Potential, which assesses the potential harm a successful exploit of the vulnerability could cause. This includes considering the extent of data loss, service disruption, financial impact, and harm to reputation that could result from the threat.

102. A cybersecurity analyst is using the PASTA (Process for Attack Simulation and Threat Analysis) methodology for threat modeling in a financial application. What is the FIRST step in the PASTA methodology?
a. Define technical scope.
b. Identify and prioritize assets.
c. Analyze vulnerabilities.
d. Enumerate threats.

Answer: b. Identify and prioritize assets. Explanation: The first step in the PASTA methodology is to identify and prioritize assets. This involves understanding what data, resources, or system components are most critical to the organization's operation and could be potential targets for attackers. This foundational step guides the subsequent phases of threat analysis and vulnerability assessment by focusing on protecting the most valuable assets.

103. In applying the VAST (Visual, Agile, and Simple Threat) model for an agile software development project, what key principle should be prioritized to ensure effective threat modeling?
a. Comprehensive documentation of all potential threats.
b. Integration of threat modeling into the daily stand-ups.

c. Scalability to accommodate large, distributed systems.

d. Alignment with user stories and iterative development.

Answer: d. Alignment with user stories and iterative development. Explanation: The VAST model is designed to align with agile and iterative development practices, making it suitable for integration into agile projects. By aligning threat modeling with user stories and sprints, security considerations are embedded into the development process, ensuring that threats are considered and mitigated in step with the project's evolution.

104. A security architect is evaluating different threat modeling methodologies to be used across various projects in the organization. Which methodology emphasizes a data-centric approach, focusing on the flow of data through the system?

a. STRIDE

b. PASTA

c. Trike

d. Data Flow Diagrams (DFD)

Answer: d. Data Flow Diagrams (DFD) Explanation: Data Flow Diagrams (DFD) are used in threat modeling to visually represent the flow of data through an information system. This methodology helps in identifying potential security vulnerabilities and threats by analyzing how data moves between components, where it is stored, and how it is processed, making it a data-centric approach.

105. When conducting threat modeling for a cloud-based infrastructure, which of the following threats should be considered SPECIFIC to the cloud environment?

a. Insecure interfaces and APIs.

b. Physical theft of server hardware.

c. Social engineering attacks on help desk staff.

d. Malware infections on user devices.

Answer: a. Insecure interfaces and APIs. Explanation: In cloud-based infrastructures, insecure interfaces and APIs are a specific concern because they can provide external attackers with a pathway to interact with the cloud services directly. Ensuring the security of these interfaces is crucial in protecting against unauthorized access and data breaches in the cloud environment.

106. In the context of threat modeling for an IoT device ecosystem, which of the following would be a PRIMARY focus due to the nature of IoT devices?

a. Buffer overflow vulnerabilities in desktop applications.

b. Firmware updates and patch management.

c. SQL injection attacks on web platforms.

d. Cross-site scripting (XSS) vulnerabilities.

Answer: b. Firmware updates and patch management. Explanation: For IoT devices, firmware updates and patch management are critical due to the direct impact on the device's security posture. IoT devices often operate with limited user interaction, making automated and secure mechanisms for updating and patching firmware essential to protect against vulnerabilities and ensure the ongoing security of the device ecosystem.

107. A threat model for a mobile banking application should PRIORARILY focus on which of the following threat vectors due to the application's nature and usage?
a. DDoS attacks on the backend servers.
b. Man-in-the-middle (MitM) attacks on public Wi-Fi networks.
c. SQL injection attacks on the application's database.
d. Physical security of data center facilities.

Answer: b. Man-in-the-middle (MitM) attacks on public Wi-Fi networks. Explanation: For mobile banking applications, Man-in-the-middle (MitM) attacks on public Wi-Fi networks are a significant concern because users often access their banking services on the go. MitM attacks can intercept and manipulate data in transit, making secure communication channels like HTTPS and VPNs critical for protecting user data.

108. In enhancing the threat model for a corporate intranet portal, the security team decides to focus on insider threats. Which of the following measures would be MOST effective in mitigating this specific type of threat?
a. Implementing a Web Application Firewall (WAF)
b. Enforcing strict password policies and two-factor authentication
c. Deploying anti-virus solutions on all endpoints
d. Conducting regular security awareness training for employees

Answer: d. Conducting regular security awareness training for employees Explanation: Insider threats often stem from employees' actions, whether malicious or unintentional. Regular security awareness training is effective in mitigating insider threats by educating employees on secure practices, the importance of data protection, and how to recognize and respond to security incidents, thereby reducing the risk of internal breaches.

109. A security team is threat modeling for an application that will handle highly sensitive information. What type of threat is MOST critical to address to ensure the confidentiality of the data?
a. Physical security breaches leading to server access.
b. Social engineering attacks targeting customer support.
c. Unauthorized data access through exploitation of software vulnerabilities.
d. Environmental threats such as floods or fires in the data center.

Answer: c. Unauthorized data access through exploitation of software vulnerabilities. Explanation: For applications handling highly sensitive information, the most critical threat to address is unauthorized data access through the exploitation of software vulnerabilities. This directly impacts the confidentiality of the data. Ensuring that the application is secure against such attacks through secure coding practices, regular vulnerability assessments, and effective access controls is paramount.

110. When implementing a Data Loss Prevention (DLP) system, which of the following is MOST crucial to protect sensitive information from unauthorized access?
a. Ensuring that all data is encrypted at rest and in transit.
b. Defining and classifying what constitutes sensitive information.
c. Implementing strong password policies across the organization.
d. Deploying anti-virus software on all end-user devices.

Answer: b. Defining and classifying what constitutes sensitive information. Explanation: A DLP system's effectiveness hinges on its ability to accurately identify sensitive information. Defining and classifying data ensures that the DLP system can correctly detect and protect the specific types of information deemed sensitive by the organization, thereby preventing unauthorized access or exfiltration.

111. A company's policy requires the secure deletion of electronic files containing personally identifiable information (PII) after they are no longer needed. Which of the following methods is MOST appropriate for this purpose?
a. Renaming the files before deletion
b. Moving the files to a different directory and then deleting them
c. Using software to overwrite the files multiple times
d. Compressing the files before deletion

Answer: c. Using software to overwrite the files multiple times. Explanation: Secure deletion of electronic files containing PII necessitates that the data cannot be recovered. Overwriting the files multiple times with software designed for secure deletion ensures that the data is irrecoverable, adhering to the company's policy on the secure handling of PII.

112. In a multinational corporation, an Information Security Officer is tasked with implementing a consistent data classification scheme. What is the FIRST step in establishing this scheme across all departments?
a. Training employees on the importance of data classification
b. Identifying the various types of data handled by the corporation
c. Purchasing data classification software tools
d. Creating labels for different data classification levels

Answer: b. Identifying the various types of data handled by the corporation. Explanation: The first step in establishing a data classification scheme is to identify the different types of data the corporation handles. Understanding the types of data is essential to determining how they should be classified, which then informs the development of policies, procedures, and training.

113. A security manager is evaluating the risks associated with the storage of sensitive data on mobile devices within the organization. Which of the following controls would BEST mitigate the risk of data leakage?
a. Remote wiping capabilities
b. Geofencing technology
c. Mandatory screen locks
d. Biometric authentication

Answer: a. Remote wiping capabilities. Explanation: Remote wiping capabilities allow an organization to remotely erase data on a mobile device if it is lost or stolen, effectively mitigating the risk of sensitive data leakage. While other controls like screen locks and biometric authentication help secure the device, remote wiping addresses the risk of data exposure directly.

114. An organization plans to decommission and dispose of old hard drives that stored sensitive information. Which of the following disposal methods is MOST secure?
a. Degaussing followed by physical destruction
b. Formatting the drives multiple times
c. Deleting all files and folders from the drives
d. Selling the drives to a third-party recycler

Answer: a. Degaussing followed by physical destruction. Explanation: Degaussing, which demagnetizes the hard drive, coupled with physical destruction, such as shredding, is the most secure method of disposing of drives that contained sensitive information. This process ensures that data cannot be recovered, protecting sensitive information even after disposal.

115. During a review of asset management practices, it was noted that several devices with access to confidential data lacked proper asset tags and tracking. What is the PRIMARY risk associated with this oversight?
a. Increased likelihood of data breaches
b. Inefficiencies in asset allocation
c. Difficulty in performing routine maintenance
d. Challenges in identifying unauthorized devices

Answer: d. Challenges in identifying unauthorized devices. Explanation: Proper asset tagging and tracking are crucial for identifying authorized devices within an organization. The lack of such measures poses a primary risk of difficulty in distinguishing between authorized and unauthorized devices, potentially allowing unauthorized devices to access and compromise confidential data.

116. In the context of asset security, why is it important to maintain an accurate inventory of all organizational assets?
a. To ensure compliance with software licensing agreements
b. To facilitate the rapid deployment of security patches
c. To enable effective risk assessment and management
d. To streamline the onboarding process for new employees

Answer: c. To enable effective risk assessment and management. Explanation: Maintaining an accurate inventory of all organizational assets is crucial for effective risk assessment and management. Knowing what assets exist and their criticality allows for proper prioritization of security measures, ensuring that resources are allocated effectively to protect the most valuable or at-risk assets.

117. A financial institution is reviewing its procedures for handling customer data to ensure compliance with the General Data Protection Regulation (GDPR). What aspect of asset security is MOST directly impacted by GDPR compliance?
a. Physical security controls for data centers
b. Encryption of customer data both at rest and in transit
c. The process for securely disposing of paper records
d. Employee training on social engineering defense

Answer: b. Encryption of customer data both at rest and in transit. Explanation: GDPR emphasizes the protection of personal data, requiring that appropriate technical measures, like encryption, be applied to secure personal data both at rest and in transit. This ensures the confidentiality and integrity of customer data, directly aligning with the regulation's requirements for data protection.

118. A company allows employees to use their personal devices for work (BYOD). What is the MOST critical consideration to ensure the security of corporate data on these devices?
a. Ensuring that all personal devices are equipped with the latest hardware.
b. Implementing a robust Mobile Device Management (MDM) solution.
c. Requiring that all personal devices use the company's Wi-Fi network.
d. Mandating personal devices to have the same make and model.

Answer: b. Implementing a robust Mobile Device Management (MDM) solution. Explanation: A Mobile Device Management (MDM) solution is crucial for securing corporate data on personal devices used for work. MDM allows the organization to enforce security policies, manage device configurations, and even remotely wipe corporate data if necessary, without impacting personal data.

119. An organization's policy mandates that data be categorized according to sensitivity and impact on the business if disclosed or altered. What process does this policy describe?
a. Data encryption
b. Data masking
c. Data classification
d. Data obfuscation

Answer: c. Data classification. Explanation: Data classification involves categorizing data based on its sensitivity and the impact on the business should that data be improperly disclosed, altered, or destroyed. This process helps in applying appropriate security controls to protect data according to its classification level.

120. When determining the classification level for a new set of documents containing trade secrets and proprietary technology, what is the PRIMARY factor to consider?
a. The cost to produce the documents.
b. The potential impact on the organization if the information were disclosed.
c. The number of employees who need access to the documents.
d. The digital or physical format of the documents.

Answer: b. The potential impact on the organization if the information were disclosed. Explanation: The primary factor in classifying information, especially sensitive information like trade secrets and proprietary technology, is the potential impact on the organization if that information were disclosed. This includes considering how the loss of confidentiality could affect the company's competitive advantage, financial stability, and market position.

121. A company is implementing a data classification policy. Which of the following is the MOST critical step to ensure the effectiveness of the policy?
a. Training all employees on the new classification labels.
b. Encrypting all data, regardless of its classification.
c. Purchasing a state-of-the-art data loss prevention (DLP) system.
d. Involving key stakeholders in the development of the classification scheme.

Answer: a. Training all employees on the new classification labels. Explanation: Training all employees on the new classification labels is crucial to ensuring that everyone understands the importance of data classification and knows how to handle data according to its classification level. Without proper training, even the best classification scheme and technical controls may not be effective if employees do not comply with the policy.

122. In the context of information classification, what is the PRIMARY purpose of labeling and handling guidelines?
a. To ensure data is encrypted at the highest possible standards.
b. To provide clear instructions on the dissemination of information.
c. To automate the process of data retention and deletion.
d. To facilitate the auditing and compliance process.

Answer: b. To provide clear instructions on the dissemination of information. Explanation: Labeling and handling guidelines are essential in an information classification system as they provide clear instructions on how different classes of information should be disseminated, stored, and destroyed. These guidelines ensure that sensitive information is handled appropriately and in accordance with its classification level to prevent unauthorized access or disclosure.

123. A multinational corporation needs to comply with various international data protection regulations. In this scenario, what is the MOST critical aspect of information classification?
a. Aligning classification levels with the strictest regulation.
b. Ensuring that all data is classified at the highest level for maximum protection.
c. Tailoring classification levels to match the cultural norms of each country.
d. Harmonizing classification schemes to facilitate cross-border data transfers.

Answer: a. Aligning classification levels with the strictest regulation. Explanation: When dealing with various international data protection regulations, the most critical aspect is to align classification levels with the strictest regulation among those applicable. This ensures compliance across different jurisdictions and minimizes the risk of non-compliance penalties while facilitating cross-border data transfers under a unified classification scheme.

124. During a security audit, it's discovered that some confidential files were stored in a publicly accessible location. This scenario indicates a failure in what aspect of information classification?
a. The initial classification of the information.
b. The enforcement of access controls based on classification.
c. The periodic review and reclassification of stored information.
d. The technical measures used to protect classified information.

Answer: b. The enforcement of access controls based on classification. Explanation: Storing confidential files in a publicly accessible location points to a failure in enforcing access controls according to the information's classification. Proper enforcement would ensure that confidential or higher classification levels are stored securely with restricted access, preventing such incidents.

125. An organization is revising its information classification policy to include a new category for sensitive personal data in response to recent privacy regulation updates. What is the MOST important factor to consider in this revision?
a. The scalability of the classification system to accommodate future data types.
b. The impact of the new category on data storage and encryption requirements.
c. The training needs for employees to understand the new category.
d. The compatibility of the new category with existing data protection technologies.

Answer: c. The training needs for employees to understand the new category. Explanation: While all the listed factors are important, the most critical is ensuring that employees are trained and understand the new category for sensitive personal data. Proper training ensures that employees can correctly classify data, which is foundational to enforcing appropriate protection measures and maintaining compliance with privacy regulations.

126. In a law firm, client-related documents are classified as "Confidential." Which of the following controls is LEAST likely to be required for handling these documents?
a. Encryption of digital files containing client-related information.
b. Two-factor authentication for access to digital client files.
c. Public posting of client-related information for marketing purposes.
d. Secure disposal of physical client documents.

Answer: c. Public posting of client-related information for marketing purposes. Explanation: Public posting of client-related information, especially when classified as "Confidential," is a clear violation of confidentiality principles and is least likely to be an appropriate control. Encryption, two-factor authentication, and secure disposal are all controls that support the confidentiality and secure handling of such documents.

127. When classifying data in a healthcare setting, which type of data requires the MOST stringent controls due to regulatory requirements and privacy concerns?
a. Employee contact information.
b. Publicly available healthcare research.
c. Patient health records.
d. Internal policy documents.

Answer: c. Patient health records. Explanation: Patient health records contain sensitive personal and health information that is protected under laws such as HIPAA in the United States. Due to the privacy concerns and regulatory requirements, these records require the most stringent controls to ensure their confidentiality, integrity, and availability.

128. A new project involves the collection of user data from an online platform. What should be the FIRST step in classifying this data?
a. Determining the storage requirements for the data.
b. Identifying the sensitivity and privacy implications of the data.
c. Implementing encryption mechanisms for data at rest.
d. Training the project team on general data protection best practices.

Answer: b. Identifying the sensitivity and privacy implications of the data. Explanation: The first step in classifying data, especially when collecting user data from an online platform, is to identify the sensitivity and privacy implications. Understanding the nature of the data and any associated regulatory or ethical obligations is crucial to determining how it should be classified and protected.

129. An organization uses a four-tier classification scheme: Public, Internal Use Only, Confidential, and Highly Confidential. Which type of information would MOST likely be classified as "Internal Use Only"?
a. Customer credit card numbers.
b. Marketing brochures.
c. Employee phone list.
d. Trade secret formulas.

Answer: c. Employee phone list. Explanation: An employee phone list, while not public, does not typically contain the level of sensitivity found in customer credit card numbers or trade secret formulas, which would likely be classified as Confidential or Highly Confidential. It is, however, sensitive enough not to be made public, making "Internal Use Only" an appropriate classification.

130. Who is PRIMARILY responsible for determining the classification level of a piece of information within an organization?
a. The IT department
b. The data owner
c. The system administrator
d. The security analyst

Answer: b. The data owner Explanation: The data owner is primarily responsible for determining the classification level of information. Data owners are typically individuals within the organization who have authority over specific sets of data and are responsible for ensuring the data is appropriately classified, protected, and handled according to its sensitivity and value to the organization.

131. In the context of information security governance, what role does a system owner play?
a. Assigns user permissions and access levels
b. Manages the technical operation of the system
c. Ensures the system meets its intended business function
d. Develops organizational security policies and procedures

Answer: c. Ensures the system meets its intended business function Explanation: A system owner is responsible for ensuring that the system meets its intended business function and complies with organizational security policies and standards. While they may work closely with IT to manage the technical aspects, their primary role is to ensure the system supports business objectives effectively and securely.

132. When transferring data ownership due to an employee leaving the company, what is the MOST critical action to take?
a. Immediately delete the former employee's user accounts
b. Conduct a review of data access and ownership assignments
c. Transfer all data to a central administrative account
d. Archive the data until a new owner is assigned

Answer: b. Conduct a review of data access and ownership assignments Explanation: Conducting a review of data access and ownership assignments is crucial when transferring data ownership. This ensures that data is correctly reassigned to the appropriate new owner and that access rights are updated to maintain security and continuity of business operations.

133. In a scenario where a company's data owner is unavailable (e.g., extended leave, termination), what is the BEST practice for handling the ownership responsibilities during this period?
a. Assign a temporary data owner with equivalent organizational authority
b. Suspend all data access until the data owner returns or is replaced
c. Transfer data ownership to the IT department for interim management
d. Allow system administrators to make data-related decisions

Answer: a. Assign a temporary data owner with equivalent organizational authority Explanation: Assigning a temporary data owner with equivalent organizational authority ensures continuity in managing and protecting the data. This temporary owner should have the knowledge and authority to make decisions about data classification, access controls, and other related responsibilities until the original owner returns or a permanent replacement is found.

134. What is the PRIMARY role of a data custodian in relation to data ownership?
a. Deciding who has access to the data
b. Determining the classification of the data
c. Implementing controls to protect the data
d. Establishing data retention policies

Answer: c. Implementing controls to protect the data Explanation: The primary role of a data custodian is to implement the controls necessary to protect the data, as specified by the data owner. Data custodians are typically responsible for the technical aspects of data management, including storage, backup, security measures, and access controls, based on the guidelines and classification determined by the data owner.

135. In an organization, who is typically responsible for defining the acceptable use of the organization's IT systems and data?
a. System administrators
b. Data processors
c. Data owners
d. End-users

Answer: c. Data owners Explanation: Data owners are typically responsible for defining the acceptable use of the organization's IT systems and data. They set the policies and guidelines for how their data can be accessed, shared, and used within the organization, ensuring that data is handled in a manner that maintains its confidentiality, integrity, and availability.

136. When establishing a new cloud-based service for storing customer data, who should be designated as the data owner?
a. The cloud service provider
b. The chief information officer (CIO)
c. The head of the customer service department
d. The chief privacy officer (CPO)

Answer: c. The head of the customer service department Explanation: The head of the customer service department, being closely involved with customer data and interactions, is typically best positioned to be designated as the data owner for a cloud-based service storing customer data. This role would have the authority and knowledge to classify the data, determine access permissions, and ensure compliance with privacy regulations, making them the ideal data owner.

137. In a situation where sensitive project data is shared with external consultants, what is the MOST important consideration for the data owner?
a. Ensuring the consultants have the necessary clearances
b. Limiting access to data to read-only
c. Establishing a non-disclosure agreement (NDA)
d. Training the consultants on the company's data handling policies

Answer: c. Establishing a non-disclosure agreement (NDA) Explanation: Establishing a non-disclosure agreement (NDA) is the most important consideration when sharing sensitive project data with external consultants. An NDA legally binds the consultants to confidentiality, ensuring they understand and agree to the terms regarding the use and protection of the shared data.

138. When a data owner delegates the responsibility of data protection to a data custodian, what aspect of data ownership CANNOT be delegated?
a. Implementation of encryption
b. Regular data backup procedures
c. Accountability for data breaches
d. Access control management

Answer: c. Accountability for data breaches Explanation: While a data owner can delegate various data protection tasks such as encryption, backups, and access control management to data custodians, the ultimate accountability for data breaches remains with the data owner. Accountability for ensuring the data's security and compliance with policies and regulations cannot be transferred.

139. In a large enterprise, the role of a system owner is often assigned to a department head or manager. What is the PRIMARY expectation from a system owner in this context?
a. Technical maintenance of the system
b. Daily operational management of the system
c. Strategic oversight and compliance alignment of the system
d. Development and coding of system enhancements

Answer: c. Strategic oversight and compliance alignment of the system Explanation: The primary expectation from a system owner, especially when assigned to a department head or manager, is to provide strategic oversight and ensure the system's alignment with organizational policies and compliance requirements. While they may not be involved in the technical or daily operational aspects, their role is crucial in ensuring the system supports business objectives and meets regulatory standards.

140. In implementing Privacy by Design principles, what should be the PRIMARY focus during the development phase of a new application?
a. Ensuring the application is scalable to handle large amounts of data.
b. Integrating strong encryption algorithms to secure data at rest.
c. Embedding privacy controls and measures from the outset.
d. Maximizing data collection to improve user experience.

Answer: c. Embedding privacy controls and measures from the outset. Explanation: Privacy by Design is a framework that advocates for privacy to be taken into account throughout the whole engineering process. The primary focus during the development phase of a new application should be on embedding privacy controls and measures from the outset, ensuring that privacy is an integral part of the application rather than an afterthought.

141. When evaluating a third-party service provider for data processing, what is the MOST important privacy consideration to ensure compliance with regulations like GDPR?

a. The geographical location of the service provider's data centers.
b. The service provider's capability to provide detailed usage analytics.
c. The cost-effectiveness of the service provider's solutions.
d. The service provider's adherence to privacy laws and data protection standards.

Answer: d. The service provider's adherence to privacy laws and data protection standards. Explanation: When engaging with a third-party service provider for data processing, ensuring that the provider adheres to relevant privacy laws and data protection standards, such as GDPR, is crucial. This compliance is vital to protect personal data and avoid legal and reputational risks associated with non-compliance.

142. Under GDPR, an individual requests the deletion of their personal data from a company's database. This request is an exercise of the individual's right to:
a. Be informed.
b. Data portability.
c. Object.
d. Erasure.

Answer: d. Erasure. Explanation: The right to erasure, also known as the "right to be forgotten," is a provision under GDPR that allows individuals to request the deletion of their personal data from a company's records without undue delay under certain conditions. This right ensures individuals can have their data removed if it's no longer necessary for the purpose it was collected or if the individual withdraws consent.

143. In the context of privacy protection, what is the purpose of data minimization?
a. To limit the use of data processing and storage resources.
b. To reduce the amount of data collected to the minimum necessary for the specified purpose.
c. To minimize the risk of unauthorized access by reducing user privileges.
d. To decrease the time data is retained before being archived.

Answer: b. To reduce the amount of data collected to the minimum necessary for the specified purpose. Explanation: Data minimization is a principle that aims to ensure that only the data which is necessary for the specified purpose is collected, processed, and stored. This principle is part of privacy protection strategies to limit the risk of data breaches and ensure compliance with privacy laws by not collecting excess personal information.

144. A company's privacy policy is being updated to comply with new regulations. What is the MOST important aspect to communicate to data subjects in the policy?
a. The technical specifications of the data storage systems.
b. The company's revenue model and financial information.
c. The purposes for which personal data is processed.
d. The list of software used for data analysis.

Answer: c. The purposes for which personal data is processed. Explanation: Transparency about the purposes for which personal data is processed is crucial in a privacy policy. This ensures data subjects are informed about how their data will be used, which is a requirement under many privacy regulations, including GDPR. This helps build trust and ensures informed consent from the data subjects.

145. A healthcare provider is implementing additional privacy measures to protect patient information. Which action would be MOST effective in enhancing privacy?
a. Increasing the frequency of system audits.
b. Adopting a strict data retention policy.
c. Requiring two-factor authentication for system access.
d. Conducting regular privacy awareness training for staff.

Answer: d. Conducting regular privacy awareness training for staff. Explanation: While all the options contribute to the overall security and privacy posture, regular privacy awareness training for staff is the most effective in enhancing privacy. Training ensures that employees are aware of privacy policies, data handling practices, and the importance of protecting patient information, which is critical in healthcare settings.

146. In a multinational corporation, how should data privacy regulations be handled when transferring personal data across borders?
a. By applying the strictest privacy regulation across all operations.
b. By ensuring data transfers comply with the privacy laws of the transferring and receiving countries.
c. By using encryption as the sole measure for cross-border data transfer.
d. By obtaining consent from data subjects for each transfer.

Answer: b. By ensuring data transfers comply with the privacy laws of the transferring and receiving countries. Explanation: When transferring personal data across borders, it's essential to ensure that the data transfers comply with the privacy laws and regulations of both the transferring and receiving countries. This might involve mechanisms like Standard Contractual Clauses, Privacy Shield (for transfers from the EU to the US), or Binding Corporate Rules, depending on the jurisdictions involved.

147. What is the primary purpose of implementing Privacy Enhancing Technologies (PETs) in an organization's data processing activities?
a. To speed up the data processing activities.
b. To enhance the accuracy of data analytics.
c. To minimize personal data usage and maximize data privacy.
d. To increase the storage capacity for personal data.

Answer: c. To minimize personal data usage and maximize data privacy. Explanation: The primary purpose of Privacy Enhancing Technologies (PETs) is to minimize the use of personal data and maximize data privacy. PETs are designed to allow organizations to perform data processing and analytics while protecting individual privacy, often by anonymizing or pseudonymizing data that could be used to identify individuals.

148. A company is developing a new app that collects users' location data. Under privacy by design principles, what measure should be taken to protect this sensitive information?
a. Collect all possible data for future use.
b. Store the data indefinitely in case it's needed.
c. Obtain explicit consent and provide clear opt-out options.
d. Share the data with third parties to improve user experience.

Answer: c. Obtain explicit consent and provide clear opt-out options. Explanation: Privacy by design principles emphasize proactive privacy measures. For an app that collects sensitive information like location data, obtaining explicit consent from users before collecting their data and providing clear and easily accessible opt-out options are essential measures to ensure users' privacy is respected and protected.

149. When dealing with Personally Identifiable Information (PII), what is the MOST important factor to consider in its lifecycle management?
a. The scalability of storage solutions for PII.
b. The encryption algorithms used to protect PII.
c. The legal and regulatory requirements governing PII.
d. The efficiency of data processing systems handling PII.

Answer: c. The legal and regulatory requirements governing PII. Explanation: The most important factor to consider in the lifecycle management of Personally Identifiable Information (PII) is compliance with legal and regulatory requirements. These requirements dictate how PII should be collected, processed, stored, shared, and disposed of, ensuring its protection throughout its lifecycle.

150. What is the PRIMARY reason for an organization to implement data retention policies?
a. To ensure data is available for marketing analysis indefinitely.
b. To minimize storage costs by deleting unnecessary data.
c. To comply with legal and regulatory requirements.
d. To improve system performance by regularly archiving old data.

Answer: c. To comply with legal and regulatory requirements. Explanation: The primary reason for implementing data retention policies is to ensure compliance with legal and regulatory requirements that dictate how long certain types of data should be retained. This can include financial records, employee records, customer data, etc., and varies by jurisdiction and industry.

151. When establishing a data retention policy for employee emails, which factor is MOST critical to consider?
a. The storage capacity of the email server.
b. Employee preferences for email retention.
c. Regulatory requirements for email archiving.
d. The impact on email system performance.

Answer: c. Regulatory requirements for email archiving. Explanation: Regulatory requirements are the most critical factor to consider when establishing a data retention policy for employee emails. Many industries and jurisdictions have specific regulations that dictate how long emails must be retained, especially if they contain business records or other significant information.

152. A healthcare provider is reviewing its data retention policy for patient records. According to HIPAA, what is the MINIMUM retention period for these records?
a. 1 year
b. 3 years
c. 6 years
d. 10 years

Answer: c. 6 years Explanation: Under HIPAA (Health Insurance Portability and Accountability Act), covered entities are required to retain patient records for a minimum of 6 years from the date of creation or the date when it was last in effect, whichever is later. This ensures that patient information is adequately preserved for legal, regulatory, and operational purposes.

153. In the context of GDPR, what is a key consideration for data retention policies regarding personal data of EU citizens?
a. Data must be retained indefinitely for historical analysis.
b. Data should be retained for at least 10 years for audit purposes.
c. Data must be anonymized after the retention period expires.
d. Data should be retained only as long as necessary for the purposes for which it was collected.

Answer: d. Data should be retained only as long as necessary for the purposes for which it was collected. Explanation: GDPR emphasizes data minimization and retention limitation, stipulating that personal data should be kept only as long as necessary to fulfill the specific purposes for which it was collected. This requires organizations to evaluate the need for retaining personal data and establish retention periods accordingly.

154. A multinational corporation needs to define a global data retention policy. What is the MOST significant challenge in this process?
a. Aligning the policy with the preferences of the corporation's senior management.
b. Ensuring the policy accommodates the data storage technologies in use.
c. Reconciling the diverse data protection and retention laws of different countries.
d. Training employees across different regions to follow the policy.

Answer: c. Reconciling the diverse data protection and retention laws of different countries. Explanation: The most significant challenge in defining a global data retention policy is reconciling the diverse data protection and retention laws across different countries where the corporation operates. This requires a comprehensive understanding of various legal frameworks and creating a policy that complies with all applicable laws, which can vary greatly in terms of retention requirements.

155. For financial institutions, data retention policies must align with specific regulatory standards. Which regulation typically dictates the retention period for transaction records in the financial sector?
a. HIPAA
b. Sarbanes-Oxley Act
c. GDPR
d. SEC Rule 17a-4

Answer: d. SEC Rule 17a-4 Explanation: SEC Rule 17a-4, which pertains to the Securities and Exchange Commission's requirements for broker-dealers, dictates the retention period for transaction records in the financial sector. It requires that records be preserved in a non-rewriteable, non-erasable format for specific periods, typically not less than six years.

156. When designing a data retention policy for a cloud-based CRM system, which stakeholder's input is MOST critical?
a. Cloud service provider
b. Sales team members
c. Legal department
d. IT department

Answer: c. Legal department Explanation: The legal department's input is most critical when designing a data retention policy for a cloud-based CRM system. They ensure that the policy complies with relevant data protection laws, regulations, and contractual obligations, minimizing legal risks associated with data handling and retention.

157. After a merger, a company is consolidating its data retention policies. What should be the FIRST step in this process?
a. Selecting a unified data storage solution.
b. Identifying and understanding the legal requirements applicable to all types of data held by the merged entities.
c. Training employees on the importance of data retention.
d. Deleting all redundant or duplicate data from both companies.

Answer: b. Identifying and understanding the legal requirements applicable to all types of data held by the merged entities. Explanation: The first step in consolidating data retention policies after a merger is to identify and understand the legal requirements applicable to all types of data held by the merged entities. This ensures that the unified policy complies with all relevant laws and regulations, which is essential for legal and regulatory compliance.

158. In an organization, who is typically RESPONSIBLE for enforcing data retention policies?
a. Data owners
b. IT support staff
c. End-users
d. Data custodians

Answer: d. Data custodians Explanation: Data custodians are typically responsible for enforcing data retention policies. They manage and protect the data according to the policies set by data owners, ensuring that data is retained for the required periods and securely deleted when its retention period expires.

159. A law firm is revising its data retention policy in light of new legislation requiring longer retention periods for certain case files. What is the MOST important factor to consider in this revision?
a. The impact on data storage costs.
b. The preferences of the firm's partners.
c. Compliance with the new legal requirements.
d. The efficiency of the firm's document management system.

Answer: c. Compliance with the new legal requirements. Explanation: The most important factor to consider when revising a data retention policy in response to new legislation is compliance with the new legal requirements. Ensuring that the policy meets the mandated retention periods for specific types of case files is critical to avoid legal penalties and ensure regulatory compliance.

160. In a distributed network environment, which data security control is MOST effective in ensuring data integrity during transmission?
a. Data masking
b. Digital signatures
c. Antivirus software
d. Firewall protection

Answer: b. Digital signatures Explanation: Digital signatures are crucial for ensuring data integrity during transmission in a distributed network environment. They provide a means to verify that the data has not been altered from its original form, thus ensuring its integrity. Unlike antivirus software or firewalls that protect against malicious software and unauthorized access respectively, digital signatures specifically safeguard the authenticity and integrity of the data being transmitted.

161. Which data security control is primarily used to prevent unauthorized disclosure of sensitive information within a database?
a. Encryption at rest
b. Role-based access control
c. Network segmentation
d. Intrusion detection system

Answer: b. Role-based access control Explanation: Role-based access control (RBAC) is a data security control that restricts access to information within a database based on the roles of individual users. It is primarily used to prevent unauthorized disclosure of sensitive information by ensuring that only users with the necessary permissions, based on their roles, can access specific data. Encryption at rest protects data storage, while network segmentation and intrusion detection systems are more focused on network-level security.

162. For an organization subject to GDPR, what data security control is essential for protecting personal data and ensuring compliance?
a. Data minimization
b. Redundant data backups
c. Public key infrastructure
d. Secure shell protocols

Answer: a. Data minimization Explanation: Data minimization is a principle of GDPR that mandates organizations to collect only the personal data that is absolutely necessary for the purposes for which it is processed. This control is essential for protecting personal data under GDPR, as it limits the amount of data collected and stored, thereby reducing the risk of data breaches and ensuring compliance with the regulation.

163. When securing data at rest, which of the following controls provides the STRONGEST protection against unauthorized access?
a. Data classification
b. Full disk encryption
c. File-level permissions
d. Regular data audits

Answer: b. Full disk encryption Explanation: Full disk encryption provides the strongest protection for data at rest by encrypting the entire storage medium. This ensures that all data stored on the disk is encrypted, making it inaccessible without the correct encryption key, even if an unauthorized individual gains physical access to the storage device.

164. In a scenario where an organization's sensitive data must be shared with an external partner, what data security control should be implemented to protect the data in transit?
a. Data anonymization
b. Secure socket layer (SSL) encryption
c. Offsite data backups
d. Hardware security modules

Answer: b. Secure socket layer (SSL) encryption Explanation: Secure socket layer (SSL) encryption is the most appropriate data security control for protecting data in transit, especially when sharing sensitive data with an external partner. SSL encrypts the data during transmission, ensuring that it remains confidential and intact, preventing eavesdropping, tampering, and forgery by unauthorized parties.

165. For protecting data integrity and authenticity in a software development environment, which control is MOST effective?
a. Code obfuscation
b. Version control systems
c. Digital watermarking
d. Application whitelisting

Answer: b. Version control systems Explanation: Version control systems are most effective in protecting data integrity and authenticity in a software development environment. They track and manage changes to the codebase, ensuring that changes are documented, reversible, and traceable to specific contributors, thus safeguarding the integrity and authenticity of the software being developed.

166. In the event of a data breach involving personal data, what control should be in place to ensure timely notification to the affected individuals?
a. Incident response plan
b. Data loss prevention (DLP) tools
c. Automated log analysis
d. Two-factor authentication

Answer: a. Incident response plan Explanation: An incident response plan is a critical control for ensuring timely notification to affected individuals in the event of a data breach involving personal data. The plan should include clear procedures for breach detection, assessment, containment, and notification processes that comply with legal and regulatory requirements, ensuring that individuals are promptly informed of breaches that may impact their personal data.

167. To protect against unauthorized changes to data by internal users, which of the following is the MOST effective control?
a. Database activity monitoring
b. User awareness training
c. Biometric access controls
d. Secure coding practices

Answer: a. Database activity monitoring Explanation: Database activity monitoring is the most effective control for protecting against unauthorized changes to data by internal users. It involves the continuous monitoring and analysis of database activity, enabling the detection and prevention of unauthorized access and changes to the data, ensuring data integrity and compliance with internal policies.

168. In a cloud computing environment, what control is essential for ensuring the confidentiality of data processed and stored by cloud service providers?
a. Multifactor authentication
b. Client-side encryption
c. Network intrusion detection systems
d. Virtual private network (VPN) access

Answer: b. Client-side encryption Explanation: Client-side encryption is essential in a cloud computing environment for ensuring the confidentiality of data processed and stored by cloud service providers. By encrypting data on the client's side before it is transferred to the cloud for storage or processing, client-side encryption ensures that the data remains confidential and accessible only to authorized users, even if the cloud service provider's systems are compromised.

169. When implementing data retention policies, what security control is critical for ensuring that data is not retained beyond its required retention period?
a. Automated data lifecycle management
b. Continuous data encryption
c. Periodic manual data review
d. Data warehousing

Answer: a. Automated data lifecycle management Explanation: Automated data lifecycle management is critical for ensuring that data is not retained beyond its required retention period. This control automates the processes of classifying, archiving, and securely deleting data in accordance with the organization's data retention policies, ensuring compliance and minimizing the risk of data breaches by eliminating unnecessary data storage.

170. When sensitive documents are to be disposed of, which method ensures the highest level of security?
a. Recycling
b. Shredding into confetti-sized pieces
c. Deleting the electronic files
d. Burning

Answer: b. Shredding into confetti-sized pieces Explanation: Shredding documents into confetti-sized pieces provides a high level of security by making it virtually impossible to reconstruct the documents. While burning is also secure, shredding is often preferred for environmental reasons and ease of handling. Deleting electronic files may not be as secure due to the potential for data recovery.

171. What is the PRIMARY purpose of labeling sensitive documents?
a. To ensure they are aesthetically pleasing
b. To facilitate easier archiving
c. To indicate the level of sensitivity and handling requirements
d. To track the document's location

Answer: c. To indicate the level of sensitivity and handling requirements Explanation: The primary purpose of labeling sensitive documents is to clearly indicate their level of sensitivity and the specific handling requirements. This ensures that individuals who come into contact with the documents are aware of how they should be securely handled, stored, and disposed of.

172. In an organization that deals with classified information, what is the most appropriate way to handle the storage of Top Secret documents?
a. In a locked drawer in a common office area
b. Within a secure, access-controlled vault
c. On a password-protected computer network

d. At an employee's home for safekeeping

Answer: b. Within a secure, access-controlled vault Explanation: Top Secret documents require the highest level of security. Storing them within a secure, access-controlled vault ensures that only authorized personnel with the necessary clearance can access them, thus maintaining their confidentiality and integrity.

173. Which of the following is NOT a recommended practice for handling sensitive electronic data?
a. Using strong encryption for data at rest and in transit
b. Storing backups in a secure, offsite location
c. Allowing employees to store data on personal USB drives
d. Implementing strict access controls based on the principle of least privilege

Answer: c. Allowing employees to store data on personal USB drives Explanation: Allowing employees to store sensitive electronic data on personal USB drives is not recommended due to the high risk of loss, theft, or unauthorized access. This practice contradicts secure data handling requirements, which emphasize control, accountability, and protection of sensitive data.

174. When determining the appropriate storage conditions for sensitive data, what factor is LEAST likely to be considered?
a. The data's classification level
b. The cost of storage solutions
c. The physical environment of the storage location
d. The color coding of storage containers

Answer: d. The color coding of storage containers Explanation: While color coding can be used for quick identification, it is the least critical factor when determining storage conditions for sensitive data. More important considerations include the data's classification level, which dictates security requirements; the cost of secure storage solutions; and the physical environment, which needs to protect against environmental hazards.

175. What is the BEST practice for ensuring the secure transmission of classified information over the internet?
a. Sending the information in a password-protected zip file via email
b. Using a secure file transfer protocol such as SFTP or FTPS
c. Posting the information on a secure website for download
d. Transmitting the information via instant messaging applications

Answer: b. Using a secure file transfer protocol such as SFTP or FTPS Explanation: The best practice for secure transmission of classified information over the internet is to use secure file transfer protocols like SFTP (Secure File Transfer Protocol) or FTPS (File Transfer Protocol Secure). These protocols provide encryption for data in transit, ensuring confidentiality and integrity. Password-protected zip files and secure websites may offer some level of security, but they may not be sufficient for classified information. Instant messaging applications are generally not secure enough for transmitting classified information.

176. For a company handling a mix of classified and unclassified data, what is the most effective way to prevent accidental disclosure of classified information?
a. Implementing physical barriers between areas handling different classification levels
b. Providing general security awareness training to all employees
c. Applying strict access controls and data handling protocols based on data classification
d. Using a single, high-security standard for all company data

Answer: c. Applying strict access controls and data handling protocols based on data classification Explanation: The most effective way to prevent accidental disclosure of classified information is to apply strict access controls and data handling protocols based on the classification level of the data. This ensures that only authorized personnel can access classified data and that it is handled in accordance with its sensitivity. While physical barriers and security training support this goal, tailored access controls and handling protocols directly address the risk of accidental disclosure.

177. When decommissioning a device that stored sensitive information, which step is CRUCIAL to ensure data confidentiality?
a. Performing a factory reset on the device
b. Physically destroying the device's storage media
c. Updating the device to the latest software version
d. Transferring the data to a new device

Answer: b. Physically destroying the device's storage media Explanation: Physically destroying the device's storage media is crucial when decommissioning a device that stored sensitive information. This method ensures that the data cannot be recovered, thereby maintaining its confidentiality. While a factory reset can remove many settings and data, it may not be sufficient to prevent data recovery by sophisticated means.

178. In the design of a secure network infrastructure, which principle ensures that a breach in one segment does not compromise the entire network?
a. Defense in depth
b. Least privilege
c. Segmentation and isolation
d. Fail-safe defaults

Answer: c. Segmentation and isolation Explanation: Segmentation and isolation are key principles in secure network design that involve dividing the network into separate segments or zones, each with its own security controls. This approach ensures that if one segment is breached, the attack cannot easily spread to other parts of the network, thereby limiting the potential damage.

179. When implementing a new cryptographic system, what factor is MOST critical to ensuring its long-term security?
a. The speed of the encryption and decryption processes
b. The length and complexity of the cryptographic keys

c. The user interface design of the cryptographic software

d. The storage capacity required for encrypted data

Answer: b. The length and complexity of the cryptographic keys Explanation: The security of a cryptographic system largely depends on the length and complexity of the cryptographic keys used. Longer and more complex keys are harder for attackers to break through brute force or other cryptographic attacks, making them critical for the system's long-term security.

180. In the context of secure software development, what is the PRIMARY purpose of implementing a secure coding standard?

a. To ensure the software is compatible with all operating systems

b. To prevent common security vulnerabilities in the software code

c. To reduce the time required for code reviews

d. To comply with industry-specific regulations

Answer: b. To prevent common security vulnerabilities in the software code Explanation: The primary purpose of implementing a secure coding standard in software development is to prevent common security vulnerabilities such as injection flaws, cross-site scripting (XSS), and buffer overflows. Secure coding standards provide guidelines and best practices that help developers write code that is more secure against potential attacks.

181. In an enterprise environment, which security control is MOST effective in preventing unauthorized access to sensitive systems?

a. Intrusion Detection Systems (IDS)

b. Role-based Access Control (RBAC)

c. Antivirus software

d. Firewalls

Answer: b. Role-based Access Control (RBAC) Explanation: Role-based Access Control (RBAC) is most effective in preventing unauthorized access to sensitive systems within an enterprise environment. RBAC assigns permissions to roles rather than individual users, ensuring that only authorized users can access specific systems based on their roles, thereby enhancing security.

182. When designing a security architecture for cloud-based services, which of the following is a key consideration for ensuring data privacy?

a. The physical location of data centers

b. The use of virtual private networks (VPNs)

c. Data encryption, both at rest and in transit

d. The scalability of cloud resources

Answer: c. Data encryption, both at rest and in transit Explanation: A key consideration for ensuring data privacy in cloud-based services is data encryption, both at rest and in transit. Encrypting data protects it from unauthorized access and ensures privacy, even if data is intercepted during transmission or accessed by unauthorized individuals in the cloud.

183. In the implementation of a secure network architecture, what is the purpose of deploying a demilitarized zone (DMZ)?
a. To isolate internal networks from the internet
b. To provide a secure area for users to access internet services
c. To host public-facing services while protecting the internal network
d. To encrypt all data transmitted between the internal network and the internet

Answer: c. To host public-facing services while protecting the internal network Explanation: The purpose of deploying a demilitarized zone (DMZ) in a secure network architecture is to host public-facing services, such as web servers and email servers, while protecting the internal network. The DMZ acts as a buffer zone, providing an additional layer of security by separating external-facing services from the rest of the internal network.

184. In a secure system design, what is the significance of implementing the principle of "fail-secure"?
a. The system remains operational even when security controls fail.
b. The system defaults to a secure state in the event of a failure.
c. The system alerts administrators immediately upon any security control failure.
d. The system maintains user accessibility to ensure business continuity.

Answer: b. The system defaults to a secure state in the event of a failure Explanation: Implementing the principle of "fail-secure" in system design ensures that in the event of a system failure, the system defaults to a secure state, preventing potential unauthorized access or data leakage. This principle prioritizes security over functionality during failures, ensuring that sensitive data remains protected.

185. When integrating an Intrusion Prevention System (IPS) into an organization's security architecture, what is the PRIMARY function of the IPS?
a. To monitor network traffic and generate alerts for suspicious activities
b. To actively prevent and block potential security threats in real-time
c. To serve as a physical barrier to unauthorized network access
d. To encrypt data transmissions across the network

Answer: b. To actively prevent and block potential security threats in real-time Explanation: The primary function of an Intrusion Prevention System (IPS) is to actively prevent and block potential security threats in real-time. Unlike an Intrusion Detection System (IDS) that only monitors and alerts, an IPS has the capability to take immediate action to stop recognized threats, enhancing the security posture of the organization.

186. In the development of a security-focused operating system, what mechanism ensures that processes operate with only the privileges necessary to perform their required tasks?
a. Mandatory Access Control (MAC)
b. Sandboxing
c. Kernel hardening
d. Secure boot process

Answer: a. Mandatory Access Control (MAC) Explanation: Mandatory Access Control (MAC) is a mechanism in security-focused operating systems that ensures processes operate with only the privileges necessary to perform their tasks. MAC policies enforce strict controls over resource access based on established security policies, limiting the capabilities of processes to the minimum required, thereby reducing the risk of privilege escalation and other security breaches.

187. What principle is MOST important when designing a system to ensure it remains secure even when some security controls fail?
a. Open design
b. Defense in depth
c. Economy of mechanism
d. Fail-safe defaults

Answer: d. Fail-safe defaults Explanation: The principle of fail-safe defaults ensures that, in the event of a failure, the system defaults to a secure state. This principle is crucial for maintaining security even when certain controls fail, as it prevents the system from defaulting to a less secure or insecure state, potentially exposing vulnerabilities.

188. In the context of secure software engineering, what is the PRIMARY purpose of implementing the principle of least privilege?
a. To enhance the performance of the software
b. To minimize the risk of unauthorized access or actions
c. To simplify the codebase for easier maintenance
d. To reduce the cost of software development

Answer: b. To minimize the risk of unauthorized access or actions Explanation: The principle of least privilege is aimed at minimizing the risk of unauthorized access or actions within a system by ensuring that users, processes, and programs are granted only the minimum privileges necessary to perform their required functions. This limits the potential damage from accidents, errors, or malicious exploits.

189. When designing a new application, why is input validation considered a critical security control?
a. It ensures user-friendly error messages are generated.
b. It prevents unauthorized users from accessing the application.
c. It safeguards the application against various forms of injection attacks.
d. It optimizes the application's performance by rejecting unnecessary data.

Answer: c. It safeguards the application against various forms of injection attacks. Explanation: Input validation is a critical security control in application design because it helps safeguard the application against various forms of injection attacks, such as SQL injection, by verifying that the input data conforms to expected parameters. Proper input validation ensures that malicious data cannot exploit the application's processing logic, thereby enhancing its security.

190. In the secure development lifecycle, at what stage should security requirements be defined?
a. After the first prototype is developed
b. During the testing phase
c. Before the design phase begins
d. At the deployment stage

Answer: c. Before the design phase begins Explanation: Security requirements should be defined early in the secure development lifecycle, ideally before the design phase begins. This ensures that security considerations are integrated into the application from the outset, influencing the design, implementation, and testing of the application, leading to a more inherently secure product.

191. What secure design principle is being applied when a system is designed to operate safely without relying on the secrecy of its internal workings?
a. Security through obscurity
b. Open design
c. Complete mediation
d. Separation of privilege

Answer: b. Open design Explanation: The open design principle dictates that a system's security should not depend on the secrecy of its design or implementation. This principle asserts that a system should be secure even if its internal workings are publicly known, relying on robust security mechanisms and controls rather than the obscurity of its design.

192. In designing a critical infrastructure system, why is redundancy an important consideration for security?
a. It ensures that the system can handle large volumes of data efficiently.
b. It prevents unauthorized access by providing multiple authentication mechanisms.
c. It provides a backup in case one component fails, ensuring system availability.
d. It reduces the overall cost of the system by using duplicated resources.

Answer: c. It provides a backup in case one component fails, ensuring system availability. Explanation: In the context of critical infrastructure systems, redundancy is vital for ensuring system availability and reliability. By incorporating redundant components or pathways, the system can continue to operate even if one part fails, thereby maintaining its critical functions and enhancing its resilience against failures and attacks that could compromise availability.

193. How does implementing modularity in system design contribute to security?
a. By allowing systems to be easily updated with the latest security patches
b. By enabling the system to process data more quickly and efficiently
c. By facilitating the isolation of components, limiting the impact of a security breach
d. By reducing the overall complexity of the system, making it less attractive to attackers

Answer: c. By facilitating the isolation of components, limiting the impact of a security breach Explanation: Modularity in system design contributes to security by facilitating the isolation of components. This means that if a security breach occurs in one module, the impact can be contained within that module, preventing the breach from affecting the entire system. This isolation helps in managing and mitigating risks more effectively.

194. What is the key benefit of incorporating the principle of "complete mediation" in a secure system design?
a. Ensuring all access requests to resources are authenticated every time
b. Reducing the system's attack surface by limiting user access
c. Improving the system's response time to security incidents
d. Streamlining the process of applying security updates and patches

Answer: a. Ensuring all access requests to resources are authenticated every time Explanation: The principle of complete mediation requires that every access request to a system's resources is fully authenticated, authorized, and audited each time the request is made. This prevents unauthorized access by ensuring that access controls are applied consistently and cannot be bypassed, enhancing the security of the system.

195. When employing the principle of "security by design" in software development, what is the MOST significant advantage?
a. It ensures that the software is free from all vulnerabilities.
b. It integrates security considerations throughout the software development lifecycle.
c. It guarantees that the software will be compliant with all industry standards.
d. It significantly reduces the time required for user acceptance testing.

Answer: b. It integrates security considerations throughout the software development lifecycle. Explanation: The principle of "security by design" integrates security considerations throughout the software development lifecycle, from the initial design phase to deployment and maintenance. This approach ensures that security is a foundational aspect of the software, rather than an afterthought, leading to more secure products by addressing potential security issues early in the development process.

196. Which security model is primarily focused on ensuring that access controls cannot be modified by unauthorized users?
a. Bell-LaPadula Model
b. Biba Integrity Model
c. Clark-Wilson Integrity Model
d. Brewer and Nash Model

Answer: a. Bell-LaPadula Model Explanation: The Bell-LaPadula Model is primarily focused on maintaining confidentiality and includes the "*-property" (star property), which ensures that subjects (users) cannot write down to objects (resources) at lower security levels, effectively preventing unauthorized users from modifying access controls or data that they should not have access to.

197. In the context of security models, which principle is central to the Biba Integrity Model?
a. No read up (no read-up)
b. No write down (*-property)
c. Integrity verification procedures
d. Separation of duties

Answer: b. No write down (-property) Explanation: The Biba Integrity Model is designed to prevent data from being written to a lower integrity level, known as the "no write down" or "-property." This principle helps to maintain the integrity of data by ensuring that information cannot be corrupted by less trustworthy sources.

198. What is the PRIMARY purpose of the Clark-Wilson Integrity Model?
a. To enforce confidentiality of classified information
b. To prevent unauthorized data disclosure
c. To ensure data integrity through well-formed transactions
d. To provide a framework for role-based access control

Answer: c. To ensure data integrity through well-formed transactions Explanation: The Clark-Wilson Integrity Model is focused on ensuring data integrity through the use of well-formed transactions. It defines a set of access control rules and certification rules that ensure any transaction brings the system from one consistent state to another, maintaining the integrity of the data within the system.

199. The Brewer and Nash Model, also known as the Chinese Wall Model, is designed to prevent:
a. Conflicts of interest in access to corporate data
b. Data tampering by system administrators
c. Unauthorized access to top-secret documents
d. Brute force attacks on encrypted data

Answer: a. Conflicts of interest in access to corporate data Explanation: The Brewer and Nash Model, or Chinese Wall Model, is designed to prevent conflicts of interest by segregating access to data based on the user's prior access to potentially conflicting information. It dynamically controls access based on the user's access history to ensure that sensitive information from competing parties cannot be accessed by the same individual, thus preventing conflicts of interest.

200. In the Bell-LaPadula Model, which rule states that a subject at a certain security level may not read data at a higher security level?
a. The Simple Security Rule (no read up)
b. The *-property (no write down)
c. The Discretionary Security Property
d. The Tranquility Principle

Answer: a. The Simple Security Rule (no read up) Explanation: The Simple Security Rule, also known as "no read up," is a fundamental rule of the Bell-LaPadula Model. It states that a subject (user) at a certain security level cannot read data at a higher security level, ensuring the confidentiality of information by preventing unauthorized access to sensitive data.

201. Which security model is specifically designed to address the integrity of transactions and ensure that only authorized users can make changes to data?
a. Take-Grant Model
b. Information Flow Model
c. Clark-Wilson Integrity Model
d. Graham-Denning Model

Answer: c. Clark-Wilson Integrity Model Explanation: The Clark-Wilson Integrity Model is specifically designed to ensure the integrity of transactions and data within a system. It requires that only authorized users can make changes through well-formed transactions and enforces separation of duties and auditing to maintain data integrity.

202. In which security model is the concept of "separation of duties" most explicitly defined to prevent fraud and error?
a. Biba Model
b. Bell-LaPadula Model
c. Clark-Wilson Model
d. Chinese Wall Model

Answer: c. Clark-Wilson Model Explanation: The Clark-Wilson Model explicitly defines the concept of "separation of duties" as part of its integrity enforcement mechanisms. This model uses a transaction-based approach to ensure that no single individual has the authority to modify data inappropriately, thereby reducing the risk of fraud and error.

203. The Information Flow Model focuses on:
a. Ensuring data does not flow from high integrity levels to low integrity levels
b. Preventing data leakage between different security domains
c. Mapping user roles to specific data access permissions
d. Enforcing access controls based on the state of the system

Answer: b. Preventing data leakage between different security domains Explanation: The Information Flow Model is concerned with ensuring that information does not flow in an unauthorized manner between different security domains, effectively preventing data leakage. It focuses on controlling the paths along which information can flow and applies constraints to ensure that information only flows in ways that comply with the defined security policy.

204. In the Take-Grant Model, what does the "take" operation allow?
a. A subject to grant access rights to an object
b. A subject to remove access rights from an object
c. A subject to transfer an object to another domain
d. A subject to obtain access rights from another subject

Answer: d. A subject to obtain access rights from another subject Explanation: In the Take-Grant Model, the "take" operation allows a subject to obtain access rights from another subject or object. This model is used to describe how rights can be transferred between subjects and objects in a system, and the "take" operation specifically deals with the acquisition of rights, enhancing the understanding of how access control can be dynamically managed in a system.

205. What is a key feature of the Graham-Denning Model?
a. It defines secure state transitions for digital systems.
b. It focuses exclusively on the confidentiality of data.
c. It outlines eight primitive operations for secure information flow.
d. It provides a framework for public key infrastructure.

Answer: c. It outlines eight primitive operations for secure information flow. Explanation: The Graham-Denning Model is known for outlining eight primitive operations that define how subjects (users or processes) can securely interact with objects (resources like files or data segments) in a system. These operations cover aspects such as creating/deleting objects and subjects, granting/revoking access rights, and transferring rights, providing a comprehensive framework for understanding and designing secure access control mechanisms.

206. What is the primary purpose of the Common Criteria (CC) in security evaluation?
a. To provide a clear set of guidelines for user password complexity
b. To establish a standard framework for evaluating the security properties of IT products
c. To define the roles and responsibilities of security personnel
d. To outline the process for responding to security incidents

Answer: b. To establish a standard framework for evaluating the security properties of IT products Explanation: The Common Criteria for Information Technology Security Evaluation (CC) is an international standard (ISO/IEC 15408) that provides a common framework for evaluating the security features and capabilities of information technology products. The goal is to ensure that the process of specifying, implementing, and evaluating security features is standardized and consistent across different products and vendors.

207. In the context of security evaluation models, what does the term "assurance level" refer to?
a. The number of vulnerabilities found in a system
b. The degree of confidence that a system's security features meet certain standards
c. The frequency of security audits conducted on a system
d. The percentage of system uptime guaranteed by the vendor

Answer: b. The degree of confidence that a system's security features meet certain standards Explanation: Assurance level in security evaluation models refers to the degree of confidence that a system's security features are correctly implemented and meet specific security standards. Higher assurance levels indicate more rigorous testing and validation, providing greater confidence in the system's security posture.

208. The Trusted Computer System Evaluation Criteria (TCSEC), also known as the Orange Book, classifies systems into how many main divisions?
a. Two
b. Four
c. Six
d. Seven

Answer: d. Seven Explanation: The Trusted Computer System Evaluation Criteria (TCSEC), commonly known as the Orange Book, classifies systems into four main divisions (D, C, B, A), each with certain subdivisions, leading to a total of seven categories. These range from the lowest level of trust (D) to the highest (A), with specific criteria for security features and assurance levels at each division.

209. Which evaluation model introduced the concept of "Protection Profiles" (PP)?
a. The Rainbow Series
b. The Common Criteria
c. The ITSEC
d. The Red Book

Answer: b. The Common Criteria Explanation: The Common Criteria introduced the concept of "Protection Profiles" (PP), which are standardized documents that outline the security requirements and objectives for a category of products or systems. PPs enable consumers to specify their security needs and vendors to demonstrate how their products meet these specific requirements.

210. What distinguishes the Information Technology Security Evaluation Criteria (ITSEC) from the Common Criteria?
a. ITSEC is solely focused on hardware evaluation, while Common Criteria covers both hardware and software.
b. ITSEC provides a fixed set of security levels, whereas Common Criteria allows for more flexible and tailored evaluations.
c. ITSEC evaluations are conducted by the product vendors, whereas Common Criteria evaluations are performed by independent labs.
d. ITSEC only applies to military systems, while Common Criteria is applicable to both commercial and governmental systems.

Answer: b. ITSEC provides a fixed set of security levels, whereas Common Criteria allows for more flexible and tailored evaluations. Explanation: One key distinction between ITSEC and the Common Criteria is the flexibility in evaluation. ITSEC, being an earlier model, provided a fixed set of security levels for evaluating products, which could be somewhat rigid. The Common Criteria, on the other hand, introduced the concept of Protection Profiles and Security Target, allowing for more tailored evaluations based on the specific security needs and objectives of the product or system being evaluated.

211. How do "Security Targets" (ST) in the Common Criteria framework benefit vendors and purchasers?

a. They specify the minimum password length and complexity requirements for system users.

b. They outline the specific security requirements and measures for a particular product or system.

c. They guarantee that a product is free from all security vulnerabilities.

d. They provide a detailed incident response plan for the product in case of a breach.

Answer: b. They outline the specific security requirements and measures for a particular product or system. Explanation: Security Targets (ST) in the Common Criteria framework are documents that detail the specific security properties, requirements, and measures of a particular IT product or system. They benefit vendors by providing a clear and structured way to claim what their product can do in terms of security, and they benefit purchasers by offering a detailed and standardized way to assess whether a product meets their specific security needs.

212. In the TCSEC (Orange Book) model, what does the A1 rating signify?

a. The system has minimal security controls and is intended for low-security environments.

b. The system has some discretionary access controls suitable for protecting confidential information.

c. The system meets the highest level of trust, incorporating formal security policies and verification.

d. The system is designed for military applications with classified information.

Answer: c. The system meets the highest level of trust, incorporating formal security policies and verification. Explanation: In the TCSEC (Orange Book) model, an A1 rating signifies the highest level of trust. Systems classified at this level have been formally verified to meet comprehensive security models, incorporating formal methods to ensure that the security policies are correctly implemented. This level of classification is intended for environments where security is of utmost importance.

213. What role do "Evaluation Assurance Levels" (EALs) play in the Common Criteria?

a. They define the different colors of books in the Rainbow Series.

b. They specify the operational roles of personnel within a secure system.

c. They provide a standardized scale for the depth and rigor of an evaluation.

d. They categorize different types of security incidents based on severity.

Answer: c. They provide a standardized scale for the depth and rigor of an evaluation. Explanation: Evaluation Assurance Levels (EALs) in the Common Criteria provide a standardized scale for assessing the depth and rigor of a security evaluation. Ranging from EAL1 to EAL7, higher levels indicate more comprehensive testing, analysis, and formal verification, offering a measure of the confidence that can be placed in a product's security properties.

214. Which of the following best describes the relationship between Protection Profiles (PP) and Security Targets (ST) in the Common Criteria?
a. PPs define general security requirements for a class of products, while STs tailor those requirements to specific products.
b. PPs are used exclusively for software products, while STs are used for hardware products.
c. STs outline the security functions of a product, while PPs provide the test cases for those functions.
d. PPs and STs are interchangeable terms that refer to the same documents.

Answer: a. PPs define general security requirements for a class of products, while STs tailor those requirements to specific products. Explanation: Protection Profiles (PP) in the Common Criteria framework define a set of security requirements and objectives for a category or class of products, such as firewalls or operating systems. Security Targets (ST), on the other hand, are specific to individual products and tailor the general requirements outlined in a PP (or define their own requirements) to describe the security properties and capabilities of that specific product.

215. What is the primary security capability of a network-based Intrusion Detection System (IDS)?
a. Preventing malware infections by scanning email attachments
b. Detecting and responding to abnormal traffic patterns or behaviors
c. Encrypting data transmissions between network nodes
d. Authenticating users before granting access to network resources

Answer: b. Detecting and responding to abnormal traffic patterns or behaviors Explanation: A network-based Intrusion Detection System (IDS) primarily focuses on monitoring network traffic to detect and possibly respond to abnormal traffic patterns or behaviors indicative of potential security threats or attacks. Unlike firewalls or encryption tools, an IDS serves as a surveillance system that alerts administrators to suspicious activities.

216. In the context of information systems security, what role does a Security Information and Event Management (SIEM) system play?
a. It serves as a primary firewall to block unauthorized external access.
b. It aggregates and analyzes log data from various sources to identify security incidents.
c. It provides physical security controls for data center environments.
d. It encrypts data stored on endpoint devices to prevent data leakage.

Answer: b. It aggregates and analyzes log data from various sources to identify security incidents. Explanation: A Security Information and Event Management (SIEM) system aggregates and analyzes log and event data from various sources within an organization's IT environment to identify, report, and potentially respond to security incidents and anomalies, providing a comprehensive view of the security status of an information system.

217. Which capability is MOST directly associated with a Data Loss Prevention (DLP) system?
a. Detecting and preventing unauthorized data transfers outside the organization
b. Conducting penetration tests on the network to identify vulnerabilities
c. Managing cryptographic keys used for data encryption
d. Auditing user activities to ensure compliance with access control policies

Answer: a. Detecting and preventing unauthorized data transfers outside the organization Explanation: A Data Loss Prevention (DLP) system is specifically designed to detect and prevent unauthorized attempts to copy or transfer sensitive data outside the organization. It monitors and controls data in use, in motion, and at rest, ensuring that sensitive information is not leaked, misused, or lost.

218. What is the primary purpose of implementing an Endpoint Detection and Response (EDR) solution?
a. To provide a secure virtual environment for testing malware
b. To manage the installation of software patches across endpoints
c. To monitor endpoints for malicious activities and facilitate incident response
d. To serve as a gateway for secure remote access to the corporate network

Answer: c. To monitor endpoints for malicious activities and facilitate incident response Explanation: The primary purpose of an Endpoint Detection and Response (EDR) solution is to continuously monitor endpoints (such as workstations, servers, and mobile devices) for suspicious or malicious activities and to provide tools for incident investigation and response, thereby enhancing the organization's ability to detect and respond to cyber threats at the endpoint level.

219. In information system security, what is a honeypot primarily used for?
a. Acting as a decoy to attract and analyze attacks
b. Filtering spam from incoming email messages
c. Encrypting data in transit to protect it from eavesdropping
d. Balancing network load to prevent service outages

Answer: a. Acting as a decoy to attract and analyze attacks Explanation: A honeypot is a security mechanism set up to act as a decoy to attract and analyze attacks and malicious activities. By mimicking vulnerable systems, honeypots can divert attackers from real targets and provide valuable insights into attack methods and strategies, without the risk to actual data or services.

220. How does a Web Application Firewall (WAF) enhance security for online applications?
a. By detecting and preventing SQL injection and cross-site scripting (XSS) attacks
b. By ensuring secure, encrypted connections using SSL/TLS protocols
c. By providing a backup and recovery solution for application data
d. By managing user access rights and authentication to the application

Answer: a. By detecting and preventing SQL injection and cross-site scripting (XSS) attacks Explanation: A Web Application Firewall (WAF) is specifically designed to protect online applications by monitoring and filtering HTTP traffic between the application and the Internet. It helps to enhance security by detecting and preventing attacks such as SQL injection and cross-site scripting (XSS), which are common threats to web applications.

221. What feature distinguishes Next-Generation Firewalls (NGFW) from traditional firewalls?

a. The ability to filter traffic based on MAC addresses
b. The capacity to perform stateful packet inspection
c. The integration of intrusion prevention systems (IPS) and deep packet inspection
d. The use of static routing to direct traffic flow

Answer: c. The integration of intrusion prevention systems (IPS) and deep packet inspection Explanation: Next-Generation Firewalls (NGFW) distinguish themselves from traditional firewalls by integrating advanced features such as intrusion prevention systems (IPS) and deep packet inspection. These capabilities allow NGFWs to inspect and make decisions about traffic based on application-level information, providing more granular and effective security controls.

222. What security capability is MOST essential in a Public Key Infrastructure (PKI) for ensuring the authenticity of digital certificates?
a. Symmetric key encryption
b. Certificate revocation lists (CRL)
c. Digital signature validation
d. Two-factor authentication

Answer: c. Digital signature validation Explanation: In a Public Key Infrastructure (PKI), digital signature validation is the most essential capability for ensuring the authenticity of digital certificates. Digital signatures, created using the private key of the certificate issuer (Certification Authority), are used to verify that a certificate is genuine and has not been tampered with, thereby ensuring the integrity and authenticity of the certificate.

223. What is the primary function of an Identity and Access Management (IAM) system in securing information systems?
a. To encrypt data stored within the system
b. To detect and prevent network intrusions
c. To manage user identities and control access to resources
d. To back up data to ensure recoverability in case of loss

Answer: c. To manage user identities and control access to resources Explanation: The primary function of an Identity and Access Management (IAM) system is to manage user identities and control their access to resources within an information system. IAM systems enable the enforcement of security policies related to user authentication, authorization, roles, and privileges, ensuring that only authorized users can access specific resources based on their roles and permissions.

224. Which of the following represents a significant vulnerability in a web application architecture that relies heavily on third-party components?
a. The increased computational overhead of encryption algorithms
b. The potential for unpatched security flaws within the third-party components
c. The physical security controls at the data center hosting the application
d. The strength of the network's firewall rules governing outbound traffic

Answer: b. The potential for unpatched security flaws within the third-party components Explanation: Relying heavily on third-party components in a web application architecture can introduce significant vulnerabilities, particularly if these components are not regularly updated or patched. Unpatched security flaws within these components can be exploited by attackers, leading to potential security breaches. It's crucial for organizations to maintain an up-to-date inventory of all third-party components and ensure they apply security patches promptly.

225. In a distributed system design, which vulnerability is MOST likely to arise from inadequate session management controls?
a. Inefficient use of network bandwidth
b. Unauthorized access to sensitive information through session hijacking
c. Data corruption due to unsynchronized database transactions
d. Reduced system performance due to memory leaks

Answer: b. Unauthorized access to sensitive information through session hijacking Explanation: Inadequate session management controls in a distributed system design can lead to vulnerabilities such as unauthorized access to sensitive information through session hijacking. Attackers can exploit weak session management practices, such as predictable session IDs or insecure token storage, to take over a legitimate user's session and gain unauthorized access to the system.

226. What vulnerability is MOST associated with the use of outdated cryptographic algorithms in a security architecture?
a. Increased latency in data processing
b. Vulnerability to cryptanalysis and potential decryption of confidential data
c. Compatibility issues with newer communication protocols
d. Higher costs due to the need for specialized hardware

Answer: b. Vulnerability to cryptanalysis and potential decryption of confidential data Explanation: The use of outdated cryptographic algorithms in a security architecture introduces a vulnerability to cryptanalysis, where attackers could potentially decrypt confidential data. As cryptographic algorithms age, their resistance to various attack methods can diminish, making them more susceptible to being broken, especially as computational power increases.

227. Which vulnerability is introduced by implementing a Single Sign-On (SSO) solution without adequate session timeout policies?
a. Increased risk of brute force attacks due to single authentication point
b. Potential for denial-of-service attacks due to increased authentication traffic
c. Unauthorized access due to abandoned sessions remaining active
d. Encryption overhead leading to decreased system performance

Answer: c. Unauthorized access due to abandoned sessions remaining active Explanation: Implementing a Single Sign-On (SSO) solution without adequate session timeout policies introduces the vulnerability of unauthorized access due to abandoned sessions remaining active. If a user fails to log out and the session does not automatically timeout after a period of inactivity, an attacker could potentially gain access to the user's session and thereby access multiple applications or services authenticated through the SSO system.

228. In a microservices architecture, what vulnerability is MOST likely to be exacerbated by the lack of effective service isolation?
a. The complexity of managing API versioning
b. The risk of a single point of failure affecting the entire system
c. The propagation of a breach from one service to others in the network
d. Resource contention among services leading to performance bottlenecks

Answer: c. The propagation of a breach from one service to others in the network Explanation: In a microservices architecture, the lack of effective service isolation can exacerbate the vulnerability of a breach propagating from one service to others in the network. If services are not adequately isolated, an attacker who gains access to one service could leverage that access to move laterally within the system, potentially compromising additional services.

229. What is the primary security concern with implementing default configurations in network devices?
a. The devices may not support the latest security protocols
b. Default configurations are often well-known and can be easily exploited
c. Custom configurations tend to be less stable and more prone to errors
d. Default settings may not be optimized for performance, leading to latency

Answer: b. Default configurations are often well-known and can be easily exploited Explanation: The primary security concern with implementing default configurations in network devices is that these configurations are often well-known and can be easily exploited by attackers. Many default usernames, passwords, and settings are publicly documented, making devices with default configurations vulnerable to unauthorized access and attacks.

230. How does the lack of secure coding practices in software development introduce vulnerabilities?
a. By increasing the time required for code compilation
b. By leading to the inclusion of hard-coded credentials and susceptible code to injection attacks
c. By requiring additional hardware resources for deployment
d. By making the application incompatible with certain browsers or operating systems

Answer: b. By leading to the inclusion of hard-coded credentials and susceptible code to injection attacks Explanation: The lack of secure coding practices in software development introduces vulnerabilities such as the inclusion of hard-coded credentials and code that is susceptible to injection attacks. Without adherence to secure coding standards, developers might inadvertently write code that exposes the application to various forms of attack, such as SQL injection, cross-site scripting, or the unauthorized use of embedded credentials.

231. What security issue arises from the improper implementation of an API gateway in a service-oriented architecture?
a. Unnecessary duplication of services leading to increased costs
b. Inadequate load balancing resulting in service outages
c. Exposure to API-based attacks due to insufficient input validation
d. Increased latency due to additional hops in the network traffic

Answer: c. Exposure to API-based attacks due to insufficient input validation Explanation: The improper implementation of an API gateway in a service-oriented architecture can lead to exposure to API-based attacks due to insufficient input validation. If the API gateway does not adequately validate incoming requests, it can become a vector for attacks such as SQL injection, command injection, or other exploits that leverage improperly handled input.

232. Which of the following vulnerabilities is MOST likely to be found in a legacy system that has not been regularly updated?
a. Incompatibility with modern encryption standards
b. The presence of undocumented backdoor accounts
c. The exploitation of unpatched software vulnerabilities
d. Over-reliance on physical security measures

Answer: c. The exploitation of unpatched software vulnerabilities Explanation: A legacy system that has not been regularly updated is most likely to be vulnerable to the exploitation of unpatched software vulnerabilities. Over time, vulnerabilities in software are discovered and patched by vendors; however, systems that do not receive these updates remain susceptible to attacks that exploit known vulnerabilities.

233. What security risk is MOST associated with the use of containerization in application deployment without proper container management and isolation?
a. The high cost of scaling containerized applications
b. The potential for "container breakout," where an attacker gains access to the host system
c. The difficulty in monitoring the performance of individual containers
d. The complexity of network configuration for container communication

Answer: b. The potential for "container breakout," where an attacker gains access to the host system Explanation: The use of containerization in application deployment without proper container management and isolation introduces the risk of "container breakout." In such scenarios, an attacker who compromises one container could exploit vulnerabilities to escape the container environment and gain unauthorized access to the host system or other containers, posing a significant security risk.

234. What vulnerability is most commonly exploited in web-based systems through unsanitized user input?
a. Denial of Service (DoS)
b. SQL Injection
c. Buffer Overflow
d. Cross-Site Scripting (XSS)

Answer: b. SQL Injection Explanation: SQL Injection exploits occur when an attacker is able to insert or "inject" a SQL query via the input data from the client to the application. This happens in web-based systems that do not properly sanitize user input, allowing attackers to execute malicious SQL statements that can read sensitive data from the database, modify database data, execute administration operations, or even issue commands to the operating system in some cases.

235. Which vulnerability can be exploited by an attacker to impersonate another user's session in a web-based application?
a. Cross-Site Request Forgery (CSRF)
b. Session Hijacking
c. Man-in-the-Middle Attack
d. Cross-Site Scripting (XSS)

Answer: b. Session Hijacking Explanation: Session Hijacking involves an attacker exploiting the web session control mechanism to steal or impersonate a legitimate user's session token. By obtaining the session token, an attacker can gain unauthorized access to the web application as the legitimate user, bypassing authentication mechanisms.

236. In web-based systems, what vulnerability arises from allowing unrestricted file uploads?
a. Poor network performance
b. Uncontrolled format string
c. Arbitrary file execution
d. Insufficient logging and monitoring

Answer: c. Arbitrary file execution Explanation: Allowing unrestricted file uploads in web-based systems can lead to arbitrary file execution vulnerabilities. Attackers might upload malicious files that can be executed on the server, potentially leading to unauthorized access, data leakage, or server compromise. This underscores the importance of validating and sanitizing all uploaded files, including checking file types and content.

237. What is the main security risk of Cross-Site Scripting (XSS) in web applications?
a. Unauthorized access to server configuration files
b. Execution of malicious scripts in the browser of a user
c. Physical damage to the server hardware
d. Overloading the server with requests

Answer: b. Execution of malicious scripts in the browser of a user Explanation: Cross-Site Scripting (XSS) vulnerabilities allow attackers to inject malicious scripts into web pages viewed by other users. These scripts run in the context of the user's browser, potentially leading to session hijacking, defacement of web sites, redirection to malicious sites, or phishing attacks, among other threats.

238. How does a Cross-Site Request Forgery (CSRF) attack exploit web-based systems?

a. By decrypting encrypted data transmitted over SSL/TLS
b. By exhausting system resources through repeated requests
c. By tricking a user into executing unwanted actions on a web application where they are authenticated
d. By intercepting and altering communication between two parties

Answer: c. By tricking a user into executing unwanted actions on a web application where they are authenticated
Explanation: A Cross-Site Request Forgery (CSRF) attack tricks the victim into executing unwanted actions on a web application in which they are currently authenticated. An attacker could potentially exploit this vulnerability to submit a malicious request through the victim's browser, unknowingly performing actions on behalf of the attacker, such as transferring funds or changing email addresses.

239. Which type of vulnerability is specifically addressed by implementing Content Security Policy (CSP) headers in web-based systems?
a. SQL Injection
b. Cross-Site Scripting (XSS)
c. Insecure Direct Object References
d. Security Misconfiguration

Answer: b. Cross-Site Scripting (XSS) Explanation: Content Security Policy (CSP) is a security standard introduced to prevent Cross-Site Scripting (XSS) attacks. By implementing CSP headers, web developers can control the resources that the browser is allowed to load for a given page, effectively reducing the risk of XSS attacks by specifying which scripts are allowed to run and from where.

240. In web-based systems, what vulnerability results from inadequate encryption of sensitive data during transmission?
a. Information Disclosure
b. Broken Authentication
c. Sensitive Data Exposure
d. Insecure Deserialization

Answer: c. Sensitive Data Exposure Explanation: Sensitive Data Exposure occurs in web-based systems when sensitive data, such as financial, healthcare, or personal information, is inadequately protected during transmission. This can happen if encryption is not used or if weak encryption algorithms are employed, allowing attackers to intercept and read the data, leading to potential data breaches and privacy violations.

241. What is the primary security concern with Directory Traversal vulnerabilities in web applications?
a. Unauthorized access to restricted directories and files on the server
b. Flooding the server with traffic to disrupt service
c. Injecting malicious code into the server's database
d. Forging the authentication tokens of other users

Answer: a. Unauthorized access to restricted directories and files on the server Explanation: Directory Traversal vulnerabilities, also known as Path Traversal vulnerabilities, allow attackers to access restricted directories and execute commands outside of the web server's root directory. This can lead to unauthorized access to system files, directories, and sensitive information, potentially compromising the security of the entire system.

242. How does a web application firewall (WAF) mitigate the risk of application-layer attacks on web-based systems?
a. By encrypting data at rest on the server
b. By analyzing HTTP/HTTPS traffic and blocking malicious requests
c. By physically securing the server in a locked facility
d. By performing regular backups of the web application's data

Answer: b. By analyzing HTTP/HTTPS traffic and blocking malicious requests Explanation: A web application firewall (WAF) is designed to monitor, filter, and block HTTP/HTTPS traffic to and from a web application. By analyzing the traffic, a WAF can identify and block malicious requests that aim to exploit vulnerabilities in the application layer, such as SQL injection, XSS, CSRF, and other common web-based attacks, thereby mitigating the risk of these threats.

243. What risk does the use of insecure third-party libraries pose to web-based systems?
a. Increased load times due to inefficient code
b. Compatibility issues with modern web browsers
c. Introduction of vulnerabilities that can be exploited by attackers
d. Legal ramifications due to licensing conflicts

Answer: c. Introduction of vulnerabilities that can be exploited by attackers Explanation: The use of insecure third-party libraries in web-based systems introduces vulnerabilities that can be exploited by attackers. These libraries may contain security flaws that, if not properly vetted and updated, can compromise the security of the entire application. Regularly auditing and updating third-party libraries is essential to maintaining the security integrity of web-based systems.

244. What vulnerability is primarily introduced by "jailbreaking" or "rooting" a mobile device?
a. Decreased battery life
b. Unauthorized access to device administrative privileges
c. Incompatibility with official app stores
d. Increased data usage rates

Answer: b. Unauthorized access to device administrative privileges Explanation: Jailbreaking (iOS) or rooting (Android) a mobile device removes manufacturer or carrier restrictions, allowing the user to gain unauthorized access to the device's administrative privileges. This can introduce significant security vulnerabilities, such as the ability to bypass security mechanisms, install unauthorized apps, and modify system settings, potentially exposing the device to malware and other threats.

245. Which of the following represents a significant security risk specific to mobile devices when connecting to unsecured Wi-Fi networks?
a. Excessive data charges from the mobile carrier
b. Automatic synchronization of all cloud-based accounts
c. Interception of data transmission by unauthorized third parties
d. Involuntary participation in a botnet

Answer: c. Interception of data transmission by unauthorized third parties Explanation: Connecting to unsecured Wi-Fi networks on mobile devices poses a significant security risk as it can allow unauthorized third parties to intercept data transmission. This can lead to the exposure of sensitive information such as login credentials, personal data, and other confidential communications, making it a critical vulnerability in mobile security.

246. What is the main security concern with mobile apps that request excessive permissions beyond their functionality needs?
a. Reduced device performance due to resource overutilization
b. User dissatisfaction and poor app reviews
c. Potential for privacy breaches and unauthorized access to sensitive data
d. Increased storage requirements on the device

Answer: c. Potential for privacy breaches and unauthorized access to sensitive data Explanation: Mobile apps that request excessive permissions beyond what their functionality would reasonably require pose a significant security concern. These permissions can provide the app, and potentially malicious actors, access to sensitive data and device features (such as contacts, camera, microphone, location), leading to privacy breaches and unauthorized data access.

247. In mobile device security, what vulnerability does "side-loading" of apps introduce?
a. Compatibility issues with the device's operating system
b. Circumvention of official app store security screenings
c. Automatic deletion of less frequently used apps
d. Conflict with pre-installed device applications

Answer: b. Circumvention of official app store security screenings Explanation: "Side-loading" refers to the installation of apps from sources other than the device's official app store. This practice introduces vulnerabilities by circumventing the security screenings and checks that official app stores typically perform, potentially exposing the device to malicious apps that could contain malware or exploit device vulnerabilities.

248. How does the use of outdated mobile operating systems contribute to system vulnerabilities?
a. Incompatibility with modern mobile applications
b. Increased likelihood of exploiting unpatched security flaws
c. Reduction in device resale value
d. Limited access to newer, more secure communication protocols

Answer: b. Increased likelihood of exploiting unpatched security flaws Explanation: Using outdated mobile operating systems contributes to system vulnerabilities by increasing the likelihood of exploiting unpatched security flaws. Manufacturers release updates to fix known vulnerabilities; when devices do not receive these updates, they remain susceptible to attacks that target these unpatched flaws, compromising device security.

249. What is a common vulnerability associated with the use of third-party app stores on mobile devices?
a. Elevated data consumption due to ad-supported apps
b. Distribution of apps with potentially malicious code
c. Loss of warranty coverage for the mobile device
d. Decreased availability of app updates

Answer: b. Distribution of apps with potentially malicious code Explanation: A common vulnerability associated with the use of third-party app stores is the distribution of apps that may contain potentially malicious code. Unlike official app stores that typically have strict app review processes, third-party stores may have laxer security standards, making it easier for apps with malicious intent to be distributed, posing significant security risks to users.

250. What security risk is posed by mobile devices that auto-connect to previously used Wi-Fi networks?
a. Unintended data sharing via peer-to-peer connections
b. Automatic download of large files, consuming data allowances
c. Connection to rogue networks masquerading as legitimate ones
d. Inability to connect to newer, more secure Wi-Fi networks

Answer: c. Connection to rogue networks masquerading as legitimate ones Explanation: Mobile devices that auto-connect to previously used Wi-Fi networks pose a security risk by potentially connecting to rogue networks that masquerade as legitimate ones. Attackers can set up rogue access points with the same SSID as trusted networks, tricking devices into connecting automatically, which can then be exploited to intercept sensitive data or launch attacks.

251. How do mobile ad networks potentially introduce security risks to mobile devices?
a. By consuming excessive battery life due to ad display
b. Through the inadvertent distribution of malicious ads (malvertising)
c. By using excessive device storage for ad caching
d. By limiting the functionality of ad-blocking software

Answer: b. Through the inadvertent distribution of malicious ads (malvertising) Explanation: Mobile ad networks can potentially introduce security risks through the inadvertent distribution of malicious ads, known as malvertising. These malicious ads can exploit vulnerabilities in the mobile device's software to deliver malware or perform other malicious activities without the user's knowledge or consent, posing a significant security threat.

252. What vulnerability is particularly concerning for mobile devices equipped with Near Field Communication (NFC) technology?
a. Incompatibility with older, non-NFC-enabled devices
b. Unauthorized data access or eavesdropping in close physical proximity
c. Interference with other wireless communication technologies
d. Increased battery consumption due to constant signal broadcasting

Answer: b. Unauthorized data access or eavesdropping in close physical proximity Explanation: Near Field Communication (NFC) technology introduces a vulnerability concerning unauthorized data access or eavesdropping when in close physical proximity. Since NFC is designed for short-range communication, an attacker could potentially access data or initiate unauthorized transactions if they come physically close enough to the target device, exploiting the NFC feature.

253. What risk is associated with the "Bring Your Own Device" (BYOD) policy in corporate environments, particularly concerning mobile devices?
a. Increased costs for mobile device management solutions
b. Difficulty in enforcing uniform security policies across diverse devices
c. Reduced employee satisfaction and productivity
d. Over-reliance on cloud-based storage solutions

Answer: b. Difficulty in enforcing uniform security policies across diverse devices Explanation: The "Bring Your Own Device" (BYOD) policy introduces the risk of difficulty in enforcing uniform security policies across diverse personal devices used in a corporate environment. This diversity can create challenges in managing and securing corporate data, as each device may have different security capabilities, operating systems, and levels of user control, making it harder to ensure that all devices adhere to the organization's security standards.

254. What vulnerability is most commonly associated with embedded devices that utilize hard-coded credentials?
a. Brute-force attacks
b. Physical tampering
c. Unauthorized remote access
d. Electromagnetic interference

Answer: c. Unauthorized remote access Explanation: Embedded devices that utilize hard-coded credentials are particularly vulnerable to unauthorized remote access. Attackers can exploit these static, unchangeable credentials, often found through reverse engineering or leaked documentation, to gain unauthorized access to the device. This vulnerability underscores the importance of implementing changeable and secure authentication mechanisms in embedded systems.

255. In the context of cyber-physical systems, what risk does the lack of timely firmware updates pose?
a. Decreased system performance over time
b. Incompatibility with newer hardware components
c. Exposure to known exploits and vulnerabilities
d. Increased power consumption

Answer: c. Exposure to known exploits and vulnerabilities Explanation: The lack of timely firmware updates in cyber-physical systems poses a significant risk by exposing these systems to known exploits and vulnerabilities. Firmware updates often contain patches for security vulnerabilities that have been discovered since the last update. Without these updates, systems remain vulnerable to attacks that could compromise their functionality and safety.

256. Which vulnerability is most concerning in embedded devices connected to the Internet of Things (IoT)?
a. Insufficient data encryption
b. Over-reliance on cloud-based storage solutions
c. Limited user interface options
d. Obsolescence of hardware components

Answer: a. Insufficient data encryption Explanation: Insufficient data encryption is a significant vulnerability in embedded devices connected to the Internet of Things (IoT). Without strong encryption, data transmitted to and from these devices can be intercepted and read by unauthorized parties, leading to potential data breaches and privacy violations.

257. What is a primary security concern with embedded devices used in industrial control systems?
a. The inability to function in high-temperature environments
b. The use of proprietary communication protocols
c. The potential for disruption of physical processes through cyber attacks
d. The requirement for continuous power supply

Answer: c. The potential for disruption of physical processes through cyber attacks Explanation: A primary security concern with embedded devices used in industrial control systems is the potential for disruption of physical processes through cyber attacks. These systems often control critical infrastructure and manufacturing processes; thus, a successful cyber attack could have severe real-world consequences, including damage to equipment, environmental harm, and risks to human safety.

258. How does the integration of embedded devices in medical equipment introduce vulnerabilities?
a. By increasing the complexity of the user interface
b. By enabling unauthorized access to patient data and device controls
c. By requiring frequent recalibration of the devices
d. By consuming excessive amounts of electrical power

Answer: b. By enabling unauthorized access to patient data and device controls Explanation: The integration of embedded devices in medical equipment introduces vulnerabilities by enabling unauthorized access to patient data and device controls. If these systems are not properly secured, attackers could potentially access sensitive health information or manipulate the functioning of medical devices, posing serious risks to patient privacy and safety.

259. What risk is associated with the use of legacy operating systems in embedded devices within critical infrastructure?
a. Incompatibility with modern networking standards
b. High replacement costs for outdated hardware
c. Exposure to unpatched security vulnerabilities
d. Difficulty in integrating with renewable energy sources

Answer: c. Exposure to unpatched security vulnerabilities Explanation: The use of legacy operating systems in embedded devices within critical infrastructure is associated with exposure to unpatched security vulnerabilities. These older systems may no longer receive security updates, leaving known vulnerabilities unaddressed and the infrastructure at risk of exploitation by attackers.

260. In cyber-physical systems, what vulnerability arises from inadequate segmentation of control networks?
a. Reduced efficiency due to network congestion
b. Potential for widespread system compromise from a single point of entry
c. Legal liability for non-compliance with industry standards
d. Increased maintenance costs due to network complexity

Answer: b. Potential for widespread system compromise from a single point of entry Explanation: Inadequate segmentation of control networks in cyber-physical systems creates a vulnerability where a single point of entry can lead to widespread system compromise. Without proper network segmentation, an attacker gaining access to one part of the network can more easily move laterally to other parts, potentially taking control of critical system functions.

261. What security challenge is presented by the increasing use of wireless communication in embedded industrial devices?
a. The physical obstruction of signal transmission
b. The susceptibility to eavesdropping and interception of data
c. The need for line-of-sight between communication endpoints
d. The high cost of wireless infrastructure deployment

Answer: b. The susceptibility to eavesdropping and interception of data Explanation: The increasing use of wireless communication in embedded industrial devices presents a security challenge in the form of susceptibility to eavesdropping and interception of data. Wireless signals can be intercepted by unauthorized individuals beyond the physical boundaries of the facility, making it crucial to implement strong encryption and other security measures to protect the transmitted data.

262. How do "backdoor" vulnerabilities in embedded systems pose a risk to organizational security?
a. By enabling unauthorized users to bypass normal authentication processes
b. By causing the system to reboot unexpectedly
c. By limiting the functionality available to the system administrator
d. By increasing the system's vulnerability to power surges

Answer: a. By enabling unauthorized users to bypass normal authentication processes Explanation: "Backdoor" vulnerabilities in embedded systems pose a significant risk to organizational security by enabling unauthorized users to bypass normal authentication processes. These hidden pathways, intentionally or unintentionally created, can be exploited by attackers to gain access to the system without detection, allowing them to carry out malicious activities, access sensitive information, or take control of the system.

263. What is the impact of "firmware rollback" attacks on embedded devices?
a. Premature depletion of the device's power source
b. Reversion to a previous firmware version with known vulnerabilities
c. Physical damage to the device's hardware components
d. Corruption of data stored on the device

Answer: b. Reversion to a previous firmware version with known vulnerabilities Explanation: "Firmware rollback" attacks on embedded devices involve forcing a device to revert to a previous firmware version that contains known vulnerabilities. Attackers exploit these vulnerabilities to compromise the device, bypassing the security improvements and patches that were implemented in later firmware versions. This type of attack underscores the importance of secure firmware update mechanisms that prevent unauthorized downgrades.

264. What is the primary function of asymmetric cryptography in secure communications?
a. To ensure message integrity and non-repudiation with digital signatures
b. To compress data for faster transmission
c. To symmetrically encrypt large volumes of data for storage
d. To detect and prevent intrusion attempts on the network

Answer: a. To ensure message integrity and non-repudiation with digital signatures Explanation: Asymmetric cryptography, also known as public-key cryptography, uses a pair of keys (public and private) for secure communications. Its primary functions include ensuring message integrity and providing non-repudiation through the use of digital signatures. A digital signature, created using the sender's private key, can be verified by anyone having the corresponding public key, proving that the message was not altered (integrity) and was indeed sent by the holder of the private key (non-repudiation).

265. Which cryptographic attack involves trying every possible key until the correct one is found?
a. Man-in-the-middle attack
b. Birthday attack
c. Brute force attack
d. Side-channel attack

Answer: c. Brute force attack Explanation: A brute force attack in cryptography involves trying every possible key or password until the correct one is discovered. This type of attack can be time-consuming and resource-intensive but is guaranteed to find the key given enough time and computational resources. The feasibility of such an attack depends largely on the length and complexity of the key.

266. In the context of cryptographic hash functions, what property ensures that any change to the input will produce a significantly different output?
a. Collision resistance
b. High entropy
c. Avalanche effect
d. Perfect forward secrecy

Answer: c. Avalanche effect Explanation: The avalanche effect in cryptographic hash functions is a desirable property that ensures even a small change in the input (like changing a single bit) will produce a significantly different output (hash value). This property is crucial for security purposes, as it makes it infeasible to predict how a change in input will affect the output, thereby ensuring the integrity of the data.

267. What is the main purpose of a Diffie-Hellman key exchange in a secure communication protocol?
a. To digitally sign a document ensuring non-repudiation
b. To establish a shared secret over an insecure channel
c. To encrypt data using a symmetric key algorithm
d. To authenticate the identity of a message sender

Answer: b. To establish a shared secret over an insecure channel Explanation: The Diffie-Hellman key exchange is a method used in cryptography to establish a shared secret between two parties over an insecure communication channel. This shared secret can then be used to encrypt further communications using a symmetric key algorithm. The protocol allows secure key exchange without the need for the parties to have had prior interactions.

268. Which type of cryptographic algorithm is considered unbreakable when used correctly?
a. RSA algorithm
b. Elliptic Curve Cryptography (ECC)
c. One-Time Pad (OTP)
d. Advanced Encryption Standard (AES)

Answer: c. One-Time Pad (OTP) Explanation: The One-Time Pad (OTP) is considered unbreakable when used correctly, adhering to its three main rules: the key must be truly random, at least as long as the message, and used only once. The absolute randomness and single-use nature of the key ensure that there is no pattern or repetition to exploit, making it theoretically secure against any form of cryptanalysis.

269. What cryptographic principle is primarily used in blockchain technology to ensure the integrity of the transaction chain?
a. Homomorphic encryption
b. Hash functions linking blocks
c. Quantum key distribution
d. Steganography

Answer: b. Hash functions linking blocks Explanation: Blockchain technology uses cryptographic hash functions to link blocks in the chain, ensuring the integrity of the transaction history. Each block contains a hash of the previous block, creating a secure chain where altering a single block would invalidate all subsequent blocks' hashes, thereby protecting against tampering and ensuring data integrity.

270. Which cryptographic protocol is commonly used to secure web transactions indicated by "https://" in a web browser?
a. Secure Shell (SSH)
b. Transport Layer Security (TLS)
c. Pretty Good Privacy (PGP)
d. Internet Protocol Security (IPSec)

Answer: b. Transport Layer Security (TLS) Explanation: The Transport Layer Security (TLS) protocol is commonly used to secure web transactions, as indicated by "https://" in a web browser's address bar. TLS provides confidentiality, integrity, and authenticity for data communications over the internet, ensuring secure exchanges between web servers and clients.

271. In Elliptic Curve Cryptography (ECC), what is the significance of the "curve" used in cryptographic operations?
a. It determines the algorithm's speed and efficiency.
b. It acts as the public key for encrypting messages.
c. It provides the mathematical foundation for generating keys and encrypting data.
d. It represents the physical path data takes when encrypted.

Answer: c. It provides the mathematical foundation for generating keys and encrypting data. Explanation: In Elliptic Curve Cryptography (ECC), the "curve" refers to the elliptic curve used, which provides the mathematical foundation for cryptographic operations such as key generation and data encryption. The properties of the curve, defined by its equation, are crucial for the security and efficiency of the ECC system.

272. What is the main advantage of using symmetric key cryptography over asymmetric key cryptography?
a. It provides a method for digital signatures.
b. It is more secure against quantum computing attacks.
c. It is generally faster and requires less computational power.
d. It allows for secure key exchange over an insecure channel.

Answer: c. It is generally faster and requires less computational power. Explanation: The main advantage of using symmetric key cryptography over asymmetric key cryptography is its efficiency. Symmetric key algorithms are generally faster and require less computational power than asymmetric algorithms, making them more suitable for encrypting large volumes of data or for use in environments with limited processing capabilities.

273. How does a Certificate Authority (CA) contribute to the security of a Public Key Infrastructure (PKI)?

a. By distributing symmetric keys to users
b. By ensuring the physical security of the network infrastructure
c. By issuing digital certificates that verify the ownership of public keys
d. By encrypting data stored on the server

Answer: c. By issuing digital certificates that verify the ownership of public keys Explanation: In a Public Key Infrastructure (PKI), a Certificate Authority (CA) contributes to security by issuing digital certificates that verify the ownership of public keys. These certificates bind a public key to the identity of the entity that owns the corresponding private key, facilitating secure communication, data encryption, and digital signatures among parties that trust the CA.

274. What principle is most important when designing the physical layout of a data center to ensure security?
a. Open floor plans to facilitate ease of access for maintenance personnel
b. Zoning to separate different levels of security and restrict access accordingly
c. Centralized placement of server racks for efficient cooling
d. Glass walls for visibility and transparency

Answer: b. Zoning to separate different levels of security and restrict access accordingly Explanation: Zoning is a critical principle in the secure design of data centers, as it involves dividing the facility into different areas or zones with varying security levels. This approach restricts access to sensitive areas, ensuring that only authorized personnel can enter specific zones based on their security clearance and the principle of least privilege, thereby enhancing the overall security of the facility.

275. In the context of physical security, what is the primary purpose of employing mantraps in a secure facility?
a. To provide a rest area for security personnel
b. To detect and prevent tailgating by unauthorized individuals
c. To facilitate the evacuation of personnel in emergencies
d. To serve as a reception area for visitors

Answer: b. To detect and prevent tailgating by unauthorized individuals Explanation: Mantraps are security devices that consist of two or more interlocking doors. They are employed in secure facilities to control access points and prevent tailgating, where an unauthorized individual follows an authorized person into a restricted area. By allowing only one door to open at a time and often requiring authentication before proceeding, mantraps effectively reduce the risk of unauthorized access.

276. What is the key consideration when implementing perimeter security controls such as fences and gates around a facility?
a. Aesthetics and the architectural theme of the surrounding area
b. The speed at which individuals can enter and exit the facility
c. The ability to withstand and delay unauthorized access attempts
d. Cost-effectiveness compared to electronic security measures

Answer: c. The ability to withstand and delay unauthorized access attempts Explanation: The key consideration when implementing perimeter security controls like fences and gates is their ability to withstand and delay unauthorized access attempts. The primary function of these physical barriers is to protect the facility by providing a robust first line of defense that deters, detects, and delays intruders, giving security personnel time to respond to potential breaches.

277. How do environmental controls contribute to the secure design of a site or facility?
a. By ensuring comfortable working conditions for employees
b. By optimizing the energy efficiency of the facility
c. By protecting sensitive equipment from environmental hazards
d. By enhancing the aesthetic appeal of the facility

Answer: c. By protecting sensitive equipment from environmental hazards Explanation: Environmental controls in the context of secure site or facility design are crucial for protecting sensitive equipment and systems from environmental hazards such as excessive heat, humidity, water damage, and dust. These controls, including HVAC systems, fire suppression systems, and dust filters, help maintain optimal operating conditions and prevent equipment failure, data loss, or other damages that could compromise security.

278. What role does surveillance play in the secure design of a facility's access points?
a. To provide a live feed for public viewing and transparency
b. To record daily operations for productivity analysis
c. To monitor and record access for security reviews and incident investigations
d. To entertain and inform visitors in waiting areas

Answer: c. To monitor and record access for security reviews and incident investigations Explanation: Surveillance systems, particularly cameras positioned at access points, play a critical role in the secure design of a facility by monitoring and recording who enters and exits. This footage is invaluable for security reviews, incident investigations, and verifying compliance with access control policies, thereby enhancing the overall security posture of the facility.

279. In securing a facility, why is it important to implement lighting around the perimeter and access points?
a. To create an inviting atmosphere for visitors and employees
b. To highlight architectural features of the facility
c. To deter unauthorized access by increasing visibility
d. To reduce the energy consumption of indoor lighting

Answer: c. To deter unauthorized access by increasing visibility Explanation: Adequate lighting around the perimeter and access points of a facility is a fundamental security measure designed to deter unauthorized access. Well-lit areas increase visibility, making it more difficult for intruders to approach or tamper with the facility unnoticed. This visibility acts as a deterrent and also aids surveillance efforts by ensuring clear camera footage.

280. What is the significance of implementing redundancy in the power supply systems of critical facilities?
a. To ensure continuous operation during power outages

b. To reduce the facility's carbon footprint
c. To comply with local building codes and regulations
d. To decrease operational costs over time

Answer: a. To ensure continuous operation during power outages Explanation: Implementing redundancy in power supply systems, such as having backup generators and uninterruptible power supplies (UPS), is crucial for critical facilities to ensure continuous operation during power outages. This redundancy is vital for maintaining the availability of critical systems and services, preventing downtime, and mitigating the risk of data loss or other adverse consequences resulting from power interruptions.

281. In site and facility security design, what is the purpose of using biometric access control systems?
a. To provide a backup method of access in case of lost keys or cards
b. To offer a personalized experience to each facility user
c. To enhance security by verifying individuals' unique physical or behavioral traits
d. To streamline the check-in process for large volumes of visitors

Answer: c. To enhance security by verifying individuals' unique physical or behavioral traits Explanation: Biometric access control systems enhance the security of a site or facility by verifying individuals based on their unique physical or behavioral traits, such as fingerprints, facial recognition, or iris scans. Unlike traditional keys or cards, which can be lost, stolen, or shared, biometrics provides a more secure and non-transferable method of authentication, significantly reducing the risk of unauthorized access.

282. How does the principle of "defense in depth" apply to the physical security of a facility?
a. By focusing all security measures at the main entrance to create a single, impenetrable barrier
b. By employing a single, advanced security technology throughout the facility for consistency
c. By layering multiple security controls throughout the facility to provide redundancy
d. By prioritizing aesthetic considerations to disguise security measures

Answer: c. By layering multiple security controls throughout the facility to provide redundancy Explanation: The principle of "defense in depth" in physical security involves layering multiple security controls and measures throughout a facility to provide redundancy and increase the overall security posture. This approach ensures that if one security layer is breached or fails, additional layers provide continued protection, making it more challenging for unauthorized access to occur and giving security personnel more time to respond to incidents.

283. What is the primary consideration when designing the emergency evacuation routes for a secure facility?
a. The routes should be complex to confuse potential intruders
b. The routes should be discreet and only known to a select few for security reasons
c. The routes should be clearly marked and easily accessible for all occupants
d. The routes should pass through the most secure areas to protect sensitive information

Answer: c. The routes should be clearly marked and easily accessible for all occupants Explanation: The primary consideration when designing emergency evacuation routes for a secure facility is to ensure that the routes are clearly marked and easily accessible for all occupants, regardless of their location within the facility. In the event of an emergency, such as a fire, natural disaster, or security threat, it is crucial that individuals can quickly and safely exit the facility to minimize the risk of injury or loss of life.

284. What is the primary purpose of a Virtual Private Network (VPN) in organizational communications?
a. To reduce the cost of long-distance telephone charges
b. To increase the speed of data transmission over the internet
c. To secure communications over untrusted networks such as the internet
d. To broadcast messages to a large number of recipients simultaneously

Answer: c. To secure communications over untrusted networks such as the internet Explanation: A Virtual Private Network (VPN) is primarily used to secure communications over untrusted networks, such as the internet, by establishing encrypted tunnels between devices. This ensures that data transmitted over these tunnels remains confidential and secure from eavesdropping, even when traversing potentially insecure or public networks.

285. Which protocol is essential for securing HTTP traffic between a web server and a client?
a. FTPS
b. SSH
c. TLS
d. SNMP

Answer: c. TLS Explanation: Transport Layer Security (TLS) is the protocol essential for securing HTTP traffic between a web server and a client, commonly referred to as HTTPS when used with HTTP. TLS provides confidentiality, integrity, and authentication for web communications, ensuring that data exchanged between the web server and the client is encrypted and secure from interception or tampering.

286. In network security, what is the function of an Intrusion Detection System (IDS)?
a. To filter out spam from email traffic
b. To provide a secure channel for VoIP communications
c. To monitor network traffic for suspicious activities and potential threats
d. To allocate bandwidth efficiently among different applications

Answer: c. To monitor network traffic for suspicious activities and potential threats Explanation: An Intrusion Detection System (IDS) is designed to monitor network traffic for suspicious activities and potential threats. By analyzing traffic patterns and comparing them against a database of known attack signatures, an IDS can identify and alert administrators to possible intrusions or security breaches, contributing to the overall security posture of the network.

287. What principle does the Secure Sockets Layer (SSL) protocol use to ensure the confidentiality and integrity of data transmission?

a. Tokenization
b. Public key encryption
c. Subnet masking
d. Bandwidth throttling

Answer: b. Public key encryption Explanation: The Secure Sockets Layer (SSL) protocol, which is the predecessor to Transport Layer Security (TLS), uses public key encryption to ensure the confidentiality and integrity of data transmission. In this process, SSL uses asymmetric cryptography for key exchange and symmetric encryption for data transmission, providing a secure channel over the internet.

288. How do firewalls contribute to network security?
a. By accelerating data transfer rates for authorized services
b. By serving as a distribution point for software updates
c. By inspecting and filtering incoming and outgoing network traffic based on predefined security rules
d. By providing redundant connections to critical network resources

Answer: c. By inspecting and filtering incoming and outgoing network traffic based on predefined security rules Explanation: Firewalls contribute to network security by inspecting and filtering incoming and outgoing network traffic based on predefined security rules. They act as a barrier between secure internal networks and untrusted external networks, such as the internet, allowing or blocking traffic based on the firewall's configuration and security policies.

289. What is the primary security concern addressed by the implementation of Secure/Multipurpose Internet Mail Extensions (S/MIME) in email communications?
a. Email address spoofing
b. Unwanted email advertisements
c. Confidentiality and integrity of email messages
d. Congestion control on email servers

Answer: c. Confidentiality and integrity of email messages Explanation: Secure/Multipurpose Internet Mail Extensions (S/MIME) is a standard used to secure email communications by providing encryption for message confidentiality and digital signatures for message integrity and authentication. S/MIME ensures that email content is encrypted, so only the intended recipient can read it, and that the message has not been altered in transit, addressing the primary security concerns of confidentiality and integrity in email communications.

290. In the context of network security, what role does a demilitarized zone (DMZ) play?
a. To provide a secure area for the storage of sensitive data
b. To act as a buffer zone between the public internet and an internal network
c. To encrypt data before it is stored on cloud servers
d. To distribute network traffic evenly across multiple servers

Answer: b. To act as a buffer zone between the public internet and an internal network Explanation: A demilitarized zone (DMZ) in network security serves as a buffer zone or perimeter network that separates the public internet from an organization's internal, more secure network. The DMZ hosts public-facing services (such as web servers and email servers) that need to be accessible from the internet but also need to be isolated from the internal network to reduce the risk of external attacks reaching the internal network.

291. What is the primary function of the Internet Protocol Security (IPSec) suite in a network?
a. To manage IP addresses dynamically
b. To prioritize certain types of network traffic
c. To secure IP communications by authenticating and encrypting each IP packet
d. To compress IP packets to reduce bandwidth usage

Answer: c. To secure IP communications by authenticating and encrypting each IP packet Explanation: The primary function of the Internet Protocol Security (IPSec) suite is to secure IP communications across an IP network by authenticating and encrypting each IP packet of a communication session. IPSec provides a secure tunnel for data transmission, ensuring confidentiality, integrity, and authenticity of the data as it traverses insecure networks such as the internet.

292. In network design, what is the purpose of implementing network segmentation?
a. To combine voice and data networks for easier management
b. To isolate different types of traffic for security and performance reasons
c. To allow for the use of legacy networking equipment
d. To reduce the overall cost of network infrastructure

Answer: b. To isolate different types of traffic for security and performance reasons Explanation: Network segmentation is the practice of dividing a computer network into subnetworks, each being a network segment, to isolate different types of traffic for security and performance reasons. This isolation helps contain security breaches within a segment, reduces the attack surface, and can improve performance by limiting broadcast traffic, thereby enhancing the overall security and efficiency of the network.

293. What technology is primarily used to prevent eavesdropping on wireless networks?
a. Quality of Service (QoS)
b. Wireless Access Points (WAPs)
c. Wired Equivalent Privacy (WEP) and Wi-Fi Protected Access (WPA/WPA2)
d. Virtual LANs (VLANs)

Answer: c. Wired Equivalent Privacy (WEP) and Wi-Fi Protected Access (WPA/WPA2) Explanation: Wired Equivalent Privacy (WEP) and Wi-Fi Protected Access (WPA/WPA2) are technologies primarily used to secure wireless networks and prevent eavesdropping. WEP is an older, less secure protocol, while WPA and WPA2 provide stronger security measures by encrypting data transmitted over wireless networks, ensuring that the data cannot be easily intercepted or understood by unauthorized individuals.

294. How does implementing VLANs contribute to secure network architecture?
a. By encrypting data packets transmitted over the network
b. By physically separating network devices based on function
c. By controlling broadcast domains within a larger network
d. By increasing the bandwidth available to network devices

Answer: c. By controlling broadcast domains within a larger network Explanation: VLANs (Virtual Local Area Networks) contribute to secure network architecture by logically segmenting networks into smaller broadcast domains. This segmentation allows for better control over who can access specific parts of the network, enhancing security by isolating sensitive data and devices from the rest of the network. VLANs enforce segmentation policies without the need for physical separation, making them a flexible and effective security tool.

295. In the context of secure network design, what is the primary purpose of a DMZ (Demilitarized Zone)?
a. To provide a public Wi-Fi network for visitors
b. To host external services that need to be accessible from the internet
c. To serve as a backup storage area for sensitive data
d. To monitor and filter outbound employee internet traffic

Answer: b. To host external services that need to be accessible from the internet Explanation: The primary purpose of a DMZ in secure network design is to host external services, such as web servers, email servers, and DNS servers, that need to be accessible from the internet. The DMZ acts as a buffer zone between the untrusted public internet and the internal trusted network, providing an additional layer of security by isolating these services from direct access to the internal network.

296. What role does network segmentation play in enhancing network security?
a. To consolidate network resources and reduce hardware costs
b. To distribute internet traffic evenly across all network devices
c. To limit the spread of attacks and breaches within a network
d. To provide redundant network paths for data backup

Answer: c. To limit the spread of attacks and breaches within a network Explanation: Network segmentation plays a crucial role in enhancing network security by dividing the network into smaller, isolated segments. This segmentation limits the spread of attacks and breaches within the network, as attackers gain access to only a portion of the network, protecting other segments from compromise. It also allows for more granular enforcement of security policies and controls, tailored to the specific needs of each segment.

297. Why is it important to secure network devices with protocols like SSH (Secure Shell) instead of Telnet?
a. SSH provides faster data transfer rates than Telnet
b. SSH allows for the transmission of multimedia content, while Telnet does not
c. SSH encrypts the entire session, including login credentials, while Telnet transmits data in plaintext
d. SSH is compatible with more operating systems than Telnet

Answer: c. SSH encrypts the entire session, including login credentials, while Telnet transmits data in plaintext
Explanation: Securing network devices with SSH instead of Telnet is crucial because SSH encrypts the entire communication session, including login credentials, providing confidentiality and integrity. In contrast, Telnet transmits all data, including passwords, in plaintext, making it susceptible to eavesdropping and interception. SSH ensures that sensitive information remains secure, even over untrusted networks.

298. What is the significance of using IPsec for securing IP communications between networks?
a. It provides a mechanism for dynamic IP address allocation
b. It compresses IP packets to optimize bandwidth usage
c. It authenticates and encrypts each IP packet in a data stream
d. It prioritizes IP packets for quality of service (QoS)

Answer: c. It authenticates and encrypts each IP packet in a data stream Explanation: The significance of using IPsec (Internet Protocol Security) for securing IP communications lies in its ability to authenticate and encrypt each IP packet in a data stream. This ensures the confidentiality, integrity, and authenticity of data as it traverses untrusted networks, such as the internet. IPsec is widely used in VPNs and site-to-site connections to secure data communications between networks.

299. How does implementing an intrusion prevention system (IPS) enhance network security?
a. By increasing the data transfer speeds across the network
b. By providing a backup solution for data storage
c. By actively detecting and preventing potential threats in real-time
d. By reducing the physical distance between network nodes

Answer: c. By actively detecting and preventing potential threats in real-time Explanation: An intrusion prevention system (IPS) enhances network security by actively monitoring network traffic for suspicious activities and known attack patterns. Unlike an intrusion detection system (IDS), which only alerts on potential threats, an IPS can actively block or prevent these threats in real-time, thereby reducing the risk of successful attacks and enhancing the overall security posture of the network.

300. In secure network architecture, what is the purpose of using end-to-end encryption?
a. To reduce the overhead caused by encryption and decryption processes
b. To ensure that data remains encrypted and unreadable from source to destination
c. To increase the speed of data transmission over the network
d. To provide a centralized encryption service for all network devices

Answer: b. To ensure that data remains encrypted and unreadable from source to destination Explanation: The purpose of using end-to-end encryption in secure network architecture is to ensure that data remains encrypted and unreadable from the source to the destination, regardless of the intermediaries it traverses. This type of encryption protects the confidentiality and integrity of data as it moves across potentially insecure networks, ensuring that only the intended sender and recipient can access the unencrypted information.

301. What is a key advantage of using stateful firewalls in network security?
a. They allow all inbound and outbound traffic by default
b. They track the state of active connections and make decisions based on context
c. They only filter traffic based on source and destination IP addresses
d. They require manual updates to firewall rules for each new application

Answer: b. They track the state of active connections and make decisions based on context Explanation: The key advantage of using stateful firewalls in network security is their ability to track the state of active connections and make decisions based on the context of the traffic. Unlike stateless firewalls, which only inspect individual packets in isolation, stateful firewalls monitor the entire communication session, allowing them to apply more sophisticated and dynamic security policies based on the ongoing state of network traffic.

302. Why is it important to implement anti-spoofing measures at the network perimeter?
a. To prevent the internal network from being overloaded with traffic
b. To ensure the network remains accessible to remote users at all times
c. To prevent attackers from masquerading as legitimate internal devices
d. To facilitate the seamless integration of third-party services

Answer: c. To prevent attackers from masquerading as legitimate internal devices Explanation: Implementing anti-spoofing measures at the network perimeter is crucial to prevent attackers from masquerading as legitimate internal devices by forging IP addresses. These measures, such as packet filtering and ingress/egress filtering, help ensure that incoming and outgoing traffic is legitimate and originates from or is destined for authorized network addresses, thereby protecting the network from various spoofing attacks and potential security breaches.

303. What role does protocol security play in the design of secure network architectures?
a. It standardizes the physical layout of network components
b. It ensures the secure transmission of data between protocols
c. It provides guidelines for the aesthetic design of network interfaces
d. It secures the data transmission over network protocols by applying cryptographic standards and practices

Answer: d. It secures the data transmission over network protocols by applying cryptographic standards and practices Explanation: Protocol security is integral to the design of secure network architectures as it involves applying cryptographic standards and practices to secure the data transmission over network protocols. This includes the use of secure versions of protocols (e.g., HTTPS, SSH, SFTP), implementing encryption, authentication, and integrity checks to protect data in transit from interception, tampering, and unauthorized access.

304. What is the primary security function of a network firewall?
a. To detect and remove malware from network traffic
b. To authenticate users accessing the network
c. To encrypt data transmissions across the network
d. To control incoming and outgoing network traffic based on a set of security rules

Answer: d. To control incoming and outgoing network traffic based on a set of security rules Explanation: The primary security function of a network firewall is to control incoming and outgoing network traffic based on a predetermined set of security rules. This ensures that only authorized traffic is allowed to enter or leave the network, which helps protect the network from unauthorized access and various types of cyber attacks.

305. In a secure network design, what is the purpose of using an Intrusion Prevention System (IPS)?
a. To provide a backup for data stored on the network
b. To monitor network traffic for malicious activities and block them in real-time
c. To increase the bandwidth available for network communications
d. To serve as a physical barrier to unauthorized network access

Answer: b. To monitor network traffic for malicious activities and block them in real-time Explanation: An Intrusion Prevention System (IPS) is designed to monitor network traffic for signs of malicious activities and block those activities in real-time. Unlike an Intrusion Detection System (IDS), which only detects and alerts on potential security threats, an IPS takes active measures to prevent the threat from causing harm to the network.

306. What role does a Network Access Control (NAC) system play in secure network architecture?
a. To optimize network traffic flow and reduce congestion
b. To encrypt data transmissions across the network
c. To enforce security policies by controlling the access to the network based on device compliance and user credentials
d. To physically isolate network segments for enhanced security

Answer: c. To enforce security policies by controlling the access to the network based on device compliance and user credentials Explanation: A Network Access Control (NAC) system enforces security policies by controlling the access to the network based on device compliance with security policies and user authentication credentials. NAC systems can assess and enforce the security posture of all devices attempting to connect to the network, ensuring that only compliant and authorized devices and users are allowed access.

307. How do Secure Web Gateways (SWGs) contribute to network security?
a. By providing additional storage space for web content
b. By managing the distribution of network bandwidth among users
c. By filtering unwanted software/malware from web traffic and enforcing company policies on internet usage
d. By acting as an intermediary for all outgoing and incoming emails

Answer: c. By filtering unwanted software/malware from web traffic and enforcing company policies on internet usage Explanation: Secure Web Gateways (SWGs) contribute to network security by filtering unwanted software and malware from web traffic, as well as enforcing company policies regarding internet usage. SWGs are positioned between users and the internet, inspecting web traffic for malicious content and ensuring compliance with organizational web access policies, thus protecting the network from web-based threats.

308. What is the function of a Data Loss Prevention (DLP) system in a secure network environment?
a. To ensure the physical security of network hardware
b. To prevent sensitive data from being transmitted outside the organization's network
c. To provide redundant data storage solutions
d. To increase the speed of data retrieval from networked resources

Answer: b. To prevent sensitive data from being transmitted outside the organization's network Explanation: A Data Loss Prevention (DLP) system is designed to prevent sensitive or critical information from being transmitted outside the organization's network. DLP systems monitor, detect, and block the transfer of sensitive data across the network, ensuring that proprietary or confidential information is not lost, misused, or accessed by unauthorized individuals.

309. In the context of secure networking, what is the primary purpose of deploying a honeypot?
a. To serve as a redundant data storage solution
b. To act as a decoy to attract and analyze attacks
c. To enhance the speed of the network
d. To filter spam from email communications

Answer: b. To act as a decoy to attract and analyze attacks Explanation: In the context of secure networking, a honeypot is deployed to act as a decoy that mimics a legitimate part of the network but is actually isolated and monitored. The primary purpose of a honeypot is to attract attackers, thereby diverting them from valuable network resources while allowing security professionals to analyze the attack patterns and methods used by the attackers.

310. What advantage does a Next-Generation Firewall (NGFW) offer over traditional firewalls?
a. Lower operational costs due to reduced power consumption
b. The ability to filter traffic based on applications, in addition to ports and protocols
c. Increased data storage capacity for logging traffic
d. Simplified network topology and reduced need for other security devices

Answer: b. The ability to filter traffic based on applications, in addition to ports and protocols Explanation: A Next-Generation Firewall (NGFW) offers several advancements over traditional firewalls, with the key advantage being its ability to filter traffic not just based on ports and protocols but also on applications. This enables more granular control over the traffic that is allowed or blocked, enhancing the overall security posture by taking into account the specific characteristics and behaviors of applications.

311. Why is it important to implement redundant network paths in a secure network design?
a. To ensure consistent monitoring of user activity
b. To provide an alternative route for data transmission in case of a path failure, ensuring availability
c. To increase the network's data storage capacity
d. To reduce the overall cost of network maintenance

Answer: b. To provide an alternative route for data transmission in case of a path failure, ensuring availability
Explanation: Implementing redundant network paths in a secure network design is important to ensure the availability of network services. Redundancy provides alternative routes for data transmission in case of a path failure, such as a hardware malfunction or a security incident, thereby maintaining the continuous operation of critical network functions and services.

312. What is the significance of implementing SSL/TLS inspection at network security appliances?
a. To reduce the encryption overhead on web servers
b. To enable the appliance to analyze encrypted traffic for potential threats
c. To increase the data transfer rate across the network
d. To serve as a backup encryption method in case primary encryption fails

Answer: b. To enable the appliance to analyze encrypted traffic for potential threats Explanation: The significance of implementing SSL/TLS inspection at network security appliances lies in the ability of these appliances to decrypt, analyze, and then re-encrypt SSL/TLS-encrypted traffic. This process allows the inspection of encrypted traffic for potential threats such as malware and intrusions, which might otherwise go undetected, thereby enhancing the security of encrypted communications.

313. What is the main purpose of implementing SSL/TLS in web communications?
a. To increase the speed of web page loading
b. To ensure the confidentiality and integrity of data exchanged between a web browser and server
c. To authenticate users accessing websites
d. To compress web traffic and reduce bandwidth usage

Answer: b. To ensure the confidentiality and integrity of data exchanged between a web browser and server
Explanation: SSL (Secure Sockets Layer) and TLS (Transport Layer Security) are cryptographic protocols designed to provide communications security over a computer network, with TLS being the successor to SSL. Their main purpose in web communications is to ensure the confidentiality and integrity of data exchanged by encrypting the information transmitted between the web browser and server, thereby preventing eavesdropping and tampering.

314. In a secure VoIP communication, which technology is most commonly used to encrypt voice data?
a. MPLS (Multiprotocol Label Switching)
b. SRTP (Secure Real-time Transport Protocol)
c. SIP (Session Initiation Protocol)
d. PPTP (Point-to-Point Tunneling Protocol)

Answer: b. SRTP (Secure Real-time Transport Protocol) Explanation: SRTP (Secure Real-time Transport Protocol) is an extension of the Real-time Transport Protocol (RTP) that provides encryption, message authentication, and integrity for the data in VoIP communications. SRTP is widely used to secure VoIP communications by encrypting the voice data packets, thereby ensuring that the voice communications are confidential and protected from eavesdropping.

315. Which component is essential in a VPN to ensure that data remains secure as it travels across a public network?

a. Router
b. Firewall
c. VPN gateway
d. Load balancer

Answer: c. VPN gateway Explanation: A VPN gateway is an essential component in a VPN that facilitates the secure connection between the VPN client and the VPN network. It is responsible for establishing, managing, and maintaining the encrypted tunnel through which the data travels across the public network. The VPN gateway ensures that data remains secure by encrypting it before it enters the public network and decrypting it upon arrival at the destination.

316. What is the primary security advantage of using quantum key distribution (QKD) in secure communications?
a. It allows for unlimited data transfer speeds.
b. It provides an unconditionally secure key exchange mechanism based on the principles of quantum mechanics.
c. It compresses data to minimize bandwidth usage.
d. It simplifies the key management process.

Answer: b. It provides an unconditionally secure key exchange mechanism based on the principles of quantum mechanics. Explanation: Quantum key distribution (QKD) is a secure communication method that uses quantum mechanical properties to exchange encryption keys between parties in a way that is immune to eavesdropping. The primary security advantage of QKD is its ability to provide an unconditionally secure key exchange mechanism, as any attempt to intercept the key would inevitably alter the quantum state of the system, alerting the parties to the presence of an eavesdropper.

317. How does the use of digital signatures enhance secure email communications?
a. By compressing email messages to reduce their size
b. By providing non-repudiation and verifying the sender's identity
c. By increasing the email delivery speed
d. By filtering spam and malicious content automatically

Answer: b. By providing non-repudiation and verifying the sender's identity Explanation: Digital signatures enhance secure email communications by providing non-repudiation and verifying the sender's identity. A digital signature is created using the sender's private key and can be verified by the recipient using the sender's public key. This ensures that the message was indeed sent by the purported sender and has not been altered in transit, thereby adding a layer of trust and authenticity to email communications.

318. What role does a Session Border Controller (SBC) play in secure VoIP communications?
a. It reduces the cost of VoIP calls by optimizing the routing of voice traffic.
b. It serves as an intermediary device that manages and secures VoIP traffic at the network border.
c. It compresses voice data to improve call quality over low-bandwidth connections.
d. It translates between different VoIP protocols to ensure compatibility between devices.

Answer: b. It serves as an intermediary device that manages and secures VoIP traffic at the network border.
Explanation: A Session Border Controller (SBC) is a device deployed at the network border to manage and secure VoIP communications. It acts as an intermediary between the internal and external VoIP networks, controlling signaling and media streams to ensure secure and efficient communication. SBCs provide security functions such as firewall traversal, call admission control, and fraud prevention, making them crucial for the integrity and security of VoIP communications.

319. In secure communications, what is the primary function of a Certificate Authority (CA)?
a. To distribute public keys to all network users
b. To provide a backup for encrypted data
c. To issue and manage digital certificates for public key encryption
d. To monitor network traffic for malicious activities

Answer: c. To issue and manage digital certificates for public key encryption Explanation: A Certificate Authority (CA) is a trusted entity that issues and manages digital certificates for public key encryption. The primary function of a CA is to verify the identity of entities (such as individuals, organizations, or devices) and issue them a digital certificate that links the entity's identity with their public key. This process is essential for establishing trust in secure communications, as it allows parties to confidently encrypt data and verify each other's identities using public key infrastructure (PKI).

320. What is the purpose of implementing a mesh network topology in secure communications?
a. To provide a single point of control for easier network management
b. To ensure there are multiple paths for data transmission, enhancing reliability and fault tolerance
c. To centralize data storage for better security
d. To minimize the number of devices involved in the network for cost savings

Answer: b. To ensure there are multiple paths for data transmission, enhancing reliability and fault tolerance
Explanation: A mesh network topology is characterized by each node in the network being connected to multiple other nodes. This setup ensures that there are multiple paths for data transmission, enhancing the reliability and fault tolerance of the network. In the context of secure communications, this means that even if one path is compromised or becomes unavailable, data can still be securely transmitted through alternative routes, thereby maintaining the integrity and availability of communications.

321. How does link encryption differ from end-to-end encryption in securing communication channels?
a. Link encryption secures each part of the communication path individually, while end-to-end encryption secures data from the origin to the destination.
b. Link encryption is faster than end-to-end encryption due to less computational overhead.
c. End-to-end encryption is used only for email communications, while link encryption is used for all types of data.
d. Link encryption requires manual key exchange, whereas end-to-end encryption uses automated key exchange mechanisms.

Answer: a. Link encryption secures each part of the communication path individually, while end-to-end encryption secures data from the origin to the destination. Explanation: Link encryption involves encrypting data at each hop along the communication path, with the data being decrypted and re-encrypted at every intermediate device, such as routers or switches. End-to-end encryption, on the other hand, encrypts data at the source and keeps it encrypted until it reaches the final destination, where it is decrypted. This ensures that the data remains confidential and intact throughout its entire transit, visible only to the sender and the intended recipient, providing a higher level of security compared to link encryption.

322. How can a network mitigate the risk of Distributed Denial of Service (DDoS) attacks?
a. Implementing strict password policies
b. Deploying DDoS protection solutions like rate limiting and traffic analysis
c. Enforcing physical access controls
d. Using antivirus software on all client machines

Answer: b. Deploying DDoS protection solutions like rate limiting and traffic analysis Explanation: DDoS protection solutions, such as rate limiting and traffic analysis, are effective in mitigating the risk of DDoS attacks. These solutions can identify unusual traffic patterns indicative of a DDoS attack and take action to limit or block malicious traffic, thereby ensuring that legitimate traffic can continue to access network resources.

323. Which method is effective in preventing man-in-the-middle (MitM) attacks in network communications?
a. Implementing network segmentation
b. Utilizing strong encryption for data in transit
c. Installing anti-malware software on servers
d. Conducting regular user security awareness training

Answer: b. Utilizing strong encryption for data in transit Explanation: Utilizing strong encryption protocols for data in transit, such as TLS/SSL, can effectively prevent man-in-the-middle (MitM) attacks. Encryption ensures that even if an attacker is able to intercept the communications, they cannot decipher the content, thereby protecting the confidentiality and integrity of the transmitted data.

324. What is a primary defense mechanism against SQL injection attacks on a network's databases?
a. Configuring web application firewalls (WAFs)
b. Regularly updating network router firmware
c. Enabling SSID broadcasting on wireless access points
d. Implementing strict file permissions on web servers

Answer: a. Configuring web application firewalls (WAFs) Explanation: Web Application Firewalls (WAFs) are designed to monitor, filter, and block HTTP traffic to and from a web application and can be configured to protect against SQL injection attacks by detecting and blocking malicious SQL queries before they reach the database server. This helps in preventing attackers from exploiting vulnerabilities in web applications to execute unauthorized SQL commands.

325. How can networks prevent eavesdropping on data transmissions?

a. By using quality of service (QoS) controls
b. Through the application of port security on switches
c. By employing encryption protocols like IPSec or TLS
d. Through the use of non-repudiation techniques

Answer: c. By employing encryption protocols like IPSec or TLS Explanation: Encryption protocols like IPSec (for network communications) and TLS (for web communications) are essential for preventing eavesdropping on data transmissions. By encrypting the data, these protocols ensure that even if data is intercepted, it cannot be read or understood by unauthorized parties.

326. What technique can effectively minimize the risk of ARP poisoning attacks within a LAN?
a. Subnetting the network into smaller segments
b. Deploying static ARP tables where feasible
c. Enforcing two-factor authentication for network access
d. Regularly clearing the DNS cache on servers

Answer: b. Deploying static ARP tables where feasible Explanation: Deploying static ARP (Address Resolution Protocol) tables can effectively minimize the risk of ARP poisoning attacks, where an attacker sends falsified ARP messages over a local area network. Static ARP entries are manually configured and do not change, preventing attackers from associating their MAC address with the IP address of another host, such as the default gateway.

327. To protect against phishing attacks, what measure should a network implement?
a. Intrusion Prevention Systems (IPS)
b. Email filtering and anti-phishing solutions
c. Biometric access controls
d. VLAN trunking

Answer: b. Email filtering and anti-phishing solutions Explanation: Email filtering and anti-phishing solutions are crucial in protecting against phishing attacks. These solutions can scan incoming emails for known phishing indicators, such as suspicious links or attachments, and quarantine or block malicious emails before they reach the end-users, thus reducing the risk of successful phishing attempts.

328. In combating ransomware attacks, what is a key preventative strategy for network security?
a. Enabling broadcast storm control
b. Conducting regular data backups and implementing robust recovery procedures
c. Deploying honeypots to distract attackers
d. Utilizing static routing protocols exclusively

Answer: b. Conducting regular data backups and implementing robust recovery procedures Explanation: Regular data backups and robust recovery procedures are key preventative strategies against ransomware attacks. By maintaining up-to-date backups of critical data and ensuring that recovery processes are in place and tested, organizations can reduce the impact of a ransomware attack and restore affected systems and data without succumbing to ransom demands.

329. What is an effective countermeasure against Zero-day exploits?
a. Disabling unused network ports and services
b. Applying virtual LANs (VLANs) to segregate network traffic
c. Implementing intrusion detection and prevention systems with heuristic analysis capabilities
d. Restricting internet access to a whitelist of approved websites

Answer: c. Implementing intrusion detection and prevention systems with heuristic analysis capabilities Explanation: Intrusion detection and prevention systems (IDPS) with heuristic analysis capabilities can effectively counter Zero-day exploits by identifying and mitigating suspicious activities or behavior patterns that deviate from the norm, even if the specific exploit has not been previously identified or has no available patch.

330. How do organizations reduce the risk of insider threats on their networks?
a. By exclusively using wired connections instead of wireless
b. Implementing strict network access controls and monitoring user activities
c. Increasing the signal strength of wireless access points
d. Using only proprietary software applications

Answer: b. Implementing strict network access controls and monitoring user activities Explanation: Reducing the risk of insider threats involves implementing strict network access controls to ensure users have only the necessary permissions to perform their job functions, along with monitoring user activities for any unusual or unauthorized actions. This approach helps in identifying and mitigating potential insider threats by limiting access to sensitive information and detecting possible malicious behavior.

331. To safeguard against session hijacking, which measure is most effective?
a. Regularly updating website content
b. Utilizing session tokens and secure cookies
c. Deploying additional wireless access points
d. Limiting the length of user sessions to a few minutes

Answer: b. Utilizing session tokens and secure cookies Explanation: Utilizing session tokens and secure cookies is most effective in safeguarding against session hijacking. These tokens are unique to each session and user, and secure cookies are encrypted, making it difficult for attackers to intercept and reuse them to hijack a user session. This ensures that even if session data is intercepted, it cannot be used to gain unauthorized access to the user's session.

332. What principle is primarily enforced by implementing segregation of duties within an identity and access management framework?

a. Least privilege
b. Mandatory access control
c. Role-based access control
d. Non-repudiation

Answer: a. Least privilege Explanation: The principle of least privilege is primarily enforced by implementing segregation of duties within an identity and access management framework. This principle ensures that individuals have only the minimum levels of access – or permissions – needed to perform their job functions, thereby reducing the risk of unauthorized access or misuse of information.

333. In an IAM system, what is the primary purpose of multi-factor authentication (MFA)?
a. To reduce the complexity of password management
b. To increase the speed of the authentication process
c. To enhance security by requiring multiple forms of verification from the user
d. To simplify user access for remote employees

Answer: c. To enhance security by requiring multiple forms of verification from the user Explanation: The primary purpose of multi-factor authentication (MFA) in an IAM system is to enhance security by requiring users to provide multiple forms of verification before gaining access. This typically involves a combination of something the user knows (like a password), something the user has (like a security token), and something the user is (like a fingerprint), making unauthorized access significantly more difficult.

334. Which access control model is based on a user's job functions within an organization?
a. Discretionary Access Control (DAC)
b. Role-Based Access Control (RBAC)
c. Mandatory Access Control (MAC)
d. Attribute-Based Access Control (ABAC)

Answer: b. Role-Based Access Control (RBAC) Explanation: Role-Based Access Control (RBAC) is an access control model that assigns permissions to roles rather than individual users, with roles created based on job functions within an organization. Users are then assigned roles, and through those roles, they inherit the permissions necessary to perform their job functions, streamlining access management and enforcing the principle of least privilege.

335. What is the primary function of a directory service in identity and access management?
a. To encrypt data transmissions between clients and servers
b. To monitor and log user activities on the network
c. To store and manage user information and provide authentication and authorization services
d. To filter and block malicious internet traffic

Answer: c. To store and manage user information and provide authentication and authorization services Explanation: The primary function of a directory service in identity and access management is to store and manage user information, such as usernames, passwords, and group memberships, and to provide authentication and authorization services. Directory services like Microsoft Active Directory and LDAP (Lightweight Directory Access Protocol) are central repositories for user information and play a critical role in managing access to network resources.

336. How does federated identity management improve user experience in a multi-domain environment?
a. By consolidating all user credentials into a single password
b. By allowing users to use a single set of credentials to access resources across multiple domains
c. By automatically assigning user roles based on their activity
d. By reducing the number of password reset requests

Answer: b. By allowing users to use a single set of credentials to access resources across multiple domains Explanation: Federated identity management improves user experience in a multi-domain environment by allowing users to use a single set of credentials – often referred to as single sign-on (SSO) – to access resources across multiple domains or systems. This approach eliminates the need for multiple usernames and passwords, simplifying the authentication process for users who need to access resources from different organizations or systems.

337. In an IAM context, what is the purpose of a provisioning system?
a. To monitor network traffic for security threats
b. To create, manage, and delete user accounts and access rights automatically
c. To encrypt sensitive data stored in user accounts
d. To track software licenses and usage within the organization

Answer: b. To create, manage, and delete user accounts and access rights automatically Explanation: The purpose of a provisioning system in an IAM context is to automate the process of creating, managing, and deleting user accounts and their access rights across various systems and applications. This not only streamlines the onboarding and offboarding processes but also helps in ensuring that access rights are consistently and accurately managed throughout the user lifecycle.

338. What is the advantage of using Single Sign-On (SSO) in an enterprise environment?
a. It increases the complexity of the authentication process to enhance security
b. It allows users to access multiple applications with one set of credentials, improving convenience and productivity
c. It restricts users to accessing only one application at a time to reduce the risk of data breaches
d. It eliminates the need for passwords, relying solely on biometric authentication

Answer: b. It allows users to access multiple applications with one set of credentials, improving convenience and productivity Explanation: The advantage of using Single Sign-On (SSO) in an enterprise environment is that it allows users to access multiple applications and services with one set of credentials (e.g., username and password). This significantly improves user convenience and productivity by reducing the number of times users have to log in when accessing various systems and applications.

339. Which IAM practice helps in minimizing the risk of orphaned accounts?
a. Periodic user access reviews
b. Implementing password complexity requirements
c. Using CAPTCHA challenges for online forms
d. Enforcing network-level segmentation

Answer: a. Periodic user access reviews Explanation: Periodic user access reviews are an IAM practice that helps in minimizing the risk of orphaned accounts, which are accounts belonging to former employees or users who no longer need access. By regularly reviewing and auditing user accounts and their access rights, organizations can identify and deactivate orphaned accounts, thereby reducing potential security risks.

340. How does attribute-based access control (ABAC) differ from role-based access control (RBAC)?
a. ABAC uses machine learning algorithms to assign user roles, while RBAC uses predefined role assignments.
b. ABAC bases access decisions on a wide range of attributes, including user, environment, and resource attributes, while RBAC relies solely on predefined user roles.
c. ABAC is used exclusively in cloud environments, while RBAC is used in on-premises systems.
d. ABAC requires physical tokens for authentication, while RBAC uses digital certificates.

Answer: b. ABAC bases access decisions on a wide range of attributes, including user, environment, and resource attributes, while RBAC relies solely on predefined user roles. Explanation: Attribute-Based Access Control (ABAC) offers a more granular and flexible approach compared to Role-Based Access Control (RBAC) by basing access decisions on a wide range of attributes related to the user, environment, and resources, among others. This allows for dynamic and context-aware access control policies that can adapt to complex and changing requirements, unlike RBAC, which relies on static role assignments.

341. What mechanism in IAM ensures that users cannot deny their actions, such as transactions or data access?
a. Anonymization
b. Non-repudiation
c. Transitive trust
d. Mutual authentication

Answer: b. Non-repudiation Explanation: Non-repudiation in IAM ensures that users cannot deny their actions, such as transactions or data access. This is achieved through mechanisms such as digital signatures and audit trails, which provide irrefutable evidence of a user's actions, thereby ensuring accountability and traceability within the system.

342. What is the primary purpose of implementing biometric access control systems at data center entrances?
a. To monitor temperature and humidity within the data center
b. To ensure only authorized personnel can gain physical access based on unique biological traits
c. To log the digital activities of users within the network
d. To facilitate easier access for maintenance personnel without security checks

Answer: b. To ensure only authorized personnel can gain physical access based on unique biological traits
Explanation: Biometric access control systems at data center entrances use unique biological traits, such as fingerprints, facial recognition, or iris scans, to identify and authenticate individuals. The primary purpose of these systems is to ensure that only authorized personnel can gain physical access to sensitive areas, thereby enhancing security by preventing unauthorized entry.

343. In the context of securing a server room, what is the advantage of using mantrap entry systems?
a. They allow multiple individuals to enter simultaneously for efficiency.
b. They provide a secure space for package deliveries without main area access.
c. They prevent tailgating by allowing one authorized entry at a time.
d. They serve as a rest area for personnel working long hours.

Answer: c. They prevent tailgating by allowing one authorized entry at a time. Explanation: Mantrap entry systems, consisting of two or more interlocking doors, are designed to control access to secure areas such as server rooms. By allowing only one individual to pass through at a time and requiring authentication at each door, mantraps prevent tailgating, where an unauthorized person might follow an authorized user into a restricted area.

344. What is the primary security function of an access control list (ACL) in a network environment?
a. To list all users currently logged into the system
b. To define which resources a user or group can access and what actions they can perform
c. To inventory all hardware devices connected to the network
d. To record the temperature and humidity levels of network storage areas

Answer: b. To define which resources a user or group can access and what actions they can perform Explanation: An Access Control List (ACL) is a list used by routers and switches to define which resources (such as files, systems, or devices) a user or group can access within a network and what actions (read, write, execute) they are permitted to perform. ACLs are crucial for maintaining the security and integrity of network resources by ensuring that only authorized users can access specific network services or information.

345. How do smart cards contribute to both physical and logical access control systems?
a. By providing a backup power source for access control systems
b. By serving as a visual identification badge only
c. By storing user credentials and cryptographic keys for secure authentication
d. By enhancing the aesthetic appeal of access control hardware

Answer: c. By storing user credentials and cryptographic keys for secure authentication Explanation: Smart cards contribute to both physical and logical access control systems by embedding a microchip that stores user credentials and cryptographic keys, which can be used for secure authentication processes. These cards can facilitate physical access to buildings or secure areas and logical access to computers, networks, and other digital resources, thereby ensuring a high level of security through two-factor authentication or more.

346. What role does a security information and event management (SIEM) system play in logical access control?
a. It acts as a physical barrier to server rooms.
b. It aggregates and analyzes log data from various sources to identify suspicious activities.
c. It replaces the need for passwords with a more advanced technology.
d. It physically audits the inventory of all network devices.

Answer: b. It aggregates and analyzes log data from various sources to identify suspicious activities. Explanation: A Security Information and Event Management (SIEM) system plays a crucial role in logical access control by collecting, aggregating, and analyzing log data from various sources within a network, such as servers, firewalls, and intrusion detection systems. By doing so, it can identify patterns indicative of suspicious or unauthorized activities, thereby helping to detect and respond to security incidents more effectively.

347. Why are visitor logs considered a critical component of physical access control in secure facilities?
a. They provide a historical record of all Internet activity within the facility.
b. They offer a detailed inventory of all physical assets within the facility.
c. They maintain a record of all individuals who have entered and exited the facility.
d. They ensure all visitors are provided with Wi-Fi access.

Answer: c. They maintain a record of all individuals who have entered and exited the facility. Explanation: Visitor logs are a critical component of physical access control as they maintain a detailed record of every individual who enters and exits the facility, including their name, the time of their visit, and the purpose of their visit. This documentation is essential for security audits, investigations, and ensuring that only authorized individuals have access to sensitive or restricted areas.

348. What is the significance of implementing VLANs (Virtual Local Area Networks) in enhancing logical access control within a network?
a. They allow for unrestricted access between all network devices.
b. They physically separate network hardware to different locations.
c. They enable the segmentation of a network into separate, isolated logical groups to control access.
d. They increase the bandwidth available for each network user.

Answer: c. They enable the segmentation of a network into separate, isolated logical groups to control access. Explanation: VLANs (Virtual Local Area Networks) enhance logical access control by allowing network administrators to segment a network into separate, isolated logical groups. Each VLAN can have its access controls and policies, thereby limiting the ability of users to access resources on other VLANs without proper authorization. This segmentation helps in reducing the risk of unauthorized access and limiting the scope of potential security breaches.

349. In the deployment of a CCTV surveillance system, what is the primary consideration to ensure effective monitoring?
a. The aesthetic integration of cameras into the environment
b. The strategic placement of cameras to cover critical areas and blind spots
c. The color scheme of the camera casings to match corporate branding
d. The use of the highest possible resolution cameras regardless of cost

Answer: b. The strategic placement of cameras to cover critical areas and blind spots Explanation: The primary consideration in deploying a CCTV surveillance system for effective monitoring is the strategic placement of cameras to ensure comprehensive coverage of critical areas and eliminate blind spots. This involves assessing the layout of the premises, identifying potential security vulnerabilities, and positioning cameras in a way that maximizes visibility and effectiveness in detecting unauthorized activities or security incidents.

350. How does the principle of least privilege apply to controlling access to network resources?
a. By granting all users administrative privileges to simplify management
b. By ensuring users have only the access necessary to perform their job functions
c. By allowing open access to all resources for maximum collaboration
d. By requiring biometric verification for all users, regardless of their role

Answer: b. By ensuring users have only the access necessary to perform their job functions Explanation: The principle of least privilege is a fundamental security concept that applies to controlling access to network resources by ensuring that users, systems, and applications have only the minimum levels of access – or permissions – necessary to perform their job functions. This restricts the potential for abuse of privileges or access to sensitive information, thereby reducing the risk of data breaches or other security incidents.

351. What is a primary security benefit of using time-based access controls on a network?
a. They ensure that network speeds are fastest during peak business hours.
b. They restrict user access to network resources based on predefined schedules.
c. They synchronize all network devices to the same clock for consistency.
d. They provide unlimited access to all users to prevent bottlenecks.

Answer: b. They restrict user access to network resources based on predefined schedules. Explanation: Time-based access controls are a security measure that restricts user access to network resources based on predefined time schedules. For example, an employee may only be granted access to certain systems or data during their regular working hours. This approach minimizes the risk of unauthorized access during off-hours and helps in maintaining tighter control over sensitive resources.

352. What is the primary purpose of implementing a Public Key Infrastructure (PKI) in an organization?
a. To facilitate physical access controls
b. To manage digital certificates for encrypting and digitally signing information
c. To increase the processing speed of network devices
d. To monitor and log all user activities on the network

Answer: b. To manage digital certificates for encrypting and digitally signing information Explanation: Public Key Infrastructure (PKI) is used to manage digital certificates and public-key encryption, enabling secure exchange of information over networks, including the Internet. PKI provides a framework for creating a secure method of exchanging information, ensuring confidentiality, integrity, and authentication of data and communications.

353. In a multi-factor authentication system, which of the following constitutes a "something you are" factor?
a. A PIN code
b. A security token
c. A fingerprint
d. A password

Answer: c. A fingerprint Explanation: A "something you are" factor in multi-factor authentication systems refers to biometric identifiers that are unique to an individual, such as fingerprints, facial recognition, iris scans, or voice patterns. These biometric factors provide a high level of security as they are difficult to replicate or steal compared to knowledge-based (something you know) or possession-based (something you have) factors.

354. How does a RADIUS server enhance network security?
a. By providing a routing mechanism for data packets
b. By encrypting data stored on the server
c. By managing network access with centralized authentication, authorization, and accounting
d. By scanning email attachments for malware

Answer: c. By managing network access with centralized authentication, authorization, and accounting Explanation: RADIUS (Remote Authentication Dial-In User Service) servers enhance network security by centralizing the authentication, authorization, and accounting (AAA) for users who are connecting to a network service. RADIUS allows network devices to communicate with a central server to authenticate users, authorize their access levels, and log their activities, which simplifies the management of network access and improves security.

355. What role does an Identity Provider (IdP) play in a Single Sign-On (SSO) system?
a. It increases the signal strength of wireless access points
b. It serves as a centralized repository for user credentials and access management
c. It acts as a firewall to block unauthorized network traffic
d. It manages the physical security of server hardware

Answer: b. It serves as a centralized repository for user credentials and access management Explanation: In a Single Sign-On (SSO) system, an Identity Provider (IdP) serves as a centralized service that stores and manages digital identities and user credentials. The IdP is responsible for authenticating users and providing them with tokens that allow them to access multiple applications or services without needing to log in separately to each one, thereby streamlining the user experience and enhancing security.

356. What is the main security benefit of using smart cards as part of an authentication system?
a. They provide an uninterruptible power supply
b. They offer a user-friendly interface for data entry
c. They store cryptographic keys that can be used for strong two-factor authentication
d. They simplify the network topology

Answer: c. They store cryptographic keys that can be used for strong two-factor authentication Explanation: Smart cards enhance security by storing cryptographic keys or digital certificates that are used in conjunction with a PIN (something the user knows) to perform two-factor authentication. This combination of something the user has (the smart card) and something the user knows (the PIN) provides a higher level of security than simple password-based authentication methods.

357. Which authentication method relies on a user's physical actions or behaviors?
a. Token-based authentication
b. Cognitive authentication
c. Biometric authentication
d. Behavioral authentication

Answer: d. Behavioral authentication Explanation: Behavioral authentication is an advanced method that relies on the unique patterns in a user's physical or behavioral actions, such as keystroke dynamics, mouse movements, or even patterns in how they interact with devices and applications. This form of authentication assesses risk and authenticity by analyzing these patterns, which are difficult to replicate or forge, thus providing a dynamic and secure authentication mechanism.

358. How does the use of Single Sign-On (SSO) impact user experience and security in an enterprise environment?
a. It decreases security by using a single password for all applications
b. It improves user experience by reducing password fatigue without compromising security
c. It complicates user access by requiring multiple authentication steps for each application
d. It reduces the need for security by centralizing user data

Answer: b. It improves user experience by reducing password fatigue without compromising security Explanation: Single Sign-On (SSO) improves the user experience by allowing individuals to log in once and gain access to multiple related but independent software systems without being prompted to log in again at each of them. This reduces password fatigue and simplifies the user's access while maintaining security by centralizing the authentication process and allowing for more stringent authentication mechanisms in one place rather than multiple weaker ones across many systems.

359. What is the primary function of a Certificate Authority (CA) in a PKI system?
a. To distribute hardware tokens to users
b. To issue and manage digital certificates for entity authentication
c. To encrypt all data transmitted over the network
d. To monitor network traffic for suspicious activities

Answer: b. To issue and manage digital certificates for entity authentication Explanation: In a Public Key Infrastructure (PKI) system, a Certificate Authority (CA) is a trusted entity that issues and manages digital certificates. These certificates are used to authenticate the identity of entities (such as users, computers, or organizations) and to facilitate secure communication and data exchange by providing a means to establish trust through the use of public key cryptography.

360. What advantage does adaptive authentication offer in identity and access management?
a. It uses a static set of rules for all users, simplifying the authentication process
b. It provides the same level of security checks regardless of the user's location or device
c. It adjusts the level of authentication required based on the user's context and risk profile
d. It eliminates the need for passwords, using only biometrics for all users

Answer: c. It adjusts the level of authentication required based on the user's context and risk profile Explanation: Adaptive authentication, also known as risk-based authentication, enhances security by dynamically adjusting the level of authentication required based on the context of the access request and the risk profile of the user. Factors such as the user's location, device, network, and behavior patterns are analyzed to determine the appropriate authentication mechanism, providing a balance between security and user convenience.

361. In what way does the implementation of OAuth contribute to secure authentication processes?
a. By providing unlimited data storage capacity for user credentials
b. By allowing applications to share user data without requiring passwords
c. By broadcasting authentication requests to all network devices for verification
d. By mandating physical security measures for all authentication servers

Answer: b. By allowing applications to share user data without requiring passwords Explanation: OAuth is an open standard for access delegation commonly used as a way for internet users to grant websites or applications access to their information on other websites but without giving them the passwords. This framework allows third-party services to exchange web resources on behalf of a user, facilitating secure and passwordless authentication processes that enhance security by minimizing the sharing and exposure of user credentials.

362. What is the primary benefit of implementing Identity as a Service (IDaaS) in an enterprise environment?
a. To decentralize identity management and distribute it across various departments
b. To enhance the physical security of the enterprise's data centers
c. To provide centralized, cloud-based identity management services for authentication and access control
d. To eliminate the need for any form of digital authentication

Answer: c. To provide centralized, cloud-based identity management services for authentication and access control Explanation: IDaaS offers centralized, cloud-based services for managing identities and access controls, streamlining authentication, authorization, and user management processes across multiple applications and systems. This model allows for efficient, scalable, and flexible identity management solutions that can be easily integrated with various cloud and on-premises applications, enhancing security and user experience.

363. How does Single Sign-On (SSO) within an IDaaS solution improve user productivity?
a. By requiring users to memorize more complex passwords
b. By allowing users to access multiple applications with a single authentication process

c. By disabling access to critical applications to enhance security

d. By increasing the number of authentication steps for each application

Answer: b. By allowing users to access multiple applications with a single authentication process Explanation: SSO simplifies the user experience by enabling individuals to log in once and gain access to a suite of applications without the need to re-authenticate for each service. This reduces password fatigue, decreases the time spent on login procedures, and minimizes the potential for security breaches due to weaker password practices, thereby enhancing productivity and security.

364. In the context of IDaaS, what is the role of a federation service?

a. To physically secure servers and networking equipment

b. To distribute cryptographic keys to users for data encryption

c. To enable interoperability and shared authentication between disparate identity systems

d. To monitor and filter internet traffic for malicious content

Answer: c. To enable interoperability and shared authentication between disparate identity systems Explanation: Federation services in IDaaS environments allow different identity management systems to trust each other by enabling users from one domain to securely access resources and applications in another domain without needing separate credentials. This interoperability is crucial for businesses that use multiple cloud services or collaborate with external partners, as it streamlines access while maintaining security standards.

365. What security advantage does Multi-Factor Authentication (MFA) offer in an IDaaS model?

a. It simplifies the authentication process by using a single security factor

b. It eliminates the need for any form of digital encryption

c. It provides an additional layer of security by requiring two or more verification methods

d. It reduces the overall cost of the IT infrastructure by consolidating authentication servers

Answer: c. It provides an additional layer of security by requiring two or more verification methods Explanation: MFA enhances security in IDaaS by requiring users to present multiple forms of evidence to verify their identity before granting access to resources. These factors can include something the user knows (password), something the user has (security token), and something the user is (biometric verification). By combining these factors, MFA significantly reduces the risk of unauthorized access.

366. How does IDaaS facilitate compliance with data protection regulations such as GDPR or HIPAA?

a. By completely outsourcing data storage to third-party services

b. By providing tools and services to manage user identities, access controls, and audit trails in line with regulatory requirements

c. By encrypting all data, making it unreadable and non-compliant

d. By allowing unlimited data access to all users, regardless of their role

Answer: b. By providing tools and services to manage user identities, access controls, and audit trails in line with regulatory requirements Explanation: IDaaS solutions offer features like automated user provisioning/de-provisioning, access management, and detailed logging and reporting, which are essential for maintaining compliance with data protection regulations. These capabilities help ensure that only authorized users can access sensitive data and that all access events are properly documented for audits.

367. What is a primary consideration when integrating an on-premises application with an IDaaS solution?
a. Ensuring that the application has a graphical user interface
b. The geographical location of the IDaaS provider's data centers
c. Compatibility and secure integration between the on-premises application and the IDaaS platform
d. The color scheme of the IDaaS user interface

Answer: c. Compatibility and secure integration between the on-premises application and the IDaaS platform Explanation: When integrating an on-premises application with an IDaaS solution, a key consideration is ensuring compatibility and secure integration between the two. This involves assessing the application's authentication protocols, data exchange mechanisms, and security requirements to ensure seamless and secure connectivity with the IDaaS platform, thereby extending cloud-based identity management capabilities to on-premises applications.

368. How do IDaaS solutions support scalability in growing organizations?
a. By limiting the number of users who can access the system
b. By offering flexible, cloud-based services that can easily adapt to increasing numbers of users and applications
c. By requiring additional on-premises hardware for each new user
d. By decreasing network bandwidth to conserve resources

Answer: b. By offering flexible, cloud-based services that can easily adapt to increasing numbers of users and applications Explanation: IDaaS solutions are inherently scalable due to their cloud-based nature, allowing organizations to easily add or remove users, manage access to an increasing number of applications, and adjust their identity and access management capabilities as the organization grows. This scalability is crucial for maintaining efficiency and security in dynamic business environments.

369. What challenge is addressed by implementing consolidated identity management through IDaaS in a hybrid cloud environment?
a. The complexity of managing multiple identity stores and authentication mechanisms
b. The need for physical security guards at data center locations
c. The requirement for all users to be located in the same geographic region
d. The use of a single, shared password for all cloud resources

Answer: a. The complexity of managing multiple identity stores and authentication mechanisms Explanation: In hybrid cloud environments, where resources are spread across on-premises data centers and multiple cloud platforms, managing disparate identity stores and authentication mechanisms can become complex and insecure. IDaaS provides a consolidated identity management solution that simplifies this complexity by offering a unified platform for managing identities and access across all environments, thereby enhancing security and efficiency.

370. In what way does an IDaaS solution enhance the user experience for remote or mobile employees?
a. By requiring complex, multi-step authentication processes for each application
b. By enabling secure, seamless access to corporate resources from any location or device
c. By restricting access to corporate resources to on-premises use only
d. By mandating the use of physical tokens for authentication

Answer: b. By enabling secure, seamless access to corporate resources from any location or device Explanation: IDaaS solutions enhance the user experience for remote or mobile employees by providing secure, seamless access to corporate resources regardless of the user's location or the device being used. This is achieved through technologies such as SSO and MFA, which facilitate easy yet secure access to applications and data, supporting the mobility and flexibility required in modern work environments.

371. What is a primary concern when integrating third-party identity services with an organization's on-premise systems?
a. Increasing the physical space for server hardware
b. Ensuring interoperability and secure data exchange between systems
c. Reducing the variety of available identity services
d. Implementing identical user interfaces across all platforms

Answer: b. Ensuring interoperability and secure data exchange between systems Explanation: When integrating third-party identity services with on-premise systems, the primary concern is ensuring that these systems can work together seamlessly and securely. This involves confirming that data exchange protocols, authentication mechanisms, and security standards are compatible and can support secure and efficient interoperability between the cloud-based identity services and the organization's internal systems.

372. How should an organization approach the management of user identities and access when using third-party identity services?
a. By allowing the third-party service complete control over all user identities and access management.
b. By establishing a hybrid identity management framework that includes both internal and third-party controls
c. By discontinuing all internal identity management practices
d. By manually synchronizing user accounts on a daily basis

Answer: b. By establishing a hybrid identity management framework that includes both internal and third-party controls Explanation: Organizations should adopt a hybrid approach to identity management when incorporating third-party identity services. This framework combines the strengths of third-party services with internal controls, allowing for centralized management of user identities and access while leveraging the scalability and expertise of third-party solutions. This approach ensures that the organization maintains control over its critical identity and access management functions while benefiting from the third-party services' capabilities.

373. What is a key advantage of using third-party identity services for authentication in a distributed environment?
a. Elimination of all internal security controls

b. Centralized management of diverse identity repositories
c. Dependency on a single authentication method
d. Requirement for additional on-premise authentication hardware

Answer: b. Centralized management of diverse identity repositories Explanation: One of the key advantages of using third-party identity services in a distributed environment is the ability to centrally manage diverse identity repositories. This centralization simplifies the authentication process across different systems and applications, enabling a unified and consistent approach to identity management across the organization's distributed IT landscape, which can include cloud, on-premises, and hybrid systems.

374. In dealing with third-party identity services, what is a critical factor to consider for maintaining data privacy and compliance?
a. The color scheme and branding of the identity service interface
b. The physical location of the third-party service's data centers and adherence to jurisdictional privacy laws
c. The speed of the identity verification process
d. The number of supported languages by the identity service

Answer: b. The physical location of the third-party service's data centers and adherence to jurisdictional privacy laws Explanation: When utilizing third-party identity services, it's crucial to consider the physical location of the service's data centers and their compliance with applicable jurisdictional privacy laws and regulations. Data sovereignty and compliance with laws such as GDPR, HIPAA, or CCPA, depending on the organization's location and operational scope, are essential to protect user data privacy and ensure the organization's compliance with legal requirements.

375. How can organizations mitigate risks associated with third-party identity service providers?
a. By exclusively using in-house developed identity solutions
b. Through regular security assessments, audits, and adherence to industry best practices
c. By avoiding any form of digital identity verification
d. By employing a single-factor authentication method for all access

Answer: b. Through regular security assessments, audits, and adherence to industry best practices Explanation: Organizations can mitigate risks associated with third-party identity service providers by conducting regular security assessments and audits of the providers and ensuring that they adhere to industry best practices and standards. This proactive approach allows organizations to identify and address potential vulnerabilities and ensure that the third-party services maintain high levels of security and reliability.

376. What role does a Service Level Agreement (SLA) play in the use of third-party identity services?
a. It outlines the aesthetic requirements for the service interface
b. It specifies the performance, availability, and security standards expected from the service
c. It eliminates the need for any form of security assessment
d. It dictates the physical layout of the third-party service's office space

Answer: b. It specifies the performance, availability, and security standards expected from the service Explanation: A Service Level Agreement (SLA) is crucial when using third-party identity services as it formally outlines the performance metrics, availability, security standards, and responsibilities that the third-party service is expected to meet. The SLA serves as a binding contract that ensures the service provider meets the organization's requirements for reliability, performance, and security, thereby protecting the organization's interests and ensuring accountability.

377. How do federated identity systems enhance the integration of third-party identity services with enterprise systems?
a. By requiring separate logins for each system to increase security
b. By enabling users to use a single set of credentials across multiple systems
c. By physically isolating enterprise and third-party systems
d. By limiting access to only a few selected enterprise applications

Answer: b. By enabling users to use a single set of credentials across multiple systems Explanation: Federated identity systems enhance the integration of third-party identity services with enterprise systems by allowing users to use a single set of credentials to access multiple systems and applications, both internal and provided by third parties. This approach streamlines the user experience, simplifies access management, and maintains security by enabling seamless and secure single sign-on (SSO) capabilities across a federated ecosystem of services.

378. What is an essential security consideration when integrating third-party identity services with internal applications?
a. The compatibility of color schemes between the identity service and internal applications
b. Ensuring secure API connections and data encryption during transmissions
c. The alignment of brand logos between the third-party service and the enterprise
d. The provision of recreational facilities for the third-party service's staff

Answer: b. Ensuring secure API connections and data encryption during transmissions Explanation: A critical security consideration when integrating third-party identity services with internal applications is ensuring that API connections between the services and applications are secure and that data transmissions are encrypted. This safeguard protects sensitive identity and authentication data from interception or exposure during the integration and communication processes, maintaining the integrity and confidentiality of the data.

379. What strategy should be employed to ensure continuity of access in the event of a third-party identity service failure?
a. Disabling all digital access controls
b. Implementation of redundant identity services and failover mechanisms
c. Complete reliance on physical security measures only
d. Manual verification of all user identities by the IT department

Answer: b. Implementation of redundant identity services and failover mechanisms Explanation: To ensure continuity of access in the event of a third-party identity service failure, organizations should implement redundant identity services and failover mechanisms. This strategy involves having backup systems or alternative identity services that can automatically take over in case the primary service becomes unavailable, thereby ensuring uninterrupted access to critical applications and services for users.

380. In what way can third-party identity services facilitate regulatory compliance for an organization?
a. By providing an unlimited number of user licenses
b. By ensuring that identity management practices meet specific regulatory requirements
c. By focusing solely on the aesthetic aspects of user authentication processes
d. By broadcasting user authentication events publicly for transparency

Answer: b. By ensuring that identity management practices meet specific regulatory requirements Explanation: Third-party identity services can facilitate regulatory compliance by ensuring that their identity management and authentication practices are designed to meet specific regulatory standards and requirements relevant to the organization's industry and operational jurisdiction. These services can help manage complex compliance requirements related to user authentication, access control, and data protection, thereby aiding organizations in adhering to laws and regulations such as GDPR, HIPAA, or SOX.

381. Which of the following is most effective in preventing tailgating in a secure facility?
a. Implementing a strict dress code
b. Using biometric access control systems
c. Providing open access during business hours
d. Deploying CCTV cameras at all exits

Answer: b. Using biometric access control systems Explanation: Biometric access control systems, which require unique physical characteristics such as fingerprints or iris scans, effectively prevent unauthorized individuals from tailgating authorized users into secure areas. Unlike traditional methods that could be bypassed or shared (like badges or PINs), biometrics ensures that only registered individuals gain access, significantly reducing the risk of tailgating.

382. How can an organization mitigate the risk of phishing attacks aimed at stealing access credentials?
a. Decreasing the frequency of password changes
b. Implementing multi-factor authentication (MFA)
c. Reducing the complexity of password requirements
d. Encouraging the use of the same password across multiple sites

Answer: b. Implementing multi-factor authentication (MFA) Explanation: MFA adds layers of security by requiring additional verification methods beyond just a password, such as a code from a smartphone app or a fingerprint scan. This approach significantly mitigates the risk of phishing attacks because even if attackers obtain the password, they still need the second factor to gain access.

383. What is the best strategy to prevent brute force attacks on user accounts?
a. Removing account lockout policies
b. Enforcing complex password policies
c. Allowing unlimited login attempts
d. Disabling logging of authentication attempts

Answer: b. Enforcing complex password policies Explanation: Complex password policies that require a mix of characters, symbols, and lengths make it difficult for attackers to successfully carry out brute force attacks, as the number of possible combinations increases exponentially, thereby protecting user accounts from unauthorized access.

384. To prevent privilege escalation attacks, an organization should:
a. Grant all users administrative privileges to simplify access control
b. Regularly review and adjust user permissions to adhere to the principle of least privilege
c. Use a single shared account for all system administrators
d. Avoid updating software to maintain system stability

Answer: b. Regularly review and adjust user permissions to adhere to the principle of least privilege Explanation: Adhering to the principle of least privilege, by ensuring users have only the permissions necessary to perform their roles, reduces the risk of privilege escalation attacks. Regular audits and adjustments of user rights prevent unauthorized access to sensitive functions and data.

385. What technique can effectively reduce the risk of session hijacking?
a. Enabling HTTP everywhere
b. Implementing session timeouts and secure cookie handling
c. Increasing the session lifetime
d. Using predictable session IDs

Answer: b. Implementing session timeouts and secure cookie handling Explanation: Session timeouts and secure cookie handling, including attributes like Secure and HttpOnly, protect against session hijacking by limiting the duration of a session and preventing client-side scripts from accessing the session cookies, making it more difficult for attackers to hijack active sessions.

386. Which method best prevents an attacker from exploiting a SQL injection vulnerability to bypass authentication?
a. Using simple input validation
b. Employing parameterized queries or prepared statements
c. Increasing the length of user input fields
d. Encouraging users to use complex passwords

Answer: b. Employing parameterized queries or prepared statements Explanation: Parameterized queries or prepared statements ensure that SQL commands are defined and executed with user input being treated strictly as data, not as part of the SQL command. This approach effectively mitigates SQL injection risks, including those that could bypass authentication mechanisms.

387. To defend against man-in-the-middle (MitM) attacks in a network, an organization should:
a. Rely solely on antivirus software
b. Utilize unencrypted communication protocols

c. Implement and enforce the use of strong encryption protocols like TLS
d. Disable network monitoring tools

Answer: c. Implement and enforce the use of strong encryption protocols like TLS Explanation: Strong encryption protocols like TLS (Transport Layer Security) provide secure communication channels by encrypting the data transmitted over the network, thus preventing attackers from intercepting and modifying the data in transit, which is a common tactic in MitM attacks.

388. What is a proactive measure to prevent the exploitation of zero-day vulnerabilities?
a. Waiting for public disclosure before taking action
b. Implementing a robust patch management process
c. Using outdated software to avoid new vulnerabilities
d. Avoiding the use of third-party software

Answer: b. Implementing a robust patch management process Explanation: While zero-day vulnerabilities are unknown to vendors at the time of exploitation, a robust patch management process ensures that once a patch is available, it is quickly tested and applied. This process, combined with other preventive measures like intrusion detection systems and regular vulnerability assessments, helps in mitigating the risk of zero-day exploits.

389. Which of the following best ensures the prevention of unauthorized data access through removable media?
a. Encouraging the use of personal USB devices for data transfer
b. Disabling write access on all removable media devices
c. Implementing strict data encryption policies for data stored on removable media
d. Allowing free access to USB ports for convenience

Answer: c. Implementing strict data encryption policies for data stored on removable media Explanation: Enforcing encryption for data stored on removable media ensures that even if the media is lost or stolen, the data remains inaccessible to unauthorized users. This approach, coupled with controlled access to USB ports and the use of managed removable media, significantly reduces the risk of data leakage.

390. How can an organization prevent unauthorized access to sensitive systems through social engineering attacks?
a. Eliminating all forms of user authentication
b. Conducting regular security awareness training for employees
c. Sharing all passwords among team members for transparency
d. Relying solely on physical security measures

Answer: b. Conducting regular security awareness training for employees Explanation: Regular security awareness training equips employees with the knowledge to recognize and respond appropriately to social engineering tactics, such as phishing or pretexting. This human-centric approach to security significantly reduces the likelihood of employees inadvertently granting access to sensitive systems or information.

391. In the identity and access provisioning lifecycle, what is the primary purpose of the provisioning review process?
a. To ensure that all users have administrative access
b. To assess and adjust user access rights to align with current roles and responsibilities
c. To increase the number of user accounts for redundancy
d. To decentralize the access control system for easier management

Answer: b. To assess and adjust user access rights to align with current roles and responsibilities Explanation: The provisioning review process is integral to maintaining security and compliance within an organization. It involves regularly assessing user accounts and their access rights to ensure they accurately reflect the individual's current role and responsibilities. This process helps to prevent privilege creep and ensures that users do not retain access to resources that are no longer relevant to their position, thereby minimizing the risk of unauthorized access.

392. What is a critical step in the identity and access provisioning lifecycle when a new employee joins an organization?
a. Granting the employee guest access indefinitely
b. Immediately providing access to all systems for efficiency
c. Conducting a thorough needs-based analysis to determine necessary access
d. Assigning random access levels to expedite the onboarding process

Answer: c. Conducting a thorough needs-based analysis to determine necessary access Explanation: When a new employee joins an organization, it's crucial to conduct a needs-based analysis to ascertain the specific systems and data the employee requires access to, based on their role and responsibilities. This targeted approach ensures that employees are equipped with the necessary tools and information to perform their duties efficiently while adhering to the principle of least privilege, thereby reducing the risk of internal threats and data breaches.

393. During the offboarding process, what is a key step to ensure the security of organizational assets?
a. Keeping the accounts active for historical data analysis
b. Revoking all access rights and returning any company-owned devices
c. Increasing access rights to expedite knowledge transfer
d. Copying user data to public archives for transparency

Answer: b. Revoking all access rights and returning any company-owned devices Explanation: A critical component of the offboarding process is to revoke all access rights the departing employee has to organizational systems and resources, and ensure the return of any company-owned devices. This step is crucial to maintaining the security and integrity of the organization's assets and information, as it prevents former employees from accessing sensitive data or systems post-departure.

394. How does regular auditing of user accounts and access rights support the identity and access provisioning lifecycle?
a. By ensuring that all users have equal access rights
b. By identifying and rectifying any inconsistencies or inappropriate access levels
c. By encouraging the use of shared accounts for simplicity

d. By permanently locking accounts after the first audit for security

Answer: b. By identifying and rectifying any inconsistencies or inappropriate access levels Explanation: Regular auditing is a fundamental practice in the identity and access provisioning lifecycle that helps in identifying any discrepancies, inconsistencies, or instances of inappropriate access levels among user accounts. Through these audits, organizations can ensure that access rights are aligned with current job functions and responsibilities, and take corrective actions to amend any issues, thereby enhancing the overall security posture.

395. What role does automation play in the identity and access provisioning lifecycle?
a. To eliminate the need for passwords
b. To streamline the process of granting, updating, and revoking access rights efficiently
c. To allow unlimited access to all users for ease of use
d. To replace all human decision-making in the access control process

Answer: b. To streamline the process of granting, updating, and revoking access rights efficiently Explanation: Automation plays a crucial role in the identity and access provisioning lifecycle by streamlining the processes of granting, updating, and revoking access rights. It enables organizations to manage these tasks more efficiently and accurately, reducing the likelihood of human error and ensuring timely updates to access rights in response to role changes, thereby enhancing security and operational efficiency.

396. In what way does the principle of least privilege impact the identity and access provisioning lifecycle?
a. By granting all users unrestricted access to ensure operational efficiency
b. By ensuring users are provided only with the access necessary to perform their job functions
c. By requiring manual approval for every access request, regardless of urgency
d. By permanently disabling user accounts after a set period of inactivity

Answer: b. By ensuring users are provided only with the access necessary to perform their job functions Explanation: The principle of least privilege is a fundamental security concept that impacts the identity and access provisioning lifecycle by ensuring that users are granted only the access necessary to perform their specific job functions. This approach minimizes the risk of unauthorized access to sensitive information and systems, thereby enhancing the overall security posture of the organization.

397. How does the integration of role-based access control (RBAC) enhance the identity and access provisioning lifecycle?
a. By assigning the same level of access to all users
b. By simplifying the process of assigning access rights based on predefined roles
c. By eliminating the need for authentication mechanisms
d. By making the access provisioning process more complex and time-consuming

Answer: b. By simplifying the process of assigning access rights based on predefined roles Explanation: Role-based access control (RBAC) enhances the identity and access provisioning lifecycle by simplifying the assignment of access rights. Access permissions are granted based on predefined roles within the organization, which correspond to the tasks and responsibilities associated with those roles. This structured approach streamlines the provisioning process, ensures consistency in access rights assignments, and makes it easier to manage and update access rights as roles evolve or personnel change.

398. What is the significance of periodic access reviews in the identity and access provisioning lifecycle?
a. To increase the number of user accounts for redundancy
b. To ensure that access rights remain aligned with current roles, responsibilities, and security policies
c. To discourage the use of strong authentication methods
d. To permanently archive user activities for historical research

Answer: b. To ensure that access rights remain aligned with current roles, responsibilities, and security policies Explanation: Periodic access reviews are crucial in the identity and access provisioning lifecycle as they ensure that the access rights of users continue to align with their current roles, responsibilities, and the organization's security policies. These reviews help in identifying any discrepancies or outdated access rights that may pose security risks, allowing for timely remediation and adjustments to maintain a secure and compliant access environment.

399. How does the implementation of a centralized identity and access management (IAM) system benefit the identity and access provisioning lifecycle?
a. By allowing each department to implement its own access standards
b. By providing a unified platform for managing user identities, access rights, and provisioning processes
c. By eliminating the need for access control altogether
d. By enforcing a single password for all systems to simplify access

Answer: b. By providing a unified platform for managing user identities, access rights, and provisioning processes Explanation: A centralized identity and access management (IAM) system offers significant benefits to the identity and access provisioning lifecycle by providing a unified platform through which user identities, access rights, and the entire provisioning process can be managed efficiently. This centralization facilitates better visibility, control, and consistency across the organization's systems and applications, simplifying the management of access rights and enhancing security.

400. What is the primary goal of a vulnerability assessment within the Security Assessment and Testing domain?
a. To identify the physical security measures in place
b. To determine the effectiveness of the organization's training programs
c. To identify, quantify, and prioritize vulnerabilities in a system
d. To assess the organization's compliance with industry regulations

Answer: c. To identify, quantify, and prioritize vulnerabilities in a system Explanation: The primary goal of a vulnerability assessment is to identify, quantify, and prioritize vulnerabilities within a system. This involves scanning systems, networks, and software to detect vulnerabilities and then evaluating the potential impact and likelihood of exploitation to prioritize remediation efforts. This process helps organizations understand their security posture and focus their efforts on mitigating the most critical vulnerabilities.

401. Which technique is used in penetration testing to simulate attacks from someone with no inside knowledge of the network?
a. White box testing
b. Black box testing
c. Gray box testing
d. Red teaming

Answer: b. Black box testing Explanation: Black box testing in penetration testing simulates attacks from an external attacker who has no prior knowledge of the internal systems or network. The tester is given no information beforehand and must find and exploit vulnerabilities purely from an external perspective, similar to how an actual attacker might operate. This approach helps identify weaknesses that could be exploited by someone without insider access.

402. When conducting a security audit, which of the following is an essential step?
a. Bypassing security controls to expedite the process
b. Relying solely on automated tools without manual verification
c. Reviewing and assessing the alignment of security controls with policies and standards
d. Ignoring low-risk findings to focus on high-impact vulnerabilities

Answer: c. Reviewing and assessing the alignment of security controls with policies and standards Explanation: An essential step in conducting a security audit is reviewing and assessing how well the implemented security controls align with the organization's established policies, standards, and regulatory requirements. This involves a thorough examination of physical, administrative, and technical controls to ensure they effectively enforce the security policies and protect the organization's assets.

403. In the context of security assessments, what is the significance of using a red team?
a. To provide IT support to end-users
b. To perform routine maintenance tasks on security systems
c. To simulate real-world attacks to test the organization's defenses
d. To conduct daily backups and disaster recovery drills

Answer: c. To simulate real-world attacks to test the organization's defenses Explanation: A red team is used in security assessments to simulate real-world attacks on an organization's security infrastructure to test the effectiveness of its defenses. This adversarial approach involves a team of security experts acting as attackers to discover and exploit vulnerabilities, helping the organization identify weaknesses in their security posture and improve their response capabilities.

404. What is the role of a security code review in the Security Assessment and Testing domain?
a. To evaluate the physical security of the organization's facilities
b. To assess the organization's adherence to compliance regulations
c. To examine the source code of applications for security vulnerabilities
d. To conduct an inventory of all hardware assets within the organization

Answer: c. To examine the source code of applications for security vulnerabilities Explanation: A security code review involves a detailed examination of an application's source code to identify security vulnerabilities that could be exploited by attackers. This process is crucial for uncovering flaws such as injection vulnerabilities, insecure dependencies, and other weaknesses that automated tools might miss, thereby enhancing the application's security posture.

405. How does a blue team contribute to security assessment and testing?
a. By acting as the offensive team in penetration testing exercises
b. By defending against simulated attacks in a controlled environment
c. By conducting external audits of the organization's security measures
d. By designing and implementing new security technologies

Answer: b. By defending against simulated attacks in a controlled environment Explanation: A blue team contributes to security assessment and testing by taking on the defensive role against simulated attacks, often in exercises involving a red team. The blue team's objective is to detect, respond to, and mitigate these simulated attacks, enhancing the organization's incident response and defensive capabilities through real-world practice.

406. Which of the following best describes the purpose of a security gap analysis?
a. To compare the current state of security with desired security goals or standards
b. To catalog all software used within the organization
c. To measure the physical security of data centers only
d. To calculate the financial impact of potential security breaches

Answer: a. To compare the current state of security with desired security goals or standards Explanation: A security gap analysis is conducted to compare the current state of an organization's security measures against the desired security goals, standards, or best practices. This analysis helps identify areas where security controls are lacking or insufficient, enabling the organization to develop a roadmap for addressing these gaps and enhancing overall security.

407. What is the main focus of a security control review?
a. To ensure all employees are satisfied with the IT support
b. To verify the operational effectiveness and compliance of implemented security controls
c. To count the number of fire extinguishers in the office
d. To review the organization's budget and financial statements

Answer: b. To verify the operational effectiveness and compliance of implemented security controls Explanation: The main focus of a security control review is to verify the operational effectiveness of the security controls that have been implemented within an organization and to ensure compliance with relevant policies, standards, and regulations. This review assesses whether the controls are functioning as intended and are effective in mitigating identified risks.

408. In the Security Assessment and Testing domain, what is the significance of a post-incident review?
a. To assign blame to individuals involved in the incident
b. To review the organization's sales strategy post-incident
c. To analyze the incident's handling and identify lessons learned and improvements
d. To update the organization's website design

Answer: c. To analyze the incident's handling and identify lessons learned and improvements Explanation: A post-incident review is significant because it involves analyzing how a security incident was handled, from detection to resolution, to identify what was done well and what could be improved. This review helps in extracting valuable lessons learned, which can be used to enhance the organization's incident response procedures and overall security posture, preventing future incidents or minimizing their impact.

409. What is the purpose of continuous monitoring in the context of security assessment and testing?
a. To constantly entertain the IT staff
b. To keep track of employee attendance and punctuality
c. To provide ongoing oversight of the risk management process and security controls
d. To monitor the stock market and financial trends

Answer: c. To provide ongoing oversight of the risk management process and security controls Explanation: Continuous monitoring in the context of security assessment and testing serves the purpose of providing ongoing oversight and evaluation of an organization's risk management process and the effectiveness of its security controls. This proactive approach ensures that security controls remain effective over time and that any changes in the threat landscape or organizational environment are quickly identified and addressed.

410. What is the primary purpose of conducting a security assessment strategy within an organization?
a. To ensure all staff members receive equal bonuses
b. To identify and prioritize risks to organizational assets and data
c. To select new office locations based on employee preferences
d. To design the layout of the organization's holiday party

Answer: b. To identify and prioritize risks to organizational assets and data Explanation: The primary purpose of a security assessment strategy is to systematically identify and prioritize risks to an organization's assets and data. This involves evaluating the potential threats, vulnerabilities, and impacts to determine the most critical areas of focus for mitigation efforts, ensuring the protection of sensitive information and maintaining the integrity of organizational operations.

411. In developing a test strategy for a new software application, what is a key consideration to ensure comprehensive security testing?
a. The color scheme of the application interface
b. The inclusion of both static and dynamic analysis methods
c. The office hours of the development team
d. The brand of coffee used in the break room

Answer: b. The inclusion of both static and dynamic analysis methods Explanation: A key consideration in developing a test strategy for a new software application is the inclusion of both static (SAST) and dynamic (DAST) analysis methods. Static analysis examines the application's code without executing it, while dynamic analysis tests the application during runtime. This dual approach ensures a more comprehensive assessment of the application's security posture by identifying vulnerabilities that may not be evident through a single method of testing.

412. When selecting assessment tools for a security testing plan, what factor should be prioritized to ensure effectiveness?
a. The popularity of the tool in social media
b. The tool's compatibility with the organization's technology stack
c. The color scheme of the tool's user interface
d. The personal preferences of the company's CEO

Answer: b. The tool's compatibility with the organization's technology stack Explanation: When selecting assessment tools for a security testing plan, it's crucial to prioritize the tool's compatibility with the organization's technology stack. This ensures that the tools can effectively analyze and interact with the systems, applications, and protocols in use, thereby providing accurate and relevant security insights. Compatibility facilitates seamless integration into the existing environment, maximizing the utility and effectiveness of the testing efforts.

413. How should an organization approach the integration of security testing within its software development lifecycle (SDLC)?
a. By conducting security testing only after deployment
b. By embedding security testing at multiple stages of the SDLC
c. By outsourcing security testing to avoid internal biases
d. By limiting security testing to third-party components only

Answer: b. By embedding security testing at multiple stages of the SDLC Explanation: An organization should approach the integration of security testing within its SDLC by embedding security testing at multiple stages, from initial design and development to post-deployment. This ensures that security considerations are incorporated throughout the development process, allowing for the early identification and remediation of vulnerabilities, ultimately leading to more secure software products.

414. What role does automated testing play in a security assessment and testing strategy?
a. To replace the need for any manual testing
b. To provide a comprehensive one-time security solution
c. To supplement manual testing efforts by covering a broader range of tests efficiently
d. To serve as the sole basis for all security investment decisions

Answer: c. To supplement manual testing efforts by covering a broader range of tests efficiently Explanation: Automated testing plays a crucial role in a security assessment and testing strategy by supplementing manual testing efforts. It allows for the efficient execution of a broad range of tests, covering more ground in less time than manual methods alone. While automated testing enhances the testing process by identifying known vulnerabilities quickly, it does not replace the need for manual testing, which can uncover more complex and nuanced security issues.

415. What is the importance of defining clear objectives when planning a penetration test?
a. To ensure the test is limited to assessing the organization's party planning capabilities
b. To provide a focused and effective assessment by clearly understanding the scope and goals
c. To determine the catering menu for the post-test review meeting
d. To select the background music for the testing environment

Answer: b. To provide a focused and effective assessment by clearly understanding the scope and goals Explanation: Defining clear objectives when planning a penetration test is crucial to provide a focused and effective assessment. Clear objectives help to understand the specific scope, goals, and expected outcomes of the test, ensuring that efforts are directed appropriately to evaluate the security posture against realistic threat scenarios. This focused approach maximizes the value of the test by aligning it with the organization's security needs and priorities.

416. In the context of security assessments, why is it critical to conduct both internal and external testing?
a. To ensure the office temperature is comfortable for both employees and visitors
b. To evaluate the security posture from both an insider's and an outsider's perspective
c. To compare the efficiency of internal and external mail delivery systems
d. To decide on interior and exterior decorations for the corporate office

Answer: b. To evaluate the security posture from both an insider's and an outsider's perspective Explanation: Conducting both internal and external testing is critical in security assessments to evaluate the organization's security posture from multiple perspectives. Internal testing simulates attacks that might originate from within the organization, taking advantage of insider access, while external testing simulates attacks from outside the organization, with no special access privileges. This comprehensive approach ensures a more complete assessment of security vulnerabilities and threats.

417. What is the significance of including social engineering techniques in a security testing strategy?
a. To improve the social skills of the security team
b. To assess the human element of security and the susceptibility to manipulation
c. To organize team-building activities for the IT department
d. To enhance the company's social media presence

Answer: b. To assess the human element of security and the susceptibility to manipulation Explanation: Including social engineering techniques in a security testing strategy is significant because it assesses the human element of security, particularly the susceptibility of staff and personnel to manipulation and deceitful tactics. Social engineering tests, such as phishing simulations, help identify potential weaknesses in employee awareness and training, allowing organizations to strengthen their defenses not just technologically but also in terms of human factors.

418. How does continuous monitoring contribute to an organization's security assessment and testing strategy?
a. By constantly broadcasting the company's financial performance

b. By providing ongoing visibility into the security posture and identifying changes in real time
c. By monitoring employee break times and productivity levels
d. By tracking the stock levels in the company cafeteria

Answer: b. By providing ongoing visibility into the security posture and identifying changes in real time Explanation: Continuous monitoring is a critical component of an organization's security assessment and testing strategy as it provides ongoing visibility into the security posture, allowing for the identification of changes and emerging threats in real time. This proactive approach enables organizations to detect and respond to security incidents more swiftly, maintaining a strong security posture in the face of an ever-evolving threat landscape.

419. Why is it essential to conduct a test of security controls after any significant change in the IT environment?
a. To ensure the new coffee machine does not interfere with Wi-Fi signals
b. To verify that security controls remain effective and have not been compromised by the changes
c. To decide on new artwork for the office walls post-change
d. To celebrate the change with a company-wide party

Answer: b. To verify that security controls remain effective and have not been compromised by the changes Explanation: It is essential to conduct a test of security controls after any significant change in the IT environment to verify that the controls remain effective and have not been compromised by the changes. Changes, such as system upgrades, network reconfigurations, or the introduction of new technologies, can introduce new vulnerabilities or impact the functioning of existing security measures. Testing ensures that security controls are still functioning as intended and providing the necessary protection.

420. What is the primary objective of implementing management controls within an organization's security framework?
a. To decorate the office during holiday seasons
b. To ensure compliance with internal policies and external regulations
c. To schedule company-wide social events
d. To manage the cafeteria menu

Answer: b. To ensure compliance with internal policies and external regulations Explanation: The primary objective of implementing management controls within an organization's security framework is to ensure compliance with internal policies and external regulations. Management controls are designed to provide a structured approach to managing and mitigating risks, enforcing policy adherence, and ensuring that the organization's security practices align with legal, regulatory, and industry standards.

421. How do operational controls contribute to an organization's security posture?
a. By facilitating team-building activities among employees
b. By providing day-to-day defense against security threats
c. By organizing annual corporate retreats
d. By managing the office supply inventory

Answer: b. By providing day-to-day defense against security threats Explanation: Operational controls are essential to an organization's security posture as they provide day-to-day defense against security threats. These controls encompass the implementation of security policies, procedures, and technical measures designed to protect the organization's assets, detect security incidents, and respond to potential threats effectively. They ensure the ongoing protection of information systems and data against unauthorized access, use, disclosure, disruption, modification, or destruction.

422. In the context of security processes, what role do technical controls play?
a. To enhance the aesthetic appeal of the office environment
b. To automate and enforce security policies through technology
c. To manage employee parking allocations
d. To select entertainment options for corporate events

Answer: b. To automate and enforce security policies through technology Explanation: Technical controls play a crucial role in the context of security processes by automating and enforcing security policies through technology. These controls include firewalls, encryption, intrusion detection systems, and access control mechanisms that provide a layer of protection by preventing unauthorized access, ensuring data confidentiality and integrity, and detecting and responding to security incidents in real-time.

423. Why is it important to regularly review and update security policies and procedures?
a. To keep the office layout fresh and engaging
b. To adapt to evolving threats and changing business requirements
c. To plan the annual company picnic
d. To revise the employee dress code

Answer: b. To adapt to evolving threats and changing business requirements Explanation: It is important to regularly review and update security policies and procedures to adapt to evolving threats and changing business requirements. The threat landscape and technology environment are constantly changing, which can introduce new vulnerabilities and risks. Regularly updating security policies and procedures ensures that an organization's security measures remain effective, relevant, and capable of protecting its assets against current and emerging threats.

424. What is the significance of conducting security awareness training for all employees?
a. To prepare for the annual talent show
b. To enhance the overall security culture and reduce human error
c. To improve the quality of office potlucks
d. To organize corporate sports leagues

Answer: b. To enhance the overall security culture and reduce human error Explanation: The significance of conducting security awareness training for all employees lies in enhancing the overall security culture of the organization and reducing human error. Employees are often considered the weakest link in an organization's security chain. By providing regular and comprehensive security awareness training, employees become more aware of potential security threats, best practices, and their roles and responsibilities in maintaining security, thereby reducing the likelihood of security breaches caused by human error.

425. How does incident response planning support an organization's security strategy?
a. By organizing social events to boost morale after an incident
b. By ensuring a structured and efficient response to security incidents
c. By facilitating the annual budget allocation process
d. By coordinating office space renovations

Answer: b. By ensuring a structured and efficient response to security incidents Explanation: Incident response planning is a critical component of an organization's security strategy as it ensures a structured and efficient response to security incidents. A well-defined incident response plan outlines the procedures, roles, and responsibilities for detecting, responding to, and recovering from security incidents. This planning enables organizations to minimize the impact of incidents, restore normal operations quickly, and mitigate the risks of future occurrences.

426. What is the purpose of implementing change management in the security process?
a. To schedule holiday decorations in the office
b. To ensure secure and controlled modifications to IT systems
c. To manage seating arrangements in the open office space
d. To plan the annual company gala

Answer: b. To ensure secure and controlled modifications to IT systems Explanation: The purpose of implementing change management in the security process is to ensure secure and controlled modifications to IT systems. Change management involves a systematic approach to proposing, approving, testing, and implementing changes to information systems and technologies. This process helps in mitigating risks associated with changes, ensuring that modifications do not introduce new vulnerabilities or compromise the security posture of the organization.

427. In what way do configuration management practices enhance security?
a. By ensuring all employees have ergonomic chairs
b. By maintaining the integrity and security of system configurations
c. By organizing the layout of corporate parking
d. By curating art installations in the office

Answer: b. By maintaining the integrity and security of system configurations Explanation: Configuration management practices enhance security by maintaining the integrity and security of system configurations. These practices involve documenting, managing, and controlling the configurations of IT systems and components, ensuring they are set up and maintained according to secure baseline configurations. This prevents unauthorized changes and helps in quickly identifying and rectifying any deviations that could compromise security.

428. Why is the segregation of duties an important control in the security process?
a. To ensure diversity in the company's softball team
b. To reduce the risk of fraud and unauthorized activities

c. To distribute office cleaning responsibilities
d. To organize diverse company lunch menus

Answer: b. To reduce the risk of fraud and unauthorized activities Explanation: The segregation of duties is an important control in the security process because it reduces the risk of fraud and unauthorized activities. By dividing tasks and responsibilities among different individuals or groups, an organization can prevent any single person from having the ability to carry out and conceal inappropriate actions. This separation of functions acts as a deterrent to malicious activities and enhances the overall security and integrity of processes and systems.

429. What is the primary purpose of conducting penetration testing on an organization's network?
a. To evaluate the performance of network administrators
b. To identify vulnerabilities that could be exploited by attackers
c. To measure the network's data throughput
d. To check the efficiency of network cabling

Answer: b. To identify vulnerabilities that could be exploited by attackers Explanation: Penetration testing, often known as "pen testing," is a simulated cyber attack against an organization's network to identify exploitable vulnerabilities. The primary purpose is to identify security weaknesses that could be exploited by attackers, providing an opportunity for the organization to strengthen its defenses before a real attack occurs.

430. Why is it important to perform vulnerability scanning regularly?
a. To ensure the office Wi-Fi remains operational
b. To keep the IT department busy
c. To identify and mitigate security vulnerabilities in a timely manner
d. To monitor the usage of office printers

Answer: c. To identify and mitigate security vulnerabilities in a timely manner Explanation: Regular vulnerability scanning is crucial for identifying and mitigating security vulnerabilities within an organization's IT infrastructure. By frequently scanning for vulnerabilities, organizations can detect security weaknesses early and take appropriate measures to address them, thereby reducing the risk of exploitation by malicious actors.

431. How does dynamic application security testing (DAST) differ from static application security testing (SAST)?
a. DAST tests the application in its running state, while SAST analyzes the source code
b. DAST is only used for web applications, while SAST is used for network security
c. DAST optimizes application performance, whereas SAST focuses on functionality testing
d. DAST requires a complete application build, while SAST works on partial code snippets

Answer: a. DAST tests the application in its running state, while SAST analyzes the source code Explanation: Dynamic Application Security Testing (DAST) approaches security testing by examining the application in its running state, simulating attacks against a live application. In contrast, Static Application Security Testing (SAST) analyzes the application's source code or binary code to identify vulnerabilities without executing the program. Each method has its strengths, with DAST identifying runtime issues and SAST uncovering vulnerabilities in the codebase.

432. What role does fuzz testing play in security control testing?
a. To ensure user interfaces are intuitive
b. To test how systems handle unexpected or random input data
c. To measure the speed of database queries
d. To assess the graphical quality of application icons

Answer: b. To test how systems handle unexpected or random input data Explanation: Fuzz testing, or fuzzing, involves providing unexpected, random, or invalid data inputs to a computer program. The objective is to uncover potential security vulnerabilities that could be exploited if the system does not properly handle anomalous data. Fuzz testing helps identify buffer overflows, unhandled exceptions, and other security weaknesses that could lead to crashes or exploitable conditions.

433. What is the significance of using a security information and event management (SIEM) system in security testing?
a. To manage employee schedules and vacations
b. To aggregate and analyze security-related events from various sources
c. To track the stock market performance of the organization
d. To automate the distribution of marketing emails

Answer: b. To aggregate and analyze security-related events from various sources Explanation: A Security Information and Event Management (SIEM) system plays a crucial role in security testing by aggregating, analyzing, and correlating security-related events and logs from various sources within an organization's IT infrastructure. SIEM systems help in real-time security monitoring, incident response, and forensic analysis by providing a centralized view of the security posture and identifying anomalous activities that could indicate a security breach.

434. Why are code reviews an essential part of security control testing?
a. To ensure coding standards are aesthetically pleasing
b. To identify and rectify security vulnerabilities in the source code
c. To assess the programming skills of new hires
d. To determine the best programming language for a project

Answer: b. To identify and rectify security vulnerabilities in the source code Explanation: Code reviews are a critical aspect of security control testing because they involve a systematic examination of an application's source code. Conducted by experienced developers or security analysts, code reviews aim to identify and rectify security vulnerabilities, logical errors, and non-compliance with coding standards. This process helps improve the security and quality of the software by catching vulnerabilities early in the development lifecycle.

435. In what way does threat modeling contribute to security control testing?
a. By designing aesthetically pleasing user interfaces

b. By identifying potential threats and vulnerabilities in system designs
c. By predicting future stock market trends for cybersecurity companies
d. By planning corporate team-building events

Answer: b. By identifying potential threats and vulnerabilities in system designs Explanation: Threat modeling is a proactive approach to security control testing that involves identifying potential threats and vulnerabilities in system designs and architectures. It allows organizations to understand the attack surface, prioritize security risks, and implement appropriate security controls to mitigate those risks before the system is developed or deployed, enhancing the overall security posture.

436. What is the purpose of a security audit in the context of security control testing?
a. To review and evaluate the effectiveness of an organization's security measures
b. To audit the company's financial accounts
c. To assess the efficiency of the HR department
d. To evaluate the company's social media strategy

Answer: a. To review and evaluate the effectiveness of an organization's security measures Explanation: A security audit is a systematic evaluation of an organization's security measures, policies, and controls to determine their effectiveness and compliance with internal and external standards and regulations. Security audits help identify weaknesses, non-compliance, and improvement areas in the organization's security posture, leading to enhanced protection against threats and breaches.

437. Why is user acceptance testing (UAT) important from a security perspective?
a. To ensure the cafeteria menu meets employee preferences
b. To validate that security features meet user requirements and expectations
c. To decide on the office's interior design
d. To organize the annual company sports event

Answer: b. To validate that security features meet user requirements and expectations Explanation: User Acceptance Testing (UAT) is crucial from a security perspective because it involves testing the application in a real-world scenario to validate that the security features and controls meet user requirements and expectations. UAT helps ensure that security measures do not impede usability while still providing the necessary level of protection, leading to a balanced and effective security posture that aligns with business needs.

438. How does incorporating security testing into the software development lifecycle (SDLC) enhance an application's security?
a. By ensuring that coffee breaks are efficiently managed
b. By integrating security considerations from the initial stages of development
c. By determining the theme for the company's holiday party
d. By scheduling corporate wellness programs

Answer: b. By integrating security considerations from the initial stages of development Explanation: Incorporating security testing into the Software Development Lifecycle (SDLC) enhances an application's security by integrating security considerations and practices from the initial stages of development. This approach, often referred to as "secure by design" or "DevSecOps," ensures that security is a fundamental component of the development process, rather than an afterthought. By doing so, vulnerabilities can be identified and addressed early, reducing the risk of security issues in the final product.

439. What is the primary advantage of automated security testing tools over manual testing methods?
a. Automated tools require more specialized training to operate.
b. They can execute a large number of tests rapidly and consistently.
c. Manual methods are more effective at identifying logic errors.
d. Automated tools are less expensive in the short term.

Answer: b. They can execute a large number of tests rapidly and consistently. Explanation: Automated security testing tools are designed to perform a wide range of tests in a short amount of time, offering rapid and consistent results. This capability is particularly advantageous for repetitive tasks and regression testing, where the same tests need to be executed multiple times to ensure that previously tested software continues to perform correctly after changes. Unlike manual testing, which is time-consuming and subject to human error, automated tools enhance efficiency and coverage in security testing.

440. In the context of security testing, what is the significance of false positive results?
a. They indicate that the system is fully secure.
b. They are accurate findings that require immediate remediation.
c. They represent benign actions mistakenly flagged as security threats.
d. They confirm the effectiveness of security controls.

Answer: c. They represent benign actions mistakenly flagged as security threats. Explanation: False positives in security testing refer to benign actions or data that are incorrectly identified as security threats by testing tools or processes. While false positives do not indicate actual vulnerabilities, they are significant because they can lead to unnecessary alarm, resource wastage in investigating non-issues, and potential desensitization to real security alerts if they occur frequently. Managing and minimizing false positives is crucial to maintaining the efficiency and effectiveness of security operations.

441. How do manual security testing methods complement automated tools in a comprehensive security testing strategy?
a. Manual testing is only used when automated tools are unavailable.
b. Automated tools can replace manual methods entirely due to their efficiency.
c. Manual methods enable deeper analysis of complex security issues that automated tools might miss.
d. Manual testing is less accurate and therefore only used for preliminary assessments.

Answer: c. Manual methods enable deeper analysis of complex security issues that automated tools might miss. Explanation: Manual security testing methods play a crucial role in a comprehensive security testing strategy by providing the ability to perform in-depth analysis and exploration of complex and context-specific security issues that automated tools may overlook. Human testers can apply critical thinking, experience, and intuition to identify subtle vulnerabilities, logic flaws, and issues that require nuanced understanding, which automated tools might not be programmed to detect. This combination of manual and automated testing ensures a more thorough examination of an organization's security posture.

442. What role does the interpretation of test outputs play in the effectiveness of security assessments?
a. It is an unnecessary step since automated tools provide clear and final results.
b. Accurate interpretation is crucial for understanding the real security posture and prioritizing remediation efforts.
c. Interpretation is only required for manual testing outputs, not for automated tools.
d. Test outputs do not require interpretation; they are only used for compliance purposes.

Answer: b. Accurate interpretation is crucial for understanding the real security posture and prioritizing remediation efforts. Explanation: The interpretation of test outputs is a critical component of security assessments. It involves analyzing the results provided by both automated tools and manual testing methods to understand the real security posture of the system being tested. Accurate interpretation helps in distinguishing between false positives and genuine vulnerabilities, understanding the context and impact of each finding, and prioritizing remediation efforts based on the severity and potential impact of the identified issues. This process ensures that security efforts are focused on the most critical vulnerabilities, thereby enhancing the overall security of the organization.

443. Why is it important to review both automated and manual test outputs in a security assessment report?
a. Automated outputs are always more reliable than manual findings.
b. Manual test outputs are considered outdated and less relevant.
c. Reviewing both provides a comprehensive view of security vulnerabilities and strengths.
d. Only automated test outputs should be included in reports for efficiency.

Answer: c. Reviewing both provides a comprehensive view of security vulnerabilities and strengths. Explanation: In a security assessment report, including both automated and manual test outputs is essential to provide a comprehensive and accurate view of the security vulnerabilities and strengths of the system or application being assessed. Automated tools can quickly identify a broad range of known vulnerabilities, while manual testing can uncover more subtle, context-specific issues that automated tools may miss. Together, they offer a complete picture of the security landscape, enabling more effective decision-making regarding risk management and remediation priorities.

444. How does the level of detail in test outputs affect the subsequent remediation process?
a. More detailed outputs can lead to confusion and slow down the remediation process.
b. Detailed outputs provide the necessary information for effective vulnerability management and remediation.
c. The level of detail in test outputs has no impact on the remediation process.
d. Less detailed outputs are preferred as they require less time to review.

Answer: b. Detailed outputs provide the necessary information for effective vulnerability management and remediation. Explanation: Detailed test outputs are crucial for the remediation process as they provide in-depth information about each identified vulnerability, including its nature, location, potential impact, and, in some cases, suggested remediation actions. This level of detail is essential for security teams to understand the vulnerabilities fully, assess their criticality, and develop effective remediation plans. Without sufficient detail, the remediation process might be inefficient, as teams could spend additional time investigating the issues further to understand how to fix them properly.

445. What is the impact of test environment configuration on the reliability of security testing outputs?
a. The test environment configuration has no impact on the reliability of testing outputs.
b. A properly configured test environment ensures that testing outputs closely reflect the production environment's security posture.
c. A less realistic test environment configuration provides more conservative and safer results.
d. The more complex the test environment, the less reliable the testing outputs.

Answer: b. A properly configured test environment ensures that testing outputs closely reflect the production environment's security posture. Explanation: The configuration of the test environment plays a critical role in the reliability of security testing outputs. A test environment that closely mirrors the production environment in terms of software, hardware, network configurations, and security controls provides a more accurate reflection of the real-world security posture. This alignment ensures that vulnerabilities identified during testing are relevant and applicable to the production environment, making the results reliable and actionable for remediation efforts.

446. Why is it essential to periodically review and update the methodologies used for security testing?
a. Security testing methodologies do not require updates once established.
b. Periodic reviews ensure methodologies remain effective against evolving security threats and technologies.
c. Updating methodologies is only necessary when there is a significant change in the organization's IT infrastructure.
d. Reviewing methodologies increases the complexity of security testing, making it more challenging for attackers.

Answer: b. Periodic reviews ensure methodologies remain effective against evolving security threats and technologies. Explanation: The cybersecurity landscape is continuously evolving, with new threats, vulnerabilities, and technologies emerging regularly. Periodically reviewing and updating security testing methodologies is essential to ensure they remain effective and relevant in identifying and mitigating current and emerging security risks. This practice ensures that the methodologies adapt to changes in the organization's IT environment, threat landscape, and industry best practices, thereby maintaining the effectiveness and comprehensiveness of security assessments.

447. In what way do test output analysis tools aid in the interpretation of security testing results?
a. They eliminate the need for human analysis, making the process entirely automated.
b. These tools help in organizing, correlating, and prioritizing findings for more informed decision-making.
c. Analysis tools are only useful for large organizations with complex infrastructures.
d. These tools are primarily used for aesthetic enhancement of reports and have little practical utility.

Answer: b. These tools help in organizing, correlating, and prioritizing findings for more informed decision-making. Explanation: Test output analysis tools play a crucial role in interpreting security testing results by helping security teams organize, correlate, and prioritize the findings. These tools can automate the analysis of large volumes of data generated by security tests, identify patterns and correlations among different findings, and prioritize vulnerabilities based on their severity and potential impact. This support facilitates more informed decision-making regarding risk management and remediation efforts, enhancing the efficiency and effectiveness of the security testing process.

448. Which of the following is a common vulnerability in a monolithic architecture system?
a. Increased scalability due to its single, unified component structure.
b. High resilience to failure, as components are loosely coupled.
c. A single point of failure that can compromise the entire system.
d. Enhanced security through distributed processing.

Answer: c. A single point of failure that can compromise the entire system. Explanation: In a monolithic architecture, the application is designed as a single and indivisible unit, which makes the entire system vulnerable to a single point of failure. If one part of the system fails, it can affect the entire application's availability and functionality. This contrasts with microservices or distributed architectures, where components are loosely coupled, and the failure of one service does not necessarily bring down the entire system.

449. In a Zero Trust architecture, which of the following is considered a vulnerability?
a. Rigorous identity and access management procedures.
b. The principle of least privilege applied to all users and devices.
c. Implicit trust granted to users or devices within the network perimeter.
d. Continuous monitoring and validation of all network transactions.

Answer: c. Implicit trust granted to users or devices within the network perimeter. Explanation: Zero Trust architecture operates on the principle that no entity, either inside or outside the network perimeter, should be automatically trusted. A common vulnerability in traditional network architectures is the implicit trust granted to users and devices once they are within the network perimeter, which can be exploited by attackers who breach the perimeter defenses. Zero Trust mitigates this risk by continuously verifying the security status of all entities trying to access resources, regardless of their location.

450. What vulnerability is introduced by a lack of network segmentation in security architecture?
a. Enhanced performance due to reduced complexity.
b. Improved user experience through simplified access controls.
c. Increased risk of lateral movement by attackers within the network.
d. Decreased operational costs due to fewer infrastructure components.

Answer: c. Increased risk of lateral movement by attackers within the network. Explanation: Lack of network segmentation creates a flat network where once an attacker gains access to one part of the network, they can more easily move laterally to other areas. Segmentation divides the network into smaller, controlled zones, reducing the attack surface and limiting an attacker's ability to move freely and access sensitive information or critical systems. Proper segmentation acts as a containment mechanism, making it harder for threats to propagate across the network.

451. How does reliance on legacy systems introduce vulnerabilities into security architecture?
a. Legacy systems often have enhanced encryption methods that are not compatible with newer technologies.
b. The modern, intuitive interfaces of legacy systems improve user compliance with security policies.
c. They may contain unpatched security vulnerabilities due to end-of-support issues.
d. Legacy systems typically employ advanced AI-driven threat detection mechanisms.

Answer: c. They may contain unpatched security vulnerabilities due to end-of-support issues. Explanation: Legacy systems can become significant security liabilities as they age. Over time, vendors may cease support for older products, including updates and security patches, leaving known vulnerabilities unaddressed. Attackers can exploit these vulnerabilities to gain unauthorized access or disrupt services. The outdated nature of legacy systems often means they lack modern security features and compliance with current standards, further increasing the risk.

452. What vulnerability does "hard-coded credentials" within an application's architecture introduce?
a. They simplify the user authentication process, enhancing user experience.
b. Hard-coded credentials improve system performance by reducing authentication overhead.
c. They pose a high security risk as attackers can exploit them to gain unauthorized access.
d. Hard-coded credentials facilitate easier integration with third-party services.

Answer: c. They pose a high security risk as attackers can exploit them to gain unauthorized access. Explanation: Hard-coding credentials (such as passwords or API keys) within an application's code is a significant security risk. If the source code is exposed or can be accessed through reverse engineering, these credentials become an easy target for attackers, granting them unauthorized access to systems or sensitive data. This practice violates the basic security principle of secure credential storage and management.

453. Which vulnerability is most associated with "Shadow IT" in an organization's security architecture?
a. Improved compliance with data protection regulations.
b. Unauthorized devices or software that might not comply with security policies.
c. Enhanced data redundancy and backup solutions.
d. Increased innovation and rapid deployment of new technologies.

Answer: b. Unauthorized devices or software that might not comply with security policies. Explanation: "Shadow IT" refers to IT devices, software, and services outside the ownership or control of IT departments. These can introduce significant vulnerabilities as they might not adhere to the organization's established security policies and controls. The lack of visibility and management over these elements increases the risk of data breaches, non-compliance with regulations, and other security incidents.

454. How does the use of open-source components without proper vetting introduce vulnerabilities?
a. Open-source components are always more secure than proprietary software due to their transparency.

b. The collaborative nature of open-source projects guarantees real-time patching of vulnerabilities.

c. They may include hidden malicious code or known vulnerabilities that have not been patched.

d. Using open-source components eliminates the need for in-depth security audits.

Answer: c. They may include hidden malicious code or known vulnerabilities that have not been patched. Explanation: While open-source software offers advantages like transparency and community support, using such components without thorough vetting can introduce vulnerabilities. Some open-source projects may lack the resources to promptly address security issues, and others might not be actively maintained. Without proper vetting, there's a risk of incorporating components with known vulnerabilities or even malicious code into the organization's technology stack.

455. Implementing a Security Information and Event Management (SIEM) system primarily helps an organization with:

a. Physical security and access control to facilities.

b. Encryption key management and secure coding practices.

c. Real-time monitoring, correlation of events, and incident response.

d. Human resources management and background checks.

Answer: c. Real-time monitoring, correlation of events, and incident response. Explanation: A SIEM system is designed to provide real-time analysis of security alerts generated by applications and network hardware. It aggregates and correlates data from different sources to identify patterns that may indicate a security incident, facilitating timely incident response. This capability is central to enhancing an organization's security posture, unlike the other options which pertain to more specific or unrelated security domains.

456. In the context of security operations, the principle of least privilege is applied to:

a. Ensure that all users have administrative rights for ease of system maintenance.

b. Limit user access rights to only those necessary to perform their job functions.

c. Grant everyone unrestricted access to all system resources for transparency.

d. Allow unrestricted access to network resources during non-business hours.

Answer: b. Limit user access rights to only those necessary to perform their job functions. Explanation: The principle of least privilege is a critical security concept that involves providing users with the minimum levels of access — or permissions — needed to perform their job functions. This minimizes the potential damage from accidents or malicious acts by limiting access rights for users to the bare minimum necessary to perform their work.

457. A Security Operations Center (SOC) analyst detects an anomaly in network traffic that suggests a potential intrusion. The FIRST step they should take is to:

a. Shut down the entire network to prevent further intrusion.

b. Immediately inform the media to warn other organizations.

c. Validate the anomaly to confirm it is a true positive incident.

d. Launch a counter-attack against the source of the intrusion.

Answer: c. Validate the anomaly to confirm it is a true positive incident. Explanation: The initial step in responding to a potential security incident, such as an anomaly detected in network traffic, is to validate the anomaly to ascertain whether it is a genuine incident (true positive) or a false alarm. This involves analyzing the context and additional information to verify the nature of the anomaly. Premature actions like network shutdown or external communications can lead to unnecessary disruption or panic.

458. During a security incident, maintaining a chain of custody is essential for:
a. Ensuring that HR policies are consistently applied across the organization.
b. Keeping track of physical changes to the building's infrastructure.
c. Guaranteeing the uninterrupted operation of supply chain management.
d. Preserving the integrity of evidence for potential legal proceedings.

Answer: d. Preserving the integrity of evidence for potential legal proceedings. Explanation: The chain of custody in the context of a security incident refers to the chronological documentation or paper trail showing the seizure, custody, control, transfer, analysis, and disposition of physical or electronic evidence. Maintaining a rigorous chain of custody is crucial for ensuring that evidence is preserved in an unaltered state, which is essential for its admissibility and credibility in legal proceedings.

459. Implementing a comprehensive security awareness training program is essential for:
a. Increasing the physical security of data centers only.
b. Enhancing the technical skills of the IT department.
c. Reducing the likelihood of phishing attacks among employees.
d. Ensuring compliance with only external audit requirements.

Answer: c. Reducing the likelihood of phishing attacks among employees. Explanation: A comprehensive security awareness training program aims to educate employees about various aspects of security, including recognizing and responding to threats like phishing attacks. By increasing awareness and understanding of phishing tactics, employees are better equipped to identify suspicious emails and links, thereby reducing the risk of successful phishing attacks.

460. The primary purpose of conducting regular penetration testing is to:
a. Evaluate the effectiveness of organizational security policies and procedures.
b. Ensure that all employees adhere to their scheduled work hours.
c. Test the physical security of the organization's facilities.
d. Comply with industry standards without assessing actual security posture.

Answer: a. Evaluate the effectiveness of organizational security policies and procedures. Explanation: Regular penetration testing is a proactive and authorized attempt to evaluate the security of an IT infrastructure by safely exploiting vulnerabilities. These tests are intended to identify weaknesses in security policies, procedures, and defenses that attackers could exploit. The primary goal is to improve the organization's security posture by identifying and mitigating vulnerabilities before they can be exploited by malicious actors.

461. The process of regularly updating software and systems to address security vulnerabilities is known as:
a. Social engineering.
b. Patch management.
c. Role-based access control.

d. Biometric authentication.

Answer: b. Patch management. Explanation: Patch management is the process of distributing and applying updates to software and systems. These patches often address security vulnerabilities, fix bugs, and add features. Regular patch management is crucial for protecting systems against known vulnerabilities that attackers could exploit, thereby enhancing the organization's security posture.

462. An Incident Response Plan (IRP) is primarily designed to:
a. Outline the steps for a company picnic.
b. Detail the organization's marketing strategy for the next fiscal year.
c. Provide a predefined set of procedures for handling security incidents.
d. Describe the daily routine maintenance tasks of the IT department.

Answer: c. Provide a predefined set of procedures for handling security incidents. Explanation: An Incident Response Plan (IRP) is a document that outlines a structured approach for handling security incidents, breaches, and cyber threats. It provides a series of coordinated actions for the organization's response team to follow in the event of an incident, including detection, containment, eradication, and recovery processes, with the aim of minimizing damage and reducing recovery time and costs.

463. In the context of security operations, "tabletop exercises" are used to:
a. Design the physical layout of office spaces for maximum efficiency.
b. Test the organization's incident response procedures in a simulated environment.
c. Train employees on the correct use of office furniture to avoid workplace injuries.
d. Conduct physical fitness assessments for security personnel.

Answer: b. Test the organization's incident response procedures in a simulated environment. Explanation: Tabletop exercises are discussion-based sessions where team members meet to discuss their roles during an emergency or critical event, such as a security incident. The purpose is to test the organization's incident response procedures in a simulated, stress-free environment to identify gaps and areas for improvement, enhancing the organization's readiness and response capabilities.

464. A comprehensive Data Loss Prevention (DLP) program is essential for:
a. Ensuring that all printers in the organization are stocked with paper.
b. Monitoring, detecting, and blocking sensitive data while in use, in motion, and at rest.
c. Tracking the physical movement of employees within the office.
d. Reducing electricity consumption in data centers.

Answer: b. Monitoring, detecting, and blocking sensitive data while in use, in motion, and at rest. Explanation: A Data Loss Prevention (DLP) program is designed to detect and prevent unauthorized access and transmission of sensitive information. By monitoring data in use (endpoint actions), in motion (network traffic), and at rest (data storage), DLP helps protect against accidental or malicious data breaches, ensuring that sensitive information such as personal identification details, financial data, or intellectual property remains within the organization's control.

465. In the event of a data breach, the first step in the investigation process should be to:
a. Notify all media outlets to manage public relations.
b. Immediately terminate all compromised user accounts.
c. Initiate a legal action against the suspected attackers.
d. Secure the affected systems and preserve evidence.

Answer: d. Secure the affected systems and preserve evidence. Explanation: The initial step in responding to a data breach involves securing the affected systems to prevent further unauthorized access and preserving evidence for a thorough investigation. This includes isolating compromised systems, capturing current system states, and maintaining logs, which are crucial for analyzing the breach and identifying the attackers.

466. When collecting digital evidence, it's essential to ensure that:
a. The time zones are adjusted to the investigator's location.
b. Data is copied to a single USB drive for convenience.
c. The original evidence remains unaltered during the process.
d. All files are immediately opened to verify their contents.

Answer: c. The original evidence remains unaltered during the process. Explanation: Preserving the integrity of original digital evidence is paramount in investigations. This involves using write blockers when accessing storage devices and creating forensic images of digital evidence, ensuring that the original data is not modified, which maintains its admissibility in legal proceedings.

467. The primary purpose of a chain of custody in digital forensics is to:
a. Track the physical location of all personnel involved in the investigation.
b. Record the sequence of custody, control, transfer, and analysis of evidence.
c. Ensure that all evidence is stored in a cloud-based environment.
d. Limit evidence review to senior management only.

Answer: b. Record the sequence of custody, control, transfer, and analysis of evidence. Explanation: The chain of custody documents the chronological history of the evidence, detailing how it was collected, analyzed, preserved, and transferred. This process is critical for establishing the integrity and reliability of evidence in legal contexts, showing that it has been handled properly and has not been tampered with.

468. In digital forensics, the process of creating an exact bit-for-bit copy of a storage medium is known as:
a. Data compression.
b. Forensic imaging.
c. Disk defragmentation.
d. Data encryption.

Answer: b. Forensic imaging. Explanation: Forensic imaging involves creating an exact duplicate of a digital storage device, including all files, folders, and unallocated spaces, without altering any data on the original device. This allows investigators to analyze a precise replica of the evidence while preserving the original for legal purposes.

469. The role of log files in an investigation is to:
a. Increase the storage requirements for data retention.
b. Serve as decorative elements in the investigator's report.
c. Provide a record of system activities and user actions.
d. Encrypt data to prevent unauthorized access.

Answer: c. Provide a record of system activities and user actions. Explanation: Log files are crucial in investigations as they record detailed information about system events, user activities, and operational anomalies. Analyzing log data can help in reconstructing events, identifying unauthorized access, and understanding the scope of an incident.

470. When conducting a digital forensic investigation, the first step to preserve the integrity of evidence is to:
a. Immediately start analyzing the data on the suspect's devices.
b. Disconnect the device from the network to prevent remote access.
c. Power off all devices to stop potential data loss.
d. Call in a public relations team to manage potential media fallout.

Answer: b. Disconnect the device from the network to prevent remote access. Explanation: The initial step in preserving the integrity of digital evidence is to isolate the device from the network to prevent any remote access, alteration, or destruction of data. This step ensures that the evidence remains in its original state for accurate analysis and is not compromised by ongoing network activities or remote attackers.

471. In an investigation involving encrypted data, the most effective way to access the information would be to:
a. Use brute force attacks to break the encryption.
b. Obtain the encryption keys through legal means, such as a warrant or subpoena.
c. Physically destroy the storage device to bypass the encryption.
d. Announce the investigation publicly to pressure the data owner into compliance.

Answer: b. Obtain the encryption keys through legal means, such as a warrant or subpoena. Explanation: Accessing encrypted data in a lawful investigation typically involves obtaining the necessary decryption keys through legal processes like warrants or subpoenas. This approach ensures that the investigation remains compliant with legal standards and the integrity of the evidence is maintained, unlike brute force attacks that are time-consuming and may not always be successful.

472. The principle of "chain of custody" in investigations is crucial to ensure that:
a. The evidence can be physically chained to prevent theft.
b. Digital evidence is duplicated across multiple locations for redundancy.

c. The chronological documentation of evidence is maintained for legal proceedings.
d. All employees have unrestricted access to evidence for transparency.

Answer: c. The chronological documentation of evidence is maintained for legal proceedings. Explanation: The chain of custody refers to the documentation that records the sequence of custody, control, transfer, analysis, and disposition of physical or electronic evidence. It is crucial for maintaining the integrity of the evidence by providing a documented history that includes every person who had possession of the evidence, thus ensuring its admissibility in legal proceedings.

473. When dealing with cross-border investigations, a significant challenge is often:
a. The homogeneity of digital forensic tools used internationally.
b. Language barriers that make evidence unreadable.
c. Differing legal frameworks and privacy laws between countries.
d. Universal time zones simplifying coordination of investigative efforts.

Answer: c. Differing legal frameworks and privacy laws between countries. Explanation: Cross-border investigations involve navigating through various legal frameworks and privacy laws that differ from one country to another. These differences can pose significant challenges in terms of jurisdiction, legal authority to access data, and compliance with international legal standards, making the coordination of investigative efforts more complex.

474. For evidence to be admissible in court, it must be:
a. Available publicly on the internet for verification.
b. Handled in accordance with the principles of data protection and privacy.
c. Relevant, material, and competent, following legal standards for evidence.
d. Stored in a decentralized manner to ensure integrity.

Answer: c. Relevant, material, and competent, following legal standards for evidence. Explanation: For evidence to be admissible in court, it must meet the legal standards of being relevant to the case, material to the issues at hand, and competent, meaning it must be legally permissible. This ensures that the evidence is capable of contributing to proving or disproving a point at issue in the legal proceedings.

475. In the context of digital forensics, "write blockers" are used to:
a. Prevent unauthorized access to the investigator's reports.
b. Ensure that data on a storage medium cannot be altered during analysis.
c. Block all writing attempts by malicious software on the investigator's computer.
d. Encrypt the forensic investigator's notes for confidentiality.

Answer: b. Ensure that data on a storage medium cannot be altered during analysis. Explanation: Write blockers are devices or software tools used in digital forensics to allow read-only access to a storage medium, thereby preventing any data from being written or altered during the forensic analysis. This is crucial for preserving the original state of the evidence and ensuring its integrity throughout the investigation.

476. To ensure the authenticity of digital evidence, an investigator should:
a. Rely solely on the metadata provided by the device manufacturer.
b. Use cryptographic hashes to verify that the data has not been altered.
c. Store evidence in a cloud service for easy access by all parties involved.
d. Only use open-source forensic tools to guarantee transparency.

Answer: b. Use cryptographic hashes to verify that the data has not been altered. Explanation: Cryptographic hashes are a fundamental tool in digital forensics used to ensure the authenticity of digital evidence. By creating a unique hash value for the original evidence and comparing it with the hash value of the analyzed data, investigators can verify that the evidence has not been altered or tampered with during the investigation process.

477. During an investigation, maintaining the privacy of unrelated data is achieved by:
a. Deleting all irrelevant data immediately upon identification.
b. Using data minimization techniques to only process relevant information.
c. Publishing all data online for public verification of relevance.
d. Storing all captured data indefinitely in case it becomes relevant later.

Answer: b. Using data minimization techniques to only process relevant information. Explanation: Data minimization is a privacy-enhancing technique that involves processing only the data that is directly relevant to the investigation, thereby protecting the privacy of unrelated or non-pertinent information. This approach aligns with legal and ethical standards, ensuring that only necessary data is examined while respecting the privacy of individuals whose information is not relevant to the case.

478. In digital forensics, "live forensics" refers to the analysis of:
a. Systems that are powered off and disconnected from any network.
b. Data in a simulated environment that replicates the original system.
c. Systems that are actively running and connected to a network.
d. Historical data that has been archived for long-term storage.

Answer: c. Systems that are actively running and connected to a network. Explanation: Live forensics involves the collection and analysis of evidence from computer systems that are still operational and possibly connected to a network. This approach is necessary when dealing with volatile data or when the shutdown of a system could result in the loss of critical evidence, making it a key technique in certain investigative scenarios.

479. To ensure effective incident detection, which of the following log sources is most critical?
a. System uptime logs
b. Application debug logs
c. Firewall and intrusion detection system logs
d. Print server logs

Answer: c. Firewall and intrusion detection system logs. Explanation: Firewall and intrusion detection system (IDS) logs are crucial for identifying unauthorized access attempts, malicious activities, and potential security breaches. These logs provide visibility into network traffic patterns and can alert security teams to investigate and respond to incidents promptly, making them essential for effective incident detection and response strategies.

480. When configuring logging for critical systems, which of the following should be prioritized?
a. Storage optimization to reduce logging costs
b. Comprehensive capture of all user activities and system changes
c. Logging only error messages to simplify analysis
d. Frequency of log rotation to minimize storage requirements

Answer: b. Comprehensive capture of all user activities and system changes. Explanation: For critical systems, it's essential to have a comprehensive logging strategy that captures all user activities and system changes. This approach ensures that in the event of a security incident, there's sufficient detail in the logs to perform a thorough investigation, identify the root cause, and understand the scope of the incident.

481. What is the primary purpose of implementing log aggregation in a security operations center (SOC)?
a. To reduce the volume of logs for storage efficiency
b. To consolidate logs from various sources for centralized analysis
c. To filter out irrelevant log entries and reduce noise
d. To increase the speed of log generation for real-time monitoring

Answer: b. To consolidate logs from various sources for centralized analysis. Explanation: Log aggregation involves collecting and consolidating logs from various sources into a centralized platform. This allows SOC analysts to perform comprehensive analysis, correlate events across different systems, and identify patterns indicative of security incidents more efficiently, enhancing the organization's overall security posture.

482. In the context of security monitoring, what is the significance of anomaly detection?
a. To identify deviations from established baselines indicating potential security incidents
b. To track the number of failed login attempts for compliance reporting
c. To monitor the uptime of critical infrastructure components
d. To log the installation of new software for license management

Answer: a. To identify deviations from established baselines indicating potential security incidents. Explanation: Anomaly detection is a technique used in security monitoring to identify unusual patterns or deviations from normal behavior, which could indicate a security incident. By comparing current activities to historical baselines, anomaly detection can alert security teams to investigate potential threats, such as malware infections or unauthorized access, that might not be identified by signature-based detection methods.

483. Which of the following best describes the role of Security Information and Event Management (SIEM) systems?
a. To serve as primary storage for all organizational data
b. To manage network devices and their configurations
c. To collect, analyze, and report on security log data from various sources
d. To automate software deployments across the enterprise

Answer: c. To collect, analyze, and report on security log data from various sources. Explanation: SIEM systems are designed to provide a holistic view of an organization's information security by collecting, analyzing, and reporting on log data from various sources, such as firewalls, intrusion detection systems, and application logs. SIEM tools help in detecting, understanding, and responding to security incidents by correlating events and identifying patterns that may indicate malicious activities.

484. For maintaining the integrity of logs, which of the following practices is most effective?
a. Storing logs on a local server with limited access
b. Encrypting log files and using secure log transfer protocols
c. Printing logs and storing them in a secure physical location
d. Periodically deleting old logs to free up storage space

Answer: b. Encrypting log files and using secure log transfer protocols. Explanation: Encrypting log files and using secure log transfer protocols, such as TLS, ensures that log data is protected both at rest and in transit. This practice prevents unauthorized access and tampering, maintaining the integrity and confidentiality of log information, which is crucial for accurate incident analysis and legal compliance.

485. What is the primary function of a log parser in security operations?
a. To encrypt log files for secure storage
b. To convert log data into a standardized format for analysis
c. To decrease the volume of logs generated by systems
d. To accelerate the log deletion process for compliance

Answer: b. To convert log data into a standardized format for analysis. Explanation: A log parser is a tool used to convert log data from various formats into a standardized or uniform format, facilitating easier analysis, correlation, and review. This is particularly useful in environments with diverse systems and applications, enabling security analysts to efficiently analyze log data for potential security incidents.

486. When planning for log retention, which factor is most critical?
a. The color-coding scheme for log severity levels
b. The physical location of the log storage servers
c. Compliance with relevant legal and regulatory requirements
d. The brand of storage devices used for log archival

Answer: c. Compliance with relevant legal and regulatory requirements. Explanation: Log retention policies should be primarily guided by legal and regulatory requirements relevant to the organization's industry and jurisdiction. These requirements dictate how long certain types of log data must be retained to ensure compliance with laws and regulations, influencing decisions on log retention periods, storage, and archival practices.

487. In a distributed environment, why is it important to synchronize time sources for logging?
a. To ensure that log entries are colorful and visually distinct
b. To enable accurate event correlation across different systems and locations
c. To reduce the size of log files by standardizing time formats
d. To prevent users from changing their system clocks

Answer: b. To enable accurate event correlation across different systems and locations. Explanation: Time synchronization across all devices and systems in a distributed environment is crucial for accurate log correlation and analysis. When time sources are synchronized, security analysts can accurately sequence events that occurred across different systems, aiding in the reconstruction of security incidents and understanding the timeline of attacks.

488. How does implementing a centralized log management solution benefit an organization's security posture?
a. By providing a single point of failure for all log data
b. By ensuring that logs are only accessible to external auditors
c. By facilitating efficient analysis and correlation of log data from multiple sources
d. By automatically discarding logs that are older than a week to save storage

Answer: c. By facilitating efficient analysis and correlation of log data from multiple sources. Explanation: A centralized log management solution collects logs from various sources into a single repository, making it easier for security teams to analyze, correlate, and review log data. This centralized approach enhances the organization's ability to detect, investigate, and respond to potential security threats by providing a holistic view of the security environment.

489. In an IaaS cloud environment, which of the following best describes the process of provisioning a new virtual machine (VM) for a development project?
a. Manual installation of the operating system on physical hardware
b. Use of a hypervisor to create a VM instance from a predefined image
c. Configuration of network switches to provide connectivity for the VM
d. Physical installation of additional RAM in the server to accommodate the VM

Answer: b. Use of a hypervisor to create a VM instance from a predefined image. Explanation: In Infrastructure as a Service (IaaS) environments, virtual machines are provisioned using a hypervisor, which allows multiple VM instances to run on a single physical server. The process involves selecting a predefined image that includes the operating system and possibly other software, which simplifies and accelerates the setup for development projects.

490. When automating the provisioning of resources in a cloud environment, which technology is most commonly used?
a. Physical server cloning
b. Infrastructure as Code (IaC) tools like Terraform or AWS CloudFormation
c. Manual scripting in batch files
d. Traditional software installation CDs

Answer: b. Infrastructure as Code (IaC) tools like Terraform or AWS CloudFormation. Explanation: IaC tools such as Terraform and AWS CloudFormation allow for the automation of resource provisioning in the cloud by defining the infrastructure through code. This enables consistent and repeatable setups across environments, reduces the potential for human error, and allows for easy versioning and changes.

491. In a DevOps workflow, how does continuous integration and continuous deployment (CI/CD) facilitate the provisioning of resources?
a. By manually reviewing and deploying code changes
b. Through automated testing and deployment pipelines that provision resources as needed
c. By requiring physical server access for each deployment
d. Through periodic, scheduled updates that require downtime

Answer: b. Through automated testing and deployment pipelines that provision resources as needed. Explanation: CI/CD pipelines automate the processes of integrating code changes from multiple contributors and deploying those changes to production environments. These pipelines can include steps to automatically provision or scale resources based on the needs of the application, improving efficiency and reducing the risk of human error.

492. What role does an orchestration tool like Kubernetes play in the provisioning of resources for containerized applications?
a. Manual configuration of containers on individual servers
b. Automating the deployment, scaling, and management of containerized applications
c. Physical network configuration for container communication
d. Direct management of virtual machine hypervisors

Answer: b. Automating the deployment, scaling, and management of containerized applications. Explanation: Kubernetes is an orchestration tool designed to automate the deployment, scaling, and operation of containerized applications. It abstracts the underlying infrastructure, allowing for efficient management of containers across a cluster of machines, facilitating resource provisioning without manual intervention.

493. How does serverless computing change the approach to resource provisioning?
a. By requiring administrators to manually scale resources based on demand
b. Through pre-allocation of fixed server resources for each application
c. By automatically managing resource allocation based on the application's needs
d. Using physical servers dedicated to specific functions or services

Answer: c. By automatically managing resource allocation based on the application's needs. Explanation: Serverless computing abstracts server management and infrastructure decisions away from the developers, allowing them to focus solely on writing code. The platform automatically provisions, scales, and manages the infrastructure required to run the code, based on the application's needs, making resource provisioning dynamic and event-driven.

494. In provisioning a secure environment for sensitive data processing, which of the following is a key consideration?
a. Ensuring public internet access to all resources for ease of use
b. Implementing strict access controls and encryption for data at rest and in transit
c. Using the least expensive storage options to reduce costs
d. Sharing credentials across teams to simplify access management

Answer: b. Implementing strict access controls and encryption for data at rest and in transit. Explanation: When provisioning resources for sensitive data processing, security is paramount. Implementing strict access controls to limit who can access the data and encrypting the data both at rest and in transit are critical measures to protect sensitive information from unauthorized access or breaches.

495. What is the significance of blue/green deployment strategies in resource provisioning?
a. They require manual switching between two identical environments
b. They involve alternating resource usage between two data centers
c. They enable seamless transitions between two identical production environments
d. They mandate the use of blue and green colored cables for network infrastructure

Answer: c. They enable seamless transitions between two identical production environments. Explanation: Blue/green deployment is a strategy that involves maintaining two identical production environments, only one of which is live at any time. Resources are provisioned in the idle environment (green) while the other (blue) serves live traffic. After testing in the green environment, traffic is switched over, allowing for seamless transitions and minimal downtime during deployments.

496. In the context of resource provisioning, how does capacity planning impact operational efficiency?
a. By ensuring over-provisioning of resources to avoid potential shortages
b. Through careful analysis and prediction of resource needs to avoid under or over-provisioning
c. By exclusively focusing on current resource utilization without future planning
d. Relying on manual interventions to adjust resources as demand changes

Answer: b. Through careful analysis and prediction of resource needs to avoid under or over-provisioning. Explanation: Effective capacity planning involves analyzing current resource usage and predicting future needs to ensure that resources are neither under nor over-provisioned. This balance optimizes operational efficiency and cost, ensuring that resources are available to meet demand without unnecessary expenditure on unused capacity.

497. What is the impact of elasticity in cloud resource provisioning on cost management?
a. It increases costs due to constant over-provisioning of resources
b. It reduces cost efficiency by maintaining a fixed amount of resources
c. It enhances cost management by automatically scaling resources to match demand
d. Elasticity has no impact on costs as cloud resources are priced uniformly

Answer: c. It enhances cost management by automatically scaling resources to match demand. Explanation: Elasticity in cloud computing allows resources to automatically scale up or down based on real-time demand, which can significantly improve cost management. Organizations pay only for the resources they use, avoiding the cost of maintaining unused capacity, thereby optimizing expenses related to resource provisioning.

498. How does the adoption of policy-as-code tools like HashiCorp Sentinel impact resource provisioning?
a. By manually enforcing policies during the provisioning process
b. Through the automatic enforcement of governance policies across all provisioned resources
c. By requiring physical security assessments for each provisioned resource
d. Policy-as-code tools are unrelated to resource provisioning processes

Answer: b. Through the automatic enforcement of governance policies across all provisioned resources. Explanation: Policy-as-code tools like HashiCorp Sentinel allow organizations to define their infrastructure policies as code, which are then automatically enforced across all provisioned resources. This ensures compliance with organizational standards and regulatory requirements, enhances security, and streamlines the provisioning process by integrating policy checks into the automation workflows.

499. In an IaaS cloud environment, which of the following best describes the process of provisioning a new virtual machine (VM) for a development project?
a. Manual installation of the operating system on physical hardware
b. Use of a hypervisor to create a VM instance from a predefined image
c. Configuration of network switches to provide connectivity for the VM
d. Physical installation of additional RAM in the server to accommodate the VM

Answer: b. Use of a hypervisor to create a VM instance from a predefined image. Explanation: In Infrastructure as a Service (IaaS) environments, virtual machines are provisioned using a hypervisor, which allows multiple VM instances to run on a single physical server. The process involves selecting a predefined image that includes the operating system and possibly other software, which simplifies and accelerates the setup for development projects.

500. When automating the provisioning of resources in a cloud environment, which technology is most commonly used?
a. Physical server cloning
b. Infrastructure as Code (IaC) tools like Terraform or AWS CloudFormation
c. Manual scripting in batch files
d. Traditional software installation CDs

Answer: b. Infrastructure as Code (IaC) tools like Terraform or AWS CloudFormation. Explanation: IaC tools such as Terraform and AWS CloudFormation allow for the automation of resource provisioning in the cloud by defining the infrastructure through code. This enables consistent and repeatable setups across environments, reduces the potential for human error, and allows for easy versioning and changes.

501. In a DevOps workflow, how does continuous integration and continuous deployment (CI/CD) facilitate the provisioning of resources?
a. By manually reviewing and deploying code changes
b. Through automated testing and deployment pipelines that provision resources as needed
c. By requiring physical server access for each deployment
d. Through periodic, scheduled updates that require downtime

Answer: b. Through automated testing and deployment pipelines that provision resources as needed. Explanation: CI/CD pipelines automate the processes of integrating code changes from multiple contributors and deploying those changes to production environments. These pipelines can include steps to automatically provision or scale resources based on the needs of the application, improving efficiency and reducing the risk of human error.

502. What role does an orchestration tool like Kubernetes play in the provisioning of resources for containerized applications?
a. Manual configuration of containers on individual servers
b. Automating the deployment, scaling, and management of containerized applications
c. Physical network configuration for container communication
d. Direct management of virtual machine hypervisors

Answer: b. Automating the deployment, scaling, and management of containerized applications. Explanation: Kubernetes is an orchestration tool designed to automate the deployment, scaling, and operation of containerized applications. It abstracts the underlying infrastructure, allowing for efficient management of containers across a cluster of machines, facilitating resource provisioning without manual intervention.

503. How does serverless computing change the approach to resource provisioning?
a. By requiring administrators to manually scale resources based on demand
b. Through pre-allocation of fixed server resources for each application
c. By automatically managing resource allocation based on the application's needs
d. Using physical servers dedicated to specific functions or services

Answer: c. By automatically managing resource allocation based on the application's needs. Explanation: Serverless computing abstracts server management and infrastructure decisions away from the developers, allowing them to focus solely on writing code. The platform automatically provisions, scales, and manages the infrastructure required to run the code, based on the application's needs, making resource provisioning dynamic and event-driven.

504. In provisioning a secure environment for sensitive data processing, which of the following is a key consideration?

a. Ensuring public internet access to all resources for ease of use
b. Implementing strict access controls and encryption for data at rest and in transit
c. Using the least expensive storage options to reduce costs
d. Sharing credentials across teams to simplify access management

Answer: b. Implementing strict access controls and encryption for data at rest and in transit. Explanation: When provisioning resources for sensitive data processing, security is paramount. Implementing strict access controls to limit who can access the data and encrypting the data both at rest and in transit are critical measures to protect sensitive information from unauthorized access or breaches.

505. What is the significance of blue/green deployment strategies in resource provisioning?
a. They require manual switching between two identical environments
b. They involve alternating resource usage between two data centers
c. They enable seamless transitions between two identical production environments
d. They mandate the use of blue and green colored cables for network infrastructure

Answer: c. They enable seamless transitions between two identical production environments. Explanation: Blue/green deployment is a strategy that involves maintaining two identical production environments, only one of which is live at any time. Resources are provisioned in the idle environment (green) while the other (blue) serves live traffic. After testing in the green environment, traffic is switched over, allowing for seamless transitions and minimal downtime during deployments.

506. In the context of resource provisioning, how does capacity planning impact operational efficiency?
a. By ensuring over-provisioning of resources to avoid potential shortages
b. Through careful analysis and prediction of resource needs to avoid under or over-provisioning
c. By exclusively focusing on current resource utilization without future planning
d. Relying on manual interventions to adjust resources as demand changes

Answer: b. Through careful analysis and prediction of resource needs to avoid under or over-provisioning. Explanation: Effective capacity planning involves analyzing current resource usage and predicting future needs to ensure that resources are neither under nor over-provisioned. This balance optimizes operational efficiency and cost, ensuring that resources are available to meet demand without unnecessary expenditure on unused capacity.

507. What is the impact of elasticity in cloud resource provisioning on cost management?
a. It increases costs due to constant over-provisioning of resources
b. It reduces cost efficiency by maintaining a fixed amount of resources
c. It enhances cost management by automatically scaling resources to match demand
d. Elasticity has no impact on costs as cloud resources are priced uniformly

Answer: c. It enhances cost management by automatically scaling resources to match demand. Explanation: Elasticity in cloud computing allows resources to automatically scale up or down based on real-time demand, which can significantly improve cost management. Organizations pay only for the resources they use, avoiding the cost of maintaining unused capacity, thereby optimizing expenses related to resource provisioning.

508. How does the adoption of policy-as-code tools like HashiCorp Sentinel impact resource provisioning?
a. By manually enforcing policies during the provisioning process
b. Through the automatic enforcement of governance policies across all provisioned resources
c. By requiring physical security assessments for each provisioned resource
d. Policy-as-code tools are unrelated to resource provisioning processes

Answer: b. Through the automatic enforcement of governance policies across all provisioned resources. Explanation: Policy-as-code tools like HashiCorp Sentinel allow organizations to define their infrastructure policies as code, which are then automatically enforced across all provisioned resources. This ensures compliance with organizational standards and regulatory requirements, enhances security, and streamlines the provisioning process by integrating policy checks into the automation workflows.

509. In the context of security operations, what is the primary purpose of implementing a Security Information and Event Management (SIEM) system?
a. To physically secure data centers and server rooms
b. To provide real-time analysis of security alerts generated by applications and network hardware
c. To manage employee access to physical buildings
d. To encrypt data stored on corporate servers

Answer: b. To provide real-time analysis of security alerts generated by applications and network hardware. Explanation: SIEM systems are designed to provide real-time analysis of security alerts generated by various hardware and software applications within an organization's IT environment. They play a crucial role in identifying, monitoring, and responding to security incidents and anomalies, thus enhancing the overall security posture.

510. What role does an intrusion detection system (IDS) play in foundational security operations?
a. Monitoring network traffic and analyzing it for signs of possible incidents, violations, or imminent threats
b. Encrypting data in transit between different network segments
c. Serving as the primary firewall at the network perimeter
d. Managing user access rights and permissions across the IT infrastructure

Answer: a. Monitoring network traffic and analyzing it for signs of possible incidents, violations, or imminent threats. Explanation: An IDS is deployed within a network to monitor traffic and identify suspicious activities or known threats based on a set of defined rules or anomaly detection algorithms. Its primary function is to alert security personnel to potential security breaches or policy violations, providing a critical layer in the defense-in-depth security strategy.

511. In security operations, what is the significance of the principle of least privilege?

a. Ensuring all users have administrative access to perform their tasks efficiently
b. Limiting user access rights to the minimum necessary to perform their job functions
c. Granting every user full access to all network resources for transparency
d. Automatically escalating user privileges in response to a detected threat

Answer: b. Limiting user access rights to the minimum necessary to perform their job functions. Explanation: The principle of least privilege is a fundamental security concept that involves providing users with only the minimum levels of access—or permissions—needed to perform their job functions. This approach minimizes the potential damage from accidental or malicious actions by limiting access to sensitive information and critical systems.

512. How does a Security Operations Center (SOC) enhance an organization's security posture?
a. By providing a recreational space for IT staff to reduce stress
b. Through centralized coordination and analysis of security events across the organization
c. By offering physical security and access control to the organization's facilities
d. By deploying antivirus software on all endpoints

Answer: b. Through centralized coordination and analysis of security events across the organization. Explanation: A SOC functions as the central unit that deals with security issues on an organizational and technical level. It is equipped with specialized security software and staffed with security analysts to monitor, analyze, and respond to cybersecurity incidents, thus significantly enhancing the organization's overall security posture.

513. What is the primary objective of implementing change management in security operations?
a. To ensure all software changes are made spontaneously to keep attackers off-guard
b. To document all employee turnover within the IT department
c. To minimize the risk of unauthorized changes and potential security vulnerabilities
d. To increase the frequency of system downtime for maintenance purposes

Answer: c. To minimize the risk of unauthorized changes and potential security vulnerabilities. Explanation: Change management is a systematic approach to managing all changes made to a product or system. Its objective in the context of security operations is to ensure that standardized methods and procedures are used for efficient and prompt handling of all changes. This minimizes the risk of unauthorized changes, system failures, and potential security vulnerabilities.

514. In the implementation of a disaster recovery plan, what is the role of a hot site?
a. A location where the organization can relocate in the event of a significant disaster, fully equipped to resume operations immediately
b. A backup site that stores physical copies of all critical documents
c. A secure facility for the organization's top executives during a disaster
d. A data center that is kept at high temperatures to ensure the longevity of backup media

Answer: a. A location where the organization can relocate in the event of a significant disaster, fully equipped to resume operations immediately. Explanation: A hot site is a fully equipped alternate facility that an organization can quickly relocate to in the event of a disaster. It has all the necessary hardware, software, telecommunications, and staff arrangements needed to resume critical business operations with minimal downtime, ensuring business continuity.

515. How does regular patch management contribute to security operations?
a. By ensuring all employees adhere to the organization's dress code
b. By keeping all systems and software up to date with the latest security patches and updates
c. By physically repairing damaged network infrastructure
d. By updating the organization's website with the latest news

Answer: b. By keeping all systems and software up to date with the latest security patches and updates. Explanation: Patch management is a crucial aspect of maintaining the security and functionality of software and systems within an organization. Regularly applying patches and updates helps fix vulnerabilities, improve functionality, and protect against the exploitation of known security gaps by malicious actors.

516. What is the primary purpose of conducting a penetration test in the context of security operations?
a. To physically test the strength of the organization's building security
b. To assess the security of an IT infrastructure by safely trying to exploit vulnerabilities
c. To test the organization's employees on their knowledge of the security policy
d. To penetrate the market with new security products

Answer: b. To assess the security of an IT infrastructure by safely trying to exploit vulnerabilities. Explanation: Penetration testing, or pen testing, is a simulated cyber attack against an organization's computer system to check for exploitable vulnerabilities. In the context of security operations, its primary purpose is to identify weaknesses in an organization's security posture, including the potential for unauthorized parties to gain access to the system's features and data.

517. What is the function of a demilitarized zone (DMZ) in network security?
a. A physical barrier around the data center to prevent unauthorized access
b. A separate network that provides an additional layer of security between the public internet and an organization's internal network
c. A secure area for storing military-grade encryption keys
d. A zone within the network where all security controls are disabled to increase performance

Answer: b. A separate network that provides an additional layer of security between the public internet and an organization's internal network. Explanation: In network security, a DMZ is a physical or logical subnetwork that contains and exposes an organization's external-facing services to an untrusted network, usually the internet. The DMZ adds an additional layer of security, isolating the internal network from the external network, which can include the internet, and provides a controlled access point to services that need to be accessible from the outside.

518. What is the primary goal of data loss prevention (DLP) systems in resource protection?
a. To facilitate rapid data transfer across networks
b. To detect and prevent unauthorized access to or theft of sensitive information
c. To increase the storage capacity of data centers
d. To reduce the cost of data management

Answer: b. To detect and prevent unauthorized access to or theft of sensitive information. Explanation: DLP systems are designed to detect potential data breaches/data ex-filtration transmissions and prevent them by monitoring, detecting, and blocking sensitive data while in use (endpoint actions), in motion (network traffic), and at rest (data storage). The primary goal is to protect sensitive data from unauthorized access and ensure that it is not lost, misused, or accessed by unauthorized users.

519. In the context of resource protection, what is the purpose of implementing network segmentation?
a. To consolidate all resources into a single network for ease of access
b. To divide a network into smaller, more manageable sections to improve performance
c. To isolate critical systems and sensitive data from the rest of the network to reduce the risk of unauthorized access
d. To eliminate the need for firewalls and other security measures

Answer: c. To isolate critical systems and sensitive data from the rest of the network to reduce the risk of unauthorized access. Explanation: Network segmentation involves dividing a computer network into subnetworks, each being a network segment or network layer. The primary purpose is to improve security and performance by isolating critical systems and sensitive data, thereby limiting an attacker's ability to move laterally within the network and access sensitive information.

520. How does encryption contribute to the protection of resources in cybersecurity?
a. By making data unreadable to unauthorized users, ensuring data confidentiality and integrity
b. By physically locking down hardware devices to prevent theft
c. By increasing the speed of data transmission on a network
d. By publicly displaying data for transparency

Answer: a. By making data unreadable to unauthorized users, ensuring data confidentiality and integrity. Explanation: Encryption transforms readable data (plaintext) into unreadable data (ciphertext) using an algorithm and an encryption key. Only those with the correct key can decrypt and access the original data. This process ensures data confidentiality and integrity by making the data inaccessible and unreadable to unauthorized users, even if they manage to intercept the data.

521. What role do access control lists (ACLs) play in protecting network resources?
a. They serve as a list of employees who can physically access the server room
b. They provide a detailed inventory of all IT equipment
c. They define which users or system processes are granted access to objects, as well as what operations are allowed on given objects
d. They act as a guest list for corporate events to ensure network security

Answer: c. They define which users or system processes are granted access to objects, as well as what operations are allowed on given objects. Explanation: ACLs are a set of rules that specify which users or system processes can access and what operations they can perform on various objects in a computer system or network, such as files, directories, or individual services. By defining access permissions and restrictions, ACLs help in effectively controlling access to network resources, thus protecting them from unauthorized access or misuse.

522. How do firewalls contribute to resource protection within an organization's network?
a. By physically securing the perimeter of the organization's property
b. By monitoring and controlling incoming and outgoing network traffic based on predetermined security rules
c. By auditing financial transactions to prevent fraud
d. By increasing Wi-Fi signal strength throughout the facility

Answer: b. By monitoring and controlling incoming and outgoing network traffic based on predetermined security rules. Explanation: Firewalls are network security devices that monitor and control the incoming and outgoing network traffic based on an organization's previously established security rules. A firewall acts as a barrier between a trusted network and an untrusted network, such as the internet, and helps protect an organization's network and resources by filtering out unauthorized or potentially harmful traffic.

523. What is the significance of employing multifactor authentication (MFA) in the protection of digital resources?
a. To ensure that system login processes are more time-consuming and complex
b. To provide an additional layer of security by requiring two or more verification factors, making it harder for unauthorized users to gain access
c. To replace all other forms of security measures, as MFA is sufficient on its own
d. To monitor and log all user activities on social media platforms

Answer: b. To provide an additional layer of security by requiring two or more verification factors, making it harder for unauthorized users to gain access. Explanation: MFA enhances security by requiring two or more forms of verification to prove identity before granting access to resources. This can include something the user knows (password), something the user has (security token), and something the user is (biometric verification). By combining multiple authentication factors, MFA makes it significantly more difficult for potential intruders to access sensitive systems and data.

524. In the framework of resource protection, how does role-based access control (RBAC) enhance security?
a. By assigning network bandwidth based on job roles
b. By granting permissions to users based on their specific roles within an organization, minimizing unnecessary access to sensitive information
c. By broadcasting all user activities publicly to ensure transparency
d. By randomly assigning access rights to users to confuse potential attackers

Answer: b. By granting permissions to users based on their specific roles within an organization, minimizing unnecessary access to sensitive information. Explanation: RBAC is a policy-neutral access control mechanism defined around roles and privileges. It restricts system access to authorized users based on their roles within the organization. Users are assigned roles, and through those roles, permissions are granted to access specific resources or data. This approach minimizes the risk of unauthorized access by ensuring that users have access only to the information and resources necessary for their roles.

525. What is the purpose of implementing security incident and event management (SIEM) in an organization's security operations?
a. To organize social events for the IT security team
b. To consolidate and analyze security alerts from various sources in real time, facilitating early detection of potential security incidents
c. To replace the need for physical security measures such as locks and alarm systems
d. To manage the organization's calendar of public holidays and work schedules

Answer: b. To consolidate and analyze security alerts from various sources in real time, facilitating early detection of potential security incidents. Explanation: SIEM systems collect and aggregate log data generated throughout the organization's technology infrastructure, from host systems and applications to network and security devices such as firewalls and antivirus filters. By analyzing this data in real time, SIEM systems can identify anomalous patterns and potential security incidents, enabling rapid response and mitigation to protect organizational resources.

526. How does the principle of segregation of duties (SoD) aid in the protection of an organization's resources?
a. By ensuring all tasks are performed by a single individual to maintain consistency
b. By dividing tasks and responsibilities among multiple people to reduce the risk of error or fraud
c. By centralizing all decision-making processes to a single department
d. By outsourcing all security-related tasks to third-party vendors

Answer: b. By dividing tasks and responsibilities among multiple people to reduce the risk of error or fraud. Explanation: SoD is a key internal control that helps to prevent fraud and errors. This principle dictates that no single individual should have control over all aspects of any critical business process or system. By segregating duties among different individuals, it reduces the risk of a single person being able to commit fraudulent activities without detection, thereby protecting the organization's resources from potential abuses or security breaches.

527. What is the primary purpose of an incident response plan (IRP)?
a. To outline the recreational activities available to employees during downtime
b. To provide a structured approach for handling security incidents to minimize impact and restore operations
c. To serve as a legal document for prosecuting cybercriminals
d. To detail the company's annual budget allocation for IT expenditures

Answer: b. To provide a structured approach for handling security incidents to minimize impact and restore operations. Explanation: An incident response plan is a set of instructions designed to help IT staff detect, respond to, and recover from network security incidents. The plan outlines steps to take before, during, and after an incident to limit damage, reduce recovery time and costs, and mitigate exploitation risks.

528. During an incident response, what is the significance of the containment phase?
a. To spread the incident as widely as possible to study its impact
b. To limit the extent of the damage and isolate affected systems to prevent further unauthorized access
c. To document the incident for future reference without taking any immediate action
d. To immediately inform all external stakeholders about the incident details

Answer: b. To limit the extent of the damage and isolate affected systems to prevent further unauthorized access.
Explanation: The containment phase is crucial in incident response as it aims to limit the damage caused by the incident and prevent it from spreading. This involves isolating affected systems, cutting off malicious communication, and implementing short-term fixes to stop the immediate threat.

529. In incident management, what role does the post-incident review play?
a. To allocate blame to the team members responsible for the breach
b. To review the incident's handling to identify lessons learned and improve future response efforts
c. To update the organization's website with detailed incident information for public relations purposes
d. To provide entertainment through a detailed recounting of the incident events

Answer: b. To review the incident's handling to identify lessons learned and improve future response efforts.
Explanation: A post-incident review is conducted after an incident is resolved to evaluate the effectiveness of the incident response, identify what was done well and what could be improved. This process is crucial for refining incident response plans and enhancing the organization's overall security posture.

530. How does an organization benefit from classifying incidents based on severity levels?
a. It ensures all incidents are treated with the same level of urgency and resources
b. It allows for prioritizing response efforts based on the potential impact, ensuring efficient use of resources
c. It creates a more complex and bureaucratic incident response process
d. It provides a framework for escalating all incidents to law enforcement

Answer: b. It allows for prioritizing response efforts based on the potential impact, ensuring efficient use of resources.
Explanation: Classifying incidents by severity levels helps in prioritizing them based on their potential impact on the organization. This ensures that resources are allocated efficiently, with the most critical incidents receiving immediate attention, while less severe ones are handled accordingly.

531. What is a Security Operations Center (SOC) primarily responsible for in incident management?
a. Hosting social events for the IT security team
b. Monitoring, detecting, analyzing, and responding to cybersecurity incidents
c. Managing the organization's social media profiles
d. Conducting annual performance reviews for IT staff

Answer: b. Monitoring, detecting, analyzing, and responding to cybersecurity incidents. Explanation: A SOC is a centralized unit that deals with security issues on an organizational and technical level. It is equipped with specialized software and staffed with security analysts to monitor, detect, analyze, and respond to cybersecurity incidents using a combination of technology solutions and a strong set of processes.

532. Why is it important to have a predefined communication plan as part of incident management?
a. To ensure the incident is publicized in the media as quickly as possible
b. To facilitate clear, timely, and effective communication within the response team and with external stakeholders
c. To provide a script for social gatherings in the workplace
d. To prioritize communication with non-essential personnel over critical response activities

Answer: b. To facilitate clear, timely, and effective communication within the response team and with external stakeholders. Explanation: A predefined communication plan is crucial for ensuring that all relevant parties are informed about the incident and the response actions in a timely and effective manner. It helps in coordinating the response efforts, managing stakeholder expectations, and maintaining trust and transparency.

533. What is the role of forensic analysis in incident management?
a. To create fictional narratives about potential future incidents
b. To provide a detailed and technical review of historical incidents without current relevance
c. To meticulously analyze evidence to understand how the breach occurred and to prevent future incidents
d. To focus solely on retrieving lost data without learning from the incident

Answer: c. To meticulously analyze evidence to understand how the breach occurred and to prevent future incidents. Explanation: Forensic analysis in the context of incident management involves the collection, preservation, and analysis of digital evidence to determine how the breach occurred, the scope of the impact, and the methods used by the attackers. This information is crucial for preventing future incidents and strengthening security measures.

534. How does implementing an incident detection and analysis system benefit an organization's security posture?
a. By decorating the office with state-of-the-art security equipment
b. By providing real-time entertainment through live incident feeds
c. By enabling early detection of potential security incidents, allowing for quicker response and mitigation
d. By replacing all other security measures, as it is the only necessary protection

Answer: c. By enabling early detection of potential security incidents, allowing for quicker response and mitigation. Explanation: Implementing an incident detection and analysis system allows organizations to monitor their networks for suspicious activities continuously. Early detection of potential incidents enables quicker response and mitigation efforts, reducing the potential damage and impact of security breaches.

535. What is the importance of establishing an incident response team (IRT)?
a. To organize team-building activities unrelated to security
b. To have a dedicated group of professionals with defined roles and responsibilities ready to respond to security incidents

c. To focus solely on post-incident legal actions without preventing future incidents

d. To shift the responsibility of incident handling to a third-party service, absolving the organization of any involvement

Answer: b. To have a dedicated group of professionals with defined roles and responsibilities ready to respond to security incidents. Explanation: An incident response team is a group of IT professionals specifically trained to address and manage the aftermath of a security breach or cyberattack. Having an IRT ensures that there is a structured and effective approach to managing incidents, minimizing the impact on the organization and reducing the time to recovery.

536. Which of the following is the most effective preventative measure to protect against social engineering attacks?

a. Increasing the complexity of network passwords

b. Regularly updating antivirus software

c. Conducting security awareness and training programs for employees

d. Implementing stronger firewall rules

Answer: c. Conducting security awareness and training programs for employees. Explanation: Social engineering attacks exploit human psychology rather than technical vulnerabilities. Therefore, educating and training employees about the nature of these attacks, common tactics used by attackers, and how to respond to suspicious requests is the most effective preventative measure.

537. In designing a secure network architecture, what preventative measure can specifically protect against external attacks?

a. Deploying a network intrusion detection system (NIDS) at the network perimeter

b. Enforcing a strict password policy

c. Regular data backups

d. Implementing application whitelisting

Answer: a. Deploying a network intrusion detection system (NIDS) at the network perimeter. Explanation: A NIDS monitors network traffic for suspicious activity and known threats, acting as a preventative measure by identifying and potentially stopping external attacks at the network perimeter before they penetrate deeper into the network.

538. What is the primary purpose of employing the principle of least privilege in an organizational IT environment?

a. To minimize the workload on IT staff

b. To reduce the amount of data stored on servers

c. To limit user access rights to the minimum necessary to perform their duties

d. To increase the complexity of the IT infrastructure

Answer: c. To limit user access rights to the minimum necessary to perform their duties. Explanation: The principle of least privilege is a key preventative measure in security, aimed at reducing the risk of unauthorized access or damage by limiting users' access rights and permissions to the minimum necessary for them to perform their job functions.

539. How does encryption serve as a preventative measure in data security?
a. By detecting intrusions in real-time
b. By making data unreadable to unauthorized users, thus protecting the confidentiality and integrity of the data
c. By physically securing the hardware devices
d. By monitoring and logging user activities

Answer: b. By making data unreadable to unauthorized users, thus protecting the confidentiality and integrity of the data. Explanation: Encryption is a critical preventative measure that secures data by converting it into a coded format that is unreadable without the decryption key, thus ensuring that even if data is intercepted or accessed by unauthorized individuals, it remains confidential and intact.

540. What role does patch management play in preventative security measures?
a. It ensures all devices are running the latest operating systems
b. It provides a backup of all organizational data
c. It fixes known vulnerabilities in software and systems, reducing the risk of exploitation
d. It monitors network traffic for anomalies

Answer: c. It fixes known vulnerabilities in software and systems, reducing the risk of exploitation. Explanation: Patch management is a crucial preventative measure involving the regular update and application of patches to software and systems. This process fixes known vulnerabilities, reducing the risk of these weaknesses being exploited by attackers.

541. How do firewalls contribute to preventative measures in network security?
a. By encrypting all data transmitted over the network
b. By serving as a barrier between internal networks and external threats, controlling incoming and outgoing network traffic based on predetermined security rules
c. By backing up data stored on the network
d. By physically securing network devices

Answer: b. By serving as a barrier between internal networks and external threats, controlling incoming and outgoing network traffic based on predetermined security rules. Explanation: Firewalls are a fundamental preventative measure in network security, acting as a barrier that monitors and controls incoming and outgoing network traffic based on an organization's security policies, thereby preventing unauthorized access and attacks.

542. What preventative measure is specifically designed to detect and prevent malware infections on individual computers and networks?
a. Implementation of strong password policies
b. Use of antivirus and anti-malware software
c. Frequent change of network infrastructure
d. Use of biometric authentication systems

Answer: b. Use of antivirus and anti-malware software. Explanation: Antivirus and anti-malware software are designed to prevent, search for, detect, and remove software viruses and other malicious software like worms, trojans, adware, and more, making them essential preventative measures for individual computers and networks.

543. In the context of secure application development, what preventative measure can specifically mitigate the risk of injection attacks?
a. Conducting regular penetration testing on the network
b. Implementing input validation and parameterized queries
c. Increasing the bandwidth of the network
d. Encrypting all application data

Answer: b. Implementing input validation and parameterized queries. Explanation: Injection attacks, like SQL injection, exploit insecure application code by inserting or "injecting" malicious input. Implementing strict input validation and using parameterized queries are effective preventative measures that ensure only properly formatted data is accepted, thereby mitigating the risk of these attacks.

544. Why is it important to secure physical access to network devices as a preventative measure?
a. To ensure a neat and tidy server room
b. To prevent unauthorized physical access that could lead to data theft, device tampering, or destruction
c. To improve the aesthetics of the security environment
d. To comply with software licensing agreements

Answer: b. To prevent unauthorized physical access that could lead to data theft, device tampering, or destruction. Explanation: Securing physical access to network devices is a crucial preventative measure because it protects against direct, unauthorized interactions with the hardware, which could result in data breaches, device manipulation, or complete system compromise.

545. What is the significance of configuring secure access controls on databases as a preventative measure?
a. To ensure faster database queries
b. To limit database access to authorized users, thereby protecting sensitive information from unauthorized access and modification
c. To increase the storage capacity of the database
d. To enhance the graphical user interface of the database management system

Answer: b. To limit database access to authorized users, thereby protecting sensitive information from unauthorized access and modification. Explanation: Secure access controls on databases are a key preventative measure that ensure only authorized users can access or modify the database contents, thereby safeguarding sensitive information and maintaining data integrity and confidentiality.

546. What is the primary goal of a patch management program?
a. To ensure all software licenses are up to date

b. To monitor network traffic for anomalies

c. To keep software and systems updated with the latest patches to mitigate vulnerabilities

d. To back up data regularly

Answer: c. To keep software and systems updated with the latest patches to mitigate vulnerabilities. Explanation: Patch management is a critical security control that involves acquiring, testing, and installing multiple patches (code changes) to an administered computer system. The primary goal is to ensure systems and applications are up-to-date and protected against known vulnerabilities and exploits.

547. In vulnerability management, what is the purpose of conducting regular vulnerability scans?

a. To assess the aesthetic aspects of the system interface

b. To evaluate the system's compliance with data handling policies

c. To identify and assess the vulnerabilities within a system or network

d. To monitor real-time data transactions for performance bottlenecks

Answer: c. To identify and assess the vulnerabilities within a system or network. Explanation: Regular vulnerability scans are an integral part of vulnerability management, aimed at identifying, ranking, and providing information on vulnerabilities in systems and networks. This proactive approach helps in understanding the security posture and mitigating risks before they can be exploited.

548. Which of the following best describes the process of prioritizing vulnerabilities for remediation?

a. Arranging vulnerabilities based on the alphabetical order of system names

b. Prioritizing vulnerabilities based on their severity, impact, and the system's criticality to the business

c. Assigning random priorities to vulnerabilities

d. Focusing on the vulnerabilities reported first, regardless of their impact

Answer: b. Prioritizing vulnerabilities based on their severity, impact, and the system's criticality to the business. Explanation: Effective vulnerability management requires prioritizing vulnerabilities for remediation based on factors like severity (as indicated by scores such as CVSS), the potential impact on the organization, and the criticality of the affected system or asset to business operations.

549. What is a Zero-Day vulnerability?

a. A vulnerability that has been patched but not yet disclosed to the public

b. A vulnerability that is known to the vendor but left unpatched for strategic reasons

c. A vulnerability that is known to attackers but not yet known to the vendor or public

d. A vulnerability in the system that causes it to crash exactly at midnight

Answer: c. A vulnerability that is known to attackers but not yet known to the vendor or public. Explanation: A Zero-Day vulnerability refers to a software vulnerability that is known to attackers but has not yet been identified or addressed by the vendor. These vulnerabilities are particularly dangerous because they can be exploited before a patch or mitigation is available.

550. How does automating patch deployment benefit an organization's security posture?
a. By creating aesthetically pleasing reports on patch levels
b. By ensuring consistent and timely application of patches across all systems, reducing the window of vulnerability
c. By increasing the workload on IT staff
d. By randomly selecting which patches to apply first

Answer: b. By ensuring consistent and timely application of patches across all systems, reducing the window of vulnerability. Explanation: Automating patch deployment streamlines the process of applying patches, ensuring that all systems receive necessary updates promptly. This consistency and timeliness significantly reduce the organization's exposure to vulnerabilities.

551. What role does a patch management policy play in an organization's security framework?
a. It outlines the color scheme for the system interfaces
b. It defines the procedures for backup and data recovery
c. It provides guidelines and procedures for acquiring, testing, and installing patches
d. It dictates the office layout for optimal airflow

Answer: c. It provides guidelines and procedures for acquiring, testing, and installing patches. Explanation: A patch management policy is a foundational element of an organization's security framework, detailing the systematic approach to managing patches, including the responsibilities, timelines, testing procedures, and approval processes to ensure effective and secure patch management.

552. In the context of vulnerability management, what is the significance of a vulnerability feed?
a. It is a decorative element in the security operations center
b. It serves as a continuous source of information on the latest vulnerabilities, threats, and exploits
c. It is a social media tool used for entertainment by the security team
d. It tracks the dietary preferences of the security staff

Answer: b. It serves as a continuous source of information on the latest vulnerabilities, threats, and exploits. Explanation: A vulnerability feed is a critical component of an effective vulnerability management program, providing up-to-date information on emerging vulnerabilities, threats, and exploits from various sources, enabling organizations to proactively address potential security issues.

553. What is the importance of a vulnerability assessment in the context of patch management?
a. It determines the color scheme for patch management tools
b. It assesses the physical durability of hardware devices
c. It identifies vulnerabilities in systems and applications to determine which patches are needed
d. It evaluates the entertainment value of security training programs

Answer: c. It identifies vulnerabilities in systems and applications to determine which patches are needed.
Explanation: Vulnerability assessments are crucial for identifying existing weaknesses in systems and applications. This information is vital for patch management as it helps determine which patches are needed to address specific vulnerabilities, thereby enhancing the security posture.

554. How do emergency patches differ from regular patch cycles?
a. Emergency patches are released for aesthetic updates to the user interface
b. Emergency patches are released in response to immediate and severe security threats, outside the regular patch cycle
c. Emergency patches are optional and only applied at the user's convenience
d. Emergency patches are used to introduce new features rather than address security issues

Answer: b. Emergency patches are released in response to immediate and severe security threats, outside the regular patch cycle. Explanation: Emergency patches, or out-of-band patches, are issued to quickly mitigate critical security vulnerabilities that are being actively exploited or pose a significant risk to the organization, bypassing the regular patch cycle to reduce the window of vulnerability.

555. What is the role of regression testing in patch management?
a. To ensure that the application of patches does not introduce new vulnerabilities or functional issues in the system
b. To test the backward compatibility of gaming software
c. To assess the visual appeal of system updates
d. To measure the decrease in system performance after patches are applied

Answer: a. To ensure that the application of patches does not introduce new vulnerabilities or functional issues in the system. Explanation: Regression testing in the context of patch management is critical to ensure that newly applied patches do not adversely affect existing system functionalities or introduce new vulnerabilities, thereby maintaining the integrity and reliability of the system post-patch application.

556. What is the primary purpose of implementing secure coding practices in software development?
a. To enhance the graphical interface of applications
b. To ensure software meets performance benchmarks
c. To prevent the introduction of security vulnerabilities during development
d. To reduce software development time

Answer: c. To prevent the introduction of security vulnerabilities during development. Explanation: Secure coding practices are essential in software development to prevent security vulnerabilities such as injection flaws, buffer overflows, and cross-site scripting (XSS) from being introduced. These practices include input validation, proper error handling, and adherence to security principles, thereby enhancing the security posture of the software.

557. In the context of software development, what is the function of a Static Application Security Testing (SAST) tool?
a. To monitor the real-time performance of applications
b. To automatically fix bugs in the software
c. To analyze source code for security vulnerabilities without executing the program
d. To create graphical elements in the user interface

Answer: c. To analyze source code for security vulnerabilities without executing the program. Explanation: SAST tools are designed to analyze source code or compiled versions of code to identify security vulnerabilities. They work by inspecting the code for patterns that may indicate security issues, allowing developers to address vulnerabilities early in the development lifecycle.

558. Which software development methodology emphasizes iterative development and collaboration among self-organizing cross-functional teams?
a. Waterfall
b. Agile
c. Spiral
d. DevOps

Answer: b. Agile. Explanation: Agile methodology is characterized by iterative and incremental development, where requirements and solutions evolve through collaboration between self-organizing cross-functional teams. This approach promotes adaptive planning, evolutionary development, early delivery, and continual improvement.

559. What is the primary goal of Threat Modeling in software development?
a. To enhance the user interface design
b. To identify potential security threats and vulnerabilities in the design phase
c. To assess the software's market potential
d. To determine the software's compatibility with various operating systems

Answer: b. To identify potential security threats and vulnerabilities in the design phase. Explanation: Threat Modeling is a proactive approach used in the design phase of software development to identify and assess potential security threats and vulnerabilities. This process helps in understanding the attack surface of the application and in prioritizing security measures to mitigate identified risks.

560. In software development, what is the purpose of implementing an input validation technique?
a. To ensure user inputs meet certain criteria before processing
b. To improve the software's graphical user interface
c. To increase the processing speed of the application
d. To enhance the multimedia capabilities of the software

Answer: a. To ensure user inputs meet certain criteria before processing. Explanation: Input validation is a security measure implemented in software development to ensure that only properly formatted data is entered into the system. This technique helps prevent malicious or unintended data from causing errors or security vulnerabilities, such as SQL injection or buffer overflow attacks.

561. What role does DevSecOps play in software development?
a. To integrate security practices into the DevOps process
b. To reduce the graphical design time of applications
c. To increase the speed of network connections within the application
d. To manage the software's digital rights and licensing

Answer: a. To integrate security practices into the DevOps process. Explanation: DevSecOps is an approach that integrates security practices within the DevOps process. It aims to involve security early in the software development lifecycle, fostering collaboration between development, security, and operations teams to ensure secure code development, deployment, and maintenance.

562. Why is it important to conduct code reviews in software development?
a. To assess the aesthetic appeal of the code
b. To evaluate the software's compatibility with different hardware
c. To identify and rectify security vulnerabilities and coding errors
d. To determine the software's impact on system resources

Answer: c. To identify and rectify security vulnerabilities and coding errors. Explanation: Code reviews are a critical part of the software development process, where peers review source code to identify mistakes overlooked in the initial development phase. This practice helps in detecting security vulnerabilities, coding errors, and ensuring adherence to coding standards, thereby improving the quality and security of the software.

563. In software development, what is the principle of "least privilege"?
a. Ensuring all users have administrative access
b. Granting users only the permissions necessary to perform their tasks
c. Providing unlimited resources to the development team
d. Allowing open access to all parts of the system for ease of use

Answer: b. Granting users only the permissions necessary to perform their tasks. Explanation: The principle of least privilege is a key security concept in software development, which stipulates that users should be granted only the minimum levels of access—or permissions—needed to perform their duties. This minimizes the potential damage from accidents, errors, or unauthorized use of systems.

564. What is the significance of using encryption in software applications?
a. To improve the application's graphical interface
b. To increase the processing speed of the application
c. To protect the confidentiality and integrity of data
d. To enhance the software's compatibility with various devices

Answer: c. To protect the confidentiality and integrity of data. Explanation: Encryption is a fundamental security technique used in software applications to protect the confidentiality and integrity of data. By converting data into a coded format that is unreadable without a decryption key, encryption ensures that sensitive information remains secure from unauthorized access and tampering.

565. In the Software Development Life Cycle (SDLC), what is the main focus of the "Maintenance" phase?
a. Initial planning and design of the software
b. Development and coding of the software features
c. Correction of defects and implementation of enhancements
d. Marketing and sale of the software product

Answer: c. Correction of defects and implementation of enhancements. Explanation: The Maintenance phase of the SDLC involves the correction of defects discovered during the use of the software, as well as the implementation of enhancements to improve performance or add new features. This phase ensures the software continues to meet user needs and remains secure over time.

566. What is the primary purpose of integrating security activities throughout the Software Development Life Cycle (SDLC)?
a. To reduce the overall cost of the project
b. To ensure that security is considered at each phase of the SDLC
c. To speed up the development process
d. To increase the software's compatibility with various platforms

Answer: b. To ensure that security is considered at each phase of the SDLC. Explanation: Integrating security activities throughout the SDLC ensures that security considerations are embedded from the initial design through development, deployment, and maintenance phases. This proactive approach helps in identifying and mitigating potential security vulnerabilities early, reducing the risk of costly fixes and breaches after deployment.

567. In the context of the SDLC, what is "Threat Modeling" primarily used for?
a. Estimating the project's budget
b. Identifying and assessing potential threats to the system
c. Determining the software's market viability
d. Allocating resources for development tasks

Answer: b. Identifying and assessing potential threats to the system. Explanation: Threat Modeling is a process used in the design phase of the SDLC to systematically identify and prioritize potential threats to the system. This approach helps in understanding the attacker's perspective and guides the development of mitigations to protect the system against identified threats.

568. Which SDLC model incorporates security reviews and testing at each iteration?
a. Waterfall
b. V-Model
c. Agile
d. Spiral

Answer: c. Agile. Explanation: The Agile SDLC model is characterized by short, iterative cycles of development, known as sprints, with each sprint including planning, development, testing, and review. Security reviews and testing are integrated into each sprint, allowing for continuous assessment and improvement of security throughout the development process.

569. What is the role of Static Application Security Testing (SAST) in the SDLC?
a. To assess the network infrastructure's security posture
b. To evaluate the application's user interface design
c. To analyze the application's source code for vulnerabilities without executing it
d. To measure the application's response time and efficiency

Answer: c. To analyze the application's source code for vulnerabilities without executing it. Explanation: SAST tools are used in the development phase of the SDLC to analyze the application's source code or bytecode to identify security vulnerabilities. These tools can detect issues such as SQL injection, cross-site scripting, and other vulnerabilities early in the development process, enabling timely remediation.

570. During which phase of the SDLC is a "Security Requirements Analysis" typically conducted?
a. Maintenance
b. Implementation
c. Design
d. Testing

Answer: c. Design. Explanation: Security Requirements Analysis is conducted during the design phase of the SDLC. This process involves identifying and defining security requirements and objectives based on the system's intended functionality, data sensitivity, and potential threats. This ensures that security considerations are integrated into the system's architecture and design specifications.

571. How does the "Principle of Least Privilege" apply to software development?
a. By granting all users administrative privileges
b. By ensuring that each component of the software has only the necessary privileges to perform its function
c. By providing unlimited access to all system resources during development
d. By minimizing the use of third-party libraries and tools

Answer: b. By ensuring that each component of the software has only the necessary privileges to perform its function. Explanation: The Principle of Least Privilege is applied in software development by ensuring that software components, processes, and users operate with the minimum set of privileges necessary to complete their tasks. This reduces the potential impact of a security breach by limiting access to system resources and data.

572. What is the significance of "Peer Reviews" in the SDLC?
a. To compare the software with competitor products
b. To assess the market demand for the software
c. To evaluate the software's source code for potential vulnerabilities and coding standards compliance
d. To determine the optimal pricing strategy for the software

Answer: c. To evaluate the software's source code for potential vulnerabilities and coding standards compliance. Explanation: Peer Reviews, or code reviews, are conducted during the development phase of the SDLC to examine the software's source code by other developers or security experts. This collaborative process helps identify potential vulnerabilities, coding errors, and deviations from coding standards, contributing to the overall quality and security of the software.

573. Why is "Secure Coding" essential in software development?
a. To enhance the visual appeal of the software interface
b. To ensure the software is developed using the latest programming languages
c. To prevent the introduction of vulnerabilities through coding practices
d. To reduce the overall development time by using automated tools

Answer: c. To prevent the introduction of vulnerabilities through coding practices. Explanation: Secure Coding is a set of practices aimed at writing code that is free from vulnerabilities and security flaws. This approach is essential in software development to prevent common security issues such as injection attacks, buffer overflows, and cross-site scripting, thereby enhancing the security and reliability of the software.

574. In which phase of the SDLC are "Dynamic Application Security Testing" (DAST) tools most commonly used?
a. Requirements gathering
b. Design
c. Implementation
d. Testing

Answer: d. Testing. Explanation: DAST tools are employed in the testing phase of the SDLC to identify security vulnerabilities in a running application. These tools interact with the application from the outside, simulating an attacker's perspective to detect issues like runtime errors, input/output validation problems, and other vulnerabilities that are observable only when the application is executing.

575. What is the primary purpose of segregating development, testing, and production environments in software development?
a. To increase the speed of the development process
b. To reduce the cost of software deployment
c. To prevent unauthorized access and protect the integrity of the production environment
d. To allow developers to have unrestricted access to live user data

Answer: c. To prevent unauthorized access and protect the integrity of the production environment. Explanation: Segregating these environments is a fundamental security control that prevents inadvertent changes or unauthorized access to the production environment, where live user data is handled. It ensures that experimental code or untested changes do not compromise the stability and security of the live system.

576. In a secure development environment, what is the role of using version control systems like Git?
a. To provide a backup of the source code
b. To track and manage changes to the source code, ensuring accountability and enabling rollback of changes if necessary
c. To automate the deployment of applications
d. To enhance the performance of the development software

Answer: b. To track and manage changes to the source code, ensuring accountability and enabling rollback of changes if necessary. Explanation: Version control systems are essential for maintaining the integrity of the source code, providing a history of changes, and facilitating collaboration among developers. They allow teams to revert to previous versions if a new change introduces errors or vulnerabilities.

577. What is the significance of code signing in a development environment?
a. To increase the execution speed of the application
b. To encrypt the source code
c. To verify the authenticity and integrity of the software, confirming that it has not been tampered with
d. To compress the application files for easier distribution

Answer: c. To verify the authenticity and integrity of the software, confirming that it has not been tampered with. Explanation: Code signing uses digital signatures to assure recipients of the software that it genuinely comes from the claimed source (authenticity) and that it has not been altered or corrupted since it was signed (integrity).

578. How do automated security scans contribute to a secure development environment?
a. By replacing the need for manual code reviews
b. By identifying vulnerabilities in the code base early in the development cycle
c. By facilitating faster deployment to production
d. By encrypting the source code

Answer: b. By identifying vulnerabilities in the code base early in the development cycle. Explanation: Automated security scans are tools used to systematically review code or compiled versions of the code to detect security vulnerabilities, such as injection flaws or buffer overflows. Early identification allows for timely remediation before the software progresses too far in the development cycle or is released.

579. Why is it important to restrict developer access to production data?
a. To comply with privacy laws and regulations
b. To ensure developers have sufficient data for testing
c. To accelerate the development process
d. To increase the amount of storage available for development purposes

Answer: a. To comply with privacy laws and regulations. Explanation: Restricting access to production data helps protect sensitive and personal information, ensuring compliance with privacy laws and preventing potential data breaches. Developers should use sanitized or anonymized data for testing purposes to avoid exposure of real user data.

580. What role does static application security testing (SAST) play in development environment security?
a. It dynamically executes the code to find runtime vulnerabilities
b. It checks the source code for vulnerabilities without requiring execution
c. It monitors the network traffic for suspicious activities
d. It tests the physical security of the development hardware

Answer: b. It checks the source code for vulnerabilities without requiring execution. Explanation: SAST tools analyze the source code, byte code, or binary code of an application for vulnerabilities that can lead to security breaches. By identifying issues early in the development process, developers can address them before the software is deployed.

581. Why are hardened development workstations important in a secure development environment?
a. To improve the graphical interface for development tools
b. To ensure that the development tools run at optimal speed
c. To prevent the introduction of malware and reduce the risk of exploitation
d. To facilitate easier collaboration between team members

Answer: c. To prevent the introduction of malware and reduce the risk of exploitation. Explanation: Hardening development workstations involves configuring them to reduce vulnerabilities and protect against attacks. This includes applying security patches, disabling unnecessary services, and using security tools, which helps prevent malware infection and unauthorized access.

582. How does continuous integration/continuous deployment (CI/CD) enhance security in the development process?
a. By constantly changing the development environment to confuse attackers
b. By frequently merging code changes into a shared repository and automatically testing and deploying them, which helps identify and fix security issues promptly
c. By making the development process entirely automated, eliminating the need for security reviews
d. By decentralizing the codebase, making it harder for attackers to target

Answer: b. By frequently merging code changes into a shared repository and automatically testing and deploying them, which helps identify and fix security issues promptly. Explanation: CI/CD pipelines automate the process of integrating code changes, testing them, and deploying to production environments. This allows for rapid identification and remediation of security vulnerabilities within the development cycle.

583. What is the purpose of environment-specific configuration files in a secure development environment?
a. To provide a single, standardized configuration for all environments
b. To store all passwords and secrets in a central, easily accessible location
c. To tailor application settings to the specific requirements of each environment (development, testing, production) without hard-coding sensitive information
d. To allow developers unrestricted access to all environments

Answer: c. To tailor application settings to the specific requirements of each environment (development, testing, production) without hard-coding sensitive information. Explanation: Using environment-specific configuration files helps manage settings like database connections and API keys differently across environments, enhancing security by avoiding the inclusion of sensitive details in the source code and reducing the risk of exposing production secrets in less secure environments.

584. Why is the principle of least privilege important in a development environment?
a. To ensure that all team members have equal access to all resources
b. To provide developers with unrestricted access to enhance productivity
c. To minimize the access rights for users to the bare minimum necessary to perform their duties, thereby reducing the risk of accidental or malicious misuse
d. To increase the complexity of the environment, making it more secure

Answer: c. To minimize the access rights for users to the bare minimum necessary to perform their duties, thereby reducing the risk of accidental or malicious misuse. Explanation: Applying the principle of least privilege in a development environment limits the potential damage from compromised accounts or insider threats by ensuring that individuals have only the access necessary to fulfill their specific roles.

585. How does threat modeling enhance software security effectiveness?
a. By creating a detailed financial plan for security investment
b. By identifying potential threats early in the software development lifecycle, allowing for proactive security measures
c. By increasing the complexity of the software, making it harder to attack
d. By encrypting all data within the software application

Answer: b. By identifying potential threats early in the software development lifecycle, allowing for proactive security measures. Explanation: Threat modeling involves systematically identifying and prioritizing potential threats to a system and determining the value that potential mitigations would have in reducing or neutralizing those threats. This process helps in the early identification of security issues, enabling developers to incorporate security measures into the design and architecture of a system before it is developed, which is more effective and less costly than making changes after the software is completed.

586. What role does fuzzing play in assessing software security effectiveness?
a. It encrypts sensitive data within the application to prevent unauthorized access
b. It simulates high user traffic to test the application's performance under load
c. It involves inputting large amounts of random data to the software to find vulnerabilities that could be exploited
d. It provides a graphical interface for user-friendly software interaction

Answer: c. It involves inputting large amounts of random data to the software to find vulnerabilities that could be exploited. Explanation: Fuzzing is a dynamic code analysis technique used to discover coding errors and security loopholes in software, operating systems, or networks by inputting massive amounts of random data, called fuzz, to the system in an attempt to make it crash. Identifying how the system reacts can help uncover potential vulnerabilities, thus enhancing the software's security posture by allowing developers to fix these issues.

587. How does static application security testing (SAST) contribute to software security effectiveness?
a. By assessing the application's compliance with licensing agreements
b. By dynamically executing the application in a real-world environment to find runtime errors
c. By analyzing source code at rest to detect vulnerabilities before the software is run
d. By measuring the physical security of the hardware on which the software is executed

Answer: c. By analyzing source code at rest to detect vulnerabilities before the software is run. Explanation: SAST tools examine source code (or at times compiled versions of code) to identify areas that might be vulnerable to exploitation. This is done without executing the program, allowing vulnerabilities to be found early in the development process. It helps developers fix potential security issues before they become part of the deployed software, significantly enhancing the software's security effectiveness.

588. In what way does code obfuscation affect software security effectiveness?
a. By making the code more readable and easier to understand
b. By encrypting the code to prevent unauthorized access
c. By modifying the software's code to make it more difficult for attackers to understand and exploit
d. By compressing the code to reduce the size of the software

Answer: c. By modifying the software's code to make it more difficult for attackers to understand and exploit. Explanation: Code obfuscation is the process of modifying an application's code to make it harder to understand and analyze. While it does not fix underlying security issues, it can make it more difficult for hackers to reverse-engineer the software and discover vulnerabilities to exploit, thus providing an additional layer of security.

589. What is the significance of penetration testing in measuring software security effectiveness?
a. It helps in creating user manuals by understanding user interactions with the software
b. It involves an authorized simulated attack on the software to identify vulnerabilities
c. It focuses on the aesthetic aspects of the software to improve user interface design
d. It tests the software's compatibility with various operating systems and platforms

Answer: b. It involves an authorized simulated attack on the software to identify vulnerabilities. Explanation: Penetration testing, or pen testing, is a simulated cyber attack against your computer system to check for exploitable vulnerabilities. In the context of web application security, penetration testing is commonly used to augment a web application firewall (WAF). Pen tests can involve the attempted breaching of any number of application systems, (e.g., application protocol interfaces (APIs), frontend/backend servers) to uncover vulnerabilities, such as unsanitized inputs that are susceptible to code injection attacks.

590. How does peer code review benefit software security effectiveness?
a. By ensuring that the code meets industry standards for performance
b. By having multiple developers review the code for errors and vulnerabilities that a single developer might miss
c. By documenting the code to make future maintenance easier
d. By automating the testing process, removing the need for manual review

Answer: b. By having multiple developers review the code for errors and vulnerabilities that a single developer might miss. Explanation: Peer code review is a process where developers review each other's code for mistakes overlooked in the initial development phase. It is an effective method for catching security flaws and logical errors, as it brings different perspectives and experiences to the table, leading to more secure and robust software.

591. What impact does secure coding training have on software security effectiveness?
a. It reduces the need for security testing tools
b. It ensures that developers are aware of security best practices and common vulnerabilities to avoid in their code
c. It eliminates the need for a dedicated security team within an organization
d. It guarantees that the software will be free from any security vulnerabilities

Answer: b. It ensures that developers are aware of security best practices and common vulnerabilities to avoid in their code. Explanation: Secure coding training equips developers with the knowledge and skills to write code that is resistant to vulnerabilities. By understanding security principles and common pitfalls, developers can proactively prevent many security issues from being introduced into the software during the development phase, thus enhancing the overall security effectiveness of the software.

592. How does regression testing relate to software security effectiveness?
a. It focuses solely on testing the software's new features and ignores existing functionality
b. It involves retesting the software after patches or updates to ensure that no new vulnerabilities have been introduced
c. It is used to test the software's performance under high load conditions
d. It assesses the software's user interface design for usability issues

Answer: b. It involves retesting the software after patches or updates to ensure that no new vulnerabilities have been introduced. Explanation: Regression testing is a type of software testing that verifies that software previously developed and tested still performs correctly after it was changed or interfaced with other software. Changes could include software enhancements, patches, configuration changes, etc. This process is crucial for maintaining the security posture of the software, as updates can sometimes inadvertently introduce new vulnerabilities.

593. What is the role of automated security scanning tools in software security effectiveness?
a. They replace the need for manual security reviews and penetration testing
b. They provide a continuous assessment of the software's security posture by automatically scanning for known vulnerabilities
c. They focus on the physical security of the servers hosting the software
d. They assess the financial impact of potential security breaches

Answer: b. They provide a continuous assessment of the software's security posture by automatically scanning for known vulnerabilities. Explanation: Automated security scanning tools are software applications that help to identify and diagnose problems with web applications, networks, and servers. These tools can efficiently scan the software for known vulnerabilities, providing regular feedback on the security health of the application. While they do not replace the need for in-depth manual reviews and penetration tests, they are a critical component of a comprehensive security strategy, allowing for early detection and mitigation of potential security issues.

594. Which security model is primarily concerned with ensuring that access controls cannot be bypassed and enforces a strict layer of protection based on security levels?
a. The Bell-LaPadula Model
b. The Biba Integrity Model
c. The Clark-Wilson Model
d. The Chinese Wall Model

Answer: a. The Bell-LaPadula Model. Explanation: The Bell-LaPadula Model focuses on maintaining the confidentiality of information. It applies the concept of "no read up, no write down," ensuring that subjects at a lower security level cannot access information at a higher level, and information cannot be written down to a lower level, thereby preventing unauthorized access and ensuring that access controls cannot be bypassed.

595. In the context of security evaluation models, what does the Common Criteria (CC) provide?
a. A framework for only evaluating cryptographic modules
b. A comprehensive set of guidelines for physical security
c. An international standard for computer security certification
d. A specific protocol for network security assessments

Answer: c. An international standard for computer security certification. Explanation: The Common Criteria for Information Technology Security Evaluation (CC) is an international standard (ISO/IEC 15408) that provides a common framework for evaluating the security properties of IT products and systems. It offers a structured approach for specifying, implementing, and evaluating the security features of IT products and systems against defined criteria.

596. Which concept is at the core of the Biba Integrity Model?
a. Preventing unauthorized subjects from writing to high-integrity objects
b. Allowing free flow of information between different security domains
c. Ensuring the confidentiality of data at varying levels of security
d. Facilitating user access based on conflict of interest policies

Answer: a. Preventing unauthorized subjects from writing to high-integrity objects. Explanation: The Biba Integrity Model is designed to protect the integrity of data by preventing subjects (users, processes) from writing data to objects (files, database entries) that are at a higher integrity level than the subject itself. This "no write up" principle ensures that information at a higher integrity level remains uncorrupted by lower integrity subjects.

597. What is the primary focus of the Clark-Wilson Model?
a. Data confidentiality and secrecy
b. User authentication and identification
c. Data integrity through well-formed transactions
d. Segregation of duties and least privilege

Answer: c. Data integrity through well-formed transactions. Explanation: The Clark-Wilson Model emphasizes ensuring data integrity in commercial applications through well-formed transactions. It enforces integrity by requiring that transactions (operations on data) must be validated and adhere to certain constraints, ensuring that data remains consistent and accurate.

598. How does the Chinese Wall Model address conflict of interest in information access?
a. By preventing write operations across different security domains
b. By dynamically controlling access based on a user's previous access
c. By enforcing two-factor authentication for sensitive transactions
d. By mandating physical separation of data storage

Answer: b. By dynamically controlling access based on a user's previous access. Explanation: The Chinese Wall Model is designed to prevent conflicts of interest by controlling access to data based on a user's previous access to potentially conflicting information. It ensures that once a user accesses data from one conflict class (e.g., one company's sensitive information), they cannot access data from a conflicting class (e.g., a competitor's information), thus maintaining impartiality and preventing information misuse.

599. What role do Trusted Computing Base (TCB) concepts play in security evaluation models?
a. They define the physical security measures for data centers
b. They outline the protocols for secure network communication
c. They specify the set of all protection mechanisms within a computer system
d. They establish guidelines for user identity verification

Answer: c. They specify the set of all protection mechanisms within a computer system. Explanation: The Trusted Computing Base (TCB) encompasses all the protection mechanisms within a computer system, including hardware, firmware, and software, that are responsible for enforcing a security policy. The TCB's integrity is crucial for the overall security of the system, as it provides the foundation upon which the trustworthiness of the system is built.

600. How does the ITSEC (Information Technology Security Evaluation Criteria) differ from the Common Criteria?
a. ITSEC focuses exclusively on network security, whereas Common Criteria covers all aspects of IT security.
b. ITSEC is a predecessor to Common Criteria, offering a less unified approach to security evaluation.
c. ITSEC applies only to military systems, while Common Criteria is for civilian and commercial use.
d. ITSEC evaluations are quicker and less comprehensive than those of Common Criteria.

Answer: b. ITSEC is a predecessor to Common Criteria, offering a less unified approach to security evaluation. Explanation: The Information Technology Security Evaluation Criteria (ITSEC) is a predecessor to the Common Criteria. ITSEC provided a framework for evaluating the security of information systems but was less unified and consistent compared to the Common Criteria, which harmonized various national standards into a single, comprehensive framework for international use.

601. In the Rainbow Series of security books, what is the purpose of the "Orange Book"?
a. It outlines the standards for cryptographic algorithms.
b. It provides guidelines for environmental security controls.
c. It defines the criteria for evaluating the security of computer systems.
d. It specifies the requirements for secure software development.

Answer: c. It defines the criteria for evaluating the security of computer systems. Explanation: The "Orange Book," formally known as the Trusted Computer System Evaluation Criteria (TCSEC), is part of the Rainbow Series of security books and sets forth the criteria for evaluating the security of computer systems, particularly focusing on the assessment of operating systems' security levels.

602. What is the main objective of the Separation of Duties (SoD) concept in security models?
a. To distribute system functions among multiple components to enhance performance
b. To ensure no single individual has control over all phases of a transaction
c. To segregate network zones based on their security levels
d. To separate user data from application data for privacy reasons

Answer: b. To ensure no single individual has control over all phases of a transaction. Explanation: The Separation of Duties (SoD) is a key concept in security models designed to prevent fraud and errors by ensuring that no single individual or entity has control over all phases of a critical or sensitive transaction. By requiring that different individuals perform different roles or tasks within a process, SoD reduces the risk of malicious or accidental misuse of the system.

603. Which OSI layer is responsible for establishing, managing, and terminating sessions between two communication endpoints?
a. Transport Layer
b. Session Layer
c. Presentation Layer
d. Application Layer

Answer: b. Session Layer. Explanation: The Session Layer, the fifth level in the OSI model, facilitates the setup, coordination, and termination of conversations, exchanges, and dialogues between applications on each end.

604. In the OSI model, which layer is tasked with ensuring data is delivered across network devices?
a. Physical Layer
b. Data Link Layer

c. Network Layer

d. Transport Layer

Answer: c. Network Layer. Explanation: The Network Layer, or Layer 3, is crucial for routing packets from the source to the destination host across multiple networks, using logical addressing like IP addresses for accurate packet delivery.

605. Which protocol at the Transport Layer of the OSI model provides connection-oriented data transmission?

a. UDP

b. IP

c. ICMP

d. TCP

Answer: d. TCP. Explanation: TCP (Transmission Control Protocol) operates at the Transport Layer, ensuring reliable, sequenced, and error-checked delivery of a byte stream between applications on hosts within an IP network.

606. IGMP is utilized for what type of IP network communication?

a. Unicast

b. Broadcast

c. Multicast

d. Anycast

Answer: c. Multicast. Explanation: IGMP (Internet Group Management Protocol) is crucial for setting up multicast group memberships on IP networks, enabling a single message to be dispatched simultaneously to a group of recipients.

607. Which OSI layer converts data formats from application to network format and vice versa?

a. Application Layer

b. Presentation Layer

c. Session Layer

d. Transport Layer

Answer: b. Presentation Layer. Explanation: The Presentation Layer, or Layer 6 of the OSI model, translates data from application format to network format and back, handling encryption, decryption, and compression processes.

608. What function does the Transport Layer in the OSI model perform?

a. Ensuring reliable data transmission between end systems

b. Routing data packets between networks

c. Defining cables, cards, and physical aspects

d. Managing dialog control and synchronization

Answer: a. Ensuring reliable data transmission between end systems. Explanation: The Transport Layer, Layer 4, provides end-to-end communication services for applications within a layered architecture of network components and protocols.

609. Which OSI layer encapsulates network layer packets into frames for transmission?
a. Application Layer
b. Data Link Layer
c. Network Layer
d. Physical Layer

Answer: b. Data Link Layer. Explanation: The Data Link Layer, or Layer 2, frames packets from the Network Layer for physical network transmission, handling error checking and reliable frame delivery.

610. What role does the Physical Layer of the OSI model play?
a. It routes packets across networks.
b. It frames packets for transmission.
c. It transmits raw bit streams over physical medium.
d. It provides encryption and compression.

Answer: c. It transmits raw bit streams over physical medium. Explanation: The Physical Layer, the first layer of the OSI model, is responsible for the transmission and reception of unstructured raw data between a device and a physical transmission medium.

611. Which OSI layer defines how data is formatted for transmission?
a. Network Layer
b. Data Link Layer
c. Physical Layer
d. Presentation Layer

Answer: d. Presentation Layer. Explanation: The Presentation Layer, Layer 6, standardizes data presented to the application layer, ensuring that data sent by an application layer of one system is readable by the application layer of another system.

612. For what purpose is the Application Layer in the OSI model used?
a. Directing data packets to destination hosts
b. Providing a user interface
c. Encrypting data
d. Framing data for the network

Answer: b. Providing a user interface. Explanation: The Application Layer, Layer 7, serves as the window for users and application processes to access network services, facilitating communication between software applications and lower layers.

613. Which of the following best describes a risk-based approach to security management?
a. Focusing solely on high-risk areas and ignoring low-risk areas
b. Allocating security resources based on the potential impact of threats
c. Implementing security controls uniformly across all assets
d. Prioritizing security measures based solely on their cost

Answer: b. Allocating security resources based on the potential impact of threats. Explanation: A risk-based approach to security management involves identifying, assessing, and prioritizing risks to ensure that security resources are allocated where they can have the most significant impact in reducing potential threats, rather than spreading resources too thinly or focusing only on cost.

614. In the context of Asset Security, which of the following is the primary purpose of data classification?
a. To ensure data is encrypted
b. To speed up data access
c. To facilitate appropriate levels of data protection
d. To reduce storage requirements

Answer: c. To facilitate appropriate levels of data protection. Explanation: Data classification categorizes organizational data based on its sensitivity and value to apply suitable protection controls. This ensures that critical or sensitive information receives higher levels of security, aligning protection efforts with the importance of the data.

615. When implementing Security Architecture and Engineering principles, which factor is most crucial in designing a secure system?
a. The cost of the security technologies employed
b. The ease of use for end-users
c. The alignment with business objectives and security requirements
d. The color scheme of the user interface

Answer: c. The alignment with business objectives and security requirements. Explanation: The primary goal in designing a secure system is ensuring that the security architecture and engineering efforts align with the broader business objectives and specific security requirements, ensuring that the system supports organizational goals while protecting against relevant threats.

616. What is the primary purpose of implementing network segmentation in Communication and Network Security?
a. To increase the network's bandwidth
b. To segregate sensitive data and systems from the general network

c. To reduce the number of needed firewalls

d. To simplify network management

Answer: b. To segregate sensitive data and systems from the general network. Explanation: Network segmentation divides a network into multiple segments or subnetworks, each acting as a separate security domain. This limits access to sensitive areas, reduces the attack surface, and contains potential breaches, enhancing overall network security.

617. In Identity and Access Management (IAM), what is the main advantage of using multi-factor authentication (MFA)?

a. It eliminates the need for passwords

b. It reduces the cost of user account management

c. It provides a higher level of security by combining multiple credentials

d. It simplifies the login process for users

Answer: c. It provides a higher level of security by combining multiple credentials. Explanation: MFA enhances security by requiring two or more independent credentials for user authentication, making unauthorized access more challenging. These credentials typically include something the user knows (password), something they have (security token), and something they are (biometric verification).

618. During Security Assessment and Testing, what is the primary goal of penetration testing?

a. To check the physical security of server rooms

b. To identify vulnerabilities in a system by simulating an attack

c. To ensure all software is up to date

d. To assess the organization's compliance with security policies

Answer: b. To identify vulnerabilities in a system by simulating an attack. Explanation: Penetration testing, or pen-testing, simulates real-world attacks on systems, networks, or applications to identify vulnerabilities that could be exploited by malicious actors, providing critical insights into security weaknesses.

619. In Security Operations, what is a key purpose of implementing an incident response plan (IRP)?

a. To eliminate the need for security monitoring tools

b. To provide a structured approach for managing security incidents

c. To increase the organization's insurance coverage

d. To document employee internet usage policies

Answer: b. To provide a structured approach for managing security incidents. Explanation: An IRP outlines procedures and roles for detecting, responding to, and recovering from security incidents, ensuring a coordinated and effective approach to minimize impact and restore normal operations.

620. In Software Development Security, why is input validation crucial?
a. To enhance the graphical interface of applications
b. To ensure user data is stored in the correct database format
c. To prevent malicious data from causing harm to the application or system
d. To increase the speed of database queries

Answer: c. To prevent malicious data from causing harm to the application or system. Explanation: Input validation checks data provided by external parties or users to ensure it's within expected bounds before processing. This helps prevent common attacks like SQL injection and cross-site scripting (XSS), which exploit input vulnerabilities to compromise systems.

621. What is the primary purpose of employing least privilege principles in an organization's security strategy?
a. To ensure all users have the access they need to perform their job functions
b. To minimize the risk associated with excessive permissions by limiting user rights
c. To simplify the process of granting permissions
d. To reduce the cost of IT operations

Answer: b. To minimize the risk associated with excessive permissions by limiting user rights. Explanation: The principle of least privilege restricts users' access rights to only what's necessary for their job functions, reducing the risk of accidental or intentional misuse of permissions and limiting the potential damage from breaches.

622. Why is change management important in maintaining security within an organization?
a. It ensures that all changes to IT infrastructure are decorative
b. It guarantees that no unauthorized changes are made to systems or applications
c. It allows all employees to make changes to IT systems freely
d. It ensures that system changes are reversible

Answer: b. It guarantees that no unauthorized changes are made to systems or applications. Explanation: Change management is a systematic approach to handling all changes in a system, ensuring that no unauthorized changes are made, and that all changes are documented, tested, and approved, reducing the risk of introducing vulnerabilities.

623. In a Zero Trust architecture, which principle is MOST critical for ensuring secure access to resources?
a. Perimeter-based security
b. Trust but verify
c. Least privilege access with continuous verification
d. Open access within the internal network

Answer: c. Least privilege access with continuous verification. Explanation: Zero Trust security models operate on the principle that trust is never assumed, regardless of the network's location. It enforces strict access controls and continuous verification of all users and devices, ensuring they have the minimum necessary access and are continuously validated for security compliance.

624. When designing a secure cryptographic solution, which factor is MOST crucial in selecting an appropriate cryptographic algorithm?
a. The popularity of the algorithm
b. Compliance with regulatory standards
c. The algorithm's execution speed
d. The color scheme of the cryptographic software

Answer: b. Compliance with regulatory standards. Explanation: While factors like execution speed and popularity might influence algorithm choice, compliance with regulatory standards and security requirements is paramount. This ensures that the cryptographic solution meets legal and industry-specific data protection mandates, providing the necessary level of security.

625. In implementing secure network architecture, what role does microsegmentation play in enhancing security within a virtualized environment?
a. Increases the network's bandwidth
b. Segregates workloads for fine-grained security control
c. Simplifies the network topology
d. Reduces the overall cost of network infrastructure

Answer: b. Segregates workloads for fine-grained security control. Explanation: Microsegmentation is a technique used in virtualized environments to create secure zones in data centers and cloud deployments. It allows for fine-grained security policies to be applied to individual workloads, enhancing isolation and reducing the lateral movement of threats.

626. For advanced identity and access management, what is the primary security benefit of implementing federated identity management?
a. Centralizes all user accounts into a single directory
b. Allows users to reuse a single authentication token across multiple domains
c. Eliminates the need for passwords
d. Simplifies the user registration process

Answer: b. Allows users to reuse a single authentication token across multiple domains. Explanation: Federated identity management enables users to access multiple systems or applications across different domains using a single set of credentials, facilitated by the sharing of identity information between the federated systems. This enhances user experience and security by reducing the number of credentials users need to manage while enabling centralized control over access.

627. During a security assessment, what is the primary purpose of using a fuzzing technique?
a. To document the network topology
b. To identify potential buffer overflow vulnerabilities

c. To assess the strength of user passwords

d. To map out wireless network coverage

Answer: b. To identify potential buffer overflow vulnerabilities. Explanation: Fuzzing is an automated software testing technique that involves providing invalid, unexpected, or random data inputs to a computer program. The goal is to uncover coding errors and security loopholes such as buffer overflow vulnerabilities, where the program might crash or behave unexpectedly, potentially leading to exploitable conditions.

628. In the context of security operations, why is it critical to implement a Security Information and Event Management (SIEM) system?

a. To replace the need for manual log reviews

b. To provide real-time analysis of security alerts generated by network hardware and applications

c. To reduce the amount of storage needed for log files

d. To automate the patch management process

Answer: b. To provide real-time analysis of security alerts generated by network hardware and applications. Explanation: SIEM systems are vital for security operations as they aggregate, correlate, and analyze log data from various sources in real-time, allowing for the rapid detection of security incidents and potential threats by highlighting anomalies and patterns indicative of malicious activity.

629. In software development security, why is it essential to conduct threat modeling during the design phase?

a. To fulfill compliance requirements only

b. To ensure the user interface is intuitive

c. To identify and mitigate potential security threats early in the development lifecycle

d. To decide the programming languages used

Answer: c. To identify and mitigate potential security threats early in the development lifecycle. Explanation: Threat modeling is a proactive approach to identifying and addressing potential security issues before they are implemented in code. Conducting threat modeling during the design phase allows developers to understand the attack surface, identify security risks, and implement mitigations, ultimately leading to more secure software.

630. When considering the secure disposal of IT assets, what is the MOST secure method for ensuring data is irrecoverable from a solid-state drive (SSD)?

a. Formatting the drive

b. Degaussing

c. Physical destruction

d. Writing zeros to the drive

Answer: c. Physical destruction. Explanation: For SSDs, physical destruction (such as shredding or incineration) is often considered the most secure method of disposal, ensuring that the data stored on the chips is completely irrecoverable. Unlike traditional hard drives, methods like degaussing are ineffective on SSDs due to their lack of magnetic storage.

631. In the context of Communication and Network Security, what is the primary purpose of implementing an Intrusion Detection and Prevention System (IDPS)?
a. To increase network bandwidth efficiency
b. To monitor and analyze network traffic for malicious activities and policy violations
c. To serve as the primary method for data encryption
d. To replace the need for firewalls

Answer: b. To monitor and analyze network traffic for malicious activities and policy violations. Explanation: An IDPS is designed to continuously monitor network and system activities for malicious actions and policy breaches. It can automatically block or alert administrators about detected threats, serving as a critical layer in a comprehensive security posture, complementing other defenses like firewalls without replacing them.

632. In Asset Security, what is the significance of data classification policies?
a. To determine the entertainment value of data
b. To define the roles of users within an organization
c. To categorize data based on sensitivity and impact, guiding protective measures
d. To streamline data storage solutions

Answer: c. To categorize data based on sensitivity and impact, guiding protective measures. Explanation: Data classification policies are crucial for identifying the sensitivity and value of data assets, which in turn dictates the level of security controls and handling procedures required to protect the data from unauthorized access, disclosure, alteration, or destruction, aligning with the organization's risk management strategy.

633. In the design of a secure network infrastructure, which of the following would be the MOST effective strategy to protect against both internal and external threats?
a. Implementation of a flat network topology
b. Application of network segmentation and zoning
c. Exclusive use of wireless access points for connectivity
d. Consolidation of all servers into a single physical location

Answer: b. Application of network segmentation and zoning. Explanation: Network segmentation and zoning enhance security by dividing the network into smaller, manageable segments, each governed by its own set of access controls and security policies. This approach limits the spread of malicious activities and reduces the attack surface by isolating critical systems and data from other network segments, thereby providing effective protection against a wide range of threats.

634. When evaluating the security of cryptographic algorithms, what factor is MOST critical in determining their resistance to cryptographic attacks?
a. The length of the key used in the algorithm

b. The age of the algorithm

c. The programming language in which the algorithm is implemented

d. The color scheme of the user interface for the encryption software

Answer: a. The length of the key used in the algorithm. Explanation: The strength of a cryptographic algorithm is significantly influenced by the length of the key it uses. Longer keys provide a higher level of security as they offer a larger number of possible key combinations, making brute-force attacks more difficult. This principle holds true regardless of the algorithm's age or the programming language used for its implementation.

635. During an incident response, what role does digital forensics play in the aftermath of a security breach?

a. Enhancing the graphical user interface of security tools

b. Providing entertainment to the security team

c. Collecting and analyzing digital evidence to support the investigation

d. Reducing the overall budget for security operations

Answer: c. Collecting and analyzing digital evidence to support the investigation. Explanation: Digital forensics is crucial in the context of incident response as it involves the meticulous collection, preservation, analysis, and documentation of digital evidence from computers, networks, and storage devices. This evidence can help in understanding the breach's nature, scope, and origin, aiding in the identification of perpetrators, and can be used in legal proceedings if necessary.

636. For a multinational corporation, why is understanding data sovereignty laws critical in cloud computing environments?

a. To ensure that cloud gaming services are uninterrupted

b. To facilitate the easier sharing of data on social media

c. To comply with regulations governing data storage and transfer across borders

d. To guarantee unlimited data storage capacity

Answer: c. To comply with regulations governing data storage and transfer across borders. Explanation: Data sovereignty laws dictate how data is to be handled based on its geographic location, impacting how data is stored, processed, and transferred across national boundaries. For multinational corporations utilizing cloud services, adherence to these laws is essential to avoid legal and regulatory violations, ensuring that data handling practices align with the legal requirements of each jurisdiction in which they operate.

637. In the context of IAM, what is the significance of implementing a Single Sign-On (SSO) mechanism?

a. To ensure that users must remember multiple complex passwords

b. To provide a single point of failure for all systems

c. To enable users to access multiple systems with one set of credentials

d. To increase the time it takes for users to log in to each system

Answer: c. To enable users to access multiple systems with one set of credentials. Explanation: SSO simplifies the user authentication process by allowing individuals to access multiple applications or systems using a single set of credentials. This not only enhances user convenience and productivity by reducing password fatigue but also can improve security by enabling more robust authentication mechanisms and streamlined user access management.

638. When integrating security into the Software Development Life Cycle (SDLC), what is the primary purpose of conducting code reviews?
a. To evaluate the aesthetic appeal of the code
b. To ensure that the code compiles without errors
c. To identify and remediate security vulnerabilities in the codebase
d. To assess the software's market potential

Answer: c. To identify and remediate security vulnerabilities in the codebase. Explanation: Code reviews are a critical security practice within the SDLC, aimed at scrutinizing the source code to detect and fix security flaws, coding errors, and other vulnerabilities. This proactive measure helps in enhancing the security and quality of the software by ensuring that the code adheres to best practices and security standards before deployment.

639. In the realm of Security Operations, what is the primary objective of conducting regular security audits?
a. To entertain the audit team
b. To check compliance with security policies and standards
c. To increase the workload of IT staff
d. To reduce the efficiency of security systems

Answer: b. To check compliance with security policies and standards. Explanation: Regular security audits are essential for evaluating the effectiveness of an organization's security measures, ensuring that security controls are functioning as intended, and verifying compliance with internal policies, industry standards, and regulatory requirements. These audits help in identifying security gaps and areas for improvement, thereby strengthening the organization's overall security posture.

640. In asset security, why is data classification essential for an organization?
a. To determine the entertainment value of data
b. To allocate budget for social events
c. To categorize data based on sensitivity and dictate appropriate handling measures
d. To decide on office decoration themes

Answer: c. To categorize data based on sensitivity and dictate appropriate handling measures. Explanation: Data classification is a critical process that involves categorizing organizational data based on its sensitivity, value, and criticality. This classification guides the implementation of appropriate security controls and handling procedures, ensuring that sensitive data receives a higher level of protection, thereby mitigating the risk of unauthorized access and data breaches.

641. How does implementing the principle of least privilege in an organization's access control policy enhance security?

a. By granting all users administrative rights
b. By ensuring users have only the necessary access rights to perform their job functions
c. By allowing unrestricted access to all system resources
d. By increasing the complexity of the IT infrastructure

Answer: b. By ensuring users have only the necessary access rights to perform their job functions. Explanation: The principle of least privilege is a fundamental security concept that entails providing users only with the access rights essential for their roles, minimizing the potential damage from accidents, errors, or unauthorized use. This approach restricts the ability of attackers to exploit privileged accounts, thereby reducing the risk of critical system compromises and data breaches.

642. In a secure network design, what is the primary function of a demilitarized zone (DMZ)?
a. To provide a secure area for the installation of military equipment
b. To act as a buffer zone separating internal network and external traffic, hosting public-facing services
c. To exclusively manage internal traffic within an organization
d. To serve as a storage area for sensitive data

Answer: b. To act as a buffer zone separating internal network and external traffic, hosting public-facing services. Explanation: A DMZ is a network segment that acts as a buffer zone between the untrusted public internet and the trusted internal network. It is designed to host public-facing services, such as web servers and email servers, providing an additional layer of security by limiting external access only to services in the DMZ, thereby reducing the exposure of the internal network to potential attacks.

643. When implementing an Identity and Access Management (IAM) solution, what is the significance of federated identity management?
a. To consolidate all user identities into a single database
b. To enable single sign-on (SSO) across different organizational boundaries and systems
c. To increase the complexity of user authentication processes
d. To limit user access to a single system

Answer: b. To enable single sign-on (SSO) across different organizational boundaries and systems. Explanation: Federated identity management allows disparate organizations to share identity information, enabling users to access systems and applications across multiple domains using a single set of credentials. This facilitates seamless access, improves user experience, and enhances security by enabling organizations to manage and enforce access policies more consistently.

644. In the context of software development security, what role does static code analysis play?
a. To dynamically assess the runtime behavior of applications
b. To review the source code for potential security vulnerabilities without executing the code
c. To evaluate the aesthetic quality of the code
d. To measure the response time of applications under load

Answer: b. To review the source code for potential security vulnerabilities without executing the code. Explanation: Static code analysis involves examining the source code to identify security vulnerabilities, coding flaws, and compliance issues without running the application. It is an essential part of secure coding practices, allowing developers to detect and fix vulnerabilities early in the development lifecycle, thereby enhancing the security of the software.

645. What is the primary purpose of a Business Impact Analysis (BIA) in business continuity planning?
a. To entertain stakeholders with hypothetical disaster scenarios
b. To identify critical business functions and the impact of their disruption
c. To calculate the annual entertainment budget for the organization
d. To design the layout of corporate offices

Answer: b. To identify critical business functions and the impact of their disruption. Explanation: A Business Impact Analysis (BIA) is a critical component of business continuity planning that identifies vital business functions and assesses the potential impact of their disruption due to various events. It helps in prioritizing resources, planning recovery strategies, and ensuring the continuity of essential services during and after a disruptive incident.

646. In secure communication protocols, what is the primary security function of TLS (Transport Layer Security)?
a. To compress data to reduce bandwidth usage
b. To provide a secure channel for data transmission by encrypting data in transit
c. To increase the speed of data transmission
d. To serve as a routing protocol for data packets

Answer: b. To provide a secure channel for data transmission by encrypting data in transit. Explanation: TLS is a widely adopted protocol designed to secure communications over a computer network by encrypting data transmitted between two systems, preventing eavesdropping, tampering, and message forgery. It is used in various applications, such as web browsing, email, instant messaging, and VoIP.

647. How does employing the principle of separation of duties enhance organizational security?
a. By requiring all tasks to be performed by a single individual
b. By dividing tasks and associated privileges among multiple individuals to prevent fraud and errors
c. By consolidating all decision-making processes
d. By reducing the number of employees within the organization

Answer: b. By dividing tasks and associated privileges among multiple individuals to prevent fraud and errors. Explanation: The principle of separation of duties involves dividing responsibilities and privileges among different individuals or groups to reduce the risk of fraud, error, and misuse of resources. This control mechanism ensures that no single individual has complete control over critical processes, thereby enhancing the overall security and integrity of the organization's operations.

648. In the realm of asset security, why is data encryption considered a critical control measure?

a. To improve the aesthetic appeal of the data
b. To ensure data is readable by everyone
c. To protect the confidentiality and integrity of data by converting it into a coded form
d. To increase data storage requirements

Answer: c. To protect the confidentiality and integrity of data by converting it into a coded form. Explanation: Data encryption is a fundamental security control that transforms data into a coded format, making it unreadable to unauthorized individuals. It ensures data confidentiality and integrity by allowing only authorized parties with the decryption key to access the original data, thereby protecting sensitive information from unauthorized access, disclosure, and tampering.

649. What role does penetration testing play in security assessment and testing?
a. To physically secure the organization's premises
b. To simulate cyber attacks under controlled conditions to identify vulnerabilities
c. To assess the organization's financial performance
d. To conduct employee satisfaction surveys

Answer: b. To simulate cyber attacks under controlled conditions to identify vulnerabilities. Explanation: Penetration testing, or pen testing, involves simulating cyber attacks on an organization's computer systems, network, or web applications under controlled conditions. This proactive security measure aims to identify, exploit, and evaluate vulnerabilities, providing insights into potential security gaps and the effectiveness of existing security measures.

650. Why is user awareness training considered a vital component of security operations?
a. To ensure all employees become IT experts
b. To enhance the physical fitness of employees
c. To educate employees on security policies, procedures, and best practices, reducing human error
d. To prepare employees for careers in entertainment

Answer: c. To educate employees on security policies, procedures, and best practices, reducing human error. Explanation: User awareness training is crucial in enhancing the security posture of an organization by educating employees about security risks, policies, and best practices. It aims to reduce human error, one of the most significant security vulnerabilities, by making users aware of potential threats and teaching them how to recognize and respond appropriately, thereby fostering a culture of security within the organization.

651. IGMP operates at which layer of the OSI model, facilitating multicasting in a TCP/IP network?
a. Data Link
b. Network
c. Transport
d. Application

Answer: b. Network. Explanation: Internet Group Management Protocol (IGMP) operates at the Network layer (Layer 3) of the OSI model. It is used by IP hosts and adjacent multicast routers to establish multicast group memberships, allowing for efficient use of resources when supporting multicasting, particularly for streaming media and gaming applications.

652. Jeff uses multiple methods to authenticate himself before accessing a database as an administrator. Which authentication concept is best illustrated here?
a. Single-factor authentication
b. Two-factor authentication
c. Multifactor authentication
d. Biometric authentication

Answer: c. Multifactor authentication. Explanation: The scenario with Jeff using a secret code, thumbprint, retina scan, and terminal location verification for access control illustrates multifactor authentication. It combines something Jeff knows (code), something he has (biometric traits), and something he is (location), enhancing security by layering different authentication methods.

653. Encrypting a message with the recipient's public key primarily ensures which of the following?
a. Confidentiality
b. Integrity
c. Availability
d. Non-repudiation

Answer: a. Confidentiality. Explanation: Using the recipient's public key to encrypt a message ensures that only the holder of the corresponding private key can decrypt and read the message, thereby maintaining confidentiality. This is a fundamental aspect of public key infrastructure (PKI) and asymmetric encryption.

654. The Encapsulating Security Payload (ESP) in IPsec is primarily used for what purpose?
a. User authentication
b. Data integrity
c. Data confidentiality
d. Network routing

Answer: c. Data confidentiality. Explanation: ESP is a component of the IPsec protocol suite providing confidentiality through encryption of the IP packet payload. While ESP also offers optional integrity and authentication, its primary role is to encrypt data to protect it from unauthorized access during transmission.

655. Upon intercepting encrypted network transmissions, an attacker is likely to attempt which type of attack next?
a. Phishing attack
b. Man-in-the-middle attack
c. Cryptanalysis attack
d. Denial of Service attack

Answer: c. Cryptanalysis attack. Explanation: With access to encrypted transmissions, an attacker might employ cryptanalysis techniques to attempt to decrypt the intercepted data without the necessary keys, aiming to uncover sensitive information.

656. To address concerns from various organizational roles regarding digital asset protection, which solution is specifically suited for digital rights management?
a. Digital certificate
b. Blockchain technology
c. Digital Rights Management (DRM) systems
d. Trademark registration

Answer: c. Digital Rights Management (DRM) systems. Explanation: DRM systems are designed to protect and manage rights over digital content, making them suitable for addressing the Board of Directors' concern about digital rights protection. Other listed solutions do not directly address the specific needs related to digital rights management.

657. Layer 3 of the OSI model is responsible for which of the following functions?
a. Framing
b. Routing
c. Error detection
d. Signal modulation

Answer: b. Routing. Explanation: Layer 3, the Network layer, is chiefly concerned with routing packets across different networks, using logical addressing (IP addresses) to ensure data reaches its correct destination.

658. Configuration management is a critical activity during which phase(s) of the asset lifecycle?
a. Initiation and disposal
b. Operation and maintenance
c. Development and acquisition
d. All of the above

Answer: d. All of the above. Explanation: Configuration management is vital throughout the asset lifecycle, from initiation, development, and acquisition, through operation and maintenance, to disposal, ensuring that all changes to the asset's configuration are identified, documented, and tracked.

659. In an enterprise network, which security control would best mitigate the risk of data exfiltration through removable media?
a. Network segmentation
b. DLP systems with removable media controls
c. Implementation of WPA3 in wireless networks
d. Regular penetration testing

Answer: b. DLP systems with removable media controls. Explanation: Data Loss Prevention (DLP) systems with controls for removable media are specifically designed to prevent unauthorized copying and transfer of sensitive data to external devices like USB drives, effectively mitigating the risk of data exfiltration.

660. A multinational corporation is looking to ensure the integrity of its messages transmitted over the internet. Which of the following would provide the best solution?
a. SSL/TLS encryption
b. Digital signatures
c. Symmetric encryption with shared keys
d. VPN with IPsec

Answer: b. Digital signatures. Explanation: Digital signatures ensure the integrity and non-repudiation of messages by using a cryptographic algorithm to generate a unique signature for each message, which can be verified by the recipient to confirm that the message has not been altered in transit.

661. During a software development project, which practice most effectively ensures security is integrated throughout the lifecycle?
a. Conducting code reviews only at project completion
b. Incorporating security user stories in the agile backlog
c. Using an automated vulnerability scanner post-deployment
d. Limiting security testing to the deployment phase

Answer: b. Incorporating security user stories in the agile backlog. Explanation: Integrating security user stories into the agile backlog ensures that security considerations are included from the start and throughout the software development lifecycle, promoting a proactive approach to security.

662. In the context of IAM, which method provides the most granular level of access control for enterprise applications?
a. Role-Based Access Control (RBAC)
b. Discretionary Access Control (DAC)
c. Mandatory Access Control (MAC)
d. Attribute-Based Access Control (ABAC)

Answer: d. Attribute-Based Access Control (ABAC). Explanation: ABAC provides the most granular level of access control by using policies that evaluate a set of attributes (user, resource, and environment attributes) to make access decisions, allowing for dynamic and context-aware access control.

663. A security analyst is tasked with selecting a secure protocol for transferring files between servers in a high-security environment. Which protocol is most suitable?
a. FTP

b. SFTP

c. HTTP

d. Telnet

Answer: b. SFTP. Explanation: Secure File Transfer Protocol (SFTP) is the most suitable choice as it uses SSH to provide encrypted file transfer capabilities, ensuring confidentiality and integrity of data during transfer, unlike FTP, HTTP, or Telnet, which are less secure.

664. Which cryptographic algorithm is primarily used for secure key exchange rather than data encryption?

a. RSA

b. AES

c. ECC

d. Diffie-Hellman

Answer: d. Diffie-Hellman. Explanation: The Diffie-Hellman algorithm is specifically designed for secure key exchange over an insecure channel, allowing two parties to establish a shared secret key used for encrypted communication, rather than for encrypting or decrypting data itself.

665. In a Security Operations Center (SOC), which tool is essential for providing real-time analysis of security alerts generated by network hardware and applications?

a. GRC platform

b. SIEM system

c. Firewall

d. Data loss prevention (DLP) tool

Answer: b. SIEM system. Explanation: Security Information and Event Management (SIEM) systems are crucial in a SOC for aggregating, correlating, and analyzing security alerts from various sources in real-time, enabling rapid detection and response to potential security incidents.

666. For a company handling sensitive government contracts, which of the following would be the most appropriate method for securely disposing of outdated documents?

a. Recycling

b. Shredding to DIN Level 3

c. Deleting digital files

d. Incineration

Answer: d. Incineration. Explanation: Incineration is a secure method of disposal for sensitive documents, ensuring that they are completely destroyed and unrecoverable, which is particularly important for organizations handling highly confidential information, such as government contracts.

667. A security architect is designing a new network infrastructure. Which of the following would best ensure the confidentiality of data in transit between sites?
a. MPLS
b. Leased lines
c. End-to-end encryption
d. VLAN segmentation

Answer: c. End-to-end encryption. Explanation: End-to-end encryption ensures that data is encrypted at the source and decrypted only by the intended recipient, safeguarding the confidentiality of data in transit across any network infrastructure, including MPLS, leased lines, or VLANs.

668. In the context of cloud security, which of the following best describes the shared responsibility model?
a. The cloud provider is responsible for securing both the infrastructure and customer data.
b. The customer is solely responsible for securing their data and applications in the cloud.
c. The cloud provider secures the infrastructure, while the customer secures their data and applications.
d. Security responsibilities are entirely handled by third-party vendors, not the cloud provider or customer.

Answer: c. The cloud provider secures the infrastructure, while the customer secures their data and applications. Explanation: The shared responsibility model in cloud security delineates that cloud providers are responsible for securing the underlying infrastructure, while customers must secure their data, applications, and access management, ensuring a collaborative approach to cloud security.

669. When implementing a new identity management system, which standard should be considered to facilitate interoperability between different systems and platforms?
a. OAuth 2.0
b. SAML 2.0
c. OpenID Connect
d. Kerberos

Answer: b. SAML 2.0. Explanation: Security Assertion Markup Language (SAML) 2.0 is widely used for enabling single sign-on (SSO) across different systems and platforms, facilitating interoperability by allowing security credentials to be shared by multiple applications and services.

670. In a high-security environment, which encryption method should be used to secure data at rest on a mobile device?
a. WEP
b. AES-256
c. DES
d. RSA-1024

Answer: b. AES-256. Explanation: Advanced Encryption Standard (AES) with a 256-bit key length is considered very secure for encrypting data at rest and is recommended for high-security environments, including mobile devices, to protect sensitive information.

671. To enhance the security of a web application, which of the following headers should be implemented to prevent clickjacking attacks?
a. Content-Security-Policy
b. X-Frame-Options
c. X-Content-Type-Options
d. Access-Control-Allow-Origin

Answer: b. X-Frame-Options. Explanation: The X-Frame-Options HTTP header is specifically designed to protect against clickjacking attacks by instructing the browser not to embed the page within frames or iframes, thus preventing malicious sites from framing the content.

672. For a company that must comply with international data protection regulations, which of the following is the most critical aspect to consider when designing a data retention policy?
a. Data minimization
b. Public cloud storage
c. Third-party data sharing
d. Encryption at rest

Answer: a. Data minimization. Explanation: Data minimization, the practice of limiting the collection, storage, and retention of personal data to what is strictly necessary, is a key principle in many international data protection regulations, including the GDPR, making it crucial for compliance.

673. Which protocol is specifically designed for securing SNMP traffic, providing message integrity, authentication, and encryption?
a. SNMPv3
b. SNMPv2c
c. HTTPS
d. SSH

Answer: a. SNMPv3. Explanation: Simple Network Management Protocol version 3 (SNMPv3) includes security features that were not part of earlier versions, such as message integrity, authentication, and encryption, making it suitable for securely managing devices on IP networks.

674. In a distributed application architecture, which pattern provides the best approach for managing security tokens and facilitating secure communication between microservices?
a. API Gateway
b. Service Mesh
c. Monolithic Architecture

d. Broker Pattern

Answer: b. Service Mesh. Explanation: A service mesh provides a transparent and language-independent way to flexibly and efficiently handle service-to-service communication, including security aspects like managing security tokens and encrypting communication, which is ideal for microservices architectures.

675. For ensuring the secure disposal of SSDs, which method is considered most effective?
a. Degaussing
b. Overwriting
c. Physical destruction
d. Encryption

Answer: c. Physical destruction. Explanation: Physical destruction, such as shredding or incineration, is considered the most effective method for the secure disposal of SSDs, as traditional methods like degaussing are ineffective, and data can often be recovered even after overwriting.

676. To mitigate the risk of insider threats in a large organization, which of the following measures is most effective?
a. Mandatory vacation policies
b. Background checks
c. Role-based access control (RBAC)
d. Periodic security training

Answer: a. Mandatory vacation policies. Explanation: Mandatory vacation policies can help mitigate insider threats by ensuring that employees take time off, during which any fraudulent activities may be detected in their absence, offering an opportunity to uncover unauthorized or malicious actions.

677. When designing a secure network architecture, which concept is essential to protect sensitive data from eavesdropping on internal networks?
a. Deep Packet Inspection (DPI)
b. Network Segmentation
c. Virtual Private Network (VPN)
d. Intrusion Detection System (IDS)

Answer: b. Network Segmentation. Explanation: Network segmentation divides the network into smaller, separate segments, each with its own security controls, significantly reducing the attack surface and limiting the potential for unauthorized access to sensitive data within the network.

678. In the context of secure software development, which practice is most effective in identifying potential security flaws early in the development lifecycle?
a. Penetration testing post-deployment
b. Code reviews and static analysis
c. Relying solely on automated testing tools

d. Waiting for user feedback on security

Answer: b. Code reviews and static analysis. Explanation: Conducting code reviews and using static analysis tools during the development process allow for the early identification and remediation of security vulnerabilities, significantly improving the security of the software before deployment.

679. In the context of cloud computing, which of the following is the most effective strategy to mitigate data breaches in multi-tenant environments?
a. Implementing strong network segmentation
b. Applying strict data encryption at rest and in transit
c. Enforcing rigorous access control and identity management
d. Regularly updating the underlying cloud infrastructure

Answer: b. Applying strict data encryption at rest and in transit. Explanation: In multi-tenant cloud environments, where resources are shared among multiple users, applying strict data encryption both at rest and in transit is crucial. It ensures that even if unauthorized access occurs, the data remains unintelligible and protected against breaches.

680. To secure a large-scale Internet of Things (IoT) deployment, which of the following is the most critical consideration?
a. Ensuring all devices are running the latest firmware
b. Utilizing a centralized management platform for device monitoring
c. Implementing strong authentication mechanisms for device-to-device communication
d. Conducting regular penetration testing on all IoT devices

Answer: c. Implementing strong authentication mechanisms for device-to-device communication. Explanation: In IoT deployments, the vast number of interconnected devices increases the risk of unauthorized access. Implementing strong authentication mechanisms for device-to-device communication is critical to ensure that only authorized devices can communicate with each other, thereby significantly reducing the risk of malicious interference.

681. When designing a secure wireless network for a corporate office, which of the following would provide the highest level of security?
a. WPA2 Personal
b. WPA2 Enterprise
c. WEP
d. Open network with MAC filtering

Answer: b. WPA2 Enterprise. Explanation: WPA2 Enterprise offers a higher level of security compared to WPA2 Personal by using 802.1X authentication, which can integrate with an organization's identity management system. This allows for individual user credentials and stronger encryption methods, making it the preferred choice for corporate environments.

682. In the aftermath of a data breach, which of the following actions is most critical to prevent future incidents?
a. Notifying affected stakeholders and regulatory bodies
b. Conducting a thorough incident response investigation to identify the root cause
c. Implementing stronger encryption algorithms for data storage
d. Increasing the frequency of data backups

Answer: b. Conducting a thorough incident response investigation to identify the root cause. Explanation: While all the listed actions are important, conducting a thorough investigation to identify the root cause of the data breach is most critical. Understanding how the breach occurred allows an organization to address specific vulnerabilities and prevent similar incidents in the future.

683. For an organization subject to GDPR, which of the following measures is essential for compliance when processing personal data?
a. Obtaining explicit consent from data subjects for processing their data
b. Storing all personal data on-premises rather than in the cloud
c. Encrypting all personal data with one-way hashing algorithms
d. Limiting data access to senior management only

Answer: a. Obtaining explicit consent from data subjects for processing their data. Explanation: Under GDPR, obtaining explicit consent from data subjects for processing their personal data is a fundamental requirement. This ensures that individuals are aware of and agree to how their data is being used, providing them with control over their personal information.

684. In a digital forensics investigation, which of the following is the most important principle to maintain the integrity of evidence?
a. Documenting a clear chain of custody for all evidence collected
b. Using proprietary software tools for evidence collection
c. Conducting all investigations remotely to avoid physical tampering
d. Relying on digital copies of evidence rather than original sources

Answer: a. Documenting a clear chain of custody for all evidence collected. Explanation: Maintaining a clear and documented chain of custody for all evidence is crucial in digital forensics. It ensures the integrity and reliability of the evidence by tracking its handling, storage, and transfer, which is vital for legal proceedings.

685. When integrating a new third-party service into an existing enterprise system, which of the following is the most effective method to assess its security posture?
a. Reviewing the service provider's privacy policy
b. Conducting a comprehensive third-party security assessment
c. Relying on the service provider's reputation in the industry
d. Implementing the service on a trial basis to monitor for security issues

Answer: b. Conducting a comprehensive third-party security assessment. Explanation: Conducting a comprehensive security assessment of the third-party service allows the organization to evaluate its security controls, data handling practices, and compliance with relevant standards and regulations, providing a detailed understanding of the service's security posture.

686. In a scenario where an organization's critical systems are distributed across multiple geographic locations, which disaster recovery strategy ensures the highest availability?
a. Hot site
b. Warm site
c. Cold site
d. Mobile site

Answer: a. Hot site. Explanation: A hot site is a fully equipped alternative facility where an organization can quickly resume operations after a disaster. It includes up-to-date copies of data and is ready for immediate use, providing the highest level of availability among disaster recovery options.

687. To secure API communications in a financial application, which of the following mechanisms provides the most robust security?
a. API keys
b. Basic authentication
c. OAuth 2.0 with token-based authentication
d. SSL/TLS encryption alone

Answer: c. OAuth 2.0 with token-based authentication. Explanation: OAuth 2.0 with token-based authentication offers a secure and flexible method for controlling access to APIs. It allows granular permissions and can integrate with existing identity providers, making it highly suitable for secure and controlled API communications in sensitive environments like financial applications.

688. When designing a secure data deletion policy, which of the following is the most effective method to ensure data is irrecoverable?
a. Overwriting data multiple times
b. Deleting file references in the file system
c. Encrypting data before deletion
d. Physical destruction of the storage medium

Answer: d. Physical destruction of the storage medium. Explanation: Physical destruction of the storage medium, such as shredding or incineration, is the most effective method to ensure data is completely irrecoverable. Overwriting data or deleting file references may not guarantee that data cannot be reconstructed, especially with advanced data recovery techniques.

689. In a distributed system architecture, which mechanism is most effective for ensuring data consistency across multiple databases?
a. Implementing database shadowing
b. Utilizing a centralized database management system
c. Applying distributed transaction protocols
d. Enforcing strict access controls on all databases

Answer: c. Applying distributed transaction protocols. Explanation: Distributed transaction protocols, such as the two-phase commit protocol, ensure that all parts of a distributed transaction either commit or roll back together, maintaining data consistency across multiple databases in a distributed system.

690. To enhance the security of a web application, which of the following measures would be most effective in mitigating cross-site scripting (XSS) attacks?
a. Enabling HTTP Strict Transport Security (HSTS)
b. Implementing Content Security Policy (CSP) headers
c. Using secure cookies with the HttpOnly flag
d. Deploying a network-based intrusion detection system (IDS)

Answer: b. Implementing Content Security Policy (CSP) headers. Explanation: CSP headers allow web application developers to declare which dynamic resources are allowed to load, effectively mitigating the risk of XSS attacks by restricting where scripts can be loaded from.

691. When considering secure communications in a corporate environment, which of the following protocols provides the strongest security for email transmission?
a. SMTP over SSL/TLS
b. S/MIME
c. PGP/GPG
d. IMAP over SSL/TLS

Answer: b. S/MIME. Explanation: Secure/Multipurpose Internet Mail Extensions (S/MIME) is specifically designed for securing email communications by providing message encryption and digital signatures, ensuring confidentiality, integrity, and non-repudiation.

692. In the context of secure software development, which approach is most effective in integrating security throughout the software development lifecycle (SDLC)?
a. Adopting a waterfall model with a security review in the final phase
b. Implementing security-focused agile methodologies
c. Conducting penetration testing after software deployment
d. Relying solely on automated security scanning tools during development

Answer: b. Implementing security-focused agile methodologies. Explanation: Security-focused agile methodologies integrate security practices and testing throughout the SDLC, allowing for continuous assessment and adaptation of security measures, ensuring that security is a priority at every stage of development.

693. For an organization looking to ensure data privacy and compliance with international data protection regulations, which of the following strategies is most critical?
a. Data localization and sovereignty adherence
b. Deployment of data loss prevention (DLP) solutions
c. Regular data encryption audits
d. Exclusive use of private cloud infrastructure

Answer: a. Data localization and sovereignty adherence. Explanation: Adhering to data localization and sovereignty principles is critical for compliance with international data protection regulations, as it involves storing and processing data within the legal jurisdiction of the data subjects, respecting the local data privacy laws.

694. In a scenario where an organization needs to secure its cloud-based infrastructure, which of the following is a key consideration for protecting data at rest?
a. Network segmentation
b. Encryption using cloud provider's built-in tools
c. Multi-factor authentication for cloud access
d. Regular vulnerability scanning of cloud services

Answer: b. Encryption using cloud provider's built-in tools. Explanation: Encrypting data at rest using the cloud provider's built-in encryption tools is a key measure for securing cloud-based infrastructure, ensuring that data is unreadable to unauthorized users and protected against potential breaches.

695. Which of the following best describes a proactive approach to detect and mitigate potential insider threats within an organization?
a. Conducting exit interviews with employees leaving the company
b. Implementing strict network perimeter defenses
c. Deploying user and entity behavior analytics (UEBA) solutions
d. Focusing solely on external threat intelligence

Answer: c. Deploying user and entity behavior analytics (UEBA) solutions. Explanation: UEBA solutions analyze user behavior and detect anomalies that may indicate insider threats, providing a proactive approach to identifying and mitigating potential risks from within the organization.

696. When designing a Business Continuity Plan (BCP) for a financial institution, which of the following would be the most critical aspect to ensure operational resilience?
a. Comprehensive insurance coverage for physical assets
b. Regularly updated contact lists for all employees
c. High availability and disaster recovery solutions for IT systems
d. Detailed inventory of all office supplies

Answer: c. High availability and disaster recovery solutions for IT systems. Explanation: For a financial institution, ensuring high availability and effective disaster recovery solutions for IT systems is crucial to maintain operational resilience, minimize downtime, and ensure continuous service delivery in the event of a disruption.

697. In the context of mobile device security within an enterprise, which of the following strategies is most effective in preventing unauthorized data access in case of device loss or theft?
a. Enforcing strong password policies
b. Implementing remote wipe capabilities
c. Mandating the use of anti-virus software
d. Requiring biometric authentication for device access

Answer: b. Implementing remote wipe capabilities. Explanation: Remote wipe capabilities allow an organization to remotely erase sensitive data from lost or stolen devices, effectively preventing unauthorized access to corporate information and reducing the risk of data breaches.

698. For a multinational corporation, the alignment of cybersecurity policies with international regulations is paramount. Which approach ensures compliance with varying data protection laws across different countries?
a. Standardizing on the strictest privacy laws globally
b. Developing a flexible framework adaptable to local regulations
c. Implementing General Data Protection Regulation (GDPR) as a baseline
d. Focusing solely on the cybersecurity laws of the corporation's headquarters

Answer: b. Developing a flexible framework adaptable to local regulations. Explanation: A flexible framework allows the corporation to adjust its cybersecurity policies and practices to meet the specific legal requirements of each country in which it operates, ensuring compliance with a variety of international regulations.

699. In the development of a secure IoT ecosystem for smart city projects, what is a critical consideration to mitigate the risk of widespread system failures?
a. Ensuring high-speed connectivity for all devices
b. Implementing robust device authentication mechanisms
c. Prioritizing physical security for key infrastructure
d. Standardizing IoT protocols across all devices

Answer: b. Implementing robust device authentication mechanisms. Explanation: Robust device authentication mechanisms are crucial in IoT ecosystems to prevent unauthorized access and control, significantly reducing the risk of compromised devices leading to widespread system failures.

700. When establishing a disaster recovery plan for a cloud-based service, what aspect is most critical to ensure minimal downtime during a major outage?
a. Contractually guaranteed uptime from the cloud provider
b. Automated failover to a secondary cloud region or provider
c. On-premises backup of all cloud-stored data
d. Regularly scheduled disaster recovery drills

Answer: b. Automated failover to a secondary cloud region or provider. Explanation: Automated failover mechanisms ensure that, in the event of a major outage in one cloud region or with one provider, services can be quickly restored from another region or provider, minimizing downtime.

701. For an organization that relies heavily on open-source software, what is the most effective strategy to manage security vulnerabilities inherent to these applications?
a. Limiting the use of open-source software to non-critical systems
b. Establishing a dedicated team for continuous vulnerability scanning and patching
c. Relying on the open-source community for timely patches
d. Replacing all open-source software with proprietary solutions

Answer: b. Establishing a dedicated team for continuous vulnerability scanning and patching. Explanation: A dedicated team ensures that open-source software is continuously monitored for new vulnerabilities and that patches are promptly applied, maintaining the security of the organization's systems.

702. In the context of advanced persistent threats (APTs), what tactic is most effective for early detection and mitigation?
a. Deploying signature-based intrusion detection systems
b. Conducting regular penetration testing
c. Implementing behavioral analysis and anomaly detection tools
d. Focusing on perimeter defense mechanisms

Answer: c. Implementing behavioral analysis and anomaly detection tools. Explanation: Behavioral analysis and anomaly detection tools are capable of identifying subtle, unusual activities indicative of APTs, enabling early detection and response before significant damage occurs.

703. To enhance the security posture of an organization, which method is most effective for educating employees about social engineering attacks?
a. Distributing annual security awareness newsletters
b. Implementing strict penalties for security policy violations
c. Conducting interactive security awareness training sessions
d. Relying on automated email filters to block phishing attempts

Answer: c. Conducting interactive security awareness training sessions. Explanation: Interactive training sessions engage employees and effectively communicate the risks and indicators of social engineering attacks, fostering a proactive security culture.

704. In securing a software-defined network (SDN), what is a key factor to protect the network control plane?
a. Enforcing physical access controls to network devices
b. Segmenting the control plane from the data plane
c. Implementing end-to-end encryption for data traffic
d. Regular firmware updates for networking hardware

Answer: b. Segmenting the control plane from the data plane. Explanation: Segmentation between the control and data planes isolates the critical network management functions from the regular network traffic, reducing the risk of unauthorized access and manipulation of the control plane.

705. For a financial institution, what is the most critical aspect of securing electronic fund transfer (EFT) systems against fraudulent transactions?
a. Implementing multi-factor authentication for all transactions
b. Establishing daily transaction limits for customers
c. Encrypting transaction data both in transit and at rest
d. Conducting real-time transaction monitoring and analysis

Answer: d. Conducting real-time transaction monitoring and analysis. Explanation: Real-time monitoring and analysis of transaction patterns can quickly identify and respond to suspicious activities, significantly reducing the risk of fraudulent transactions.

706. In a BYOD (Bring Your Own Device) policy, what is essential to protect corporate data on employee-owned devices?
a. Mandating the installation of corporate-approved antivirus software
b. Enforcing device encryption and secure boot mechanisms
c. Implementing a containerization solution to separate personal and corporate data
d. Prohibiting access to corporate systems from personal devices

Answer: c. Implementing a containerization solution to separate personal and corporate data. Explanation: Containerization creates a secure, isolated environment for corporate data on personal devices, safeguarding it from unauthorized access and potential data leaks.

707. To ensure the integrity of data in transit over the internet, which of the following is most effective?
a. Using MPLS (Multiprotocol Label Switching) for network traffic
b. Implementing IPsec (Internet Protocol Security) in transport mode
c. Applying SSL/TLS encryption for all data transmissions
d. Relying on VPN (Virtual Private Network) services with PPTP (Point-to-Point Tunneling Protocol)

Answer: c. Applying SSL/TLS encryption for all data transmissions. Explanation: SSL/TLS encryption provides a secure channel for data transmission over the internet, ensuring the integrity and confidentiality of the data in transit, protecting it from interception and tampering.

As we wrap up this journey through the vast landscape of CISSP, it's remarkable to reflect on the ground we've covered together. From the intricate details of Security and Risk Management to the technical depths of Software Development Security, each chapter was a step forward in preparing you for not just an exam, but for the real-world challenges you'll face in the field of cybersecurity.

Remember, the knowledge you've gained is not just for passing a test. It's a toolkit for solving complex problems, protecting valuable assets, and making informed decisions in the face of digital threats. The principles of Asset Security, the strategies in Communication and Network Security, and the nuances of Identity and Access Management are more than just topics; they're part of a larger narrative that underscores the importance of vigilance, adaptability, and continuous learning in safeguarding our digital world.

As you move forward, take with you not just the facts and figures, but the underlying ethos of CISSP: a commitment to excellence, integrity, and a deeper understanding of the interconnectedness of our digital ecosystem. The challenges ahead are many, but with the foundation you've built, you're more than equipped to meet them head-on.

So, as you close this chapter and gear up for the next, do so with confidence. Trust in the knowledge you've acquired, lean on the principles you've embraced, and never stop pushing the boundaries of what you know. The path to becoming a CISSP professional is as much about the journey as it is about the destination. Good luck, and may your curiosity and dedication to security lead you to new heights.

bookvault
Publishing

CISSP Study Guide 2024-2025: All in One CISSP Exam Prep for the Certified Information Systems Security Professional Certification. With Exam Review Material, 700+ Practice Test Questions.

ISBN: 9781836021346
Perfect Bound

First published in 2024 by bookvault Publishing, Peterborough, United Kingdom

An Environmentally friendly book printed and bound in England by bookvault, powered by printondemand-worldwide